SOCIAL HISTORY
AND
SOCIAL POLICY

SOCIAL HISTORY
AND
SOCIAL POLICY

Edited by

DAVID J. ROTHMAN

Department of History
Columbia University
New York, New York

STANTON WHEELER

Yale Law School
New Haven, Connecticut

ACADEMIC PRESS
A Subsidiary of Harcourt Brace Jovanovich, Publishers
New York   London   Toronto   Sydney   San Francisco

ACADEMIC PRESS, INC.
111 Fifth Avenue, New York, New York 10003

United Kingdom Edition published by
ACADEMIC PRESS, INC. (LONDON) LTD.
24/28 Oval Road, London NW1 7DX

Library of Congress Cataloging in Publication Data
Main entry under title:

Social history and social policy.

   Includes bibliographical references and index.
   1. History--Addresses, essays, lectures.
2. Social policy--Addresses, essays, lectures.
3. United States--Social conditions--Addresses,
essays, lectures. 4. Social problems--History--
Addresses, essays, lectures. I. Rothman, David J.
II. Wheeler, Stanton, 1930–
HM36.S63   973   80–1772
ISBN 0–12–598680–7

PRINTED IN THE UNITED STATES OF AMERICA

81 82 83 84   9 8 7 6 5 4 3 2 1

RM
6-10-82

CONTENTS

I The History of Social Institutions

II   The History of Social Problems

III The Uses of History in the Making of Social Policy

LIST OF CONTRIBUTORS

Numbers in parentheses indicate the pages on which the authors' contributions begin.

JOHN DEMOS (301), Department of History, Brandeis University, Waltham, Massachusetts 02154

ROBERT M. FOGELSON (145), Department of Urban Studies and Planning, Massachusetts Institute of Technology, Cambridge, Massachusetts 02138

LAWRENCE M. FRIEDMAN (203), Stanford Law School, Stanford University, Stanford, California 94305

HERBERT G. GUTMAN (239), Department of History, The Graduate School and University Center, City University of New York, New York, New York 10036

MICHAEL B. KATZ (57), Graduate School of Education and Department of History, University of Pennsylvania, Philadelphia, Pennsylvania 19104

SEYMOUR J. MANDELBAUM (275), Department of City and Regional Planning, University of Pennsylvania, Philadelphia, Pennsylvania 19104

CHARLES E. ROSENBERG (19), Department of History, University of Pennsylvania, Philadelphia, Pennsylvania 19104

DAVID J. ROTHMAN (1, 103), Department of History, Columbia University, New York, New York 10027

SHEILA M. ROTHMAN (175), Center for Policy Research, 475 Riverside Drive, New York, New York 10027

STANTON WHEELER (1), Yale Law School, New Haven, Connecticut 06520

PREFACE

This collection of chapters represents a pioneering effort to explore the links between social history and social policy, to analyze the advantages and disadvantages of this collaboration. It performs this task not through exhortation but through exemplification. Here are efforts by a group of historians concerned with the origins and structure of health systems, criminal justice, urban planning, pension programs, and schooling to contribute to the formation of social policy.

The chapters demonstrate the variety of perspectives that historians may bring to this assignment. Their work provides a vital sense of options and opportunities available to the decision makers. They also reveal how history can demystify a subject by challenging the notion that since an institution has always been with us it must always be with us. The historians are well suited to explaining the dynamics that have shaped policies. They can work at the microlevel, whether the subject be pensions or hospitals or prisons; in this way, they have much to tell those concerned with policy about the players, the strategies, and the rules of the game.

Historians, too, can correct the often misconceived ideas that policymakers carry about history, ideas that do deeply affect their programs. At the least, historians can help ensure that policymakers are using an accurate history. At best, they can suggest new ways of thinking about problems that break out of standard molds.

Each of these contributions reorients policymakers and analysts to their fields. Few disciplines are better suited than history to challenge inherited wisdoms and received truths.

The substantive chapters in this volume were prepared by social historians. However, our interest in ensuring that the chapters be relevant to those working more closely in social policy led us to hold a conference at Seven Springs Center, Mount Kisco, New York, at which the chapters were discussed and critiqued by reviewers who are closer to the world of policy than most of the authors. We wish to thank all of those reviewers and discussants: Judith Blake, Milton Burdman, Kenneth B. Clark, Eliot Freidson, Bernard R. Gifford, Mitchell I. Ginsberg, Geoffrey C. Hazard, Jr., Gilbert Y. Steiner, Robert Tilove, and Robert C. Wood.

The work reported in this volume was initiated with the support of a grant from the Russell Sage Foundation. We wish to acknowledge the support of the foundation and its then president, Hugh F. Cline, for their interest in examining the relationship between history and social policy.

Finally, we owe a special debt of gratitude to Bern Fasse, whose help at all stages of the project is gratefully acknowledged.

1

INTRODUCTION

DAVID J. ROTHMAN
STANTON WHEELER

The attempt to make historical studies relevant to the concerns of social policy often provokes two contradictory types of response. To some, a latitudinarian spirit ought to prevail. Social policy analysis and implementation seem to be so open-ended and freewheeling an enterprise that it would be presumptuous to rule out the potential contribution of the historian. Indeed, given the morass that now permeates public policy in so many areas, any and all attempts to bring some guidance to a beleaguered official, from whatever quarter, should be welcomed. But others adopt a far more restricted view. They compare a decision maker to a ship's captain who is trying to dock his boat in a swirling current. He has an immediate need to know which way to steer, and, hence, some rule of parsimony must, and appropriately does, prevail. History, then, is something of a luxury if not a distraction. It may offer some interesting background information. But when it comes down to the core of issues, to the hard process of reaching a decision, the historian has no central role to play.

As such divergent positions suggest, the appropriate links between history and social policy have been neither well defined nor thoroughly explored. Not that historians are for the first time discovering their potential impact on social policy. At the opening of the twentieth century, many Progressive historians shared an explicit commitment to influencing public programs. To choose the most famous example, Charles

1

Beard clearly intended *An Economic Interpretation of the Constitution* to shake judges loose from a strick constructionist interpretation of the Constitution that was obstructing progressive social welfare legislation. Nevertheless, despite this tradition, the interaction of history and social policy—what history can and should do—has not been systematically examined. At this moment, a permissive attitude seems to prevail. Exhortations to historians to enter the arena of policy abound, perhaps because the discipline is undergoing a crisis of relevance or perhaps because of more mundane considerations: When graduate students cannot find jobs in universities, it is advantageous to place them in state or federal bureaucracies. In all events, exhortation cannot substitute for careful consideration, for presenting the advantages and disadvantages of such a collaboration.

To clarify the ways by which the following chapters address this issue, let us describe the origins of this project. For several years the two editors of this volume served together on a policy committee charged with investigating incarceration and its alternatives. In the course of that service, we often debated the respective policy roles of our disciplines, particularly whether historians could go beyond the concluding lines of many of their articles ("and these findings have implications for today") and actually detail the consequences of their findings. It has been said that contemporary novels begin where old-fashioned ones left off; we wondered whether contemporary histories too might begin where others left off. Accordingly, we invited a group of historians to address the problem and asked a group of people involved in social policy, either with day-to-day responsibilities for administration or with a concern for analysis, to comment on the result. We recognized that such a format had a built-in imbalance: The historians would present findings, and those from social policy would pass judgment. The imbalance, however, did fit with an important reality for us. Our question was not whether history might be useful in some abstract sense but whether those immersed in policy would find it so. Thus, despite some discomfort with the arrangement, we believed that it was a suitable way to test the potential contribution of history, a way to move from exhortation to exemplification.

The design of the project also reflected an initial optimism about the results. We were relatively confident that historians could do more than provide background music for social policy decisions. Yet, it should be clear from the outset that the enterprise has in many ways been chastening. Our initial optimism has by now been well qualified; we have a much sharper sense of the limits of the collaboration. By no means do we conclude that history has no significant contribution to make to social policy. We are, however, more keenly aware of the barriers to cooperation and the difficulties of the enterprise. We remain convinced of the viability of uniting history and social policy, but we recognize how complicated and even discomforting it is to accomplish this task.

Let us present the darker side first, the major problems that emerged in the course of discussion between historians and social policy analysts and administrators. As might be expected, we had little difficulty in identifying historians whose work seemed relevant to social policy. As the Contents of this book makes immediately apparent, health systems, criminal justice, urban planning, pension programs, and schooling are all subjects with a high priority among historians. Indeed, the list could easily have been expanded to include science policies, agriculture, transportation, housing, and a variety of other topics. To locate common areas of concern to both groups was simple. However, the interest of the historian in these matters is not identical to or easily linked with the concerns of those in social policy. Diverse motives brought historians into one or another of these areas. Some were simply curious about the origins of a program, others were quite alert to the problematic state of public policy in a given area, and still others were frankly determined to exert a direct influence over social policy, at least to the extent of informing social policy analysts of strategies that an historical analysis might suggest. But none of the historians, it seems fair to say, were first and foremost concerned with *solving* a public policy problem. None of them took as their assignment the formulation of specific policy alternatives that would be immediately implemented.

This stance put the historian at odds with the social policy analysts and adminstrators. Some wanted the historian to assume that there was a client with a pressing need; they wanted the historian to imagine that the target audience was an official confronted with a series of alternatives and to design and carry out the research in such a way as to help policymakers decide among alternatives. In other words, those from the world of social policy anticipated an immediate pay-off from the historians in the form of answers to clients' questions of what should be done now. In fact, a few of the social policy analysts believed that historians could actually carry out this task. The past record did appear relevant to contemporary problems. But it soon became clear that the social policy analysts wanted to frame the questions to suit their particular agendas, which were not necessarily identical to those of the historians. In a sense, the historian was about to become the research assistant for the analysts.

The historians were immediately uneasy with this formulation and advanced all sorts of objections. Some of the policy questions were poorly framed, others were based on misinformation. Moreover, since historians did not meet on a sustained basis with those in authority or those in policy departments, how could they ever come to know the needs of the field? An even more fundamental issue was emerging here: The historians were determined to set their own priorities. They had anticipated a collaboration between equals, not one group carrying out assignments given by the other. In the end, it became altogether apparent that historians were not by training or inclination client oriented. They were far more sensitive to disciplinary than to policy agendas. They were accustomed to a freedom of action that was not easily limited or even mildly constrained. This conflict might have reflected the idiosyncratic views of these particular historians. However, we think not. Despite the historians' exceptionally strong interest in social policy, only a few had actually devoted a significant amount of time to such efforts as serving on a task force addressing a major policy issue. If in the future historians' contributions to social policy become better recognized and more integral to policy making, this might change. Still, for the moment, the distance between disciplinary concerns and policy concerns remains substantial. The problem is not unknown in the relationship of other academic disciplines with social policy, but it is probably more acute in history than in political science or sociology.

The issue of who sets the questions was only one (and not the most important) of the divisions between the two groups. The social policy analysts were also uneasy with the scope and types of data that historians relied upon for their findings. They feared that historians selected their cases on the basis of accidents of survival. Because this institution kept meticulous records or that legislative history was particularly complete, historians decided to examine them—not because they were typical or directly relevant to the problems that social policy was confronting, but because the material was available. (There is a classic story worth telling here: One night a policeman encountered a drunk who was searching the pavement under a street lamp. He asked what the drunk was doing; the drunk replied that he was looking for his wallet. The policeman then asked where he lost it, to which the drunk replied, "One block away." "But then why are you looking here for it," the policeman demanded? To which the drunk responded: "Because this is where the light is.") And the doubts of the policy people were not without some basis. For historians to enter into an analysis that is sufficiently detailed and enlightening to meet their own standards of evidence and to be of immediate relevance, they must have access to an especially rich body of documentation. Certainly more than those working in most other social sciences, they are dependent upon the accidents of survival and cannot generate their own data.

Thus, again and again, the policy analysts wanted to be assured that these particular hospitals, or prisons, or congressional debates, or pension battles were truly representative of the class of institutions or controversies that were under discussion. Or, if not typical, could the historians specify the direction of the atypicality? These concerns emerged, for example, in Charles E. Rosenberg's study of hospitals in the late nineteenth century, which drew heavily on the experience of a few leading eastern institutions. Rosenberg argued that although these institutions were hardly representative of hospitals in other states or cities, they were the models, the exemplary cases, that others tried to emulate. Hence, their very unusualness gave them special importance. This discussion also took place around David Rothman's analysis of the experience of one Massachusetts prison in the 1930s. Rothman, like Rosenberg, contended that the very atypicality of the prison, its special effort to translate Progressive reform precepts into action, made it an important enterprise for policy analysts to understand. Thus, historians were prepared to defend the validity of their selections and their generalizations based upon them. Yet, it remained unclear whether the policy analysts were convinced. The historians were prepared to give such assurances, but the policy analysts may not have been persuaded.

The problem went even deeper. Those from the world of social policy were often doubtful whether the critical determinants of contemporary policies usually (or really ever) had much relationship to events that had occurred 20, 30, or 40 years ago. Their own sense of time was, at least to historians, narrow. If one wishes to debate and promote changes in health care today, is it important to know the history of the Sheppard–Towner Act in the 1920s (Chapter 6) or the organization of hospitals in the Progressive era (Chapter 2)? If one wishes to alter the present sentencing system, must one be informed about California's experiences of 1880–1920 (Chapter 7) or about Norfolk as a model institution established in the 1930s (Chapter 4)? If one wishes to change the structure of public schools, is the record of the Jacksonian period at all meaningful (Chapter 3)? To shape family policy today, is it important to rediscover the world of the plantation or the errors of the black sociologist E. Franklin Frazier (Chapter 8)? At times a tone of scepticism and impatience crept into the responses of the policy analysts and administrators. As one of them exclaimed in a moment of exasperation: "When I have a problem, I want it addressed; I want costs calculated, solutions proposed. Historians bleed too much!"

This sense of immediacy and urgency on the part of policymakers reappeared at innumerable points. One of them declared,

> Imagine you are the mayor of New York City. It's Sunday night. Tomorrow a group of welfare mothers are going to be in your office at 10 A.M., a major case of Medicaid fraud has just been discovered at a city hospital, and Albert Shanker and the teacher's union are threatening a strike. What can the historian do to help? He probably *can't* help, at least not in an immediate sense. A history of welfare, of Medicaid, of the teacher's union, would probably not solve these particular problems. And even if it could, by the time the history was completed some other problem would have top priority.

As another participant put it, "Sometimes you can have *too much* information." Or, sometimes the information can be irrelevant. To those closest to social policy, the historian was often examining variables that were impossible for the policymaker to manipulate. To the extent that an analysis focuses on aspects of the problem that are beyond the control of those in charge of the system, it may be good history as history, but not germane to the options facing the administrator.

The impatience was not all one way. The historians were often unsatisfied with the responses of those from social policy. In some cases, they were surprised at the ignorance of policy analysts about the past and their readiness, with the "experts" sitting right next to them, literally to make up their own history, to pronounce on the past with a degree of confidence that seemed disturbing. Their knowledge of slavery, for example, was outdated by some 20 years of new research, but they clung to older views with surprising tenacity. And at points the historians were frustrated by the inability of some of the policy analysts to appreciate the structure of an argument for its own sake. Relevance was the order of the day, and policy concerns had brought the groups together, but surely, the historians argued, there was some time left for intellectual appreciation, for an admiration of craftsmanship, for the findings themselves as opposed to their implications. Furthermore, the historians had little sympathy for a view of policymakers as ships' captains. From the historians' perspective, many of the problems had been around for a long time, and they were not convinced that the felt urgency of action was necessarily a legitimate ground for neglecting the potential of historial research. The lament "I have to act" might sometimes be justified, but often it could be an excuse, a means to insulate the bureaucracy from probing deeply into questions and analyses, an irresponsible withdrawal or abnegation of responsibility for the present system. It took decades for the South Bronx to degenerate into an urban wasteland. Why measure the historians' potential contribution in hours and minutes?

Something of a polarization did take place between the "intellectuals" and the "real world" people, although these historians knew far more about the real world than do most of their colleagues and this group of policymakers were far more comfortable in an academic setting than are the great majority of their colleagues. Nevertheless, both groups often accentuated their differences, marking off their own territory, rather than emphasizing what was no less obvious, their common purposes. This dynamic was probably not specific to the composition of these two groups. At work was a difference of discipline and role, not of personality.

All these problems said and recognized, the results of the encounters, and the chapters that follow here, point to the relevance of history to social policy and justify not only this effort in particular but also the larger endeavor in general. The dialogue between historians and those in social policy promoted a more penetrating view of what history can contribute to the decision maker and the analyst. Despite all the difficulties in communication, the struggle to collaborate seemed to almost everyone concerned worthwhile.

The historian's perspective on contemporary issues provided a sharp and vital sense of options, opportunities, and abilities to maneuver. As opposed to some social science research that appears better able to analyze the forces upholding a system than the forces that might promote change, the historians consistently analyzed the past record in ways that expanded the range of choices available to decision makers. In their work, the elements that compose the present situation appear to be far less determined and fixed. An aura of inevitability gives way to a sense of experimentation. Thus, the historian's sense of the contingencies that went into the construction of present policies and practices is a much-needed corrective to the more closed constructs of other disciplines. It is important that policy analysts and administrators recognize that the federal government funded a major health program in the 1920s, not because the precedent itself should be faithfully copied today but because the very notion of an alternative system is liberating.

To take this point one step further, historical analysis often serves to demystify a subject. It challenges one fundamental source of legitimacy— the notion that since an institution or practice has always been with us, it must necessarily always be with us. The dead weight of the past prompts inertia when survival comes to be confused with desirability. The historian can counter such an orientation, thereby stimulating attempts at change.

The historian's analysis is also well suited to explain the dynamics that shaped policies, to identify the critical elements in the decision-making process. Historians can work at the microlevel; sufficient records do survive in enough detail to provide historians with the necessary data on which to base such an analysis. Whether the case on hand be the organization of the hospital, the operation of a public pension system, or the presumptions that underlie urban design, the historian has much to tell the social policy analyst about the players, the strategies, and the rules of the game. To ignore such data is to miss some of the most illuminating and important moments in the implementation of social policy—and the chapters that follow should go far toward substantiating this point.

Moreover, policymakers, in informed and uninformed ways, are already using history. But too frequently this history is an invented one; many administrators carry with them an image of the past that exerts a powerful influence on their design of programs. Both the long history of policy toward the black family and the short history of such a group as the Carnegie Council on Children demonstrate that, for better or worse, history is often integral to the formulation of public policy. Historians can, at least, help to make certain that policy people are using an accurate history. Furthermore, historians can bring their own sense of the past to bear directly on the framing of policy choices. It is simply not true that the nineteenth century was the golden age of family cohesion or that the black family totally disintegrated under slavery. And a policy that presupposes otherwise, may well be mischievous and counterproductive.

The chapters that follow do not merely sound these general themes, but present a rich and complex set of variations on them. To address, albeit briefly, each of the contributions in turn provides at least an initial sense of the points and counterpoints integral to the historical presentations and an occasion to raise some of the questions that might concern policymakers in their use of these chapters.

The chapters in Part I examine three of the most important organizations in modern society: the hospital, the school, and the prison. Charles E. Rosenberg's analysis of the origins of the American hospital 1880–1914 explores the critical role of physicians in the shaping of the institution's present structure. Under the ideology of "scientific medicine," physicians modernized the hospital or, put another way, shifted its control from lay to professional hands. The consequences of this alteration for patient care and for institutional functioning is at the heart of Rosenberg's chapter—and he makes clear that this change was neither inevitable nor beneficial. Indeed, substantial evidence suggests that the hospital came to serve the needs of doctors, which were by no means identical to the needs of patients. Thus, Rosenberg's contribution is large scale and radical—at once liberating and demystifying. He helps to remove barriers to change (by clarifying the political role of the doctors). Yet, at the same time, there is a tone of pessimism: The forces that uphold the present system are deeply rooted and will not be removed easily.

Michael B. Katz's chapter on education and inequality is a further example of the historian's ability to help expose the ideological underpinnings of institutional practices. Like Rosenberg, his is a "third party" approach, which demonstrates the historian's usefulness as an outsider evaluating the insider's claims. Katz does not attempt to spell out a program for a new kind of schooling or to give details on specific policies that should in his opinion be enacted. But in clarifying the width of the gap between educational rhetoric and school reality, he is clearly encouraging a search for new practices. Still, in his writing too, a note of pessimism is inescapable. The particular style of American schools seems so overdetermined that it is difficult to imagine how fundamental change can occur. There can be frustration in historians' forays into social policy: They at once marshal our enthusiasm for change and then dampen it.

David J. Rothman's chapter is an effort to use an extraordinary document, a 700-page "diary" of reform efforts at the Norfolk prison (1932–1933), to examine what happened when the hopes of a generation of Progressive reformers were put into practice. His presentation is historical in a traditional sense: What were Progressive reformers attempting to accomplish, how well did they succeed, how should we understand the causes of failure? But he also moves directly into social policy. What does an understanding of the dynamics that operated at Norfolk tell us about current efforts to alter the system of incarceration? His answers also are on the negative side. He is sceptical about anyone's ability to deliver effective treatment in an institution; his text leads him to conclude that "the Norfolk experience does raise the complex issue of whether the difficulties of administering a humane prison *system* are not insurmountable." Whether the Norfolk experience can sustain the weight of such conclusions can be argued. But clearly the historical record of past efforts at social engineering is complete enough to allow for a whole series of illuminating case studies.

Taken together, these three chapters begin to suggest both the limitations and the potential of historical analysis for the policymaker. Anyone faced with the actual operation of these institutions, or with setting broad policy for them, would have to be discouraged given the conclusions of the chapters. Ideals and reality remain far apart, and even under what would appear to be exemplary conditions, organizational reform is extraordinarily difficult. This theme of pessimism and failure is so strong in all the chapters that we conclude this Introduction with a more detailed analysis of the theme's sources.

The policymaker must also be struck by the powerful effect of ideology on the operation of the institutions and by its constraining effects on reform, for it appears that major ideological shifts have to take place before basic change in the hospital, the school, or the prison can occur. Current institutional practices might be examined in an effort to discern which are most likely to be resistant to reform efforts and which might not require major shifts in the ideologies or belief systems of the principal actors. In any event, it should encourage a healthy sense of realism about the institutions and their capacity for change.

Finally, these three chapters exemplify the diversity and range of forms that historical analysis may take. Rothman uses a distinctive set of historical documents to trace one brief period in the life of a single prison. Rosenberg enlarges the scope to a small set of institutions in one area of the country, and over a third of a century, whereas the Katz chapter ranges over some 200 years of educational philosophy and schooling, bounded no more tightly than by the boundaries of the North American continent. Of course, these three styles by no means exhaust the range. As historical analyses are extended to a wider variety of institutions, we may come to learn which styles of work seem best suited to each of the variety of issues confronting the policymaker.

In Part II, the focus shifts from organizations to the history of specific social problems and policies. Robert M. Fogelson's inquiry addresses the morass that now affects public pension programs. His starting point is a contemporary crisis in policy. Then, in the traditional methodology of historians, he looks back to find the roots of the dilemma—using Los Angeles as a case in point, he asks how the police and fire department's pension system took on its contemporary characteristics? Fogelson's effort is not particularly aimed at apprising us how to solve the problem. In this sense, he does not have a client in mind. Yet, those with responsibility for present pension policies would not want to ignore his analysis. His evidence on how political considerations undercut cost–benefit considerations is masterly; it is, in effect, a primer for anyone who would have to see a program through the maze of urban politics.

Sheila M. Rothman examines the fate of the first federal program to fund maternal and child health care. This program of the 1920s was the creation of women determined to bring a new kind of preventive health care to the working classes. But their efforts failed, Rothman argues, in large measure because of the takeover of medical professionals. Sometimes in cooperation with the women reformers and sometimes in outright antagonism to them, the private doctors came to dominate maternal and child health care. As a result, programs that Progressive women initiated to raise the standard of health of the poor gave way to programs that private doctors administered, which enhanced their own prestige and promoted the welfare of paying, middle-class patients to the neglect of lower-class patients. Her analysis invites specific comparison with the Rosenberg essay, as each focuses on the power of the organized professions.

The chapter by Lawrence M. Friedman addresses the criminal justice system. Friedman self-consciously uses history to contradict the notion that some procedures are so deeply rooted as to be immutable to change. He demonstrates that laws prohibiting certain types of "victimless crimes," such as fornication, are relatively new, the invention of one generation that need not be binding on the next. Abolishing such statutes would not tear apart the fabric of morality. Yet, Friedman's chapter like so many others here has a darker side. He suggests that efforts to reduce discretion or eliminate plea bargaining will (almost inevitably?) be frustrated. Once again, we are back to history as a liberating and at the same time chastening discipline.

Like the chapters in Part I, these three chapters invite speculation on their use for policymakers and, more generally, on the role of historians relative to that of other contributors in policy debates.

The Fogelson and Rothman chapters raise the question of who gets to *define* the situation that policymakers confront? Often it is precisely those insiders—the police and firemen, the physicians—whose lives and careers stand to be most affected by any policy change. That hardly comes as a surprise, but its long-term consequence is surely something to be pondered by those who wish policymaking to reflect the public interest.

The Friedman chapter in particular raises the problem of piecemeal reforms. Unlike the institutions examined in Part I in which there is an identifiable center and core (albeit one that may be difficult to change), the criminal justice system has been called by some a "nonsystem" precisely because of the gangling and disjointed qualities noted in the Friedman chapter. Particularly in such systems, successful change in one part may be offset by compensating moves in another, making significant overall change nearly impossible.

These chapters lead us to speculate also on the role of historians compared with that of others in the policy field, specifically those engaged in some form of cost–benefit analysis. Is the policymaker always wise to pursue a cost–benefit analysis if a choice must be made? Does the emergence of policy analysis as a discipline mean that historical examinations will become still less relevant? We think the evidence in these chapters clearly suggests a negative answer. In many instances, ideology and power have mattered far more than the newer forms of policy analysis would suggest. It is still too early to tell what mix of history and other disciplines will yield the most powerful analysis. Perhaps we will need some form of cost–benefit analysis to generate solutions and some form of historical analysis to explain why the solutions are rarely adopted, or if adopted rarely work as planned.

Part III addresses a different question: The use of history by those whose primary concern is with social policy. Herbert G. Gutman's analysis reveals how a distorted view of the black past influenced the design of social policy, with the work of E. Franklin Frazier as case in point. Gutman's essay is one of the strongest statements of the need to bring good history directly to bear on social policy.

Seymour J. Mandelbaum's essay focuses on policymakers' conceptions of history in a different arena—urban social policy. He comes away unimpressed. Mandelbaum concludes that policymakers are deeply concerned with the past but are naive in their uses of the past. He does not believe that they recognize how often they manipulate the past to narrow their options in the future. There are few charges that, to historians at least, would be more damning. Put another way, Mandelbaum's chapter is an attractive invitation to historians to enter the field and to policy analysts to heed them.

The closing chapter by John Demos describes his firsthand encounter with the world of social policy—service on the Carnegie Council to examine policy toward children. He gives an intimate and revealing portrait of the way in which policy analysts use history and, not unimportantly, treat historians. He demonstrates that the impact of history is not always direct or even easily isolated; some of the influences enter in more roundabout and indirect ways: as part of a culture or as part of one's sense of self, group, and nation. Demos argues persuasively that policymakers and analysts are more influenced by their sense of the past than they would admit; the Carnegie Council, for example, was certain that since the family had survived so many rapid social transformations before, it was likely to do it again, and hence policy appropriately should attempt to buttress the family. The Demos chapter, uniquely among these contributions, shows the historian actively experiencing and contributing to the making of policy. As such, it is a fitting conclusion to this volume.

These final chapters offer the most direct evidence on the role of history and historians in social policy. It is these chapters that portray both the explicit and the implicit dialogue between the policy community and the community of historians. They provide the beginnings of what we hope will become a rich agenda for discussion and further inquiry. Five questions strike us as crucial, and worthy of note here.

First, when is historical understanding rich or deep enough to be taken seriously by those developing social policy? Put differently, how can those in policy circles be certain that the "past" they are using is accurate? As the Gutman chapter suggests, E. Franklin Frazier and, later, Daniel P. Moynihan thought they were relying on the best literature and evidence of the day. It was only later that these histories were exposed as inadequate. But what then about the current understanding? Will evidence a decade hence lead to yet a different and perhaps conflicting picture? Any understanding of the moment is necessarily incomplete, but to wait for the final definitive history would mean to abandon the enterprise. If Mandelbaum is right, the policy community wants "as little history as necessary," but even that must meet standards of adequacy for policy purposes. Are those standards different from any other the historian might employ?

A second theme is also evident in the Gutman and Mandelbaum chapters. Gutman implies that some of the inadequacies in Frazier's historical analysis were the result not of his ignorance but of his attempt, in a self-conscious way, to use history to the ends of social policy. And Mandelbaum argues that the urban planning community used history more to legitimate present policy than to explain past policies. There is no doubt that this concern for contamination—the fear that objectivity will be lost to the historian who moves into the policy world—keeps some historians away from the world of social policy. If this does constitute a problem, as these chapters surely suggest, are there strategies to minimize and control the risks?

Third, when history is used, is it to direct a particular policy, as implied in the Gutman and Mandelbaum chapters, or subtly to change the broad public understanding of an issue, as suggested in the Demos chapter? Clearly, the uses are many, only some of which are developed in this volume. But we suggest that the kind of influence described by Demos—a change in the general climate or zeitgeist within which policy issues are debated—is a much more frequent impact of historical understanding than is reflected in these particular chapters. And it is this potential for a diffuse and subtle impact that makes it so hard, as Demos notes, to articulate clearly the relevance of history for social policy.

Fourth, under what conditions will a historical analysis lead to an essentially "conservative" position, an effort to preserve and give support to past practices, and when will it cast doubt on those practices? The contrast is reflected in the Carnegie Council's general posture of support for the historic institution of the family, compared with chapters in Part I that tend to greater pessimism about the functioning of the hospital, the school, and the prison. Are these differences compelled by the actual differences of the institutions in question? May they be explained more readily by the difference between historians functioning on their own in contrast to a policymaking commission representing diverse specialties and interests?

A final, related question concerns the role the historian is to play in policy analysis. Specifically, how involved in the policy process should the historian be? Varying degrees of engagement and disengagement are suggested throughout this volume. Fogelson, for example, provides a rich and detailed description of the policy failures in public pension programs. But he does not feel compelled to offer his own recommendations. Friedman examines problems in criminal justice without revealing any strong preferences for solutions. At the other extreme is Demos, participating actively in the formulation of a social policy for children. We may expect that historians, like others, will contribute in a variety of different ways according to their own individual styles and preferences. But are there any preferred ways—ways that promise a greater impact from historians in the making of social policy? And, given the reservations reflected in our first two points in this brief list, would that greater impact necessarily be an unmixed blessing?

These questions raise only a few of the issues touched on variously by the different contributors to this volume. We make no claim to a complete canvassing of the range of substantive issues, of styles of historical work, or of policymakers' concerns for the use of history. But we do feel the chapters are rich and varied enough to be treated as a rough sampler of this complex field. And we suggest that the reader will get most out of the volume not by reading for a particular solution to a particular problem but by reading comparatively, to sense the similarities and differences in the intellectual problems each type of contribution confronts.

Let us conclude with one final observation on the feature, unanticipated in the design of this volume but now pervading it, that a majority of the chapters in Parts I and II trace policy failures. For all the claims that history is a liberating discipline, the accounts generally do tell a dispiriting story. The federal program in health care under Sheppard–Towner was defeated at the end of the 1920s; the grand hopes for reform at the Norfolk penitentiary fell short of realization. The pension system in Los Angeles is a mess; hospital administrators all too typically erect barriers to change; public schooling has not enhanced social mobility; the criminal justice system in California turns on itself in ways that discourage innovation. The reader is almost entitled to the conclusion that if in the nineteenth century economics earned the designation of a "dismal science," in the twentieth century the title belongs to history.

Quite possibly, the "failure" quality of the programs analyzed in the chapters here is accidental. It just so happened that these particular historians selected negative cases. Were chapters included on the ways that cities over the course of the nineteenth century reduced the risk of fires, improved their water supply, or minimized a host of public health dangers, the balance would be righted. But more than accident, we suspect, is at stake.

One possibility is that these historians in particular (it may or may not be characteristic of the discipline) tended to compare the reforms they were studying against the ideals set out for them by their originators. By taking the original rhetoric so seriously, the historians may have been prone to find failure. Different standards might have led to different overall judgments. For example, a more explicitly comparative perspective in examining the experience in other nations might have led to different conclusions in some cases. But, then again, what constitutes an approriate comparison is itself problematic and often controversial.

An alternative way to evaluate programs is to compare the particular reform in question against conditions that would have held in its absence. The development of the common public school traced by Katz may have had only a limited redistributive effect, as he suggests. But may it not have promoted greater opportunity than did the academy or apprenticeship systems it replaced? These observations simply remind us that the choice of a reference for comparison is a crucial step in an overall assessment. Our historians may have picked a tough standard for any program to meet.

Another possibility is that historians select for study those very institutions, policies, or practices that are beginning to lose their legitimacy or effectiveness. Historians, consciously or not, may well share in a public attitude of disquiet in a way that prompts them to ask: If this institution or procedure is so problematic today, then how did we first construct or devise it? It is just when the hospital, the prison, the delivery of health care, the school, or the pension program seems to be something other than appropriate, wise, and necessary that the historian turns his attention to the issue. In this sense, one effective way to know what is troubling a society is to read what the historians are investigating.

This process, we argue, makes the historian's contribution to the world of social policy all the more significant and relevant. A predisposition to select "failures" is an asset precisely because it helps to bring history directly to bear on the most difficult and problematic areas in public policy. In this way, a historical analysis is not at all restrictive of action or paralyzing. It does not hamper innovation or experimentation. To the contrary, its very ability to identify the elements that first created the problem is an excellent starting point for any effort to attempt to ameliorate it.

In sum, the chapters that follow represent accurately both the limitations and the promises of the collaboration between history and social policy. Those who would define policy relevance in narrow terms, who are seeking guidance in reaching immediate decisions, will find the approaches here of only limited interest; the chapters typically raise more questions than they resolve. On the other hand, each of these contributions reorients policymakers and analysts to their fields. Few disciplines are better suited than history is to challenge inherited wisdoms and received truths.

I

THE HISTORY OF SOCIAL INSTITUTIONS

2

INWARD VISION AND OUTWARD GLANCE: THE SHAPING OF THE AMERICAN HOSPITAL, 1880-1914[1]

CHARLES E. ROSENBERG

It is natural for us to see the hospital as central to the provision of medical care, to medical education, and to clinical investigation. For historians concerned with such matters, it is equally natural to see the hospital as reflecting in its evolution and present shape all those factors that have made the modern world modern—increases in scale, the dominance of professional elites, the bureaucratization of human relationships, the tendency toward technological approaches to social problems, and the legitimation of social roles and policies in terms of that technology. Contemporary social criticism has made this image familiar indeed.

Inasmuch as these clichés reflect reality, it is a relatively recent situation. A century ago the hospital was still a marginal aspect of medical care (although already significant to the ambitions of elite urban physicians). Even in the nation's largest cities, dispensaries and the hospitals' own outpatient divisions treated a far greater number of the poor than were ever admitted as inpatients. In 1873 the first American hospital survey located only 178 hospitals (including mental institutions), con-

[1]This chapter is drawn partially from materials collected during the author's tenure as a Rockefeller Foundation Humanities Fellow, 1976–1977, in preparation for a general history of medical care in America. A longer and more elaborately documented version of this chapter appeared in the *Bulletin of the History of Medicine* 53 (1979): 346–391, and appears here with the permission of that journal and the Johns Hopkins University Press.

SOCIAL HISTORY AND SOCIAL POLICY
ISBN 0-12-598680-7

taining a total of less than 50,000 beds.[2] Only a few of these institutions were consistently hospitable to medical school instruction, while in none was research an explicit commitment.

In a nation of some 40 million, this comparative handful of hospitals provided only a small proportion of the medical care Americans received. Not only did the hospital play a marginal role in the delivery of care, but it was also in its internal structure a far different institution from that which has become familiar in the twentieth century.[3] It was no monolith, certainly not one dominated by the medical profession and its needs. Lay trustees still felt that it was their duty to oversee every aspect of the hospital's internal life. Physicians could do little to intervene in the patient's biological reality and almost as little to shape the quality of life on the ward. Nurses and attendants could not be presumed to identify with medical men and medical values, and available therapeutics could ordinarily do little to alter the course of a patient's illness or the quality of his hospital experience. Stays were lengthy and most inpatients were not critically ill; keeping moribund patients alive was simply not an option.

Much of this had changed substantially by the first decade of the twentieth century. The hospital itself had become far more central in both the provision of medical care and the careers of ambitious physicians. In 1909 a census of American hospitals listed 4359, with 421,065 beds (a total that did not include mental or chronic-disease hospitals).[4] The hospital had become not only more widely distributed throughout the United States but also a potential recourse for a much larger proportion of Americans; the respectable and prosperous as well as the indigent might be treated in hospitals, frequently by their regular physicians. The hospital had become an institution easily recognizable to late-twentieth-century eyes. It had grown in size and had become more formal and bureaucratized, increasingly monolithic in authority structure, and more consistently reflective of medical needs and perceptions. All this had occurred without dramatic conflict, without formal planning or even informal concert, but within a set of social perceptions, economic relationships, and professional values that dictated a pattern of development as precise as anything that might have resulted from formal planning.

[2] J. M. Toner, "Statistics of Regular Medical Associations and Hospitals of the United States," *Transactions of the American Medical Association* 24 (1873): 287–333.

[3] The following conclusions are drawn from Charles E. Rosenberg, "And Heal the Sick: The Hospital and Patient in 19th-Century America," *Journal of Social History* 10 (1977): 428–447.

[4] E. H. L. Corwin, *The American Hospital* (New York, 1946), p. 8.

These developments reflect, at least in retrospect, a clear and consistently understood vision. The vision looked inward toward the needs and priorities of the medical profession, inward toward the administrative needs of the individual hospital, and inward toward a view of the body as mechanism and away from that of the patient as social being and family member. It was a vision, moreover, so deeply felt as to preclude conscious planning, replacing it instead with a series of seemingly necessary actions.

The decisions that shaped the modern hospital cannot be understood without a knowledge of the peculiar world of medical ideas and values, what might be called the culture of medicine. It has become fashionable in recent years to see medical self-conceptions as best explicable in marketplace terms. And obviously economic realities do explain much of what we see in past medical behavior; individuals do not ordinarily act in ways contrary to their perceived economic interest. Interest, however, cannot be understood in economic terms alone. The formal values of medicine were not simply a means of legitimating demands for control of the therapeutic marketplace. Why did at least some early nineteenth-century physicians work long hours to perform autopsies and publish their results, master an increasingly elaborate clinical literature, and treat large numbers of indigent patients without thought of fee? Such behavior is not comprehensible in purely material terms. The honor accorded innovation and the satisfaction of intellectual competence in a world of pervasive mediocrity, for example, are meaningful compensations—if perhaps no more transcendent than dollars and cents. One can hardly understand the evolution of the hospital without some understanding of the power of ideas, of the allure of innovation, of the promise of healing, and of the amelioration of painful and incapacitating symptoms through an increasingly hospital-based technology. This was the ethos of a medical community as eager to establish its own legitimacy as a profession with formalized standards of achievement as to increase its wealth. The self-consciousness that accompanied this emerging professionalism encouraged a necessarily inward vision among those aspiring practitioners concerned more with the establishment and definition of their own particular role than with any larger social context. The ethos of the medical profession elicited change as it defined behavior. The germ theory, antiseptic surgery, immunology, and the X ray were evidence of that change and seeming proof of the value of medical aspirations. That there could be conflict between the specific demands of the medical culture and other needs of human beings rarely occurred to those physicians who dominated hospital medicine.

As we shall see, there were advocates among late nineteenth- and early twentieth-century physicians and administrators for a hospital oriented toward community needs. An understanding of the patient's social environment, such critics contended, was necessary to a full understanding of both the cause of sickness and appropriate therapeutics. But this view was not to prevail. Those aspects of late-nineteenth-century institutional medicine not centered in the hospital's wards—the independent dispensary and the hospital's own outpatient facilities—actually decreased in significance to the medical world as the hospital and its inpatient service grew increasingly prominent both in the culture of medicine and in the delivery of medical care.[5]

Despite our late-twentieth-century assumption that the hospital is a necessarily central social institution, we know little, aside from its most general aspects, about the evolution of American hospitals between the Civil War and the first decade of the twentieth century. We do not have a good general history of the American hospital; we do not even have a study presuming to fulfill such a need. We do, on the other hand, have a number of chronicles of particular hospitals. Yet even the most dogged and monumental of these are by intent monuments to far-sighted philanthropists and discerning clinicians.[6] This is hardly an accident; nor is it happenstance that such histories are written from a narrowly internal perspective. This inward-looking historical canon is entirely consistent with the hospital's evolution. It is to be expected that we should have numerous histories of hopsitals but no history of *the* hospital in America. To write about *the* hospital is to see it as a social institution, but to write about *a* hospital is ordinarily to chronicle its internal

[5]For a more detailed discussion, see Charles E. Rosenberg, "Social Class and Medical Care: The Rise and Fall of the Dispensary." *Journal of the History of Medicine* 29 (1974): 32–54.

[6]We have no synthesis of American hospital history comparable to Brian Abel-Smith's *The Hospitals, 1880–1948: A Study in Social Administration in England and Wales* (Cambridge, Mass, 1964). A general study by the Commission on Hospital Care, *Hospital Care in the United States* (New York, 1947), provides a useful overview. There have been several significant monographs by professional historians: Morris Vogel, "Boston's Hospitals, 1870–1930: A Social History" (Ph.D. diss., University of Chicago, 1974), and "Patrons, Practitioners and Patients: The Voluntary Hospital in Mid-Victorian Boston," in *Victorian America*, ed. Daniel W. Howe (Philadelphia, 1976), pp. 121–138; David Rosner, "A Once Charitable Enterprise: Health Care in Brooklyn, 1890–1914" (Ph.D. diss., Harvard University, 1978); and William H. Williams, *America's First Hospital: The Pennsylvania Hospital, 1751–1841* (Wayne, Pa., [1976]). These studies have been extremely useful, especially Vogel's work, which emphasizes the period covered in this chapter and evaluates many of the same issues. See also Leonard K. Eaton's excellent *New England Hospitals, 1790–1833* (Ann Arbor, Mich., [1957]). For prominent examples of the older variety of hospital history, see Nathaniel T. Bowditch, *A History of the Massachusetts General Hospital . . .* 2d ed. (Boston, 1872); Thomas G. Morton and Frank Woodbury, *The History of the Pennsylvania Hospital* (Philadelphia, 1895).

development. Most hospital histories, including those of recent vintage, define their scope, logically enough, in terms of the accomplishments and dedication of skilled clinicians, the adoption of an increasingly elaborate technical armamentarium, and, of course, the building of buildings.

This chapter will concern itself with the years of transition between 1880 and World War I. Obviously these few pages cannot pretend to comprehensiveness. They will instead emphasize certain areas of change and conflict. One is the shifting pattern of authority within the hospital, especially the changing relationship between lay and medical administrators. Another is the role of inpatient as opposed to outpatient care and the place of both in the interaction between hospital and medical profession. And a third area is the conscious discussion of policy options as understood by contemporaries.

DECISIONS AND DECISION MAKERS

At no time in the nineteenth century was the hospital dominated by one group or one point of view. It was a creature of neither physicians nor laymen. Physicians had played a key role in the organization and shaping of America's earliest hospitals and dispensaries. Lay trustees, even though they might oppose specific demands of medical staff members, always conceded a general legitimacy to the claims of medical education; opportunities for clinical training had been an explicit aim in the founding of all our pioneer hospitals. Yet lay authorities throughout the late eighteenth and first half of the nineteenth centuries maintained a secure control over hospital policy and personnel.[7] To do less would have been a denial of their responsibility as stewards. Through this day-to-day commitment, community values and perceptions necessarily played a prominent role in shaping the antebellum hospital.

Perhaps the most helpful way of looking at authority within the nineteenth-century American hospital is to imagine a feudal division of responsibility, with conflict implicit in the differing perceptions of laymen and physicians—a conflict, however, ordinarily suppressed by the institution's fragmented quality. But a word of caution is necessary. Authority within the hospital should not be seen in entirely dichotomous terms, medical as opposed to lay. Day-to-day life on the ward was

[7]This was normally exerted by a subcommittee of the lay board, styled variously the attending, visiting, or inspecting committee, whose members would visit the hospital once or twice a week to oversee its workings and admit patients. This was true of both voluntary hospitals and municipal almshouse hospitals.

dominated by a "third force," the hospital subculture of patients, nurses, and attendants—laymen, certainly, but differing significantly in attitudes and origin from the trustees who retained formal control. There is, nevertheless, analytic purpose in emphasizing the continuing conflict between lay trustees and physicians. If we do so, a marked shift toward an increasing role for medical men and medical perceptions is to be seen even in the first three-quarters of the nineteenth century. In its last decades, this shift was to become far more dramatic.

The conflict must not be seen as simply a series of trivial squabbles between individuals with differing perceptions yet an equal desire to shape the institution to their will; it was ultimately a conflict between two cultures. In most respects, physicians' life-styles and world views were no different from those of the laymen who served on hospital boards of trustees or of those less secure members of the middle class who served as hospital stewards or superintendents. All were drawn from a similar social background and often shared religious, as well as class, identity. But as members of a profession, staff physicians were provided with particular values, particular ways of behaving, and particular ways of achieving a legitimate status within that profession. For ambitious and well-connected young physicians, the hospital had played a central role throughout the nineteenth century (although it played little or no role in the education or subsequent career of most ordinary practitioners).

Historians of medicine emphasize the sketchy quality of medical education in the first half of the nineteenth century and especially its lack of clinical training. Although these strictures probably do apply to the education of the vast majority of American physicians, they do not describe the opportunities available to the prosperous and ambitious. These young men were able to pay the preceptorial fees demanded by their generation's leading practitioners (many of whom enjoyed hospital appointments and the teaching privileges that normally accompanied them).[8] After completing their apprenticeships, they were able to compete for the scarce and unpaid hospital resident physicianships. Many such young men studied in Europe as well, creating an *ad hoc* but demanding course of clinical education—one based on the guidance of a skilled preceptor, hospital residence, and European training.

Although leading urban physicians did not pursue their private practice in the hospital, and while most did not contemplate the kind of clinical investigation recognizable as research today, the hospital nevertheless remained central to their ambitions. First, the hospital was, as

[8]In the eighteenth and early nineteenth century, apprenticeship was still a normal part of medical training, even for those would-be physicians who also attended formal medical lectures. Only those preceptors with hospital appointments as visiting or attending physicians could offer their students access to the hospital's wards.

has been suggested, a key locus for the teaching of clinical medicine. Second, hospital and dispensary physicianships allowed young medical graduates to accumulate needed clinical experience in a period when there were no formal residency programs, no speciality boards, and no certification examinations. Moreover, insofar as a physician's standing was related to scholarship (not research, but scholarship in the sense of mastering an existing literature and integrating that literature with clinical experience), a hospital attending post meant the opportunity to acquire that experience and to perform "important" operations for a surgeon or to describe and treat obscure and critical ills for the physician. Perhaps most importantly, in a society with few formal attributes of medical status—no government grants, endowed chairs, memberships in national academies or board certifications—a hospital attending position was (along with a medical school professorship) the most significant badge of professional achievement.

These professional needs implied specific demands within the hospital. And such demands might often clash not only with the trustees' personal desire for control but also with their sense of what constituted an appropriate stewardship. In the generations before the 1880s, such conflicts appeared and reappeared in a number of predictable areas: conditions for medical instruction and student access to patients, admission procedures, control of autopsy policies, staff discipline and performance, and even seemingly technical aspects of therapeutics.

The most frequent conflicts developed and reoccurred over medical education and its impact on patient care—and patient dignity. Trustees of both private and municipal hospitals consistently objected to an excessive amount of student contact with patients. When the Massachusetts General Hospital sought in 1824 to attract students, it warned that they could be admitted to its wards only with the understanding that they "carefully abstain from any gesture or remark which may tend to alarm the sick." They could examine patients only with specific authorization from the attending surgeon or physician. "It is obvious that the greatest inconveniences must arise, if such examinations are commonly made by the pupils." Philadelphia's Board of Guardians of the Poor emphasized in 1845, "There are rights possessed even by the recipients of charity which should be guarded, and feelings which should be respected."[9]

[9]Massachusetts General Hospital (hereafter abbreviated as MGH), *The Subscribers . . . rules for the Admission and Conduct of Pupils. May, 1824* (Boston, 1824), circular signed by James Jackson and John Collins Warren; Charles Lawrence, *History of the Philadelphia Almshouses and Hospitals . . .* (Philadelphia, 1905), pp. 156–157. For a similar action by Pennsylvania Hospital that limited students, see Board of Managers Minutes, 27 October 1845, Pennsylvania Hospital Archives, Philadelphia (hereafter abbreviated as PHA).

At the same time, however, all these antebellum hospitals tolerated clinical teaching programs—limited and unsatisfactory as such opportunities may have seemed to many physicians. The pupils of visiting physicians at the New York Hospital, for example, served as "walkers" and "dressers"—clinical assistants—in its medical and surgical wards; at other hospitals the pupils of visiting physicians could attend clinical lectures and "observe the practice" on the wards without paying a fee. Students at neighboring medical colleges were, however, required to pay a fee to attend clinical lectures at the hospitals; but the charges were modest, and the students could and did attend.

Even at the Philadelphia almshouse hospital, where the struggle between politically oriented lay managers and medical school teachers was most intense and where all teaching was banned for a dozen years at mid-century, special lecturing facilities had been arranged as early as the 1820s, and small clinical wards for medical and surgical cases had been established close to the clinical amphitheater, wards in which cases for "demonstration" could be chosen by the lecturers.[10] The relationship, in other words, between lay and medical authority, was complex. Lay trustees at all the hospitals felt called upon at times to circumscribe teaching, although they rarely challenged the need for clinical instruction as such.[11] Physicians could still less plausibly question the authority of lay trustees but nevertheless sought ever-expanding teaching opportunities. Thus the recurrent quibbles over the number of students to be admitted to wards, their bearing and decorum while in the hospital, and the right of patients to refuse to serve as "clinical material."

The logical connection—logical in twentieth-century terms—between medical school teaching and clinical appointments in hospitals was never accepted by nineteenth-century trustees. They were jealous of their appointing powers, and thus another conflict endemic in antebellum hospitals inevitably developed. Without a hospital appointment, a medical school professor could not lecture in its amphitheater or demonstrate cases on its wards. Some hospitals and medical schools did have

[10]The Filed Papers of the Board of Governors, New York Hospital Archives, New York City (hereafter abbreviated as NYHA), contain numerous testimonials documenting the network of association suggested here. For their formal rules, see *An Account of the New York Hospital* (New York, 1820), p. 24.

[11]Trustees did so in part because it promised benefits to the entire community, not just those few who found themselves in hospital beds. "Those physicians," as MGH trustees stated in 1822, "to whom necessity compels us to entrust the lives of our wives and children, do not witness patients for the first time in our chambers nor apply their first remedies to those whose health is so precious to us." *Address of the Trustees of the Massachusetts General Hospital, to the Subscribers and to the Public* ([Boston, 1822]), p. 22. The "us" who were potential patrons of the hospital were clearly not those who would be treated in its wards.

special relationships—Harvard and the Massachusetts General Hospital, the Pennsylvania Hospital and the University of Pennsylvania—but even in these conflict over appointments might arise. The fact that a man had been appointed professor in a medical school did not, trustees emphasized, create any obligation on their part to parallel that appointment with one as attending physician. And if trustees felt it inappropriate to have choices dictated to them, physicians on their part made it increasingly clear that they considered it inappropriate that laymen held so much power over professional matters.

In cities where more than one medical school competed for students, access to hospital facilities constituted an important element in that competition. Those medical schools without established ties to hospitals, such as Jefferson in Philadelphia or the Medical Department of the University of New York, demanded clinical privileges at least approximating those enjoyed by their more-established peers. In none of the cities, however, did the hospitals and their lay trustees provide access to clinical facilities equal to the demands of local medical schools. "A necessary connexion," one medical school teacher contended as early as 1822, "must . . . subsist between Colleges and Hospitals in order to form a complete system of medical education."[12] Not surprisingly, urban medical schools had by mid-century begun establishing their own dispensaries and even advertising for patients in an effort to provide clinical instruction. As early as the 1840s, for example, the University of Pennsylvania established its own dispensary with a few inpatient beds. Finally, in 1874, its School of Medicine was able to open the Hospital of the University of Pennsylvania—a concrete response to the desire of medical school faculty members for a hospital genuinely under their control, one that could be used both for teaching and as a setting for a portion of their private practice.[13] This was a significant event in the history of both the hospital and medical education in America.

Lay trustees also came into conflict with medical staff members when they sought to impose what seemed to them a proper discipline on their physicians. Throughout the century, senior attending physicians might prove themselves unreliable in appearing at stated visiting hours (even though such physicians rotated their tenure of responsibility, holding

[12]William Hamersley to William Bayard, Miscellaneous Manuscripts, 1822, New-York Historical Society, New York City. Origins of this assumption can be demonstrated much earlier, even in Great Britain's North American colonies.

[13]For a description of the crude dispensary of the 1840s, see Henry H. Smith to Bishop Potter, 4 January 1849, in Episcopal Hospital of the City of Philadelphia, *Appeal on Behalf of the Sick* (Philadelphia, 1851), pp. 41–42; and for a general account of the University Hospital and its origins, see George Corner, *Two Centuries of Medicine: A History of the School of Medicine of the University of Pennsylvania* (Philadelphia, 1965), pp. 133–153.

terms of 3 or 4 consecutive months in the year). It was difficult, however, for trustees to enforce hours of attendance on the senior physicians, especially since such men were prominent and influential in their own right. As if to make up for this failure of discipline, trustees sought all the more energetically to control the behavior of those fledgling practitioners who served as resident house staff. In their unquestioned view of themselves as stewards of an institution populated and staffed by moral and economic minors, lay trustees felt strongly that young physicians must submit to their authority. This meant in practice that house officers had to accept the surveillance of a lay superintendent, ask permission to leave the hospital building, and observe bylaws that forbade drinking, gambling, and the most casual socializing with nurses. Not surprisingly, young men of 20 or 22 often found such restraints confining and came into conflict with superintendents, matrons, or ward nurses. The reaction of lay authorities was often to chastise physicians but not their lay antagonists.

Even appropriate therapeutics might serve as an occasion for conflict between lay and medical authorities. Although trustees did not ordinarily presume to judge the effectiveness of particular drugs or surgical procedures, they felt it entirely within their competence to evaluate the economic and moral aspects of the physician's accustomed practice. A particularly long-standing conflict developed, for example, over the traditional medical use of alcohol as a stimulant and tonic. From the 1820s until the end of the century, staff members had to withstand the sometimes vigorous opposition of lay trustees to their use of alcoholic beverages; if alcohol was so destructive to man's health, the argument followed, how could alcohol help restore that health once it was impaired? Economic considerations, however, more frequently than temperance qualms led to the questioning of therapeutic practice. In several antebellum institutions, for example, physicians were warned against the use of costly leeches to draw blood; the lancet had served well enough in the past. At other times, lay committees were required to approve lists of drugs to be made available for hospital and dispensary practice. At mid-century, such watchdog committees often questioned an increasingly lavish use of beef tea and other dietary supplements. [14] In 1845, for example, a subcommittee of the New York Hospital's Board of Gover-

[14]On pressure to reduce the amount of alcohol administered, see, among many such examples, Board of Physicians Minutes, 18 June 1821, 4 April 1831, and Hospital Committee Minutes, 24 October 1884, both in Board of Guardians Records, Philadelphia City Archives, Philadelphia (hereafter abbreviated as PCA); Richard Cadbury to De Forrest Willard, 5 February 1885, Superintendent's Letterbooks, PHA. For attempts to reduce the number of leeches employed, see Minutes, 15 February 1836, Board of Guardians Records, PCA; Medical Staff to the President and Managers, Boston Dispensary, [February 1844], Boston Dispensary Papers, Countway Library of Medicine, Boston.

nors bemoaned the use of "very expensive medicine & in quantities which have not been used—and a prodigal use of Lint & Leeches." They did not, the report concluded, "intend to cast ... censure upon the resident Physicians & Surgeons." It seemed that "Ardent young men in the pursuit of Science are not likely to be very careful of expenditure."[15]

Although less picturesque, admissions procedures illustrate perhaps most clearly the gradual redefinition of authority within the nineteenth-century hospital. At the beginning of the century, responsibility for admissions was in reality, as well as in legal form, in the hands of laymen. Trustees appointed small subcommittees that met, usually twice a week, at the hospital to evaluate all applicants for admission (and, in the case of accidents or emergencies, to determine whether the patient might be allowed to remain). Thus, it was natural for even the eminent Benjamin Rush to assure a friend that he would appear before the Pennsylvania Hospital's visiting committee and plead the case of a prospective candidate for admission; Rush could not unilaterally admit a patient, even though he was an attending physician at the hospital.[16] Subscribers or annual contributors might as a condition of their support nominate patients for admission; in effect, such laymen controlled access to a bed for all or part of a year. Similarly, in outpatient dispensaries, a written testimonial from a contributor might be necessary before a poor man could receive medical attention. One's social place, as well as biological state, determined hospital admission. Not only the assumptions of deference and stewardship implicit in the trustees' admission power but also their willingness to exert that power—personally and in circumstances that must in many cases have been onerous— guaranteed that the hospital's patient population would not be determined by medical criteria alone.

The categories of clinical diagnosis were only one of several factors determining admission at private hospitals. (The municipal or almshouse hospitals were the legatees of all those cases deemed unacceptable by private institutions. Within the almshouse, however, ward designations reflected categories such as morality and ability to work in addition to medical diagnosis, whereas admission itself had ordinarily to be approved by lay welfare administrators, as well as by staff physicians.)[17] Until mid-century, significantly, most American hospitals did not have a specific location devoted to the physical examination of pro-

[15]"The Committee to whom was referred the subject of the increasing expenditure of the Hospital, ... Report, 4 February 1845," Filed Papers of Board of Governors, NYHA.
[16]Benjamin Rush to Ashbel Green, 26 April 1803, in Benjamin Rush, *Letters of Benjamin Rush*, ed. L. H. Butterfield, 2 vols. (Princeton, 1951), 2:863.
[17]Rosenberg, "And Heal the Sick," p. 432; Cook County (Illinois) Hospital, *Rules and Regulations. June, 1868* (Chicago, 1867), p. 15.

spective patients; admission was a process that took place as much in social as in physical space. The shift to an admission procedure in which lay trustees intruded only occasionally, but assigned their responsibility instead to medical men and the seemingly universalistic categories of medical nosology, was well underway by the 1870s, although it was not to approach completeness until the twentieth century.[18]

Less significant in terms of the hospital's day-to-day realities, but nevertheless revealing underlying attitudes, were sporadic conflicts in regard to postmortem and autopsy policies. The very recurrence of such disputes illustrates the potential for conflict in the differing imperatives of lay and medical cultures. Physicians sought throughout the century to enjoy liberal autopsy regulations, ones that would allow the performance of postmortems in ambiguous or interesting cases; trustees sought to enforce regulations that would minimize the possibility of offending the deceased patient's family—and thus the community generally. Their primary responsibility, as lay trustees understood it, was to provide medical care for a particular constituency. Popular fears that the hospital was a place where patients would be experimented upon while alive and dissected after death obviously interfered with the carrying out of that responsibility. Physicians, on the other hand, contended that the advancement of medical knowledge justified the occasional disconfiture of a particular patient's family. Such arguments recurred regularly in the history of every large American hospital; although the circumstances might differ, the conflict itself remained essentially unchanged, for it reflected the same underlying differences between lay and medical perceptions. The medical ethos dictated a vision fixed inward toward the body as mechanism and toward the profession; lay attitudes looked outward toward the place that body had occupied in society. Each saw their particular imperatives as legitimate, and neither view entirely dominated the nineteenth-century hospital.

Significantly, the arguments of physicians who sought unfettered access to patients for teaching purposes were strikingly similar to those that justified demands for liberal autopsy procedures. The particular patient was not as important, the argument followed, as the lessons his illness might impart to student physicians.[19] The momentary inconve-

---

[18]The free-bed policy of the late nineteenth century constituted something of a transition device. As late as 1890, for example, the New Haven Hospital allowed the donor of $5000 or his heirs and assigns to nominate patients to a free bed for 100 years or during the lives of any three persons the donor might nominate. New Haven Hospital, *Sixty-fourth Annual Report, 1890,* (New Haven, 1891), p. 7.

[19]Toward the end of the century, the prerogatives of research figured increasingly prominently in medical arguments. "The hospital," one MGH staffer declared in 1894, "has a duty to the future as well as to the present generation. . . . No one could have predicted the

nience of an individual patient was a small price to pay for the increased clinical competence that a whole class of students might later apply in practice (often, it was contended, in rural areas where opportunity for observing obscure cases was infrequent). As J. C. Warren explained this deeply felt medical assumption in 1845:

> Medical treatment at the hospital alleviates the sufferings of some one or two hundreds of persons who, from year to year, resort to its wards, but the advancement of medical science confers important benefits upon the community at large, and every individual, throughout the extent of our land, who becomes the victim of disease or accident, directly participates in them.[20]

Thus stated, the social benefits of clinical teaching far outweighed any problems it might create.

SOURCES OF CHANGE AND FORMS OF CONTROL

The years between 1880 and the first decade of the twentieth century constituted a period of administrative transition for the American hospital. Lay trustees increasingly limited their personal involvement. The older assumption that every detail of patient care might receive their legitimate attention seemed hardly a plausible option in the larger urban hospitals. In the twentieth century, trustees no longer felt it their place to discipline resident physicians, interview nurses, sample the house diet, or determine the necessity and financial conditions of each admission. Prospective trustees could be reassured that their responsibilities would be largely financial, limited to raising funds and perhaps attending a monthly luncheon.[21] Individual trustees might still involve themselves in particular conflicts or in particular staff appointments, but such paternalistic intrusion was no longer the routine method of arriving at such decisions. Medical men still resented the lingering power of lay

---

future of sulphuric ether in 1845, nor is it possible to foretell at this period, what bearing the disclosures made by a single autopsy may have upon the lives of thousands in years to come." H. A. Beach to W. S. Bigelow, 15 February 1894, H. A. Beach Biographical File, MGH Archives, Boston.

[20]J. Collins Warren to Henry B. Rogers, Frances C. Lowell, and Charles Amory, Committee, in "Report on a Lying-In Department, October, 1845," Obstetrics Department File, MGH Archives, Boston.

[21]"A trusteeship," a prospective member of the Philadelphia Polyclinic Hospital Board was assured in 1907, "involves no obligations save when it is possible, attending the Board meetings on the third Tuesday of each month." Board to Mr. Anderson (copy), 7 January 1907, Polyclinic Hospital Papers, Archives of the University of Pennsylvania, Philadelphia.

trustees and their frequent unwillingness to allow medical men to sit on their boards, but they must have been aware of the increasing distance of lay trustees from the hospital's daily routine.

A number of interrelated factors had helped bring about these new administrative realities. One was financial. Voluntary hospitals had always depended largely, although not exclusively, on private contributions, and especially after the difficult years of the early 1890s, trustees found their economic responsibilities demanding enough to absorb all their available energy and commitment. Allied to this financial exigency was a parallel increase in hospital size and fixed costs. Immigration and the steadily increasing size of American cities meant increasing numbers of potential patients unable to employ private physicians; for such urban workers, nursing and sickroom space were as elusive as a doctor's fees. As costs mounted, trustees sought both to decrease expenditures and increase income; almost inevitably they turned to the fees of private patients as a means of balancing chronically straitened budgets.[22] Given the determination of private boards to maintain their autonomy and the general unavailability of public funds, such calculations were a necessity; how else could a private hospital control spiralling costs except by establishing an appropriate ratio between pay and charity cases? In accepting the need for private patients, moreover, hospitals necessarily conceded an increasing influence to those staff physicians whose referrals and reputation were needed to fill private beds. Second, increasing size and a parallel growth in bureaucracy within the institution placed formal and inevitably self-conscious and self-interested layers of reassuring experts between the trustees and the hospital's wards. To define trustee responsibilities in financial terms alone seemed by the beginning of the present century a prudent, even moral, division of authority. Finally, an increasingly elaborate level of technical and intellectual capability underscored the seeming necessity for medical autonomy within the institution, while at the same time increasing the hospitals' costs. Clinical laboratories, X-ray apparatus, and more sophisticated surgical facilities inflated hospital expenses as they changed the hospital's public image. To alert and ambitious physicians, the hospital was becoming the only appropriate place for the highest level of clinical practice. Their patients gradually came to share this view.

In 1874, the year the Hospital of the University of Pennsylvania

[22]MGH, for example, found its income increasing from $123,251 in 1891 to $136,997 in 1894, whereas its expenses increased from $135,656 to $178,924. By 1896 the trend was such that the trustees felt that they had to limit expenses to balance their budget even if it meant closing wards. "If we prove ourselves bad economists we shall lose the confidence of our friends. They will not give money which appears to be wasted." Edmund Dwight to J. Collins Warren, Visiting Staff Correspondence, Box 1, MGH Papers, Countway Library, Boston.

opened its doors as America's first university-controlled hospital, its already aged and honored peer, the Pennsylvania Hospital, instituted a seemingly trivial, but in retrospect significant, change. Its Board of Managers appointed a medical "Officer of Hygiene" to inspect the hospital, ward by ward, and report its condition.[23] No longer would a subcommittee of the trustees walk methodically from floor to floor, approve invoices, and verify admissions. Like all its sister institutions, even the conservative and atypically patriarchal Pennsylvania Hospital had evolved far from the personal stewardship exerted by its trustees at the beginning of the century.

Perhaps most significant in this shift was the redefining of the superintendent's role; for it was his intermediary and managerial presence that became central in the gradual delimiting of trustee authority. By the turn of the century, superintendents of the nation's largest hospitals had come to think of themselves as professionals, competent in a new and highly challenging discipline. Yet, as late as the Civil War, hospital superintendents had normally been men of wide business experience (if of no great success); only infrequently was it assumed that they should have had previous institutional experience. Their wives still routinely served as matrons, overseeing the domestic work—the hospital's cleaning, cooking, laundering—as a competent wife would her husband's home. By 1900 the superintendent of a large urban hospital had to deal with an already complex economic world—purchasing, accounting, labor management—and this within an ever more intricate organizational structure.

Both medical and nursing staff, for example, presented a very different aspect from that that they had assumed at mid-century. In the larger hospitals, attending medical staff members had organized themselves into boards, and in some of the largest, into separate medical, surgical, and outpatient units. Their staff meetings provided a unified platform for the formulation of medical goals and needs. Changes in nursing were even more dramatic. Nursing now constituted its own "estate," represented in organizational terms by a superintendent of nursing eager to control the nursing staff and to act as intermediary between trustees, medical staff, and superintendent. The nurse training school, moreover, had by the end of the century become almost universal in American hospitals of any size; in some ways it was a financial necessity. For the unpaid labor of student nurses had become indispensable if the hospital was to balance its books.[24] Even the hospital's physical plant had become larger and more complex; by the turn of

---

[23]Board of Managers Minutes, 25 May 1874.
[24]Ratios of 1 graduate to 10 student nurses were typical in large hospitals at the turn of the century.

the century, the skilled work of electricians, plumbers, and steam fitters, the maintenance of elevators and electric ambulances meant new problems and new kinds of personnel relationships for the hospital superintendent.

Many hospitals sought to solve the problem of a divided authority and minimize conflict between lay and medical views by hiring a full-time salaried physician as "chief resident"; he would be responsible for purely medical administration, whereas a lay superintendent or administrator exerted the trustees' responsibility over routine financial and personnel matters. Most of the large hospitals, however, attempted to centralize administrative responsibility in the hands of one individual, usually a layman. Ordinarily, organizational wisdom endorsed the policy of what came to be called "dual management," the separation of lay from medical areas of control, with lay trustees assuming responsibility for the institution's economic well-being and medical boards for matters relating to admissions, therapeutics, and house staff discipline. This did not protect the hospital from occasional internal friction, especially between superintendent and medical staff, but did tend to keep such conflict within the institution. Even in municipal hospitals, administrators and medical staff exerted an ever-increasing autonomy. The combined influence of an increasingly bureaucratized structure and the removal of lay trustees from day-to-day intervention in the hospital implied an institution increasingly inward looking, one less and less amenable to pressures originating outside the institution itself and the culture of medicine.[25]

As the superintendent became more self-consciously professional the relationship of the physician to the hospital changed as well. This hinged, as I have suggested, on two related developments: the increasing technical resources of the profession and the parallel increases in the financial demands made upon the hospital's traditional sources of voluntary support, demands that could be met only by finding new benefactors or enforcing a prudent ratio of pay to indigent patients.[26] Most of the larger hospitals pursued both options.

Not surprisingly, all of the older voluntary hospitals had by the 1890s

[25]It would be no difficult task, of course, to find isolated examples of a vestigial paternalism. Physicians might still be suspended or even discharged as a result of patient complaints; trustees might still intervene in behalf of favored patients; and in occasional cases trustees chastised physicians for inhumanity toward patients or chronic tardiness. The youthful indiscretions of house officers still demanded discipline; the penchant of resident physicians for alcohol and the occasional destruction of furniture seems to have been endemic.

[26]In April 1899, for example, St. Luke's Hospital in Chicago instituted a policy whereby the total number of free cases would not exceed half that of "full pay patients." In the years immediately following, the hospital was consistently able to show a small surplus. St. Luke's Hospital, *Thirty-sixth Annual Report, 1898–99; Thirty-eighth Annual Report, 1900–*

begun to seek increased numbers of private patients. The only major exception to this policy was the small, conservative, and still Quaker-dominated Pennsylvania Hospital, which stated explicitly that its resources were to continue to be devoted primarily to the poor—for whom the hospital had been founded—and not to the well-to-do (who had, by the 1880s, an assortment of private hospitals among which they might choose). The Massachusetts General Hospital also experienced a late nineteenth-century split between those physicians and lay trustees who sought to increase private bed utilization and those staff members who thought this inconsistent with the hospital's social mission. In newer hospitals and away from the more tradition-oriented East Coast, the emphasis on paying patients was never questioned.[27]

Indeed, most hospitals established in the late nineteenth century were founded on the assumption that a major portion of their operating budget would come from private patients. Significantly as well, almost all provided elaborate private bed facilities before they were able to achieve a satisfactory level of occupancy. Hospital publications emphasized not only their superior clinical facilities but also the comfort and convenience of their rooms and the attentiveness of their resident staff. No hotel suite, particularly enthusiastic administrators gushed, could offer more comfort than their private hospital rooms.[28]

These new realities implied a new kind of relationship between visiting staff and hospital. It was a relationship of mutual accommodation and dependence—and one in which the hospital became inevitably more central not only to the ambitions of the physicians who treated the rich and dominated hospital attending physicianships and medical school appointments but also to an increasingly large number of urban physicians generally. As early as the 1890s, a few prominent and enterprising urban surgeons had begun to limit their practice to the hospital; they were still only a few but, at least in retrospect, were an influential few.[29] Thus, a symbiosis between physician and hospital had begun to

---

1902, p. 70. Newly established voluntary hospitals made it clear that although they did not hope to make a profit, they could admit only that number of "worthy and impecunious patients, as its resources from paying patients and its endowments will permit." In the great majority of cases, endowments were small or nonexistent. Lane Hospital (San Francisco), *First Annual Report 1894–1895*, (San Francisco, 1895) p. [1].

[27]Cf. Richard Cadbury to Mrs. J. D. Armstrong, 30 March 1885, Superintendent's Letterbooks, PHA. As early as 1905, even the comparatively well-endowed MGH collected $74,538.20, nearly one-third of its operating expenses, from private patients. George Day, "Abuse of Medical Charity," *Boston Medical and Surgical Journal* 152 (1905): 297.

[28]See, for example, the comments of Louis R. Curtis, Superintendent of St. Luke's Hospital (Chicago), "The Modern Hotel–Hospital," *Transactions of the American Hospital Association* 9 (1907): 132–138.

[29]In 1894, for example, Nicholas Senn, Chicago's most prominent surgeon, could explain to J. Collins Warren that he enjoyed "continuous service" at St. Joseph's and Presbyterian hospitals (that is, he did not serve a 3- or 4-month tour of duty). "It is here I earn

develop well before the publication of the Flexner Report (1910), the movement for formal hospital accreditation, and the systematic incorporation of American hospitals into a reformed pattern of medical education. In this case, at least, formal procedures merely reflected and intensified already-established economic and institutional relationships.

Not surprisingly, many physicians found this growing dependence on the hospital a convenient, profitable, and honorific pattern. There were some exceptions, however; not all medical men were pleased with these developments. Among the dissatisfied were attending physicians at that minority of hospitals that refused to allow staff members to accept fees for treating inpatients. Equally unhappy were the much larger number of physicians denied admitting privileges in major urban hospitals; by the time of the World War I, the denial or limitation of such privileges had already become a controversial issue in a number of cities. Finally, there were the least prosperous, least well-educated physicians who could not aspire to admitting privileges and who saw all of institutional medicine as an unfair and undemocratic mode of competing for patients.

The Massachusetts General was the hospital most conspicuously and atypically unwilling to allow its physicians to accept fees for treating inpatients. Despite rising costs in the 1890s, some of its trustees and certain Brahmin attending physicians held fast against this intrusion of materialism into what they saw as a fundamentally charitable enterprise. In the course of a sometimes bitter internal debate, it became apparent that Massachusetts General represented a small minority among contemporary hospitals; perhaps even more significantly, it became apparent as well that its own visiting staff members were sending their private patients to other hospitals, institutions in which physicians could accept payment for professional services. Far more typical, even among older institutions, was the New York Hospital, which not only built special rooms for private patients at the turn of the century but also moved to extend admitting privileges to certain nonstaff physicians who might provide private referrals. At the same time, it adjusted rates to keep them competitive with New York's other private hospitals.[30] In many

---

my daily bread," he elaborated, "because I have not the time to operate in private houses. This arrangement is a great help to the hospitals as it brings them wealthy and influential patients who later show a deep interest in their prosperity." Senn to Warren, 28 February 1894, Phillips House File, MGH Archives. In a letter of transmittal (undated) to the trustees' secretary Edmund Dwight, Warren noted that "Dr. Senn is one of the most prominent men in the country. He told me recently he 'paid no visits'. He is said to have an income of $75,000 a year." Phillips House File.

[30]Howard Townsend to Visiting Committee, 27 September 1901, Filed Papers of Board of Governors Papers; Executive Committee Minutes, 23 October 1901, 6 November 1901, NYHA; and George Ludlam to Visiting Committee, 25 September 1901, Visiting Committee File, NYHA.

less prestigious voluntary hospitals, the private patients of any regularly licensed practitioner were welcome, and the physician was allowed to treat them and charge whatever fees seemed to him appropriate. By 1910 an older practitioner could complain that hospital trustees had ceased to evaluate staff members on the basis of their skill but judged them instead on the number of patients they could attract.[31]

By the First World War, in short, the role of American hospitals had changed drastically. The private patient was becoming part of the hospital's normal patient population—and an important factor in balancing its accounts. The hospital was becoming a significant locus for urban medical practice; hospital treatment had become a plausible option for well-to-do patients. A generation earlier their counterparts would not have entered a general hospital under any circumstances. In smaller communities, physicians and medical societies allied with local men of affairs to organize their own hospitals; even in such small cities and towns, a hospital had begun to seem a necessity to the practice of medicine. The hospital itself was becoming increasingly unified and, insofar as it was so, consistently informed by medical needs and perceptions. Although still unquestioned in their legal control of most voluntary hospitals, lay trustees exerted that control indirectly and through well-understood bureaucratic channels.

INPATIENT AND OUTPATIENT IN THE CULTURE OF MEDICINE

Since the late eighteenth century, gratuitous outpatient care had been an accepted part of urban medicine; indeed, it had become the principal form of institutional care for the working poor and the indigent and remained so throughout the century. Both pioneer hospitals and independent dispensaries offered "walk-in" care to American city dwellers unable to afford their own physicians. In the case of the more seriously ill, staff physicians paid house calls. The policy was effective, in keeping with both the needs implicit in the career patterns of physicians and the social perceptions of those benevolent stewards of society's wealth who paid the costs of dispensary care. At minimum cost, the laboring poor could be kept out of the hospital's pauperizing wards and returned to work as soon as possible; healing itself might be expected to take place more easily in the emotionally reassuring and relatively contagion-free home. Physicians, on the other hand, found volunteer work at a dis-

[31]Thomas A. Emmett, *Incidents of My Life* (New York, 1911), pp. 333–334.

pensary or hospital outpatient facility an attractive way of accumulating clinical experience while establishing those contacts—both lay and medical—that led ultimately to professional success.

In the hierarchy of professional achievement, however, outpatient appointments were always less desirable than were attending physicianships. Control of beds, the opportunity to select and monitor challenging cases, the opportunity for surgeons to perform "important" operations, and, most importantly, the traditional social distinction of the position itself guaranteed that the inpatient physician would enjoy more status than did his outpatient confrere.

Emphasis might have changed, but the distinctions between inpatient and outpatient care remained sharp. Outpatients ailments were episodic and ordinarily not life threatening and, perhaps most important, remained consistently outside the economic nexus. Inpatient care, on the other hand, was less episodic, related to more dramatic ills, and was consistently associated with the status attached to hospital physicianships. (Chronic ailments were generally treated in municipal and county institutions—often as custodial rather than as medical problems.) The gap between the two kinds of appointments grew wider as the century progressed and medicine's technical capabilities increased; especially in surgery, inpatient care seemed increasingly the only appropriate basis upon which proper treatment might be undertaken. And although providing inpatient care was through the first three-quarters of the century ordinarily unpaid, by the end of the century, as I have suggested, it was becoming increasingly clear to enterprising medical men that the hospital might soon play a significant role in private practice. Outpatient work, on the other hand, remained a formative stage in the physician's professional evolution, a stage decreasingly central as hospitals increased in number and opportunities for clinical training expanded. In the 1880s, however, outpatient and clinic work still constituted an important phase in the medical career, even though the function of such practice had changed since the beginning of the century. In the larger urban hospitals, outpatient appointments provided a recognized stage in an elite medical career, one in which ambitious young practitioners accumulated specialized skills as they waited more or less patiently to achieve the higher status of attending physician or surgeon.

Although undoubtedly important to budding specialists and their students, outpatient medicine exhibited a number of chronic shortcomings. One was the frequently poor quality of care; clinic hours were short, waiting rooms were crowded and lacking in privacy, examinations were perfunctory, records were casually kept, and attendance by senior physicians was sometimes equally casual. A second shortcoming was the organizational problem of relating outpatient staff and functions to the hospital and its senior attending staff. Such medical dynasts saw outpatient work as useful in serving to "feed clinical material" to the hospital's inpatient beds and as a necessary part of training for medical students and nurses. When these functions were not performed effectively, friction developed. Conflict also emerged as inpatient and outpatient physicians squabbled over facilities and privileges. A third problem developed at the very end of the nineteenth and beginning of the twentieth centuries: It became increasingly difficult to interest "first-class" young men in routine outpatient work. Such positions, as a New York Hospital report explained in 1906, had become comparatively undesirable as more attractive opportunities opened and clinical instruction became an integral part of medical education.[32] A fourth and particularly bitter conflict arose, finally, over the economic aspects of outpatient care. Comtemporaries increasingly assumed that many of those consulting hospital and dispensary outpatient departments were fully capable of employing their own physicians. In soliciting gratuitous care, they were participating in a kind of fraud, one generally described by contemporaries as "charity abuse." Hospital and dispensary spokesmen became increasingly defensive, as rank and file practitioners attacked what they perceived to be unfair competition.

Although it may sound judgmental, it must be understood that patient care as such was not ordinarily a consideration in these discussions—beyond the institutional and moral inertia shaped by the traditional assumption that medical care should be supplied to the deserving among the indigent (the crippled, blind, aged, and widowed) and those working poor temporarily in need. Medical care had been, in this sense, a right at the beginning of the nineteenth century. Certainly few if any physicians opposed in a categorical way the need for such gratuitous outpatient care or the responsibility of the medical profession to provide it. But the provision of such care offered neither material wealth nor intellectual glory. No one opposed outpatient care at mid-century, but neither did more than a few care intensely about it as such. The significance of outpatient work to medical men lay in the opportunities it provided for the acquisition of status and clinical experience. In some ways this orientation pervaded all decision making within the hospital. Institutional policies were determined, that is, only partially by the needs of a specific population; they were shaped far more often by

[32]"The acquirements of recent graduates of our medical school[s] have been so greatly increased that the men no longer feel the need of doing dispensary work for self-improvement." The report noted the same experience at other outpatient departments at which they had made inquiries. Executive Committee Minutes, 31 October 1906, NYHA.

some institutional dilemma, such as financial stringency, or some professional conflict, such as access to patients for teaching purposes. If
optimum care for the working poor had been an explicit priority in
shaping the delivery of medical care, clinic hours—to cite only the most
mundane of examples—would hardly have been limited to the working
day.

Let me cite several examples to illustrate these generalizations. In 1887
the New York Hospital had experienced a series of conflicts between
inpatient and outpatient staff, as well as complaints about the quality of
its outpatient care. The hospital's attending physicians felt particularly
strongly that the outpatient department should function primarily as a
feeder, as a provider of "good material," for the inpatient wards; and it
seemed clearly to have failed to fulfill this goal. The attending physicians
accordingly sought to trim some of the larger—and they charged
superfluous—outpatient departments. The arguments employed by
both sides in the controversy are illuminating. In opposing the
suggested dissolution of the outpatient gynecology service, for example,
its advocates made four points in order of decreasing significance. First,
they contended, this service supplied the hospital with valuable referrals, "the treatment of which often demands important operations."
Second, the experience it provided was essential to nursing education.
Third, it was similarly important for medical students. Fourth, and finally, physicians connected with the service noted that it was useful to
the working people in the vicinity.[33] Medical staff priorities could not
have been more precisely displayed.

At the Massachusetts General Hospital, the outpatient department
constituted a source of conflict throughout the period of this discussion,
as bright young physicians sought to rise out of the lesser status of
outpatient physicians and into that of attending physician. Outpatient
physicians had their own board but in theory could appeal to the hospital's trustees only through attending physicians and surgeons, a situation that the outpatient staff did not find to their liking.[34] Specialists
practicing without compensation in the hospital's outpatient service

[33]For the phrase "good material," see Medical Board to Board of Governors, Executive
Committee Minutes, 31 January 1887. For the itemized list of reasons for maintaining a
gynecological outpatient department, see entries for 5 November 1888 and 31 December
1888, and see also 2 June 1888, Executive Committee Minutes, NYHA.

[34]Charles Townsend to E. G. Cutter, secretary, Staff of Physicians and Surgeons, 20
January, 31 March 1898, 1 November 1897, Thomas B. Hall to Physicians and Surgeons to
Outpatients, 11 March 1898, A. Cabot, chairman of committee appointed to confer with
the Committee from the Outpatient Department, to Visiting Staff, 22 April 1898, all in
Visiting Staff Correspondence, 1881–1897, Box 1, MGH Papers.

fought repeatedly for access to inpatient beds as well; without such beds there was no way of following cases, as they saw it, or of applying particularly interesting or innovative therapeutic techniques. I do not mean to suggest that such conflict was an everyday reality in the hospital—but that it was implicit in the motives and relationships of staff physicians. Most of the outpatient physicians resigned themselves to their secondary status within the hospital hierarchy and waited until Massachusetts General's time-honored seniority system offered a vacant physicianship.

Most such pushing and shoving remained hidden from the public and often from trustees as well. In the public mind, and in the reflections of the great majority of medical practitioners as well, the central dilemma of outpatient care was that subsumed under the term "charity abuse." For the ordinary urban practitioner, the hospital was a stronghold of medical privilege, and those cases that the hospital's attending staff regarded as potential "clinical material" were his potential bread and butter. Even those administrators convinced of the need for a vigorous outpatient effort had become increasingly defensive by the late 1890s. Earlier convictions that such benevolence was a moral responsibility of the medical profession had faded by the beginning of the twentieth century. Only a minority of medical men still felt it preferable that a few dissimulators receive undeserved care than that the genuinely needy be either discouraged or humiliated by questions and investigations. By the late 1890s, critics of promiscuous charity emphasized not only the drain of unjustified demands on hospital treasuries but also the moral dangers of instilling a pauper mentality in the recipients of unearned and thus unappreciated benefits. In addition, the generation's newly self-conscious rationalizers of charity joined their voices to those of disaffected medical men in decrying the existing system of providing care without adequate financial investigation. By the opening years of the twentieth century, most hospitals and dispensaries had to an extent responded to such criticisms.[35] Some institutions arranged with professional social work organizations to check the legitimacy of patient claims

[35]In reading between the lines of this debate, it becomes apparent that many patients, especially at the outpatient departments of the largest and best-known hospitals, did have some ability to pay but came to special clinics seeking more definitive diagnoses than their regular practitioners were capable of providing. Indeed, many were referred informally by family physicians who desired a consultation their patients could not have afforded as private patients. "The patients come very largely for diagnosis," one contemporary explained, "and care little for the prescriptions. They will be treated at home, but wish to know 'if the Doctor is right.'" E. G. Cutler to Edmund Dwight, 18 November 1893, Pharmacy File, MGH Archives.

of financial inability; others conducted their own financial investigations or began to make small charges for the use of outpatient facilities.[36] Inpatients were comparatively immune from such charges of misrepresentation; for, at least to contemporary perceptions, these patients were truly in need, a need demonstrated by both the admitting physician's diagnosis and a willingness to enter the hospital's forbidding wards.

As has already been suggested, a minority of physicians and administrators sought not only to emphasize the continued need for outpatient and dispensary care but also to expand and improve it. In their arguments, truly effective medical care and a more humane urban society were inextricably related. Aspects of traditional etiological thought, as well as a motivating mixture of Christianity, socialism, and a concern for ameliorating the conditions of urban life, pointed toward the need for a medicine with roots in the family and community. Traditional medical thought had never questioned the significance of the relationship between environment and illness: Diet, work, family and economic stress, filth, and an impure atmosphere all interacted to shape either resistance or predisposition to sickness. But such assumptions, although never explicitly or entirely disavowed during the nineteenth century, grew decreasingly compelling in the century's last quarter. The germ theory and microscopic pathology provided a seemingly more precise and circumstantial framework in which to explain sickness and health. This new knowledge implied first the specificity of particular diseases as clinical entities and—ultimately—specificity of cause. Older and more inclusive ideas of disease causation seemed in comparison vague and diffuse. Questions of resistance, predisposition, and the relation between social environment and health seemed less and less relevant. Moreover, implementation of the social program implicit in environmental views demanded the difficult and unsettling consideration of political and social action. In addition, the provision of public outpatient care had always borne a low status in the medical community. It could compete neither with the prestige of academic medicine nor the rewards of private practice.

A few medical reformers did advocate an increased intervention in the social environment. Brahmin physician Richard Cabot, for example, probably the most outspoken and articulate of such social activists, pictured each patient as a kind of sampling device (like the bacteriologist's

[36]By 1901, for example, the New York Hospital paid 25 dollars each month to the Association for Improving the Condition of the Poor for investigating the financial status of prospective patients. They also charged 10 cents per prescription and a small fee for treatment, although even such small fees were remitted in "worthy" cases. George Ludlam to Francis H. McLean, 19 March 1901, Superintendent's Letterbooks, NYHA.

sample of a water supply) reflecting in his or her sickness the nature of the society that helped produce such disability:

> As a bucket let down into an artesian well or into the ocean brings up from the bottom a sample of what is widely distributed there, so a patient with lead poisoning, with tuberculosis, with a court record, brings us into touch with conditions which we should not ignore.[37]

It was entirely consistent that Cabot should have been a prime mover in establishing America's first hospital social service department (at the Massachusetts General Hospital) and that he should have condemned the disjunction between patient as citizen and family member and the same patient as hospital case; the two dimensions of experience could not be dissassociated without reducing the quality of care.[38] Such arguments paralleled the motivations and social assumptions of contemporary social welfare advocates, many of whom, like Lillian Wald or Alice Hamilton, took a professional interest in socially oriented medical care.

Michael Davis, administrator of the Boston Dispensary in the years before World War I, was perhaps the most ingenious among his contemporaries in shaping plans for outpatient medicine. Davis sought to turn the staid Boston Dispensary into something resembling a health maintenance organization, not for the indigent alone but for all Bostonians who could not afford the most advanced and specialized care. He emphasized both the need to reach into patients' homes and the unsettling reality that many among even the skilled workers and the salaried middle class of clerks and managers could not afford the services of an array of special consultants in the event of illness; he emphasized as well that such services should not be limited to the treatment of acute ills but rather should be seen as necessary preventive measures.[39] Davis sought accordingly to use the dispensary's resources to disseminate the preventive truths of cleanliness, proper diet, and appropriate clothing. The dispensary and outpatient department of a major hospital could thus be made to fill gaps in the prevailing system of urban medical care. Davis

---

[37]Richard Cabot, *The Achievements, Standards and Prospects of the Massachusetts General Hospital. Ether Day Address. 1919* (Boston, 1919), p. 19.

[38]"Beyond the special disease," Cabot argued, "of a special child or adult who comes to us in the dispensary, stands a family problem, ultimately a community problem, poverty, bad housing, bad food, bad habits and associations, ignorance of the ways and means of making a clean and healthy life on scanty means." "Why Should Hospitals Neglect the Care of Chronic Curable Disease in Out-Patients?" *St. Paul Medical Journal* 10 (1908): 6.

[39]In 1919 the Boston Dispensary initiated a Health Clinic that provided a complete medical evaluation for a nominal five-dollar fee. It included examinations by an opthalmologist and an otolaryngologist, physical diagnosis, and blood and urine tests. *Boston Dispensary, Annual Report, 1920–1921*, p. 13.

was not alone in articulating such views. Yet, just as his ideas and pilot programs were being elaborated, changes in medical ideas, institutional practices, and related medical career patterns were making the independent dispensary (such as his Boston Dispensary) well-nigh obsolete and the hospital outpatient department less and less important to the plans of aspiring young physicians.[40] Twentieth-century outpatient clinics continued and still continue to treat vast numbers, but the performance of this significant social function has not altered their comparatively low status in the culture of medicine.

As it became less relevant to the career needs of aspiring physicians, the independent dispensary was left with the residual function of providing casual and largely gratuitous medical care. The dominion of fee-for-service medicine remained essentially unchallenged—even rhetorically—by most Progressive critics of America's medical-care system. Those ambitious and often idealistic young men incapable of remaining content with the mere accumulation of fees and clinical reputation were, as the twentieth century advanced, ordinarily attracted not by social medicine but increasingly by the "higher" and seemingly less ambiguous demands of research; the hospital was inevitably the locus for those kinds of clinical investigation that bore the highest status. The reward systems of medicine and society reinforced each other, offering their highest inducements to those physicians controlling hospital access and hospital practice. The hopes of those who sought to expand and elaborate outpatient facilities were doomed to frustration.

VISIONS AND REALITIES:
THE HOSPITAL IN A NEW CENTURY

Of course, such reformers as Michael Davis and Richard Cabot were not alone in finding fault with American hospitals. Even many of the self-consciously professional leaders in the new field of hospital administration were conscious of imperfections in their proud new temples of healing and sought to make them as humane as they were by intent scientific. At the beginning of the twentieth century, certain thoughtful administrators, such as George Rowe of the Boston City Hospital, George P. Ludlam of the New York Hospital, and S. S. Goldwater of the Mount Sinai Hospital in New York, were well aware of flaws in the institutions they administered. Such men feared a hospital that would, as one critic put it, become a "great machine" reducing to cogs those

---

[40]For a more detailed discussion, see Rosenberg, "Social Class and Medical Care."

patients unfortunate enough to find themselves within it or, in the words of another contemporary, an "experiment station" of interest chiefly to a small clique of ambitious physicians.[41]

Administrators such as those cited by way of example were committed, despite occasional reservations, to the basic form assumed by the institutions they led. They rarely questioned the primacy of the hospital in urban medical care or the necessary autonomy of physicians in matters seemingly medical. Nevertheless, they were as aware as any of the hospital's most acid critics of the dangers of impersonality, of the crippling pressures implied by cost cutting, of the evils of relentless specialization, and of the danger of an unchecked medical autonomy within the hospital. As we shall see, they entertained certain solutions or, at least, emphases in policy. But all such modes of inducing change were limited by their very inability to find values and institutional forms genuinely alternative to the inexorable reality of the medical culture and its demands, on the one hand, or the dilemma implied by the voluntary hospital as an essentially isolated economic and social entity, on the other.

By 1910 almost all of the criticisms so familiar in the 1970s were already being directed toward American hospitals. From the patient's perspective, the hospital seemed often impersonal and bureaucratic. Jane Addams, for example, described such organizational inhumanity to a group of hospital administrators by citing the case of a woman suffering from a severe fever who had been admitted and in conformity with regulations had been bathed and had her hair braided—but who expired before being treated by a physician.[42] The patient had become, so the already-clichéd argument ran, not a person but a configuration of organs and potential syndromes. Richard Cabot expressed such attitudes with whimsical acidity as he quoted the words of his clinical assistant who greeted him one morning with the enthusiastic report that there awaited: "a pretty good lot of material. There's a couple of good hearts, a big liver with jaundice, a floating kidney, three pernicious anemias, and a flat-foot."[43] Hospital physicians infrequently treated the whole patient, the argument followed, certainly not as part of a specific family

---

[41]"The hospital must," as this critic stated, "realize itself to be a great social force and not content itself to be, as unfortunately it frequently is, the mere adjunct, laboratory or experiment station of some medical school or coterie of men." Leo M. Franklin, "Some Social Aspects of the Hospital," *Transactions of the American Hospital Association* 14 (1912): 105.

[42]Jane Addams, "The Layman's View of Hospital Work among the Poor," *ibid.* 9 (1907): 58–59.

[43]Richard Cabot, *Social Service and the Art of Healing*, (New York, 1909) p. 33, and cf. pp. 174, 177.

and specific community; specialists addressed themselves to a focus narrowed by their training. Paralleling this induced myopia was a disproportionate interest in acute ailments, especially those in which the hospital's technical capabilities might lead to life-saving intervention, and a corresponding lack of interest in convalescence and chronic illness. The hospital was, finally, coming to seem a province of the very rich and the extremely poor alone; the great mass of Americans of middling income would not willingly enter a hospital as ward patients but could not afford the rates charged for private patients either.

There were a number of plausible responses to the felt imperfections of the early twentieth-century hospital, or perhaps ways of rationalizing their administrators' tasks. One was the invocation of something called "efficiency." Second, and seemingly related, was a faith in the ability of science not only to provide better care in the present but also to solve existing problems by the accumulation of knowledge in the future. In addition, there was a program of increased social service, better convalescent homes, and a more sensitive response to the economic problems of patients from every social class—in sum, that is, a commitment to reasoned meliorism. All of these positions were widely endorsed; all had real, if varying, effects on the institution; and none altered those rigidities and imperfections in American hospitals already apparent to critics in the first decade of the twentieth century.

Efficiency was a term invoked so frequently and with so little precise content that one must approach it with the caution appropriate to a word so useful, yet at the same time so elusive. The word *efficiency* had a number of distinct meanings within the hospital. One centered on the mastery of an intrinsically forbidding task: reducing the complex internal life and external relationships of the hospital to an at least minimal order. It is only to have been expected that the meetings of hospital superintendents should often have been concerned with such matters as the best forms for maintaining patient records, for submitting bills, and for controlling accounts payable. Efficiency meant as well the creation of a hospital routine, one that would simplify medical care and avoid waste. If every aspect of the patient's treatment, from admission through discharge, were carefully specified, nurses, attendants, and house officers could provide an effective level of care. Mistakes could never be eliminated, nor could accidents be entirely avoided, but routinization of care and treatment, the argument followed, meant that such misadventures would be minimized. This ordering of tasks not only would shape an irreproachable level of medical care but also applied to purchasing, cleaning, and cooking, and allowed the hospital to make the most effective use of its limited financial resources.

Efficiency meant discipline as well as routine; it implied centralized control over an increasingly diverse work force. The desire to impose an ordered discipline upon the hospital was not limited to the sphere of rhetoric, not did it begin with the self-conscious vogue of efficiency at the end of the nineteenth century. It began in the 1870s with an effort by most large hospitals to impose order from above upon the institution and its sometimes intractable employees. Such efforts include demands for increased cleanliness and decreased alcohol consumption and were symbolized by administration demands that uniforms designating the status and function of the worker be worn. It meant the wresting of such strongholds of internal power as the kitchen and purchasing office away from the "untrained" and "unprofessional."

The invocation of efficiency played a legitimating role, in addition, implying devotion to a mode of decision making untainted by self-interest. E. A. Codman, a Boston surgeon and perhaps the most fanatically dedicated among American advocates of hospital efficiency, for example, was well aware of this function of the "efficiency ideal." Without such a selfless goal, he warned the president of the American College of Surgeons, the organization could offer little to differentiate it from a trade union.[44] Efficiency implied selflessness and thus moral legitimacy at a time when Americans saw little reason to accept traditional medical self-conceptions; charity, wisdom, and self-sacrifice seemed in any case less relevant than did mastery of organization and the laboratory's mysteries.

The rhetoric of efficiency was not, however, fashioned easily into a corresponding reality. Critics at the time realized that true efficiency would not easily reshape the American hospital. As Codman, for example, emphasized, uncompromising efficiency implied the evaluation of medical men, medical procedures, even medical fees; this was a goal not easily achieved. Even those administrators most committed to efficiency understood that a hospital could not be run with the relentless discipline of a factory or army barracks; it had also to be a family writ large, providing sympathy and concern, as well as economy and clinical virtuosity. The hospital, as one pioneer executive stated,

> has a peculiarity not commonly recognized: while it conducts a *business*, it is the *home* of those who live in it. . . . The management of a hospital is often likened to a business, such as that of a manufactory or a mercantile house. It is more than that by having a different human element in it; the special work of the hospital is done by a family, and should be governed with due regard for its domestic unity.[45]

[44]Codman to J. M. T. Finney, 27 December 1915, Codman Papers, Countway Library, Boston.

[45]Edward Cowles, "The Relations of the Medical Staff to the Governing Bodies in Hospitals," in *Hospitals Dispensaries and Nursing*, ed. John S. Billings and Henry M. Hurd (Baltimore, 1894), p. 72.

Finally, efficiency was hardly a realistic goal in a decentralized and un-coordinated system of medical care. Within every city, individual hospitals duplicated services and multiplied costs as they competed for both paying patients and status. As early as the 1870s, New York City hospitals had sought to cooperate rationally and had divided the city so that ambulance and outpatient services would have clearly demarcated territories; it was even suggested that hospitals might specialize in particular ailments. However, little came of this idea or of attempts to form regional hospital associations early in the twentieth century. Institutions continued to compete, not only for funds and private patients but also for medical reputation. Such rivalries in a decentralized system meant, as one well-informed contemporary contended in 1911, that cooperation between hospitals would remain on the level of rhetoric.[46] The repetition of similar criticisms in the 1960s and 1970s only underlines the tenacity of such patterns and the motivations that they reflect.

If the invoking of efficiency served in part as a means of avoiding serious consideration of the hospital as a social institution, a parallel faith in scientific medicine played a similar and perhaps even more significant role. Faith in medicine as science was well-nigh universal; the inexorable accumulation of hard knowledge promised to solve the hospital's problems as it would those of therapeutics generally. No one considered that such progress might imply new problems. Indeed, the most "advanced" and influential reformers of the 1870s and 1880s saw the principal function of the new model hospital as that of providing a necessary home for scientific medicine. John Shaw Billings, probably the most prescient of such reformers and an influential advisor to the trustees of the Johns Hopkins Hospital, saw this as a principal function of Baltimore's ambitious new institution. It would, he urged, not only educate clinicians as major hospitals always had but also train a new species of clinical investigator and serve as a laboratory for their investigations. "Appointments to the staff," as the Hopkins Hospital superintendent phrased the new standards, "should not be regarded as honors simply, but rather as imperative calls to duty and to fresh efforts to investigate disease."[47] At the Johns Hopkins Hospital and School of Medicine at least, these goals were partly realized; hospitals ambitious for scientific recognition could not permanently ignore so prominent an example.

[46]Charles Emerson, "The American Hospital Field," in *Hospital Management. A Handbook for Hospital Trustees, Superintendents, Training-School Principles, Physicians, and All Who Are Actively Engaged in Promoting Hospital Work*, Charlotte Aikens, ed. (Philadelphia, 1911); John A. Hornsby and R. E. Schmidt, *The Modern Hospital* (Philadelphia, 1913).
[47]H. M. Hurd, "Laboratories and Hospital Work," *Bulletin of the American Academy of Medicine* 2 (1896): 157.

If a late eighteenth-century understanding of the hospital's social mission was based on Christian stewardship allied with a perhaps less strongly felt commitment to medical education, the late nineteenth-century hospital and its leaders found their justifications increasingly in the claims of science. To the generation that came of age at the end of the nineteenth century, these claims were compelling indeed. Aseptic surgery, the X ray, and applied immunology all seemed to provide objective, almost overwhelming, evidence of the promise offered by continued investigation. A decade later, even more fundamental insights beckoned; to an aspiring physician in 1910, the promise of biochemistry, of physiology, and of bacteriology seemed limitless, and their application in clinical medicine, no more than a matter of time.

Not surprisingly, hospitals sought consciously to capitalize on their image as temples of science. Administrators emphasized the gleaming walls and intimidating apparatus in their operating rooms and laboratories, the startling photographs taken by the X ray "in its wonderful powers as a searchlight" as they appealed for funds, reassured paying patients, and impressed visiting committees. European visitors often commented on the opulent appearance of American operating rooms, the use of glass and marble, for example, where less expensive materials would have sufficed. Private patients and their visitors were suitably awed by displays of technical capacity; the hospital with an irreproachable scientific reputation could hope to enjoy a similarly elevated standing in the community. In the 1890s, it had already become apparent that scientific reputation would serve as an advantage in attracting the brightest and most ambitious young medical men and, it soon became clear, the support of individual and corporate benevolence. Economic reality, public relations, and scientific achievement were inextricably related.

As we have come to understand, however, the relationship between such achievement and its application in clinical medicine is hardly simple or unambiguous. Of course, real achievements obscured real inadequacies. New capabilities reinforced an interest in ills amenable to medical intervention, while ensuring a continued lack of interest in those ills for which medicine could do little. An ever-increasing faith in newfound surgical and pharmacological skills served as well to underwrite exclusively technological approaches to problems of patient care. Furthermore, the increasing faith in medicine as science created a certain rigidity within the hospital by magnifying the authority, if not necessarily the immediate efficacy, of the physician. The emphasis on medicine as science also undergirded the decentralized quality of hospital organization; the esoteric knowledge that the physician brought to bear upon his treatment of the patient loomed ever more important and became in fact a symbol of the hospital's social legitimacy—in a sense of the hospital itself. Within the mystical interaction between doctor and patient, social variables seemed increasingly insignificant and diffuse, and the physician's technical powers, correspondingly enlarged.

In the face of such powerful trends, well-meaning attempts to shape new social programs within the hospital had comparatively little impact. Special care for convalescent and chronic patients remained a low priority. (And thus voluntary hospital physicians were faced with an unrealistically narrow choice of clinical options: Was a chronically ill patient to be discharged or retained in an expensive facility oriented to acute care? In most cases there were no other options.) Medical social work, so enthusiastically advocated by Richard Cabot and many of his contemporaries did make a permanent, but in sum marginal, place for itself in the hospital.

Thoughtful administrators of the early twentieth-century hospital also feared that their institutions would become a refuge only for the rich and the poor. The municipal hospital would serve the poor, and the voluntary hospital would serve both rich and poor, but in a fashion calculated to provide different accommodations and perquisites. The middle-class patient would not willingly enter the free ward, tainted as it was by charity, nor could he afford private accommodations and the physician's fees that normally accompanied them. Hospitals thus began, naturally enough, to create facilities suitable for the large middle class. This had been a goal at the Massachusetts General Hospital since the turn of the century. At first, an informal system of graduated rates was instituted, and attending physicians might at their discretion waive or reduce fees for the worthy and genteel. Finally, the hospital was able (in 1930) to open a pavilion designed to serve this middle-income constituency. But such innovations, useful as they were, had little fundamental impact on the hospital.[48]

In retrospect, the deeply felt and often acute observations—and meliorist programs—of early twentieth critics of the hospital's social role seem to have had little impact; their commitment was a mere glance outward of little significance in comparison with the compulsion exerted by the forces that shaped the hospital in its inward vision. The outward

[48]For an account of the MGH and its attempt to answer this problem, see Frederic A. Washburn, *The Massachusetts General Hospital. Its Development, 1900–1935* (Boston, 1939), chap. 13, "Baker Memorial: Hospital for People of Moderate Means." The MGH Archives contain a scrapbook documenting in detail the background of the Baker Memorial Hospital and reactions to it in Boston and elsewhere. See also C. Rufus Rorem, *The Middle-Rate Plan for Hospital Patients. The First Year's Experience of the Baker Memorial of the Massachusetts General Hospital* (Chicago, 1931).

glance of social involvement was simply that, one peripheral aspect of a far more fundamental and radically inconsistent configuration of forces. The outward view seemed to most physicians not so much indefensible as irrelevant, diffuse, and politically unsettling, while the most prestigious scientific insights (a word chosen advisedly) looked inward to the realms of bacteriology, biochemistry, and pathology, as the century advanced to ever more precise modes of understanding the body's mechanisms in health and disease. Outpatient and dispensary medicine (and social service as well), on the other hand, were never to escape the stigma of poverty medicine; never a part of the economic structure of medical practice, they soon became a marginal concern for the profession.

CONCLUSION

Suddenly, it seemed, in the late 1960s the hospital became a problem. It has remained one. Depending on the critic's temperament, politics, and pocketbook, the hospital is a source of uncontrolled inflationary pressure, or an impersonal monolith, managing in its several ways to dehumanize rich and poor at once, if not alike. At the same time, the hospital seems to many to be the stronghold of a profession obsessed with income, status, and prerogative, and little concerned with needs that cannot be measured, probed, or radiated. Analysts choose among this smorgasbord of criticisms; some find all to their liking, others emphasize one theme or another. But few concerned Americans fail to find some fault with the social role and internal order of the American hospital. And if much criticism is overwrought, if most American hospitals do some things well, and some do most things well, such criticisms have a certain objective basis and at the same constitute in themselves a significant reality. How did this come about?

The present state of things was, as I have emphasized, already immanent in the American hospital at the turn of the century. It was implicit in the structure of American society and in the values and career patterns of the medical culture nurtured in that society.[49] Inward vision and outward glance is more than an enticing title. In the absence of a compelling assumption that hospital policies should respond in a precise way to

[49]I do not mean to contend that all of the trends discussed here were somehow peculiarly the product of American society. Generally, parallel developments in scale and consequent professionalization took place throughout Europe and in the United Kingdom. The wealth and the decentralized and entrepreneurial aspect of American society did, however, allow for a certain lushness of growth that may well be considered characteristic.

patterns of need and morbidity, it was inevitable that the pressures exerted on medical men by their profession, allied with the profit motive and the desire of hospital trustees and administrators for eminence and financial stability, would shape hospital decision making. It was hardly to be expected that the lay trustees or politically selected boards of municipal hospitals would see their responsibilities in ways inconsistent with the assumptions of their time and class. They could in practice see no greater good than the hospital's own growth in size and clinical reputation. It was rarely considered that such ends might not be entirely compatible with the optimum delivery of medical care. And state and federal governments, of course, did little in the years before World War II to reshape an atomistic world of individual hospitals competing for dollars and clinical status.

Within the hospital, increasing scale, bureaucratization, and capital costs exerted a parallel logic of their own. Like every other major institution in twentieth-century America, the hospital was dominated by the competing needs of increasingly self-conscious interest groups—in the case of the hospital, nurses, physicians, and administrators. The needs of these groups to find mutual adjustment also shaped the institution's internal order. No advocate of the patient's interest, however, figured in this evolution; not surprisingly, the patient's feelings played no prominent role in the gradual definition of the hospital's internal environment.

We have suggested how ideological emphases such as those upon professionalism, efficiency, and the all-sufficient efficacy of science all conspired to help legitimate this particular order—and seemingly to remove the hospital from the sphere of conscious policy making. The respective logics of scientific understanding and administrative rationality were left to create an effective hospital system. A lack of national and state commitment to the support and organization of medical care not only paralleled other dominant social views but also guaranteed that this situation would not be altered by shifts in governmental policy. Events in the past three decades have underlined this truth. The sacredness of the doctor–patient relationship, buttressed by both an increasing popular willingness to accept the physician at his own estimation and the growing political power of medicine, guaranteed that federal subsidization of medical care would come only gradually and indirectly. Thus, the generous support of research in the years since World War II helped underwrite medical education and patient care—but never with an explicit admission that anything other than research was being subsidized. Control of the hospital remained firmly in the hands of medical men and administrators. Hospitals were also supported through construction funds provided in the Hill–Burton Act (1946); again, the availability of Hill–Burton funds did little to affect decision making within the hospital or drastically rearrange existing hospital priorities. That is, it represented another example of that characteristically American phenomenon, the transmission of funds from the public to the private sector without the imposition of meaningful conditions or the evaluation of social consequences. The growth of third-party payment in this period exerted similar effects on the hospital; it provided economic support, encouraged the increasing dominance of hospital-based medical practice, narrowed the choice of clinical options, yet provided little in the way of evaluation or control.

Planning, even the conscious discussion of public policy and its ultimate consequences for medical care, could hardly be part of this process. Yet, as I have indicated previously, there can be policy—and certainly the continued hegemony of existing men, attitudes, and institutions must be considered a policy objective—without planning. In this case, of course, and in many others, the absence of explicit plans and projections was an aspect of policy and must be seen in such terms. But this is neither surprising nor peculiarly the medical historian's area of expert knowledge.

The medical culture and the extraordinary compulsion it exerted on its members is less concrete than such institutional and policy considerations but no less important to an understanding of hospital growth during the last century—and is more appropriately, indeed necessarily, the historian's concern. This medical culture has historically exerted a formative influence on the behavior of physicians, has defined their system of rewards, and has proved instrumental in creating the modern hospital's internal environment and social priorities. It formed, in short, what I have chosen to call an "inward vision." The lack of governmental control of medical care and the withering of traditional ideas of stewardship in the private sector only magnified the autonomy of the profession and its role in the shaping of medical care.

That physicians respond to the programmatic demands of their profession is not simply a sociological truism, but is a political reality. Insofar, for example, as physicians have internalized the self-image of medicine as science, they are committed to a particular vision of what medical care should be. On one level it implies a high status for research. In a clinical setting it implies a similarly high regard for crisis intervention. This turning inward to the body and the realm of technical capability has both structured and legitimated particular kinds of doctor–patient interactions in the twentieth century. Among other consequences, this has meant that although much institutional care is delivered through outpatient facilities, the provision of such care enjoys low status in the profession. Community medicine is seen as making minimal intellectual demands and attracts something less than maximum efforts; the majority among the most ambitious practitioners, those boasting (or suffering from) the highest levels of aspiration, turn generally to those areas of medicine that seem "hardest," that is, most intellectually demanding, and eschew the apparent softness of social medicine. With the exception of a small minority of physician activists, the delivery of medical care outside the hospital was not and is not a priority.

I do not seek to question the sincerity of the great majority of elite physicians who are committed to the centrality of the hospital and are at best tolerant of community-oriented medical practice. Such views cannot be dismissed as consciously self-serving; those who have assimilated the values of academic medicine boast a genuine conviction of intellectual and social legitimacy. Not all clinical investigators will be innovative, but all who are part of the world of scientific medicine must act as though they expected to be; not all medical care involves life-threatening ills and critical therapeutic intervention, but claims of physicians to autonomy are based on the assumption that all doctor–patient interactions are potentially such.

It would be naive to suggest that physicians act from motives of material self-interest alone. Indeed, these values of the medical culture that I have just suggested may in specific instances conflict with purely economic motives. I have, nevertheless, described a configuration of structure and motive in which economic imperatives are generally consistent with other demands made by the medical culture—and, practically speaking, in which economic needs are neatly justified in terms of the commitment and achievements of medicine as science. The hospital has in the past century become increasingly the institutional nexus for the acting out of these social and economic roles.

In the 1960s and 1970s, a variety of social critics made us aware of imperfections in this system. Even the medical community has itself begun to manifest increasing awareness of failings in contemporary hospital-oriented medicine. But the dichotomy described by the distinction between inward vision and outward glance remains fundamental—only magnified by the past half-century's advances in technical capacity. The basic inconsistencies in our hospitals—already apparent to sensitive critics three-quarters of a century ago—continue to constitute an agenda for those who would attempt to create a more flexible system of medical care.

Those reformers must be prepared not only to understand such overtly political and actuarial questions as third-party payment mechanisms or peer review but also to understand and contend with the most fundamental attitudes that characterize the medical profession. Change must imply a previous recognition of the power and tenacity of the medical culture's vision of worthy and unworthy acts. It will be no easy task to modify such a deeply internalized system of assumption, for they are a moral, as well as a cognitive, map guiding the physician in his day-to-day actions. This world of medicine has produced, moreover, a seemingly overwhelming technical capacity and has shaped institutions that promote and reward these values. Laboratories, medical schools, and hospitals all reflect the peculiar history and ethos of the profession, as well as the social attitudes and economic relationships of the larger society. None will easily be changed.

3

EDUCATION AND INEQUALITY: A HISTORICAL PERSPECTIVE

MICHAEL B. KATZ

"No one at all familiar with the deficient household arrangements and deranged machinery of domestic life, of the extreme poor and ignorant, to say nothing of the intemperate—of the examples of rude manners, impure and profane language, and all the vicious habits of low-bred idleness, which abound in certain sections of all populous districts," wrote Henry Barnard, one of the great figures in the early history of public education, in 1851, "can doubt that it is better for children to be removed as early and as long as possible from such scenes and such examples and placed in an infant or primary school, under the care and instruction of a kind, affectionate, and skillful female teacher."[1]

The object of that early education, Barnard made clear, had little to do with cognitive skills. "The primary object in securing the early school attendance of children," he observed, "is not so much their intellectual culture as the regulation of the feelings and dispositions, the extirpation of vicious propensities, the preoccupation of the wilderness of the young heart with the seeds and germs of moral beauty, and the formation of a lovely and virtuous character by the habitual practice of cleanliness, delicacy, refinement, good temper, gentleness, kindness, justice, and truth."

[1] Henry Barnard, "Sixth Annual Report of the Superintendent of Common Schools to the General Assembly of Connecticut for 1851," *American Journal of Education* 5 (1865): 293–310.

SOCIAL HISTORY AND SOCIAL POLICY

Barnard's argument would not have startled any nineteenth-century educational promoters, for they echoed its essential themes over and over again as they sold public education to North America. Contrary to popular mythology, public education did not represent the institutional culmination of a humane, democratic, egalitarian impulse. Rather, it reflected a horror at the consequences of urban poverty: crime, disorder, and immorality. Public schools embodied the attempt to alleviate the casualties of an urban capitalist social order through the reformation of character rather than through the redistribution of wealth or power. Public school systems were a conservative attempt to shore up a social structure under stress and were one element in a new institutional configuration designed to retain a structure of inequality endangered by profound social change.

In the eighteenth century, conservatives opposed mass education because they believed it to be dangerous. Once educated, the poor would revolt. Southern slaveholders in the United States used precisely this justification to keep their slaves illiterate by law. Thomas Jefferson, who supported mass education, argued in exactly the same way. Education would prevent the accumulation of political power and keep alive the capacity for revolt among a people jealous of their liberty.[2]

The achievement of the first generation of public school promoters, led most visibly by Horace Mann and Henry Barnard in the United States and Egerton Ryerson in Canada, was to reverse radically the classic connection between education and political radicalism. They succeeded in creating public school systems because they argued brilliantly that education would exert a conservative influence. In order to make their case, school promoters had to redefine the nature of schooling. To eighteenth-century conservatives schools were dangerous because they dealt with the mind; they became safe in the nineteenth century when they turned their attention to the moral. Staunchly committed to the primacy of the moral, schools have remained safe ever since.

This chapter will elaborate upon the conservative impulse at the heart of public education. It also will attempt to link the origins of public school systems with their contemporary shape and structure and to point to the implications of both continuity and discontinuity for those concerned with the relation between schools and society today.

[2]For a collection of Jefferson's thoughts on education, see Gordon C. Lee, ed., *Crusade Against Ignorance: Thomas Jefferson on Education* (New York, (1961). William R. Taylor, "Toward a Definition of Orthodoxy: The Patrician South and the Common Schools," *Harvard Educational Review* 36 (Fall 1966): 412–426; Carl F. Kaestle, "Between the Scylla of Brutal Ignorance and the Charybdis of a Literary Education: Elite Attitudes toward Mass Schooling in Early Industrial England and America," in *Schooling and Society*, ed. Lawrence Stone (Baltimore, 1977).

I will not attempt to offer programmatic suggestions about the details of school reform. That is not the function of the historian. Rather, my intent is to provide a perspective on the relations between school and society against which specific policy proposals may be assessed. As a historian commenting on education I hope to accomplish three things. First, I will give an explanation of the current situation. In part this means undermining the myths that sustain public education. Beyond that, however, it means using history as a mode of explanation. To understand anything at all we must grasp the process by which it came to be as it is. History is not a backdrop or a preface to sociology or policy analysis. It is, rather, one critical component of analysis itself.

Second, I hope to offer a rationale for the struggle in which those people who dedicate themselves to concrete educational change engage. Often, when I speak about the history of education to teachers, graduate students, or others concerned with reform, I am asked why, if schools have been ineffective levers of social change, should we continue to care? This is the question that has been uppermost in my mind as I have written this chapter.

Third, I have attempted to provide a general orientation toward certain particular issues: desegregation, the open classroom, and cognitive skills. It would be arrogant to go beyond this point because what should be done tomorrow is not a question that can or should be answered through a directive from academics. Indeed, a real answer can emerge only through a dialectical confrontation between engagement and reflection.

PUBLIC POLICY ISSUES

Specifically, the remainder of this chapter assembles historical evidence with which to address two contemporary questions: (1) What are the implications of the inequality debate for educational policy?; (2) What are the policy implications of the "failure" of educational reform? Historical analysis and contemporary social science answer these questions in partially similar ways. About inequality, the message of each is that schools do not matter very much. In this chapter I will confront that conclusion directly and attempt to show in what ways it is reasonable and in what ways it is the artifact of a question improperly asked. I shall attempt to contribute to the reformulation of the relation between education and inequality through arguing that policy is basically dialectical and that the failure to recognize the inevitable impermanence of institutional solutions continually undercuts their effectiveness by leaving debilitating contradictions unresolved. Although the major part of this chapter will point to the origins of contemporary educational patterns in the nineteenth century, I shall argue also that the relation between school and society has become discontinuous with its antecedents in critical ways. The result is a crisis of legitimacy without historical precedent.

Consider, first, a brief overview of the contemporary issues. The initial document in the recent debate was the famous Coleman Report—*Equality of Educational Opportunity*—commissioned as a result of the Civil Rights Act of 1964. In the report's most superficial and vulgar, although also most popular and widely diffused, form, the authors argued that schools have less influence than is usually believed. The report set out to examine the variation in educational facilities available to the children of different races and to measure the extent to which educational opportunity is equally distributed. Its alleged novelty stems from its redefinition of equality of educational opportunity. Hitherto, according to the authors of the report, analysts measured equality in terms of the components of the educational system ("inputs"), such as per pupil expenditure, the qualifications of teachers, or the social and racial composition of schools. The report, by contrast, focused on the results ("outputs") of schooling, measured by pupil achievement on standardized tests. The commentators on the report, largely ignorant of history, were unaware of the extent to which the outputs of education have been a recurring issue in educational controversy throughout the last century. Nonetheless, they were correct that in the years following World War II the issue of inequality has been argued primarily in terms of access and facilities.[3]

The report found that major differences in educational facilities exist between regions but not between races or classes. Moreover, major differences in educational achievement (measured by verbal scores) occur between black and white and, from a slightly different angle, between affluent and poor. Some evidence indicated to the report's authors that placing poor or black children in a school where the majority was white or affluent would boost their achievement marginally. Reanalysis of the data, however, shows that the effect of peers on performance resulted from technical errors in the analysis. However, reanalysis confirms, with only minor qualifications, the report's other conclusion: Tampering with

[3]James S. Coleman *et al.*, *Equality of Educational Opportunity* (Washington, D.C., 1966); James S. Coleman, "The Evaluation of Equality of Educational Opportunity," in *On Equality of Educational Opportunity*, ed. Frederick Mosteller and Daniel P. Moynihan (New York, 1972), pp. 147–150. For another, and in an important way similar, historical comment to mine on the issues raised by the report, see David B. Tyack, "Do Schools Make a Difference," *Andover Review* 2 (Autumn 1975): 2–9.

pupil–teacher ratios, the educational qualifications of teachers, the number of books in school libraries, the presence of science laboratories, the existence of accelerated streams, or other aspects of school life contributes virtually nothing to overall verbal achievement.[4]

The report did not prove that all innovation would fail. It measured the differences in the major varieties of innovation that currently exist within public schools. One aspect of contemporary education, however, is the relative similarity of its contours from place to place. Therefore, the report deals only with relatively minor variation, not with a wide spectrum of possibilities. Nonetheless, it makes indisputable the pointlessness of tinkering with marginal variation in pupil–teacher ratios or the number of master's degrees per teacher. It is only surprising that so many people found this conclusion startling. That, in itself, is a commentary on the investment in marginal innovation within the educational establishment.

The findings of the Coleman Report fit with the results obtained from other innovations, such as Operation Headstart, which generally have been disappointing. Most educational policy, as measured by contemporary research, appears unable to overcome the initial handicaps with which poor or black children enter school. Indeed, one analysis of all evaluations of federal programs directed at improving the skills of disadvantaged children or the economic returns of schooling has concluded that, without exception, they have failed. Although the inputs of the educational system have been equalized more than ever before, the results of schooling remain as systematically skewed as ever.[5]

Christopher Jencks's *Inequality* delivered a stunning blow to educational reformers already on the ropes. Even if the schools somehow could assure that the educational achievement of various social groups assumed a normal distribution, Jencks argued, the unequal distribution of income within society still would not alter. Education cannot be an effective policy with which to attack inequities in the distribution of wealth.[6]

Jencks intended his message to lead to radical political conclusions. Its implications are more ambiguous because he also asserted that little connection exists between family background and the eventual eco-

[4]Marshall S. Smith, "Equality of Educational Opportunity: The Basic Findings Reconsidered," in *On Equality*, ed. Mosteller and Moynihan, pp. 230–342.

[5]Henry M. Levin, "A Decade of Policy Developments in Improving Education and Training for Low-Income Populations," in Institute for Research on Poverty, *A Decade of Federal Antipoverty Programs: Achievements, Failures and Lessons* (Madison, Wis., 1977), pp. 123–188.

[6]Christopher Jencks et al., *Inequality: A Reassessment of the Effect of Family and Schooling in America* (New York, 1972).

nomic achievement of individuals. In his conclusions, economic mobility in America is an essentially random process in which the key factors are luck and on-the-job competence. Given a set of goals different from those of Jencks', this conclusion could reinforce relative complacency. If Jencks is right, American policy has removed the institutional barriers to mobility. Policy should aim at further refinement of the meritocracy by increasing the contribution of on-the-job competence and decreasing that of luck. Gross discrepancies in wealth should continue to exist, for they furnish incentives and rewards for contribution to the public good.

Jencks's conclusions about the lack of a systematic relation between class and mobility startle this student of the North American past. Virtually all historical analyses reveal a continually close association between family of origin and occupational or economic achievement throughout at least the last 2 centuries. In fact, as the French sociologist Raymond Boudon argues, good grounds exist for believing that Jencks's conclusions are partially an artifact of his method. Analyses of variance of the sort undertaken by Jencks assume linearity in a process characterized by a complex interaction among variables; they give a spuriously random cast to results that are, in fact, highly determined.[7]

Nonetheless, Boudon's alternate mode of analysis reaches one conclusion similar to Jencks. Although Boudon, unlike Jencks, believes that social inequality is reproduced systematically from one generation to another, he does concur that schools cannot alter social inequality. Boudon's conclusions rest primarily on Western European data. Similarly, Henry Levin has compared the major studies of the relationship between educational opportunity and social inequality in Western Europe and concluded:

> Whether we use the standard of equality of educational access, educational participation, educational results, or educationally induced life chances, the operation of the educational systems of Western Europe fails to meet them. The educational treatments and results... mirror the initial differences in ... social class origins as well as sex differences.... There is little doubt that the distribution of education has become more nearly equal throughout Western Europe.... But, there seems little relation between the increasing equality of educational attainments (in nominal years of schooling) and the distribution of income.

The same statement might have been written about the United States or Canada. Clearly, the Coleman Report and *Inequality* have tapped aspects

---

[7]Raymond Boudon, *Education, Opportunity, and Social Inequality* (New York, 1973), pp. 77, 200–201. See also Robert M. Hauser, "Review Essay: On Boudon's Model of Social Mobility," *American Journal of Sociology* 81 (1975–1976): 911–928, and Raymond Boudon, "Comment on Hauser's Review . . .," *ibid.*, pp. 1175–1187.

of the relation—or lack of relation—between education and equality that transcend national boundaries. That relation is not ephemeral, accidental, or, as one prominent observer absurdly claimed, a result of "mindlessness"; it is a product of the connection between schooling and a capitalist order whose contours, beneath the gloss of national differences, remain remarkably stable and alike. That is the message that has driven the optimism out of educational reform.[8]

The result has been a process familiar in American social history: Institutional reform premised on an optimistic and environmentalist view of human nature has failed to reach its promised goals. Early in the nineteenth century, reformers argued that human nature was malleable, a product of circumstances: Schools would eradicate the effects of a poor home environment; the healthy milieu of mental hospitals would cure the insane; and the rehabilitative atmosphere of prisons would transform the criminal. For predictable reasons, none of these happy outcomes occurred. The reasons rest in the way in which institutions had been created. They were too large, too crowded, too inherently punitive, and too underfinanced to operate in a manner remotely approaching their ideal, and the ideal of each was itself systematically undermined by intellectual fallacies. Nonetheless, the promoters and managers of institutions, unwilling to accept the responsibility for failure, blamed the victim. Environmentalism gave way to heredity as the theory of human nature. The problem with the children of the poor, the mentally ill, and the criminal resided in their genes, not in their environment.[9]

The same process happened in the 1960s. Writing in 1968, I predicted that if the educational enthusiasm of the War on Poverty failed to reach its goals, the clear environmentalist explanation for individual incapacity or deviance that underlay its policies would yield to a rebirth of the hereditarian position. Within a short time, Arthur Jensen's famous article appeared in the *Harvard Educational Review*, and the hereditarian assault on reform had begun.[10]

The argument that failure to learn stems from hereditary influence comforts not only racists but also schoolpeople anxious to avoid responsibility for the failures within their classrooms. On the other hand, the

[8]Boudon, *Education and Inequality*, pp. 40–65; Henry M. Levin, "Educational Opportunity and Social Inequality in Western Europe," *Social Problems* 24 (December 1976): 160. For a similar argument, see the important book, Samuel Bowles and Herbert Gintis, *Schooling in Capitalist America: Educational Reform and the Contradictions of Economic Life* (New York, 1976). The "mindlessness" diagnosis was offered by Charles E. Silberman, *Crisis in the Classroom: The Remaking of American Education* (New York, 1970). p. 10.

[9]Michael B. Katz, *The Irony of Early School Reform: Educational Innovation in Mid-Nineteenth-Century Massachusetts* (Cambridge, Mass., 1968), p. 216.

[10] Arthur R. Jensen, "How Much Can We Boost IQ and Scholastic Achievement?" *Harvard Educational Review* 39 (Winter 1969): 1–123.

pessimistic message of social science deeply troubles those people still emotionally committed to educational reform. Why innovate if it makes no difference? Why strive for integration that will not markedly increase the educational achievement of black youngsters? Why care about what happens within classrooms? Is it enough to say, as does Jencks, that we care simply because classrooms are full of children whose lives deserve to be pleasant? Should our energies be redirected to an immediate redistribution of wealth and power within the social order?[11]

ORIGINS OF PUBLIC EDUCATIONAL SYSTEMS: THE NINETEENTH-CENTURY CONTEXT

The perspective that a historian can offer to those troubled by these questions is ambiguous. It at once reinforces the argument of the Coleman Report and of *Inequality*. At the same time, it suggests that the issue has been framed incorrectly and in a misleading fashion. This situation is not new. But to understand how and why the issue of inequality has assumed its modern form, we must understand something about the origins and history of public educational systems.

One chapter cannot document adequately an interpretation of the history of a major social institution. Rather, what I attempt here is a synthesis of the recent work in the field and my own research, which has focused both on the history of education and on the history of social structure and domestic organization. My own conclusions about schools result not only from a reading of the literature of educational promotion but also from an attempt to follow the process of educational development in great detail in local communitites. Indeed, it has been my conviction for the last 15 years that only through the detailed reconstruction of social structure and institutional history in particular settings can scholars arrive at adequate general statements about social development. I have pursued that conviction through an attempt to reconstruct the population of a Canadian city, Hamilton, Ontario, during its early industrialization. That study has rested on the compilation of a massive data bank containing information about all of the people in the city listed in various sources (tax rolls, manuscript censuses, city directories, vital statistics); in some instances my colleagues and I have joined together the information about individuals from different sources to trace people across time. We also have compared patterns in Hamilton to those in Buffalo, New York, and rural Erie County, for which we have roughly

[11]Jencks et al., *Inequality*, p. 256. For useful commentary on the issues raised by Jencks, see Donald M. Levine and Mary Jo Baine, eds., *The "Inequality" Controversy: Schooling and Distributive Justice* (New York, 1975).

comparable data. The interpretation here draws upon that research, on my own work specifically on education, and on the recent relevant work in social history. Readers interested in pursuing the evidence for any of the historical points in the chapter may do so through its references.[12]

In a discussion of public educational systems, the word *systems* is crucial. For in neither Canada nor the United States were schools unusual or novel creations in the nineteenth century, and in neither place was it unusual for them to receive some sort of public support, although in most places the line between public and private was not drawn with precision until well into the nineteenth century. Indeed, in New York and Massachusetts the proportion of young people attending school achieved its greatest nineteenth-century increase in the 2 or 3 decades *prior* to the development of public school systems. Although schools existed and frequently received some public support, the haphazard arrangements of the seventeenth, eighteenth, and early nineteenth centuries cannot be considered true progenitors of the school systems that we know today. By the latter part of the nineteenth century, the organization, scope, and role of schooling had been fundamentally transformed. In place of a few casual schools dotted about town and country, there existed in most cities true educational systems: carefully articulated, age-graded, hierarchically structured groupings of schools, which were primarily free and often compulsory, administered by full-time experts, and progressively taught by specially trained staff. No longer casual adjuncts to the home or apprenticeship, schools were highly formal institutions designed to play a critical role in the socialization of the young, the maintenance of social order, and the promotion of economic development. Within the space of 40 or 50 years, a new social institution had been invented, and it is this startling and momentous development that we must seek to understand.[13]

The origins of public educational systems cannot be understood apart from their context. They formed part of four critical developments that reshaped North American society during the first three-quarters of the nineteenth century. Those developments were (*a*) industrialization and

---

[12]The work on Hamilton is contained in my *The People of Hamilton, Canada West: Family and Class in a Mid-Nineteenth-Century City* (Cambridge, Mass., 1975), in the three reports of the Social History Project, York University, Toronto, and, with Michael J. Doucet and Mark J. Stern, *The Social Organization of Early Industrial Capitalism* (Cambridge, Mass., forthcoming).

[13]David Tyack, *The One Best System* (Cambridge, Mass., 1974); Carl F. Kaestle, *The Evolution of an Urban School System: New York City 1750–1850* (Cambridge, Mass., 1974); Stanley K. Schultz, *The Culture Factory: Boston Public Schools, 1789–1860* (New York, 1973); Selwyn Troen, *The Public and the Schools: Shaping the St. Louis System, 1838–1920* (Columbia, Mo., 1975); Carl F. Kaestle and Maris A. Vinovskis, *Education and Social Change in Nineteenth-Century Massachusetts* (New York, 1980).

urbanization; (b) the assumption by the state of direct responsibility for some aspects of social welfare; (c) the invention of institutionalization as a solution to social problems; and (d) the redefinition of the family.

During the early and middle nineteenth century, industrialization, urbanization, and immigration reshaped the economic and social order of North America. The pace and timing of social development varied, of course, from region to region. However, everywhere a close temporal connection existed between social development and the creation of public educational systems. In the United States, for example, the date when the first high school opened provides a rough but convenient index of educational development that, across the country, retained a strong association with social and economic complexity.[14] Our understanding of the relationships among the introduction of industrial capitalism, the transformation of the technology of production, the redistribution of the population into cities, and the creation of systems of public education remains far from precise, and I shall speculate on the connection between them later in this discussion. At the outset, however, it is important to observe and remember the temporal connection between the economy, the social order, and the schools. In fact, educational promoters of the time made explicit connections between economic development and the introduction of public educational systems. Much in the way of comtemporary theorists of human capital, nineteenth-century school promoters argued that an investment in education would stimulate economic growth and yield a high and immediate return.[15]

The development of systems of public education did not comprise the sole thrust of governments into the area of social welfare during the early and middle nineteenth century. In England, the United States, and Canada in this period governments generally began to exchange their haphazard and minimal concern with social problems for a systematic approach to questions of welfare. At the start of the period, problems of poverty, public health, crime, insanity, disease, and the condition of labor remained more or less untended and subject to ancient legislation, custom, sporadic regulation, and public and private charity. By the end of the third quarter of the nineteenth century, each had become the subject of public debate, legislative activity, and the supervision of newly created state administrative bodies with full-time expert staffs.[16]

[14]Michael B. Katz, "Secondary Education to 1870," in *The Encyclopedia of Education* (New York, 1970), 8:159–165.

[15]Katz, *Irony of Early School Reform*, pp. 27–30.

[16]David Roberts, *Victorian Origins of the British Welfare State* (New Haven, 1960); Oscar Handlin and Mary Flug Handlin, *Commonwealth: A Study of the Role of Government in the American Economy: Massachusetts 1774–1861* (New York, 1947); Karl Polanyi, *The Great Transformation: The Political and Economic Origins of Our Time* (1944; reprinted., Boston, 1957).

The state did not enter the area of public welfare without serious opposition. Its activity commenced at a time when the very distinction between public and private had not emerged with any sort of clarity, and in this situation the definition of public responsibility became an especially elusive task. In most cases voluntary activity preceded state action. Philanthropic associations, often composed primarily of women and usually associated with the spread of evangelical religion, first undertook the alleviation of social distress. In part their activity reflected the lack of any public apparatus to cope with the increased misery that people discovered in the growing cities of the late eighteenth and early nineteenth centuries; in part, too, it reflected the belief that social distress represented a temporary, if recurring, problem that charitable activity could alleviate. The activities of voluntary associations, however, usually convinced their members that problems were both far more widespread and intractable than they had believed, and they turned, consequently, to the public for assistance, usually first in the form of grants and later in the assumption of formal and permanent responsibility.[17]

No clear models for action, however, existed, and people concerned with social policy at the time debated not only the legitimacy of public activity but also its organizational form. In the case of education, their disagreements over the nature of public organizations reflected fundamental value conflicts and alternative visions of social development. If the shape that modern society eventually assumed appears inevitable to us today, it did not appear at all clear to the people of the time, which we must remember if we are to understand the passion aroused by debates about social institutions and policies in the nineteenth century.

In fact, in the United States four distinct models for the organization of formal education coexisted and competed in the early and middle nineteenth century, and at the time the outcome of their conflict did not appear at all self-evident to many sane and responsible people. The alternative that triumphed might be called incipient bureaucracy. Although its advocates generally supported the extension of a competitive and laissez faire approach to economic issues, they encouraged as well a strong regulatory role for the state in the area of social welfare and morality. Their model organizations were controlled by bodies responsible to legislatures, financed directly through taxation, administered by experts, and relatively large in size. They were, in short, public *institutions*, in a novel and dramatic sense.[18]

[17]Carroll Smith-Rosenberg, *Religion and the Rise of the American City* (Ithaca, N.Y., 1971); Raymond Mohl, *Poverty in New York 1783–1825* (New York, 1974); Susan E. Houston "The Impetus to Reform" (Ph.D. diss., University of Toronto, 1974).

[18]Michael B. Katz, *Class, Bureaucracy and Schools: The Illusion of Educational Change in America*, expanded ed. (New York, 1973), chap. 1.

Thus, the victory of incipient bureaucracy reflected a new faith in the power of formal institutions to alleviate social and individual distress. The novelty of this commitment to institutions must be appreciated, for it represented a radical departure in social policy. Prior to the nineteenth century, institutions played a far smaller and much less significant social role: The mentally ill, by and large, lived with other members of the community or in an undifferentiated poorhouse; criminals remained for relatively brief periods in jails awaiting trial and punishment by fine, whipping, or execution; the poor were given outdoor relief or, if a nuisance, were driven from the community. By the middle or third quarter of the nineteenth century, all this had changed. In place of the few undifferentiated almshouses, jails, and schools, there now existed in most cities, states, and provinces a series of new inventions: mental hospitals, penitentiaries, reformatories, and public schools. Shapers of social policy had embodied in concrete form the notion that rehabilitation, therapy, medical treatment, and education should take place within large, formal, and often residential institutions.[19]

Lest it should seem inevitable that modern society should be an institutional state, it is worth pointing out that responsible people at the time did see alternatives. In New York, for instance, Charles Loring Brace proposed the shipment of city urchins to the West as an alternative to their institutionalization, and elsewhere opponents and skeptics at the time critically, perceptively, and with, in retrospect, an eerily modern ring, pointed to the dangers and limitations of institutions.[20]

One of their common arguments centered on the family. Both proponents and critics of institutions agreed that the ideal family provided a paradigm for social policy. Rather than supplying an alternative to the family, institutions to their supporters would become, literally, surrogate families for the mentally ill, the criminal, the delinquent, and the schoolchild. In fact, it was precisely through their embodiment of a familial environment that new institutions, according to their sponsors, would perform their rehabilitative, therapeutic, or educational work. The difficulty, as critics astutely pointed out, was that no institution could imitate a real family.[21]

---

[19]David J. Rothman, *The Discovery of the Asylum: Social Order and Disorder in the New Republic* (Boston, 1971); Gerald N. Grob, *The State and the Mentally Ill: A History of Worcester State Hospital in Massachusetts 1830–1920* (Chapel Hill, N.C., 1966), and *Mental Institutions in America: Social Policy to 1875* (New York, 1973); W. David Lewis, *From Newgate to Dannemora: The Rise of the Penitentiary in New York, 1796–1848* (Ithaca, N.Y., 1965); Robert M. Mennel, *Thorns and Thistles: Juvenile Delinquents in the United States 1825–1940* (Hanover, N.H., 1973).

[20]Charles Loring-Brace, *The Dangerous Classes of New York and Twenty Years' Work Among Them* (New York, 1872); Katz, *Irony of Early School Reform*, pt. 3.

[21]Houston, "Impetus to Reform"; Alison Prentice, "Education and the Metaphor of the

Nonetheless, in the early and middle nineteenth century, both critics and supporters of institutions shared a widespread sense that the family was in some sort of trouble, though they were vague about the exact nature of that difficulty. In fact, they probably mistook change for deterioration, because the fragments of historical evidence about the family in this period indicate not breakdown but an important shift in domestic structure and relations.

Commonly, social theorists have believed that the nuclear replaced the extended family during industrialization. The work of Peter Laslett and other historians has shown quite conclusively that, as it is usually argued, this proposition is clearly wrong for British, American, or Canadian society, and probably for Western society in general. The majority of families—or, in Laslett's terminology, coresident domestic groups—at any point in time appear to have been nuclear in structure. That is not to say, however, that their role and other aspects of their organization did not change, for they did. And it is these more subtle, but real and consequential, alterations that historians just are beginning to appreciate.[22]

The most dramatic change that occurred during industrialization has been pointed out frequently. It is, of course, the separation of home and workplace. Indeed, the gradual division of place of residence and place of work fundamentally altered the day-to-day pattern of family existence, the relationships among family members, and (sociologists would argue) the very influence of the family itself.[23]

The separation of home and workplace formed one part of the process by which the boundaries between the family and the community became more sharply drawn. As a part of the increasing specialization of institutions, the family shed its productive function, as well as its role in the treatment of deviance. Rather than diminishing in importance, however, the family gained stature through its heightened role in the socialization of its children, which earlier had been shared more widely with the community. This tightening and emotional intensification of the family fundamentally reshaped the process of growing up.

For centuries it had been customary for parents of various social ranks to send their children away from home to live as surrogate members of another household for a number of years between puberty and marriage. Young people in this stage of their lives, which I call semiautonomy, exchanged the complete control of their parents for a

---

Family: The Upper Canadian Example," *History of Education Quarterly* 12 (Fall 1972): 281–303.

[22]Peter Laslett, ed., *Household and Family in Past Time* (Cambridge, 1972), pp. 1–148; Katz, *People of Hamilton, Canada West*, chap. 5.

[23]Robert Dreeben, *On What Is Learned in Schools* (Reading, Mass., 1968).

supervised yet relatively more autonomous situation in another household. It would take me too far from my topic to elaborate here upon the evidence for this stage or upon its meaning. Rather, I wish simply to point to semiautonomy as a phase in the life cycle that virtually disappeared during the development of modern capitalist society. By the mid-nineteenth century or shortly thereafter, depending upon the pace of economic development, young people began to remain within their parents' homes after they had found work, and stayed there roughly until marriage, far longer than had been the case before. At the same time, many remained in school for prolonged periods of time, and young men began to enter their fathers' occupations far less frequently. Certainly, I am deliberately foreshortening a complex process in order to provide support for the main point I wish to make about families: namely, that they acquired an increasingly important and specialized role in the socialization of their children as part of a general sharpening of the boundaries between social institutions and between the family and the community.[24]

Popular ideas about domesticity and the role of women reflected the redefinition of the family. The "cult of true womanhood," as it has been called, urged women to create within the home a haven against the harsh world of commerce and a nest in which children could be reared with attention and affection. From one perspective, the ideal of domesticity has justified a not especially subtle attempt to keep women within the home and subservient to their husbands. However, it also elevated the importance of women as the moral guardians and spiritual saviours of an increasingly corrupt and irreligious society. Despite this tension in its meaning, popular ideology reinforced the structural changes within the family. In both social thought and reality, the family—and I suspect in time the working-class, as well as the middle-class, family—became an increasingly private, intense, and sharply defined agency for the nurture of the young.[25]

A THREE-STAGE PARADIGM

Although educational development must be viewed as part of a larger series of changes in North American society, it must become the focus of

[24]Katz, *People of Hamilton, Canada West,* chap 5; John R. Gillis, *Youth and History: Tradition and Change in European Age Relations, 1770 Present* (New York, 1974), pp. 1–3; Michael B. Katz and Ian Davey, "Youth and Early Industrialization in a Canadian City," in *Turning Points: Historical and Sociological Essays on the Family,* ed. John Demos and Sarane Spence Boocock (Chicago, 1978), pp. 839–880; Joseph F. Kett, *Rites of Passage: Adolescence in America 1790 to the Present* (New York, 1977), pp. 11–37.

[25]Barbara Welter, "The Cult of True Womanhood, 1820–1860" *American Quarterly* 18

attention in its own right. School promoters argued that the introduction of public educational systems would alleviate a number of specific and substantial problems within contemporary society. In the most general sense, school promoters shared a profound ambivalence about the emerging economic and social order in which they lived. Cities, railroads, and factories were exciting, harbingers of progress, symbols of civility, and guarantors of prosperity. At the same time, they were profoundly frightening. The example of poverty and social disorder in English industrial cities haunted American midwives to industrial capitalism. The material exuberance of the nineteenth century elevated ambition, greed, and sensuality at the expense of traditional values that by exercising restraint upon men's passions had guaranteed the perpetuation of civilized social life. The new social and economic order could become a new barbarism in which the bonds that connected men and women dissolved and were replaced by the competitive savagery of class warfare, in which the confrontation between indolent luxury and destitution could ignite a conflagration that would destroy the New World as surely as it had the great empires of the past.[26]

For influential people who were ambivalent about the world they industriously were creating, education became a mechanism for simultaneously promoting and regulating social change. School systems would promote economic growth and stave off social chaos. They would foster both economic development and social harmony.[27]

School promoters, more precisely, argued that public educational systems would solve five quite distinct problems, to which I shall turn shortly. However, without a coherent explanation it is difficult to appreciate the exact connections between the tasks that school systems were designed to undertake and the broader developments of which they formed a part. Most attempts to link the origins of education with their social and economic context remain—as do most interpretations of the relations between institutional development and social change—unsatisfying, because they reflect the inadequate conceptual framework through which early North American history usually is viewed. Most histories of the period from colonial times to, roughly, 1875 rest on a two-stage paradigm: a shift from a preindustrial to an industrial society, or from a rural to an urban one.[28] This paradigm makes difficult the

(Summer 1966): 151–174; Kathryn Kish Sklar, *Catherine Beecher: A Study in American Domesticity* (New Haven, 1973); Nancy F. Cott, *The Bonds of Womanhood: 'Woman's Sphere' in New England, 1780–1835*, (New Haven, 1977), chap. 2.

[26]Katz, *Irony of Early School Reform*, pt. 1; Alison Prentice, *The School Promoters: Education and Social Class in Mid-Nineteenth-Century Upper Canada* (Toronto, 1977), p. 25.

[27]Prentice, *School Promoters*.

[28]As an example, see Herbert G. Gutman, "Work, Culture, and Society in Industrializing America," *American Historical Review* 78 (1973): 540.

systematic relation between institutions and social change. For, though the transformation of economic structures and the creation of institutions did take place at roughly the same period, the chronological fit between industrialism and institutions is imperfect, and attempts to construct causal models or to develop tight and coherent explanations usually appear too mechanistic or vague.

When a three-stage paradigm replaces the two-stage one, the fit between social change and institutional creation becomes tighter. In the three-stage paradigm, North America shifted from a peculiar variety of a mercantile–peasant economy to a commercially based capitalist society and to an industrial capitalist society. Although the pace of change varied from region to region and stages overlapped each other, the most important aspect of the late eighteenth and early nineteenth centuries was not industrialization or urbanization but, rather, the spread of capitalism, which is defined, in Dobb's words, as "not simply a system of production for the market . . . but a system under which labor-power had 'itself become a commodity' and was bought and sold on the market like any other object of exchange." Theoretically, in this point of view capitalism is the necessary, though conceptually distinct, antecedent of industrialization.[29]

Consider the chronology of institutional development. In New York State, dissatisfaction with the existing system of poor relief led to the passage of a law creating specialized county poorhouses in 1825; the first special institution for juvenile vagrants and delinquents opened in 1827; and the New York Public School Society emerged out of the Free School Society in 1824. In Massachusetts, the first state hospital for the mentally ill opened in 1833; poor relief underwent fundamental shifts in the 1820s; and agitation for educational reform really began in the same decade. The point of these examples is to show that the drive toward institutional innovation *preceded* the industrial take-off in the Northeast.[30]

On the other hand, the similarity in the timing of movements toward innovation in public policy did not happen by accident. The policies that created institutions arose in response to shifting social conditions: most directly from pressures felt within cities and regions where capitalist relations had begun to emerge within production.

The most characteristic and important feature of capitalism for the

---

[29]Maurice Dobb, *Studies in the Development of Capitalism*, rev. ed. (New York, 1963), p. 7; Karl Marx, *Capital* (first English ed., 1887); reprinted ed., Moscow, 1954), pp. 318–347.

[30]Martha Branscombe, *The Courts and the Poor Laws in New York State, 1784–1929* (Chicago, 1943); David M. Schneider, *The History of Public Welfare in New York State, 1609–1866* (Chicago, 1938).

development of institutions, including public school systems, was its utilization of wage labor and the consequent need for a mobile, unbound labor force. The shift in the nature of social organization consequent upon the emergence of a class of wage laborers, rather than industrialization or urbanization, fueled the development of public institutions.

This interpretation must remain partly speculative, because we lack hard data on a variety of critical specific issues, especially the proportion of the work force engaged in wage labor at various points in time. However, enough clues do exist to make the three-stage paradigm at least plausible—that is, consistent with social reality as well as with social theory. For instance, the most striking change in New York City's occupational structure between 1796 and 1855, using Carl Kaestle's figures, was the increase in the proportion of men who listed themselves simply as laborers, a rise from 5.5% to 27.4%. We know, too, that apprenticeship, whose emphasis on bound labor is incompatible with capitalism, had ceased to function with anything like its traditional character well before industrialization. From a different point of view, one historian recently has pointed to an unmistakable increase in the wandering of the poor from place to place in late eighteenth-century Massachusetts. Of course, the expansion of commerce in this period has been documented extensively, and we already have observed the abandonment of mercantilist economic regulations by the state in the same period.[31]

Capitalism as a concept assists in the interpretation of institutional development for two reasons: First, institutions reflected the drive toward order, rationality, discipline, and specialization inherent in capitalism. There is a parallel in the ways in which a capitalist society processes its business and its problems. The problems themselves comprise the second reason. Even as it created its own casualties, capitalism made obsolete the usual ways in which families and communities had coped with disaster, distress, and deviance.

Consider these circumstances: The seasonality and irregularity of work in early capitalist society posed problems as great as the meager subsistence wages paid to laborers. At the same time that chronic underemployment became a permanent situation, the creation of a mobile labor force and increasing transiency sundered the ties of individuals to communities. In crises or periods of difficulty people decreasingly found themselves within a community of familiar neighbors and kin to whom they could turn for help. In this situation, state and local

[31]Kaestle, *Evolution of an Urban School System*, p. 102; Douglas Lamar Jones, "The Strolling Poor: Transiency in Eighteenth Century Massachusetts," *Journal of Social History* (Spring 1975): 28–55; Handlin and Handlin, *Commonwealth: Massachusetts.*

authorities had to innovate in order to cope with the dislocation, distress, and destitution of landless wageworkers.[32]

EDUCATIONAL CHANGE AND SOCIAL
PROBLEMS

Early and mid nineteenth-century school promoters argued that public educational systems could attack five major problems, which, with hindsight, appear to be products of early capitalist development. If these problems appear familiar, it should not be surprising. For a century and a half they have continued to haunt North American society, which repeatedly has turned unsuccessfully to public schooling for their solution. Although observers at the time were more definite about symptoms than about causes, they surely would agree with the identity and urgency of this list: (a) urban crime and poverty; (b) increased cultural heterogeneity; (c) the necessity to train and discipline an urban and industrial work force; (d) the crisis of youth in the nineteenth-century city; and (e) the anxiety among the middle classes about their adolescent children.

According to nineteenth-century social commentators, a massive increase in both crime and poverty accompanied the growth of cities and the development of modern industry. Though the actual dimensions of the problem remain unclear—that is, whether crime and poverty increased disproportionately or merely kept pace with population growth—what matters for our purposes is the widespread belief among the "respectable" classes in an epidemic of lawlessness and pauperism threatening the foundations of morality and the maintenance of social order. Like "a weltering flood," wrote Horace Mann, the secretary of the Massachusetts Board of Education, in 1848, "do immoralities and crimes break over all moral barriers, destroying and profaning the securities and sanctities of life.... The great ocean of vice and crime overleaps every embankment, pours down upon our head, saps the foundations under our feet, and sweeps away the securities of social order, of property, liberty, and life." In the formulations of the time, it is important to observe, crime and poverty did not comprise two distinct problems.

---

[32]Ian E. Davey, "Educational Reform and the Working Class: School Attendance in Hamilton, Ontario, 1851–1891" (Ph.D. diss., University of Toronto, 1975); Stephan Thernstrom and Peter Knights, "Men in Motion: Some Data and Speculations about Urban Populations in Nineteenth Century America," in *Anonymous Americans: Explorations in Nineteenth Century Social History*, ed. Tamara K. Hareven (Englewood Cliffs, N.J., 1971), pp. 17–47; Katz, *People of Hamilton, Canada West*, chap. 3.

Rather, the terms *criminal* and *pauper* overlapped and merged into synonyms for deviant and antisocial behavior that stemmed from individual moral failure.[33]

The process of causal mechanism through which urbanization worked its mischief remained vague in mid nineteenth-century social commentaries. Nonetheless, neither crime nor poverty appeared, as they once had been, to be the accidental results of misfortune or deviance among an otherwise stable and reliable population. To the contrary, the emergence of fundamentally new classes of people, it was argued, had accompanied social transformation. Criminals and paupers were not merely individuals but were representatives of the criminal and pauper class, and it was the implications of the iceberg, rather than of its tip, that frightened respectable people.

Although people concerned with the explanation of crime and poverty often relied on environmental rather than on genetic explanations, their arguments still reflected the lack of any deep understanding of the relationship between social structure and social deviance, for in the last analysis, blame fell upon the lower classes. Crime and poverty became moral problems, which arose because the lower-class urban families failed to implant earnestness and restraint within the character of their children. A Massachusetts judge observed in 1846, "There is seldom a case of a juvenile offender in which I am not well satisfied that the parents or person having the child in charge, is most blamable; they take no pains to make him attend school; they suffer him to be out nights without knowing or caring where; and, in many instances, they are incapable of taking care of themselves, much less the children; they have no home fit for a child; their residence is a grog shop; their companions drunkards and gamblers or worse; they bestow no thought upon their child." Raised in an atmosphere of intemperance, indulgence, and neglect, the lower-class urban children began life predisposed to criminality and unprepared for honest work. By definition, in this argument, lower-class families became the breeding place of paupers and criminals.[34]

Given these premises, schooling held an obvious attraction. Exposure to public education, it was widely believed, would provide lower-class children with an alternative environment and a superior set of adult

[33]Houston, "Impetus to Reform"; Harold Schwartz, *Samuel Gridley Howe: Social Reformer, 1801–1876* (Cambridge, Mass., 1956); Katz, *Irony of Early School Reform;* Mohl, *Poverty in New York;* "Twelfth Annual Report of the Secretary of the Massachusetts Board of Education (1848)," excerpted in *The Republic and the School: Horace Mann on the Education of Free Men,* ed. Lawrence A. Cremin (New York, 1957), pp. 99–100.
[34]Commonwealth of Massachusetts, Senate Document No. 86 (1946), pp. 2–16.

models. Through its effect upon the still pliable and emergent personalities of its clientele, a school system would prove a cheap and
superior substitute for the jail and the poorhouse. As some of the more
acute commentators at the time observed, the school was to become a
form of police. Thus, though expenditures on public schooling might
seem high, they would in fact ultimately lessen the burden imposed
upon society by adult crime and poverty. Orestes Brownson commented
caustically in 1839, "In the view of this respectable board [Massachu-
setts State Board of Education], education is merely a branch of general police, and schoolmasters are only a better sort of constable. The
board would promote education, they would even make it universal,
because they esteem it the most effectual means possible of checking
pauperism and crime and making the rich secure in their possessions.
Education has, therefore, a certain utility which may be told in solid cash
saved to the commonwealth."[35]

Mid nineteenth-century social policy blurred more than the distinction between poverty and criminality; it equated cultural diversity with
immorality and deviance as well. Thus, the ethnic composition of expanding cities became a source of special anxiety. At first it was the
massive immigration into North America of the famine Irish that made
the problem acute. In 1851, for instance, a writer in the *Massachusetts
Teacher* noted, "The constantly increasing influx of foreigners during the
last ten years has been, and continues to be, a cause of serious alarm to
the most intelligent of our own people." Would it, "like the muddy
Missouri, as it pours its waters into the clear Mississippi and contami-
nates the whole united mass, spread ignorance and vice, crime and
disease through our native population?" The "chief difficulty," said the
author, was "with the Irish ... down-trodden, priest-ridden of centuries." Seven years later, the Boston School Committee summarized its
task as "taking children at random from a great city, undisciplined,
uninstructed, often with inveterate forwardness and obstinacy, and
with the inherited stupidity of centuries of ignorant ancestors; forming
them from animals into intellectual beings; giving to many their first
appreciation of what is wise, what is true, what is lovely, and what is
pure—and not merely their first impressions, but what may possibly be
their only impressions."[36]

To the "respectable classes" of North America, poor Irish Catholics

[35]Orestes Brownson, *Second Annual Report of the Board of Education, together with the
Second Annual Report of the Secretary of the Board* (Boston, 1839), reviewed in *The Boston
Quarterly Review* 2 (October 1839): 393–418.

[36]"Immigration," *The Massachusetts Teacher* 4 (October 1851): 289–291; Boston School
Committee, *Annual Report, 1858* (Boston, 1859) pp. 10–11.

appeared alien, uncouth, and menacing. Once again we must confront the relationship between reality and the perception of people at the time, because most contemporary research indicates that the Irish were not as intemperate, shiftless, and ignorant as the nativists portrayed them. To the contrary, the immigrants, it now is reasonable to suppose, may have represented a select, especially highly motivated and unusually literate portion of Irish society. Whatever instability their lives in North America might have revealed probably stemmed—as Theodore Hershberg and his associates have discovered in the case of exslaves—from the harsh and discriminatory urban social structure that they encountered, rather than from any moral slackness within their culture.[37]

Nonetheless, as in the case of crime and poverty, social commentators proved unable or unwilling to connect the problem they thought they saw around them with its structural basis, and they consequently once again retreated to an explanation that traced the source of a social problem to a moral weakness, in this case embedded in a set of foreign and inferior cultural traditions. As with most cases of nativist behavior, the shrill exaggeration with which observers dwelled on the subversive potential of the immigrants' alleged sensual indulgence reveals more about the critics themselves than about the objects of their attack. It is tempting to argue that nativists projected onto the Irish the sensuality that they consciously repressed within their own lives and hated them for acting out the fantasies that they denied themselves. Certainly, the key phrases in contemporary prescriptions of the good life were restraint and the substitution of higher for lower pleasures, which are attributes precisely the opposite of those that many thought they saw in the lives of the Irish immigrant poor.[38] Whatever the truth of this speculation may be, it is quite clear that the brittle and hostile response to Irish immigrants revealed an underlying fear and distrust of cultural diversity.

Once more the implications of a widespread social problem for the role of schooling are transparent. Although the cultural predisposition of adult immigrants might prove intractable, the impending rot of Anglo–American civilization could be averted through a concerted effort to shape the still pliable characters of their children into a native mold. This massive task of assimilation required weakening the connection between the immigrant child and its family, which in turn necessitated

[37]Kaestle, *Evolution of an Urban School System;* Harvey J. Graff, "Literacy and Social Structure in the Nineteenth-Century City" (Ph.D. diss., University of Toronto, 1975); Frank F. Furstenberg, Jr., Theodore Hershberg, and John Modell, "The Origins of the Female-Headed Black Family: The Impact of the Urban Experience," *Journal of Interdisciplinary History* 6 (Autumn 1975): 211–234; Oliver MacDonagh, "The Irish Famine Emigration to the United States," *Perspectives in American History* 10 (1976): 357–448.

[38]Katz, *Irony of Early School Reform,* pp. 120–121.

the capture of the child by an outpost of native culture. In short, the anxiety about cultural heterogeneity propelled the establishment of systems of public education; from the very beginning, public schools became agents of cultural standardization.

The need to discipline an urban work force interacted with fear of crime and poverty and anxiety about cultural diversity to hasten the establishment of public educational systems. Although this problem persists today in developing societies, it perhaps first arose in its modern form during the early industrialization of Great Britain, as E. P. Thompson has described eloquently. The difficulty emerged from the incongruity between customary rhythms of life and the requirements of urban and industrial work settings. In contrast to the punctuality, regularity, docility, and deferral of gratification demanded in a modern work force, populations, both peasant and urban, usually had governed their activities more by the sun than by the clock, more by the season and customary festivities than by an externally set production schedule, and more by the relationships established within small work groups than by the regimentation of the factory.[39]

At the same time, rewards had been distributed more on the basis of ascribed than of achieved qualities. Social position devolved upon successive generations mainly as a result of heredity, and it would be considered not corrupt but correct to favor a kinsman over a more qualified stranger in the award of jobs or favors. The contrast in this respect between traditional and modern custom certainly remains less than absolute in practice. Nonetheless, the ideal that governs behavior has nearly reversed itself. For democratic ideology, with its emphasis upon merit and concepts such as equality of educational opportunity, advocates the substitution of achievement for ascription as the ideal basis for the distribution of rewards in contemporary society.

Their promoters expected public school systems to bring about precisely this substitution of achievement for ascription combined with the inculcation of modern habits of punctuality, regularity, docility, and the postponement of gratification. It is no accident that the mass production of clocks and watches began at about the same time as the mass production of public schools.[40]

A writter in the *Massachusetts Teacher* made explicit the connection between time, modern civilization, and schooling:

[39]E. P. Thompson, "Time, Work Discipline, and Industrial Capitalism," *Past and Present* 38 (December 1967): 56–97; Gutman "Work, Culture, and Society."
[40]Leo Marx, *The Machine in the Garden: Technology and the Pastoral Ideal in America* (New York, 1964), p. 248.

The habit of prompt action in the performance of the duty required of the boy, by the teacher at school, becomes in the man of business confirmed; thus system and order characterize the employment of the day laborer. He must begin each half day with as much promptness as he drops his tools at the close of it; and he must meet every appointment and order during the hours of the day with no less precision. It is in this way that regularity and economy of time have become characteristic of our community, as appears in the running "on time" of long trains on our great network of railways; the strict regulations of all large manufacturing establishments; as well as the daily arrangements of our school duties. . . . Thus, what has been instilled in the mind of the pupil, as a principle, becomes thoroughly recognized by the man as of the first importance in the transaction of business.[41]

Disciplinary goals became especially obvious in the reports of local school committees across the continent. Everywhere the major obsessions—and difficulties—were punctuality and regularity of attendance, whereas the villains were parents uneducated to the importance of schooling who allowed or encouraged their children to remain at home for what, to school promoters, appeared whimsical reasons or who took the side of their child against the teacher. At a higher level, state and provincial authorities continually complained about the refusal of local school committees to introduce universalistic criteria into the hiring of teachers who, too often, were simply kin or friends. In this way, the school system as a whole became an object lesson in the organization of modern society and a force, as its promoters were fond of pointing out, that would radiate its influence outward through entire communities. Through the establishment, organization, and correct operation of school systems, the habits of a population would be transformed to match the emerging and radically new social and economic order.[42]

Among their litany of complaints about urban populations, social commentators repeatedly included a denunciation of the masses of idle and vagrant youth roaming city streets. The school committee of the town of Roxbury, Massachusetts, for instance, worried about "a class of large boys, numerous and we fear increasing, who seldom or never go to school and have little or no visible occupation." The town's selectmen complained,

We have been called upon frequently to take charge of boys and give them a place in our Alms House, who have been in the habit of lodging in barns and

[41]*Massachusetts Teacher* 14 (September 1861): 329.
[42]Katz, *Class, Bureaucracy and Schools*, pp. 32–37; Katz, *Irony of Early School Reform*, pp. 45–46.

sheds, and exposed to everything which is bad, and dangerous to society, who have no friends to direct them and if they have cannot control them.— We have noticed the most profligate and profane, who are strolling about the streets, who never go to school because they have no one to make them.[43]

Once I was tempted to treat such observations about idleness and vagrancy as middle-class moralizing. Now, though they are moralistic to be sure, the evidence points to their firm anchor in social reality, for school promoters saw about them a real crisis of youth in the nineteenth-century city. In precapitalist Western society, long-standing customs defined with reasonable precision the expectations and duties of people throughout their life cycle. Young people left home, perhaps around age 14, to work as servants or apprentices, almost always dwelling in another household. During no span of years was it unclear where young people should live or how they should spend their time. Thus idleness, on any large scale, was an unimaginable social problem.

However, during the rapid growth of cities in the eighteenth and nineteenth centuries, the population of young people increased enormously, whereas apprenticeship gradually decayed as an effective social institution. Indeed, the demise of a prolonged, highly regulated apprenticeship accompanied the first phase of capitalist development and preceded industrialization by some decades. The practice of keeping male servants apparently had declined well before apprenticeship. Whether young women found fewer opportunities for work as domestic servants remains unclear; however, there is evidence that large numbers of young women were neither in school nor employed outside their family.

Customary practices declined not only prior to industrialization but also before the creation of any network of institutions to contain and manage young people. Those who once would have worked as apprentices or servants now had literally almost nothing to do, for in a preindustrial urban economy, contrary to what is often believed, there existed little work for young men. Their labor, in fact, was scarcely more necessary than that of adolescents today. Without schools or jobs, large numbers of youths undoubtedly remained in an unwilling state of idleness until, in the case of young men, they became old enough to find work or, in the case of young women, until they married. The existence of these idle young people is the situation that I call the crisis of youth in the nineteenth-century city.

In Hamilton, Ontario, for example, during the decade that population growth made the problem of youth most acute, about half of the young

[43]Massachusetts State Archives, Boston.

people over the age of 13 or 14 were neither in work nor at school and exactly how they spent their time remains a puzzle. Not a puzzle, though, is the timing of the creation of a school system, which took place precisely in the decade following the sudden appearance of large numbers of idle youth on the city's streets. The establishment of a school system with special provisions for young people over the age of 11 or 12 almost immediately and dramatically reduced the proportion of idle youth. However, it is apparent that many young people entered school simply because they could not find work, for when jobs in factories first became available during the next decade, large numbers of working-class young men left the schools, whereas their more affluent contemporaries—and young women—remained behind.[44]

Affluent parents had promoted the establishment of school systems partly on account of their own problems, which might be called middle-class anxiety. By middle class I mean not only professionals, entrepreneurs, and other people in nonmanual occupations but also the more prosperous and independent artisans: in short, those people who owned or controlled the means of production or, as in the case of clerks, aspired to ownership. My point is not that the working class cared less about its families but, simply, that many of its members could not share one of the two fundamental concerns that made the middle class anxious: namely, downward social mobility. For the lower segment of the working class already had hit the bottom.

The anxiety about slipping down the social ladder that permeates both nineteenth-century social commentary and fiction relates in a complex manner to actual experience. Nineteenth-century cities revealed at once a curious combination of rigidity and fluidity. Within them, sharply entrenched patterns of inequality persisted, while the experience of individual people and the very identity of the population itself changed with dazzling rapidity. Nineteenth-century cities perhaps best can be thought of as railroad stations with waiting rooms for different classes. Although the population of the station constantly changed, those who departed were replaced by people with remarkably similar characteristics. And though their populations usually increased, the proportions in the various waiting rooms remained about the same. Studies of individual social mobility within nineteenth-century cities reveal this combination of stability and transience. On the one hand, they show a high rate of status transmission from father to son: The popular image of a continent of opportunity wide open to talent simply cannot be sustained, though many men made modest gains that undoubtedly appeared critical to their lives. Few laborers, that is, replicated the rags-to-riches version of success, but many managed eventually to buy a small house. At the same time, entrepreneurs failed in business with extraordinary frequency. Indeed, entrepreneurial activity entailed enormous risks, which made the threat of catastrophe ever present. For example, almost half of one small sample of entrepreneurs around the middle of the century whose histories I followed failed in their businesses.[45]

For different reasons, the position of master craftsmen became increasingly insecure as technological development eroded the association of skill and reward that had been the hallmark of many crafts. In the 1850s, for instance, the introduction of the sewing machine suddenly brought about a deterioration in the position of shoemakers and tailors when manufacturers flooded the market with cheap goods. In this situation, master artisans no longer could assure the comfort and prosperity of their sons by passing on to them their skills. Indeed, it is poignant to observe the extent to which the sons of artisans, especially those affected by technological innovation, ceased to enter their fathers' crafts within the course of one decade. In practical terms, in order for the master artisan to assure his son a position commensurate to his own, he had to assist his entry into different occupations, particularly commerce or the expanding public bureaucracies.[46]

The establishment of public schools for adolescents—high schools—was not promoted solely in terms of middle-class interests. Although high school sponsors did point out to middle-class parents the advantages of local tax-supported secondary education, their arguments focused on the prosperity of the community and the prospects of working-class children. High schools, they argued, would raise land values through attracting to communities affluent families concerned about the education of their children. At the same time, they would provide working-class children with an avenue for social mobility. High schools would make accessible to children of the poor the educational

[45]Stephan Thernstrom, *Poverty and Progress: Social Mobility in a Nineteenth Century City* (Cambridge, Mass., 1964), and *The Other Bostonians: Poverty and Progress in the American Metropolis, 1880–1970* (Cambridge, Mass., 1973); Katz, *People of Hamilton, Canada West,* chaps. 2, 3, 4; Michael B. Katz, Michael Doucet, and Mark Stern, "Migration and the Social Order in Erie County, New York, 1855," *Journal of Interdisciplinary History* 8 (Spring 1978): 669–701, and "Population Persistence and Early Industrialization in a Canadian City," *Social Science History* 2 (Winter 1978): 208–229.

[46]Alan Dawley, *Class and Community: The Industrial Revolution in Lynn* (Cambridge, Mass., 1976), chap. 3; Michael B. Katz, "Fathers and Sons: A Comparison of Occupations, Hamilton, Ontario, 1851 and 1871, Buffalo, New York, 1855," York University, *Second Research Report* (Toronto, 1976).

qualifications previously reserved for the wealthy and thereby would equip them for careers in commerce and the professions.[47]

"Shall we," asked one town school committee trying to persuade local citizens to establish a high school, "stand still, and see our children outstripped in the race of life, by the children of those who are willing to pursue a liberal and far-sighted policy?" In Beverly, Massachusetts, a local high school promoter argued that "the best educated community" will "*always* be the most prosperous community [for] nothing so directly tends to promote the increase of *wealth* of a community as the thorough mental training of its youth." Emphasizing the relation between the high school and social mobility, another promoter in the same town contended, "The State had an interest in the education of the best talent of the community. And this talent was as often found among the middling and lower classes as among the rich." The high school would make available "preparation for college and the higher branches of learning . . . to distinguished industry and talent, in whatever condition and circumstances it might be found."[48]

Working-class parents sometimes were skeptical of the arguments advanced by high school promoters. They realized that high schools formed part of a package of economic and social development of which they were not to be the prime beneficiaries. More interested in jobs than in schools for their adolescent children, they sometimes viewed high schools as a way of siphoning their taxes to the more affluent members of the community. In various places, in fact, working-class parents opposed and delayed the introduction of high schools. Thus, despite a good deal of egalitarian rhetoric to the contrary, the anxiety of the middle classes over their children formed the driving force behind the establishment of public secondary schools and solidified (and sustained until the present) the commitment of the middle classes to public education itself.[49]

Observe that my discussion of the purposes of public schooling has omitted one area of concern: the transmission of cognitive skills. Very simply, the cultivation of skills and intellectual abilities as ends in themselves did not have nearly as much importance in the view of early school promoters as did the problems that I have outlined. It is "obvious," asserted one urban superintendent, "that heart-culture should be

[47]Katz, *Irony of Early School Reform*, pt. 1.

[48]Winchendon School Committee, *Annual Report, 1852–1853* (Winchendon, 1853), p. 15; Report of Rufus Putnam as superintendent of schools, in Beverly School Committee, *Annual Report, 1853–1854* (Beverly, Mass., 1854), pp. 24–26; Albert Boyden, *Here and There in the Family Tree* (Salem, Mass., 1949), pp. 117–120.

[49]Katz, *Irony of Early School Reform*, pt. 1.

paramount to brain-culture, moral culture to intellectual culture." Public school systems existed to shape behavior and attitudes, alleviate social problems, and reinforce a social structure under stress. In this context, the character of pupils remained of far greater concern than their minds.[50]

SOME RESULTS OF PUBLIC EDUCATION

By 1880 in larger urban settings school promoters successfully had established public school systems and reorganized teaching into a hierarchical occupation complete with its own source of training, entrance requirements, and active national organizations. The process had taken less than half a century, a truly remarkable and swift accomplishment.[51]

My argument is that American urban education had acquired its fundamental structural characteristics by about 1880. Beyond doubt, there have been educational developments and innovations of first-rate importance since the late nineteenth century. Consider, for instance, the kindergarten, the junior high school, industrial education, testing, the new math. Each has brought about change, but—and this is the important point—it is change *within* a given structure that itself has not altered. That is the basis on which we can claim continuity in American education over almost a century. By the late nineteenth century, public education was universal, tax supported, free, compulsory, bureaucratically arranged, and class biased. It has retained those characteristics ever since.

The relation between the fundamental structure of education and early twentieth-century innovation becomes somewhat clearer if we consider for a moment changes in the high school between roughly 1890 and 1920, for these were the years of the introduction of curricula differentiated by the occupational destination of students. The idea of a unitary, undifferentiated high school curriculum, defended as late as the 1890s by the Committee of Ten, gave way within a few decades to the division of students into tracks based upon an expected future, predicted by their academic performance as young children and the social class of their parents. Although they were momentous, the division of high schools into college and noncollege tracks and the establishment of

[50]Lawrence School Committee, *Annual Report, 1857–1858,* (Lawrence, 1858), p. 48.
[51]Katz, *Class, Bureaucracy and Schools,* chaps. 1, 2; Tyack, *One Best System,* pt. 2.

vocational and commercial high schools did not upset the already existing bureaucratic structure of urban education.

By the late nineteenth century, many urban school systems *already* had become fully developed bureaucratic organizations, and the introduction of vocational education did not reverse or substantially alter that development. Indeed, it even could be argued that bureaucratic structure proved more powerful than did the original concept of vocational education, which had to be reshaped before it could be incorporated permanently as a feature of urban education. Marvin Lazerson, in an important study, points to the fascinating and unsuccessful attempt in Massachusetts to institutionalize a system of vocational education distinct from the public schools and linked closely with industry. By the time that effort began in the early twentieth century, however, professional educators had formed an interest group strong enough to resist the effective implementation of a rival organization, and in a relatively short time the public-schoolmen won control of vocational education, which they incorporated in an altered fashion into *their* system.[52]

In fact, vocational education fitted well within existing educational systems because it represented the extension of the social role and structural principles of urban school systems to an altered demographic situation. Despite the common-school ideology, urban education always had been differentiated. Among young students, residential segregation managed to keep intact a fair amount of social-class division within urban schools. Until well into the twentieth century, moreover, most students left school quite early, around age 13 or 14, and only a small minority went to high school. Within the high school, no need for a differentiated curriculum existed, because the relatively few students who attended generally sought the same sort of education as preparation for university entrance, for teaching, or for commercial careers. Early in the twentieth century, for reasons that require more exploration, young people began to stay in school for longer periods, and it soon became apparent to educators that they had a new clientele within the high schools: children of immigrant and working-class parents, for whom the old curriculum appeared manifestly inadequate. Vocational education appeared to be an appropriate and egalitarian response to the entrance of large numbers of children who would work with their hands when they left high school. In fact, the introduction of vocational educa-

[52]Davey, "Educational Reform"; Michael Katz, "Who Went to School?," *History of Education Quarterly* 12 (Fall 1972): 432–454. Katz, *Irony of Early School Reform*, pp. 39–40; Marvin Lazerson, *Origins of the Urban School: Public Education in Massachusetts, 1870–1915* (Cambridge, Mass., 1971), pp. 165–171.

tion allowed school systems to continue to offer their traditional advantages to the middle classes; through vocational education, school systems formalized their long-standing participation in the reproduction rather than in the alteration of class structure.[53]

Thus, in the largest sense, vocational education permitted school systems to retain their social function; at the same time, if reflected the organizational principles upon which educational bureaucracies had been erected. Schoolmen long had stressed the importance of exact classification to the development of educational systems. Specialization and the division of labor, they argued, were the fundamental principles of modern organizational development, and upon them schoolmen spun out their plans for elaborate educational systems. At first their goal was simply the introduction of age-grading into schools; then it became the creation of a hierarchy of schools within each system; afterward, as Lazerson shows, it became the introduction of differentiated educational programs. From this perspective, vocational education represented an elaboration of the bureaucratic impulse that had been at work in urban social organization since the middle decades of the nineteenth century.

The results that public school systems achieved were mixed and difficult to measure. Indeed, the evidence for the results of education remains elusive and controversial even today. For an age before the tools of behavioral science had been invented, it is even more difficult to acquire. The problem can best be approached by decomposing the question of results into three components.

First, compare the explicit purposes of schooling with what we know about social trends over time. Schools have had little effect upon crime, delinquency, and poverty. These problems, as we all know, did not disappear after schools had been founded. Despite a massive expenditure of funds and a recurrent attempt to use the schools to alleviate social pathology, little connection ever existed between the extent of public education and the amount of distress and disorder in social life.

It is more difficult to pinpoint the relations between the schools and social mobility. However, for as long as it can be measured, the distribution of wealth in America has remained very skewed, and rates of social mobility do not appear to have changed greatly over time, Indeed, what changes did occur resulted more from shifts in industrial and occupational structure than from education. Again, despite the assertion of

[53]On the introduction of vocational education and related innovations, see Lazerson, *Origins of the Urban School*, especially chaps. 3–7; Bowles and Gintis, *Schooling in Capitalist America*. For a general discussion of secondary education, see Edward A. Krug, *The Shaping of the American High School* (New York, 1964).

promoters to the contrary, the connection between educational expansion and social process seems, at best, tangential.

Although the school attendance of young children soon became virtually universal, secondary school attendance remained largely a practice restricted to the children of at least the moderately affluent. Early working-class skeptics who worried that tax money spent on high school support would enable middle-class parents to transmit their own status to their children at minimal expense had been right. As high school attendance became nearly universal in the twentieth century, college assumed the differentiating role once played by secondary education. Schooling, to be sure, has been the source through which many individuals have achieved social mobility, but it never significantly lessened the distance between the major groupings within the class structure. Rather than opening opportunity, schools have regularized mobility and controlled competition in the world outside the classroom. The mechanisms—various forms of tracking, vocational education, guidance—have become increasingly more elaborate, but the result has remained the same. Contemporary social science has discovered, simply, that schools continue to play their historic role.

Frequently the argument about the overall lack of relation between schooling and social mobility is countered with the example of the Jews. The astounding success of the children of Jewish immigrants, it is asserted, proves the effectiveness of the school as an agency of social mobility, at least in the early twentieth century. The problem with this argument is that the Jews were a small, atypical group. In fact, on the basis of the black experience, exactly the opposite point can be made. David Tyack has pointed out that rates of black school attendance in the late nineteenth and early twentieth centuries were high. Louis Harlan has shown that southern whites feared the immense hunger of blacks for education in the same period. Indeed, it appears that from the years after Emancipation through at least the early decades of the twentieth century blacks accepted the promise of public education. In no instance was that promise proved more hollow.[54]

Schools, however, have dealt more successfully with some of the other problems that encouraged their creation. Schooling alleviated a

[54]Tyack, *One Best System*, pp. 110–125; Louis R. Harlan, *Separate and Unequal: Public School Campaigns and Racism in the Southern Seaboard States, 1901–1915* (Chapel Hill, N.C., 1958), p. 196; Herbert G. Gutman, *The Black Family in Slavery and Freedom, 1750–1925* (New York, 1976), p. 229. On Jewish social mobility, see Thernstrom, *Other Bostonians*, pp. 145–175. See also Michael R. Olneck and Marvin Lazerson, "The School Achievement of Immigrant Children, 1900–1930," *History of Education Quarterly* 14 (Winter 1974): 453–482.

good deal of middle-class parental anxiety by providing an institutional setting for adolescence and a mechanism for the transmission of status. Among all social classes, schooling has reduced massively the problem of idle youth. Whatever else they do, compulsory schools take young people off the street. Proclamations about the relation between higher education and job success, moreover, persuade many of them to stay there, not only out of sight but also out of the labor market. This has been a major accomplishment of public education since the mid-nineteenth century.

Schools undoubtedly contributed to the reduction of another problem that worried their early sponsors: the discipline of an industrial work force. This accomplishment raises the second way in which the results of education can be explored: the nature of the learning that young people took away with them from school. It is not difficult to reconstruct the nature of the curriculum, pedagogical methods, and the content of textbooks. However, it is exceedingly difficult to estimate their impact upon children.

Some speculation, however, is possible with the application of the theory advanced by Robert Dreeben, who contends that schools have their greatest impact through their structural characteristics rather than through the content of their pedagogy. What is learned in schools today, Dreeben argues, is how to behave. More specifically, within schools children learn the norms that differentiate public from private life, which govern the way people are treated in institutions and at work as opposed to within the family.[55]

Nineteenth-century educational spokesmen claimed that schools would foster regularity, punctuality, docility, and restraint. Contemporary discussions more often use terms such as universalism, independence, and achievement. Nonetheless, the message, the organization, and, by implication, even some of the results of schooling have remained similar throughout the last century. Age-grading, a stress on individual rather than on collective achievement, the application of universalistic standards, a preoccupation with time, all of these have characterized most public school experience for at least a century and a quarter. The norms learned in school have suited the bureaucratic organization of social, political, and economic activity. They are, indeed, norms without which bureaucracy cannot work.

Although the acceptance of universalism, independence, and achievement, as defined by Dreeben, cuts across class structure, the organization of schooling is in some ways differentiated. Observers have

[55]Dreeben, *On What Is Learned in Schools*, passim.

pointed to the variations in authority patterns, sanctions, and motivational techniques within schools composed primarily of students with different class backgrounds, and these variations can be shown to relate to the characteristics of the work settings that students from different classes are likely to enter. Whether this was the case in the nineteenth century is not yet known.[56]

Whether the norms that govern families and schools are as sharply differentiated as Dreeben implies also is not clear. Both Michael Zuckerman and Christopher Lasch, for instance, show a correspondence between styles of child rearing in contemporary America and the behaviors required for success in corporate bureaucracies. Those behaviors—an easygoing sociability, lack of introspection, and avoidance of conflict—also are stressed in schools. If, as Lasch contends, they have invaded the family as part of the socialization of reproduction in the twentieth century, then it may be possible that the relation between home and school has shifted from opposition to complementarity during the last 100 years. Again, the issue awaits historical study. However, the Lasch–Zuckerman thesis does not affect Dreeben's observation that the special and individual treatment of children within their families differs from their treatment as members of categories within schools. Nor does it speak to the nature of child rearing styles in families that are not part of the corporate or political bourgeoisie. For these families, the relation between home and school still may be in important ways one of opposition.[57]

There have been many ways in which schools have transmitted their messages. For example, age-grading, a key component of plans for educational systematization since the 1840s, when it first entered the Boston schools, has taught children that they are members of categories. It has enforced the lesson that people should be treated according to characteristics that they share as members of a group and that they are not entitled to special treatment on account of their individual qualities. The utility of popular commitment to this proposition for a society that shuffles its citizens between mass settings is self-evident.[58]

Early schoolmen, in fact, debated the consequences of pedagogical arrangements for the development of attitudes. Emulation, for instance,

[56]For instance, see Edgar Z. Friedenberg, *Coming of Age in America: Growth and Acquiescence* (New York, 1865), and Bowles and Gintis, *Schooling in Capitalist America*, pp. 125–148.

[57]Michael Zuckerman, "Dr. Spock: The Confidence Man," in *The Family in History*, ed. Charles E. Rosenberg (Philadelphia, 1975), pp. 179–205; Christopher Lasch, *Haven in a Heartless World: The Family Beseiged* (New York, 1977), and *The Culture of Narcissism: American Life in an Age of Diminishing Expectations* (New York, 1979), especially pp. 267–317.

[58]Katz, *Irony of Early School Reform*, pp. 55–56, and *Class, Bureaucracy and Schools*, pp. 35, 165.

was a matter of far greater concern to Horace Mann and his generation than was the teaching of mathematics. By *emulation* educators meant a common motivational device: competition. Children were spurred to learn through a desire to emulate their peers. To the architects of the common-school system in the United States (though not in Canada), emulation represented the beginning of the mad competitive scramble, the acquisitive materialism that cursed contemporary society. The award of prizes for achievement had the same effect. Students learned to work only for the sake of rewards, they were, to use a much later though entirely appropriate phrase, outer-directed.[59]

Schoolmen of the time, worried over the consequences of outer-direction for social life, believed that a major shift, an internalization of the desire to achieve for its own sake, had become urgent. A society of students weaned on emulation and prizes would require a continued reliance on external police and artificial incentives. Although acceptable in an authoritarian state, external incentives and emulation were inappropriate and insufficient in an open, democratic society. For a democratic society to function, its work to be done, the aspirations of its populace to remain decently restrained, and harmony rather than envy to govern social relations, a massive internalization of the will to achieve and the work ethic had to be learned within the schools. Those qualities, moreover, could never be taught didactically. They would emerge from an identification of students with role models and from the lessons transmitted through the organizational aspects of a carefully designed educational process. Thus, no issue was trivial, and, to take one example, whether to continue to award medals in the Boston schools emerged as a major controversy.[60]

Ultimately, the moral mission of the schools—as educators refered to the teaching of attitudes and behavior—was political, because its goal was the legitimation of inequality. The extent to which ordinary people have accepted the legitimacy of a social and economic order in which they have been the losers remains the most effective evidence that the panoply of devices securing the hegemony of industrial capitalism—among which education has been prominent—has achieved its goal. This is the third way in which the results of public education may be assessed. It again retains all the dangers of an argument that moves from

---

[59]Katz, *Irony of Early School Reform*, pp. 120–141.

[60]*Ibid.*

[61]For an example of debate over the social implications of motivational techniques, see *ibid.*, pt. 2. A recent exploration of the legitimation of inequality is Michael Lewis, *The Culture of Inequality* (Amherst, Mass., 1978). A different point of view on the same problem may be found in Michael Burawoy, "Toward a Marxist Theory of the Labor Process: Braverman and Beyond," *Politics and Society* 8 (1978): 265.

the present backwards. Yet, it is clear that the successful legitimation of inequality is a fundamental characteristic of North American society and, as such, must be explained.[61]

The hegemony of what has been termed "nonegalitarian classlessness" as the reigning conception of social order has been secured in many ways, which historians only recently have begun to appreciate. Relative weights cannot be given to socialization within the family, the organization of work, patterns of property distribution and social mobility, the messages transmitted through religion, literature, advertising, and other media, and education. Much less can a sequence, an interrelation of factors woven into an explanation, be offered with any confidence.[62] However, the question remains important because there has been no golden age in modern North American history. A sharply etched structure of inequality crystallized early and remained intact with only minor modifications throughout the last century and a half. Despite occasional protest at moments when, as Herbert G. Gutman has shown, new populations had to be incorporated into the industrial capitalist order, the most remarkable aspect of the history of inequality has been the degree to which it has been accepted not only by its beneficiaries but also by its casualties.[63]

The question is why. Although the answer is complex and involves a variety of agencies and practices, schools have been one of the important mechanisms. One way in which schooling has contributed to the legitimation of inequality has been through teaching children to blame themselves for failure. Starting in the second quarter of the nineteenth century, schoolmen waged a campaign to base promotion on achievement. Over the complaints of parents and students, they emphasized that promotion from one grade or educational level to another had to be earned. The system owed them nothing; children who did not pass examinations were entirely responsible for their own failure. Thus, for about a century and a half within school, children have learned their first lesson in political economy: The unequal distribution of rewards mirrors the unequal distribution of ability. Those who achieve deserve their success; those who fail are, simply, less worthy.[64]

[62]The concept of nonegalitarian classlessness was created by the late Stanislaw Ossowski in his brilliant book, *Class Structure in the Social Consciousness* (London, 1963). Some of the evidence for the relation of job hierarchies to the legitimation of inequality is cited in Burawoy, "Toward a Marxist Theory," pp. 262–263. The relation of both property and social mobility to the process is discussed in Katz, Doucet, and Stern, *Social Organization of Early Industrial Capitalism.*

[63]Katz, *People of Hamilton, Canada West,* chap. 2; Gutman, "Work, Culture, and Society," *passim.*

[64]Katz, *Irony of Early School Reform,* pp. 89–90.

The lesson coincides with the ideology of social mobility in America. The virtue of North American society, according to both popular thought and political rhetoric, has resided in equality of opportunity, not in equality of condition. The measure of the good society has not been the extent to which the disparities between groups have lessened; rather, the measure has been the degree to which the individual has remained free to rise as far as his talents could take him. (I deliberately use the male pronoun here. Occupational mobility primarily has been a game restricted, until very recently, to men.) In this view, social policy should be evaluated by the extent to which it removes barriers to individual achievement, not primarily by the degree to which it reduces inequity. The strength of popular commitment to an individualist definition of equality may be seen in the resistance to affirmative action, the first sustained attempt in American history to give priority to the reduction of inequality of condition, even at the expense of individual merit.

The traditional commitment to a good society, defined as equality of opportunity for the individual, has misdirected debate about the relation between educational policy and social inequality. Although inequality has resided deep within the structure of public educational systems from their very inception and although sociologists have argued persuasively that schools by themselves cannot reduce inequality and poverty or promote social mobility, attempts to reduce the inequities in their structure and operations retain an important purpose.

The purpose, however, is not the promotion of opportunity for individual social mobility, for even if policy designed to promote individual equality of opportunity could be successful, it only would reinforce the equation of individual mobility with the good society. The equation creates a sense of worthlessness within the majority of people. To some extent mobility is a zero-sum game; most people always must lose. If they believe that the inequity they suffer on account of their loss reflects their own inherent unworthiness, they are doomed to a life in which they are systematically robbed of their self-esteem.

A preoccupation with equality of opportunity engenders frustration. When each new cycle of reformers learns that the schools cannot alter the structure of inequality, it leaves the scene of the action, cynical or defeated, allowing the biases of the system flourish more easily. Those biases—inequality of resources, access, and achievement—remain critical because they represent a contradiction between political values and social institutions. Officially, North American society remains committed to goals that deny that races, classes, or sexes should experience systematic discrimination. Where discrimination can be shown to exist, it violates political and moral principles. A major contradiction, thus, exists between social and political values and public schools.

The reason for promoting integration, attempting to equalize the achievement of racial or social groups, or increasing access is that institutions should reflect widespread political and moral values. The failure to pursue egalitarian policies is a tacit admission that the values that underlie democracy have become hollow shells, resonating a rhetoric without substance.

THE DIALECTICS OF SOCIAL POLICY

Social policy is dialectical, as the early history of public schooling shows quite nicely. Policy emerges from a combination of objective circumstances and perception. In the case of public schooling, early nineteenth-century social and economic development created certain very real problems. Policymakers of the period, however, viewed those problems through a lens that reflected the limitations of their culture and the anxieties of their class. As a result, the school systems that emerged did not represent a wholly appropriate response to the problems that troubled their creators. They won acceptance through promises that could be fulfilled only partially and revealed, from their inception, serious contradictions between explicit purposes and actual results.[65]

Whether policymakers at the time seriously believed that schools would promote equality and lessen crime and poverty remains impossible to know. However, their claims were unambiguous, and, particularly as the cost of schooling increased, the contradiction between promise and results erupted into serious criticism. Beginning especially in the aftermath of the depression in 1873, across the continent a series of critics ruthlessly began to dissect the bureaucratic urban school systems that had mushroomed in the preceding 2 decades. Their themes would be familiar to anyone today: Schools had become too rigid; they did not lessen crime; they were unresponsive to the community; they taught reading and writing less effectively than had little country schools earlier in the century; they cost much too much; they required too many administrators; and schoolpeople had become martinets, unwilling to tolerate criticism and defensive of their systems.[66]

Although the contradiction between the purpose of policy and its institutional form emerged quite quickly in the case of education, a similar dialectic always is inherent in the policy process. The implementation of a policy alters the context in which that policy originated. The

[65]For a more formal discussion of the application of a dialectical approach to institutional analysis, see J. Kenneth Benson, "Organizations: A Dialectical View," *Administrative Science Quarterly* 22 (March 1977): 1–21.
[66]Katz, *Class, Bureaucracy and Schools*, chap. 2.

creation of school systems altered the objective educational situation, just as, to take another example, the creation of mental hospitals altered the relation between mental illness and society. In time altered circumstances make obsolete the original policy: A new contradiction emerges, and a demand for innovation or reform begins anew. Of course, the dialectic varies in its pace and in the amount of conflict it generates. The appropriateness of the original policy to the circumstances in which it emerged is one important factor; another is the degree of commitment to existing policy on the part of various interest groups. However, in a general sense the moral is clear: No policy can be expected to last forever; policymakers should learn to build impermanently.

The point seems almost commonsense, but it requires emphasis, for the failure to appreciate the dialectical nature of institutional development represents a major recurrent weakness of policy. Certainly, the failure to approach policy historically and dialectically has added bitterness to the often unproductive arguments between proponents of centralization and decentralization in public education. Neither side in the controversy has appreciated that no particular balance of centralization will remain appropriate forever. The struggle has been waged in moral terms with virtue invested by each side in a particular set of administrative arrangements. That sort of argument, however, misses the point: Administrative arrangements must be judged by the extent to which they foster particular goals or values at a given historical moment. Those goals—such as equality of access to public facilities and the reduction of differential achievement between children of varied social origins—will require a policy sensitive to the contradictions that emerge between principles and administrative arrangements, not one frozen for all time and defended as sacred.[67]

The existence of institutions has defined important groups: the mentally ill, paupers, and juvenile delinquents. In the case of education, to take another example, truants as a class cannot exist without compulsory schooling. At a more general level, institutions create new classes: managers and managed. Among the first chief executives of the institutional state in the nineteenth century were school superintendents and superintendents of insane asylums. The managerial class develops a vested interest in the avoidance of change and the justification of institutional policy. Early superintendents of insane asylums, for instance, fended off critics of institutionalization in the 1870s and defended the desirability of treating mental illness in large residential institutions. Similarly, school superintendents banded together to fight the first crit-

[67] *Ibid.*, chap. 3.

ics of public education in the 1870s and to justify the large, expensive, public bureaucracies over which they presided.[68]

Through the creation of a managerial class, institutions develop a built-in mechanism that enables them to mobilize resistance to fundamental change. Herein lies a complicated and subtle task for policymakers: the development of policies that will self-destruct and the formation of a core of committed managers who gracefully will dismantle their own creations.

A dialectical conception of policy has four major problems. One is the problem of implementation exacerbated by the tenacious hold of institutional beneficiaries on the status quo. A second is the contradiction that frequently exists between principles themselves. For instance, two goals of many educational reformers are to increase the influence of parents on the content and procedures of schooling and to reduce racial segregation. The implementation of one principle requires radical decentralization; the implementation of the other could lead to larger and more heterogeneous schools.

The third problem is the susceptibility of a dialectical conception of policy to a strictly pragmatic or technocratic point of view. The measure for policy should not be simply what works most easily at a given moment or political acceptability. Rather, policy should be evaluated according to the extent to which it expands the influence of a principle within social life. The point of a dialectical view is that institutionalized policy will develop contradictions with the principles it is supposed to promote. At that point shifts in policy become urgent.[69]

Institutionalized policies shape the categories in which we think. This is the fourth problem with the dialectical approach: namely, the difficulty of transcending in our imagination the set of arrangements that actually exists at any given moment. Consider the question of adolescence as an example. Defined as a stage of prolonged, institutionalized dependency, adolescence emerged only in the late nineteenth century. G. Stanley Hall's treatise *Adolescence* (1904) did not mark the belated recognition of a permanent phase in the life cycle. Rather, it reflected the shift in demographic experience that occurred when young people began to live longer than ever before in the homes of their parents and to spend large portions of their lives in specially designed institutions called schools. Ironically, prolonged institutionalized dependence is accepted as characteristic of a span of years in the life cycle, and policy is

---

[68] *Ibid.*, chap. 2; Grob, *Mental Institutions*, pp. 323–336.

[69] For a fine discussion of this point in the context of a comparative analysis of Marx and Weber, see Anthony Giddens, *Capitalism and Modern Social Theory: An Analysis of the Writings of Marx, Durkheim and Max Weber* (Cambridge, 1975), p. 235.

directed toward the question of how to make that experience more pleasant and worthwhile. Not nearly enough, however, is it asked if prolonged institutionalized dependence is itself necessary or appropriate. We are, in other words, unable to transcend the categories with which nearly a century of social policy has described the life course of young people.[70]

DISCONTINUITIES IN SOCIAL ISSUES

In three particular respects, however, the contemporary situation is discontinuous with the past in ways that make necessary the transcendence of traditional categories. The first is the women's movement and the contradictions for policy posed by the entry of a large proportion of married women into the labor force. To a substantial degree, support for the women's movement has come from people both critical of institutions and determined to overcome barriers to the achievement of women. Nonetheless, the increased participation of married women in the labor force will require institutional care of children beginning at a much younger age than ever has been customary. This will reinforce the custodial role of institutions. In these circumstances the only viable policy guide is to accept openly that one key role of public institutions should be to provide good day care. (Indeed, public schools might take the *best* day-care centers as models. They illustrate that effective, decentralized, nondestructive environments in fact can be created.)

The second historically new force affecting educational policy is the emergent rupture between schooling and occupational success among middle class young people. For the last 150 years, schools served the middle class as an agency for the transmission of status to its children. Recently, the capacity of schools to guarantee this outcome has lessened seriously. Although many jobs still require educational certification, degrees no longer guarantee genteel work. Unemployed Ph.D.'s, lawyers, and teachers who are unable to find jobs may be only the first casualties of a historic break between education and employment. If this is the case, the commitment of the middle class to the support of public schooling probably will diminish sharply. Indeed, signs exist that this already has begun to happen.

[70]On Hall, see Dorothy Ross, *G. Stanley Hall: The Psychologist as Prophet* (Chicago, 1972). See also Kett, *Rites of Passage.*

The rupture between schooling and occupational success could be permanent. Contrary to conventional wisdom, Harry Braverman has argued, occupational skill requirements do not increase with technological progress. Within industrial capitalist countries, in fact, they have declined: Jobs have been subdivided into their component parts and made easier to learn. Until recently demographic and economic growth masked this process. Sustained growth created openings for managers, teachers, scientists, engineers, and so on. However, the skills demanded within individual occupations did not increase, and for a large part of the work force, they declined. Given the decline in growth and the overproduction of highly trained specialists in a variety of fields, demand is unlikely to rise again in the foreseeable future. The result is a major contradiction between the actual operation of school systems—the continued excess production of specialized workers—and the stagnant nature of the economy. The decline in political support for education, especially post secondary education, is the first product of that contradiction.[71]

Simultaneously, and this is the third major discontinuity, schools have experienced the crisis of legitimacy that affects most social and political institutions.

Recently, for example, the American Federation of Teachers documented widespread violence—rapes and assaults of students upon each other and upon teachers—within the Houston, Texas, public schools. Although partly an attack on self-serving school officials who refuse to report incidents to the police and intimidate teachers who do, the AFTs report places the blame for violence on the inadequate financial support provided the schools by the community. Underpaid teachers face overcrowded classrooms in which they are unable to keep order, and the result is violence.[72]

Contrary to the report, however, violence, class size, and teachers' salaries have only a marginal connection with each other. In the nineteenth and early twentieth centuries, miserably paid teachers commonly taught classes of 60 or 70 students. In the monitorial schools serving children of the poor in the late eighteenth and early nineteenth

[71]Harry Braverman, *Labor and Monopoly Capital: The Degradation of Work in the Twentieth Century* (New York, 1974), p. 212–233; Levin, "Educational Opportunity and Inequality," pp. 162–164.

[72]American Federation of Teachers and Houston Federation of Teachers, "The Houston Public Schools: A Study of Violence and Cover-Up" (Report presented in the city of Houston to the Executive Council of the Houston Federation of Teachers, Local 2415 AFT/AFL–CIO, 4 May 1977).

centuries, one master sometimes presided over hundreds of pupils. In most accounts these schools were remarkable for their orderliness. Violence and disruption did not pose serious problems, and pupils generally accepted the authority of teachers. Thus, the source of contemporary violence within the schools must be sought in the recent refusal to accept willingly the authority of teachers and administrators. That refusal reflects much more than a decline in civility, manners, or respect. It is a fundamental challenge to the legitimacy of the school as a social institution.[73]

Serious attendance problems, physical assaults upon students and teachers, and the need for police to patrol school corridors are developments that signal not only a failure of traditional modes of ensuring order but also a broader refusal to accept the authority of social and political institutions. Students who riot have not learned docility, reliability, and restraint. They have not learned to accept the unequal distribution of power and rewards with grace and a fitting self-effacement. In the same way, poor parents who have attempted to make schools legally responsible for the achievement of their children have rejected a fundamental premise of the system: individual responsibility for failure. By their demand that the schools actually teach, they are making a powerful political protest that strikes directly at not only schools but also the ideology of mobility that has legitimized the structure of inequality in North American society.[74]

The failure of the schools to perform their historic role as agents of political legitimization reflects a failure common to other institutions: The rise in malpractice suits, the attack upon the welfare system, and the disillusionment following the Watergate scandal provide three examples. Without doubt, the contradiction between the promise of institutionalized policy and its results finally has begun to penetrate popular consciousness. Whether that penetration will yield cynicism and apathy or sustained political activity remains unclear.

What does stand out clearly, however, is that the forces most powerfully affecting schools do not flow from educational planning or policy. Nor have they ever. That, certainly, is one message of educational history. Rather, the source of contemporary pressure for change lies in the

---

[73]Tyack, *One Best System*, pp. 50–56; Carl F. Kaestle, ed., *Joseph Lancaster and the Monitorial School Movement* (New York, 1973).

[74]The essentially political nature of popular insurgency is made unmistakably clear in Frances Fox Piven and Richard A. Cloward, *Poor People's Movements: Why They Succeed and How They Fail* (New York, 1977).

contradictions between the schools and the social order: unequal education and democratic values, the continued production of highly skilled workers in a stagnant job market, and the demand for obedient acquiescence in failure confronted by a crisis of legitimacy. It would be unduly optimistic to predict the resolution of these contradictions in the interests of the poor or powerless. Most responses to them will attempt to defuse their explosive potential and to maintain the structural inequalities of industrial capitalism with only minor modifications.[75]

Indeed, one response to the crisis of legitimacy in education has been the adoption of open classrooms and related soft innovations. School-people have adeptly co-opted innovation before, and in the current situation the danger is that the open classroom could become a mode of repressive desublimation, a means for the defusion of conflict through the expression of emotions in an environment where controls have been hidden more subtly and power relations altered not at all. "The appearance of permissiveness," observes Christopher Lasch, "conceals a stringent system of controls, all the more effective because it avoids direct confrontations between authorities and the people on whom they seek to impose their wills." What Lasch calls the "therapeutic view of authority" permits the preservation of "hierarchical forms of organization in the guise of 'participation.'" Thus, the open classroom parallels other strains in cultural policy. As happened in the early period of industrial capitalism, a fit exists between the character structure advocated by "progressive" educators and the character structure appropriate to social and economic relations. The danger is that the open classroom could be used like the advertising in the Sunday paper: to promote the illusion of freedom in the interests of corporate capitalism and the state.[76]

The advocates of the open classroom, it is important to stress, frame their argument in ways distressingly similar to the main line of educational thought in the nineteenth and twentieth centuries. They stress the affective results of schooling and show more concern with emotions than with intellect. A true revolution in North American education would reverse this emphasis. No true division can be made between

---

[75]My argument in this paragraph has been inspired by Henry Levin, "The Limits of Educational Planning" (unpublished MS, April 1977). Of course, as Piven and Cloward, in *Poor People's Movements*, point out, the possibility of achieving specific and limited goals—which do not imply structural change—should not be overlooked. For instance, a 12-day sit-in by parents in a West Philadelphia school in December 1979 apparently succeeded in removing the principal, which was the goal of the protestors.

[76]Lasch, *Culture of Narcissism*, pp. 310, 315; Katz, *Class, Bureaucracy and Schools*, pp. 185–193; see also Zuckerman, "Dr. Spock."

moral and intellectual aspects of curriculum or pedagogy. However, it does matter whether the primary emphasis of schooling is upon the development of cognitive skills, such as reading, or the inculcation of a set of political and social attitudes.

It is important, though, to remember that the fashionable contemporary call for a return to the basics in education rarely rejects the fundamentally moral mission of the schools. The clue is that an improvement in the teaching of reading, writing, and mathematics often is thought to lie in authoritarian pedagogy. The advocates of basic education, unfortunately, are frequently the champions of rigidity, conformity, and corporal punishment as well. They seek not the intellectual emancipation of students but a solid return for their dollars invested in schools and an end to the freaky, subversive behavior that they associate with educational liberalization. The problem is that the old methods did not work very well. There is no evidence that schools ever promoted a level of reading ability higher than now exists among the population as a whole. In fact, quite the opposite probably is the case.

Schools, as has happened before, have become the scapegoats for anxieties about the younger generation and a fear of social change. The danger is that a legitimate concern about the quality of cognitive skills will foster a return to a more oppressive regimen within the schools, that the last decade's mild but unmistakable increase in the concern with human dignity, honesty, and compassion will be lost without any corresponding gain in the ability of students to read, write, or think critically and analytically about their lives.

The old days were not very good. The traditional methodology, to which a return often is advocated, was part of the problem, for its authoritarian style conveyed part of the message that schools existed to instill. The problem, thus, is to tilt the emphasis of schooling away from character and towards cognitive ability without returning to the repressiveness whose effective exposure remains the best legacy of the romantic reform that inspired us a decade ago.

In the end, the portrait is crisscrossed with contradictions. Libertarian reform becomes a new form of social control; basic education turns out to be antiintellectual. Schools cannot by themselves promote a more egalitarian society, but we must continue to work for egalitarian reform. The explosive forces in contemporary education result from contradictions between the schools and their social context, not from a cooly plotted revolutionary policy. There is no neat way to resolve the inconsistencies, to tie the conflicting threads of this chapter into a coherent, programmatic solution. We must accept the conflict and the contradiction. If we allow ourselves an illusory optimism, we are sure to suffer the disenchantment that has followed the failure of reform in other generations. Still, if we resign, we can accomplish nothing. There is a liberation that accompanies the acceptance of our own futility, the acknowledgment that we shall fail to reach our ultimate goals, for we become free to measure our efforts not by their probable success but by their moral worth. If we cannot build a new social order, we at least can try to do what is right.[77]

ACKNOWLEDGMENTS

For their advice on this chapter I would like to thank Michael Doucet, Mark Stern, Brenda Torpy, David Tyack, Henry Levin, Stanton Wheeler, and David Rothman.

[77]My phrase here is, of course, a deliberate play on George S. Counts, *Dare the Schools Build a New Social Order?* (New York, 1932), an example of the type of passionate manifesto that, I think, engenders unrealistic expectations and, in the end, despair. The argument in this chapter has referred to general changes in schooling, such as an alteration in curriculum, and to changes in the overall relation between education and society. It does not deal with specific, limited goals, such as the removal of a principal considered offensive by parents. Nor does it deal with the tactics of change. On both these levels a slightly more optimistic account is possible based on the analysis in Piven and Cloward, *Poor People's Movements.* The implications of their work for educational change require a thorough exploration.

4

THE DIARY OF AN INSTITUTION: THE FATE OF PROGRESSIVE REFORM AT THE NORFOLK PENITENTIARY[1]

DAVID J. ROTHMAN

It is commonplace for individuals, particularly those occupying the high places of politics and culture, to keep a diary of their activities and ideas. It is extraordinary, however, for an institution to do so, to maintain a running account of its successes and failures over a period of years. By a series of odd circumstances, just such a diary was created at the Norfolk, Massachusetts, penitentiary, 700 single-spaced typewritten pages that cover the 2 most critical years in its history—1932 and 1933. As is more typical than historians might like to admit, I stumbled on this document unaware of its existence (even if I did confirm the adage that good things happen to those who enter archives). Yet as soon as I began to examine it, I realized that the diary was nothing less than a text that explored intimately and explicitly, as diaries often do, exactly what happened when the hopes of a generation of reformers were translated into practice.

If diary keepers are not usually the ordinary men of their times, this penitentiary was certainly not the typical institution of its time. The Norfolk penitentiary represented a grand effort to implement the program that Progressives—the group whose ideas on social policy constituted the reform tradition from 1900 until the mid-1960s—defined as the

[1]The material in this chapter is adapted from Chapter 11 of *Conscience and Convenience: The Asylum and Its Alternatives in Progressive America,* by David J. Rothman (Boston, 1980). Copyright © 1980 by David J. Rothman. Adapted by permission of Little, Brown and Company.

 ISBN 0-12-598680-7

ideal way to organize and administer criminal punishment. Norfolk was to be the model institution, the prison that realized the most scientific and humanitarian system of incarceration. Indeed, like the nineteenth-century institutions at Philadelphia and Auburn, N. Y., the list of notables that visited Norfolk or, given the passage of 100 years, were consultants to the project, was long and impressive, including Sheldon Glueck, Thorsten Sellin, Miriam Van Waters, Elton Mayo, Edwin Sutherland, and W. I. Thomas. And my own sense of affinity with the enterprise was strong. Having just served with the Field Foundation Committee for the Study of Incarceration to devise a new agenda for prison reform, I had the distinct sense that the Norfolk group was my predecessor committee.

More than personal curiosity, however, drew me into the Norfolk penitentiary materials. The novelty of the diary lay not merely in its form but also in its content. The document is as clear and specific a statement of the Progressive program for incarceration as can be found; more important, the diary moves back and forth between principles and practices. It exposes more vividly and accurately than does any other single source that I have examined the dynamics that operated as reformers attempted to create a therapeutic institution. Thus, the diary affords the opportunity to present an historical analysis—what Progressive reformers were attempting to do, to what degree they could succeed, and what elements impeded or promoted their victories and failures—and to move directly to social policy concerns: What does an understanding of the dynamics that operated at Norfolk tell us about current attempts to alter the system of incarceration?

That the Norfolk penitentiary is a case of only one I am fully aware. The idiosyncratic elements that shaped its story are not inconsiderable. Howard Gill, who designed and ran the program, had his own special strengths (optimism and confidence) and weaknesses (an ability to delude himself and an inability to delegate authority) that helped to determine the outcome of events. Nevertheless, I am not uncomfortable in offering a series of generalizations, of both a historical and social policy sort, on the basis of Norfolk. The proof will have to be in the analysis itself, but I am persuaded that Norfolk's history speaks directly to many past and present efforts to implement reform.

*   *   *

The founding of the Norfolk Prison Colony, as it was officially designated, was no different than that of any other state prison. Agitation for a new institution in Massachusetts began in the early 1920s when state legislators and philanthropic groups, particularly women's clubs, complained of the antiquated facilities at Charlestown—and it is no wonder, since that structure dated from 1805 and was severely overcrowded, with inmates confined two to a tiny cell or sleeping in schoolrooms made into dormitories. The legislature responded in 1927, appropriating $100,000 to begin the construction of a wall for a prison that could either serve as a colony to Charlestown, holding its overflow, or perhaps come to replace it altogether. The site itself, selected in ways that are reminiscent of a process that Michel Foucault describes for early modern Europe, was a parcel of state land some 23 miles from Boston that had first held an inebriate hospital and later, after it failed to cure its charges, became a rehabilitation camp for sick and wounded World War I soldiers. The appointment to superintendent went to Howard Gill an efficiency expert who had graduated from Harvard College and Harvard Business School, had worked for Herbert Hoover in the Commerce Department, and had recently completed a survey on prison industries for the Justice Department. Gill seemed the perfect choice to oversee the construction of the new prison and its administration. In all ways, then, Norfolk had a rather unremarkable beginning.[2]

In short order, however, the institution assumed a special character. Warren Stearns, a psychiatrist, took office in Massachusetts in 1928 as commissioner of corrections. Stearns, among the first, but and certainly not the last, of his profession to hold such a post, was eager to import his techniques for treatment into the prison. His first report to the legislature noted that the existing system appeared "in general to be well managed" but that the "most serious criticism [was] the lack of work with the individual inmate according to his needs." Unless the prison adopted a social-work orientation, "unless all the available data concerning individuals is accumulated and made readily accessible, we cannot hope to handle these individuals to the best advantage."[3] Clearly, Stearns was prepared to make incarceration rehabilitative.

At the same time, Howard Gill was undergoing something of a personal transformation at Norfolk itself. For purely financial reasons, convict laborers were building the prison wall; some 100 inmates from Charles-

[2]Carl Doering, ed., *A Report on the Development of Penological Treatment at Norfolk Prison Colony in Massachusetts* (New York, 1940), pp. 71–75. The Doering volume is made up of three parts: the *Official Manual*, compiled by Walter Commons; *A History of the State Prison Colony*, by Thomas Yahkub; *Individualization of Treatment as Illustrated by Studies of Fifty Cases*, by Edwin Powers. Hereafter citations will be to the particular section, as in this case, Yahkub, *History of State Prison*, pp. 71–75. See also Massachusetts Department of Correction, *Annual Report* . . . *1927*, pp. 4–5.

[3]Massachusetts Department of Correction, *Annual Report* . . . *1929*, pp. 2–3. Stearns's predecessor, Sanford Bates, resigned to head the Federal Bureau of Prisons.

town were living in the Oval, as the old hospital buildings were called, and spent almost 2 years erecting the barriers and the buildings that would eventually enclose them. The construction and the course of daily living went well at Norfolk, really very well; perhaps the inmates were carefully selected, perhaps steady work boosted their morale, or perhaps Gill was an especially effective leader. In all events, Gill was soon ready to generalize a prison routine from this experience. It was not simply that the wall was being built on schedule; rather, the inmates seemed dependable: They could be given responsibility without abusing it and could be put on their honor and trusted. Gill, in short, was discovering for himself that convicts were human beings and, moreover, that an institutional program could appear to be healthy and productive and, therefore, rehabilitative.

These postulates, as we shall see, underlay Progressive thinking, and Gill was well aware of related attempts, such as at Virginia's Lorton Reformatory, to put them into practice. It was one thing to read about these notions and quite another to confirm them by direct experience. Exuberantly, Gill told the legislature in 1928, "We are trying not only to build a wall, but to build men." A few years later, when recounting to a visiting architect the origins of the Norfolk experiment, he declared, "We did not come here with a plan all worked out as many people imagined. The original idea was to build a bastille, but during the two years we lived down here with 150 inmates, clearing the land and building the wall, we began to get the idea of a Prison Colony."[4]

At the outset, Gill was certain that he could organize a rehabilitative prison to build new men as he was building new walls. (The construction metaphor, not surprisingly, pervaded his language.) "We are creating," he announced, "as near as possible a 'sample' institution."[5] What the components of the model should be, in all their detail, he was less sure of, but in some way the early experience at the Oval had to become a basis for a reformatory routine. And some sort of social work had to be included as well. This was not merely because Stearns, a psychiatrist, was commissioner but was because of the centrality of a casework approach to all Progressive thinking. Around these principles Gill and Stearns entered into an easy partnership: "A program can be established at the State Prison Colony to develop a plan of research and therapy in

---

[4]Massachusetts Department of Correction, *Annual Report . . . 1928*, p. 3. Norfolk Diary, 8 August 1932, p. 262, Bureau of Social Hygiene Collection, Rockefeller Foundation, Archives, North Tarrytown, N.Y. (hereafter cited as Diary). For an analysis of Progressive corrections, see David J. Rothman, *Conscience and Convenience* (Boston, 1980).

[5]Gill Memorandum "Re: Research Project" to Dr. George Vold, 7 August 1931. Unless otherwise noted, all letters and memoranda are in the Bureau of Social Hygiene Collection.

individual cases which has not only relief but reconstruction as its conscious aim."[6]

The first result of these considerations was Gill's application in January 1930 to the Bureau of Social Hygiene of the Rockefeller Foundation for a grant. After 6 months of negotiations, chiefly with University of Chicago criminologist Edwin Sutherland and Bureau staff member Leonard Dunham, Gill received a grant. The Bureau, as Sutherland successfully proposed to the board, would allot $55,000 "to defray the extraordinary expenses of a five year experiment." The state "would continue to meet the ordinary expenses of the care of the prisoners." The Bureau funds would be used "to keep a complete record of the experiment and of its results, and to assist in carrying the experiment to its logical limits." More particularly, $10,000 a year would pay the salaries of persons to investigate "the antecedent records of the prisoners" (Stearns's part), to keep a record of "activities in the Colony" (Gill's part), and to check on "the behavior of prisoners after release" (Sutherland's part, which was never carried out). Sutherland was never especially precise in describing the nature of the experiment, but he did convey Gill's sense that the Oval was to be the prototype for the prison: "Several new methods of handling the prisoners are being tested," and "extraordinary careful studies are made of the prisoners and extraordinary efforts made to develop their interests and abilities and solve their personal problems." Concluded Sutherland, "The experiment is, therefore, of interest in penology everywhere and it is important that a careful record be kept of what is done in the experiment and what results are produced by it." And he continued with a line that alone would have won for Gill the grant: "This Colony is in many ways the most interesting and promising piece of pioneer work in penology that is being carried on in America."[7]

As soon as the grant was awarded, Dunham, of the bureau staff, dispatched the foremost criminologist of his generation, Thorsten Sellin, to report on Norfolk's progress. Sellin, on the whole, liked what he saw and over the next several years served as Dunham's major evaluator of the project. In March 1931, halfway into the first year of the grant, he judged Norfolk to be a splendid piece of administrative work and gave Gill full credit for it.[8] There was nothing casual in Sellin's choice of

---

[6]Gill Memorandum to Stearns, 29 August 1930, p. 1.
[7]Gill to the Bureau of Social Hygiene to the attention of Sutherland, 14 January 1930; Sutherland Memordanum to the Board, 17 June 1930, pp. 1–2; Gill to Sutherland, 9 May 1930.
[8]Sellin Memorandum to Dunham, 23 October, 1930; Sellin Memorandum "Visit to Norfolk Prison Colony, March 10–12, 1931," to Dunham, 16 March 1931.

words—Norfolk was a splendid piece of administration, but it lacked a serious research component. Sellin and Dunham persuaded Gill to hire Minnesota criminologist George Vold to take over the research, but Gill, in what would prove to be typical fashion, would not allow anyone to operate independently on his territory. Sellin informed Dunham, "Because of the great latitude offered to Mr. Gill under the Bureau's grant and his clear and unshakable purpose, there is very little that we can do... except to keep in constant friendly contact with him, help him when he wants assistance, and wait for the report."[9]

This passive posture did not content Dunham or Sellin for long. The bureau wanted to be certain that something tangible would result from the Norfolk grant, and Sellin, whose own work was, and continues to be, acutely sensitive to the historical forces that shape the criminal justice system, did not want the Norfolk experiment to disappear without a trace. Sellin came up with a suggestion that pleased everyone. "I had a long talk with Mr. Gill," he told Dunham in December 1931:

> I pointed out again that in an institution such as Norfolk, which is constantly changing aspect, many things occur from day to day, many issues are met and decisions made... and yet are lost sight of in the course of time.... If the reports on Norfolk were to be of any help to administrators... these transient elements must be seized and embodied in some kind of permanent record.... I suggested that Mr. Gill engage a competent secretary who would day by day make the rounds of the important departments, talk to the heads and particularly to Mr. Gill himself and his deputy, ask them what significant events had occurred during the day... and then ask them to dictate for a few minutes on the points raised.[10]

Gill agreed "with alacrity" and immediately put the program as Sellin outlined it into effect. Dunham had his monthly reports, Gill had satisfied the Bureau and kept control over research, and Sellin had served the needs of future researchers.

*   *   *

Despite the tentative quality of what was to constitute the Norfolk plan, or perhaps because of it, the critical assumptions that came to make up its program represented the essentials of Progressive thinking.

[9]Sellin to Vold, 6 November 1930; Vold Memorandum to Gill, *ca.* 10 December 1930, carbon copy to the Bureau of Social Hygiene; Sellin to Dunham, 13 August 1931.
[10]Sellin Memorandum "State Prison Colony at Norfolk" to Dunham, 19 December 1931, pp. 1–3.

To be sure, shifts in policy were not infrequent at Norfolk, and Gill had a distinct aversion to being limited to a single plan of action.[11] Nevertheless, the basic ingredients of the Norfolk agenda did recapitulate the ideas that all right-thinking persons advanced for prison reform.

The *Official Manual of the State Prison Colony*, compiled in December 1932, opened with a "Statement of Fundamental Policies": "Norfolk seeks not only to guard securely the men committed to its safekeeping, but as a fundamental policy to assume its responsibility for returning them to society . . . as better men capable of leading useful, law abiding lives."[12] These lines embodied the most significant and ultimately most problematic Progressive assumption that the prison could perform both a custodial and a rehabilitative function. There was no inherent conflict between guarding men securely and making them better men, between incapacitation and reformation. The keeper and the kept were part of a common venture. "The basis of our whole social philosophy here," declared Gill, "must be that the staff and the inmates will cooperate for the good of all. I cannot see even a small wedge driven between the two if we are to build and educate men in the right social attitude."[13]

Every Progressive innovation in the field of criminal justice reflected this judgment. Probation and parole, which took hold in the opening decades of the twentieth century, also presupposed that surveillance and assistance could go together, that the roles of counselor and police officer were not divergent. And nowhere was this premise more relevant than in the organization of the juvenile court. The courts' "great discovery," noted one reformer, was that "individual welfare coincided with the well-being of the state. Humanitarian and social considerations thus recommend one and the same procedure." The court could simultaneously and without tension promote "sympathy, justice and even the self-interest of society." The judge who decided that a delinquent should be sentenced to a training school was not violating the precepts or elevating community safety over the child's welfare. To incarcerate the young, as the most important decision upholding the constitutionality of the juvenile court ruled, was not to deprive them of their liberty but to exercise "the wholesome restraint which a parent exercises over his child."[14]

With this principle established, the *Manual* next defined the characteristics of Norfolk's population and its own style of rehabilitation: "It

[11]Diary, 15 April 1932, p. 73.
[12]Commons, *Manual*, p. 3.
[13]Diary, 2 November 1933, p. 587.
[14]*Survey* 22 (1910): 607; Commonwealth v. Ames, 213 Penna. 48 (1905).

accepts its charges as delinquent, socially maladjusted human beings . . . who need help, understanding and guidance in rebuilding their lives and characters. Each man is looked upon as an individual with individual needs and problems."[15] In these brief phases, Norfolk declared its allegiance to the Progressive interpretation of the etiology of crime and prescriptions for cure. The inmate was a "delinquent," a term whose use was to signal a commitment to explore the "state of mind" of the deviant rather than the illegal "act." Just as the juvenile court did not respond to the specific behavior that brought the juvenile before the judge, so was Norfolk planning to react not to "burglars" or "robbers" but to "human beings" with "needs and problems." To label the inmate "socially maladjusted" was to confirm the point: The roots of deviant behavior reflected not inherited physical characteristics or moral failings but, to use Dr. William Healy's phrases, "bad habits of mind" and "mental imagery." (Not coincidentally, Healy's book, virtually the Progressive's bible on the causes of crime, was entitled, *The Individual Delinquent*.)[16] The Norfolk penitentiary inmates, therefore, required "guidance" (as in "guidance clinics" that were being established for the first time in the 1920s and 1930s), so that they could "rebuild" their lives. Gill never had difficulty in grafting his favorite construction metaphors onto the language of psychology.

Furthermore, by promising to treat each inmate as an "individual," Norfolk echoed the Progressives' favorite slogan, which pervaded their campaign to implement the indeterminate sentence. The traditional system of punishment, the reformers contended, had been based on a retributive rationale, and therefore judges had passed fixed sentences for specific crimes. Now that rehabilitation was to become the purpose of punishment, they declared, sentences had to be open-ended so that each case would be treated in a unique fashion. Uniformity would give way to diversity, and fixity, to discretion. At this point in the argument, Progressives invariably inserted a medical analogy: Just as the doctor should not be told when to discharge a patient as cured, so too a prison warden should not be told when to discharge a prisoner as reformed. Around this principle, the minimum–maximum term, with a parole board instead of a judge determining time of release, became the essential feature of American prison sentences.

In Norfolk's terms, this Progressive orientation promoted a commitment to become a hospital that dispensed casework as its medicine.

[15]Commons, *Manual*, p. 3; see also, Diary, 1 May 1933, 447.
[16](Boston, 1915), especially pp. 124–125, 130–132, 165, 184.

"Sometimes I liken a prison," Gill would often remark, "to a great social hospital in which there are men with all manner of diseases—the seriously sick, the men with minor ailments, the men who . . . will get well in a short time, the men who will never get well." The problem was that: "1. In the average prison nobody knows what is the matter with the people there. 2. Nobody is doing anything about it." Gill echoed the Progressive refrain: Treat the robber, do not punish the robbery; treat the rapist, do not punish the rape. "We are the last field," he concluded, "to apply casework to problems that deal with human beings. The things which the hospital considers elementary we look upon as revolutionary."[17]

There was a third and no less critical premise that Norfolk drew from the contemporary reform ideology, but its exact fit with a medical model always remained ambiguous. Prison organization, Progressives insisted, should recreate the organization of a normal community; the institution should pattern itself upon the outside society. In a significant way, this maxim represented the Progressives' answer to their Jacksonian predecessors and would allow them to succeed in making prisons rehabilitative where others had failed. The Jacksonians had designed the prison as a *model* community; its organization was to inspire the outside society to emulation—and in this sense the reform had a quasi-utopian quality about it. To the Progressives, the lines of influence were to run the other way: The community was to be the model for the penitentiary. The traditional organization of the prison was "unnatural." To move men in lockstep, with their eyes downcast under a pervasive rule of silence, was to deny the individuality of the inmate and to make his adjustment after release more difficult and perhaps impossible.[18] Thus the Progressives set out to alter the prison routine, to abolish the striped uniform, the lockstep, and the rule of silence, and to implement commissaries, freedom of the yard, prison bands, prison teams, and, most dramatic of all, under Thomas Mott Osborne's leadership, inmate self-government. In a phrase, "Temporary exile into a temporary society as nearly as possible like normal society on the outside would seem the best solution."[19]

Such an orientation fitted well with Gill's experience during the "building time." If any reform ideal had a personal meaning and immediacy for him, it was that prisons should emulate society. Thus, the *Manual*'s "Statement of Fundamental Purposes" concluded:

[17]Diary, 6 July 1932, pp. 181–182.
[18]David J. Rothman, *The Discovery of the Asylum* (Boston, 1971), Chaps. 3–4; Thomas Osborne, *Society and Prisons* (New Haven, 1916), pp. 151–156.
[19]Julia Jaffrey, ed., *The Prison and Prisoners* (Boston, 1917), pp. 153–157.

> The administrative organization and living conditions with the institution are
> made to approximate as nearly as can be in a prison the atmosphere and
> spirit of a normal community. . . . Community life within the institution is a
> common undertaking, based upon the principle of joint responsibility shared
> by administration and inmates.

Gill returned repeatedly to this notion (and in so doing raised, however inadvertently, some troubling points). Norfolk had to be "a replica of a normal community, with its industries, jail, farm, etc. . . . We should develop in men respect rather than docility." The test that had to be applied to a prison routine was "Is that thing normal in community living, will it tend to make men normal?"[20]

Neither Gill nor any of his contemporaries perceived a conflict or discrepancy between the model of the hospital and the model of the community, and they moved easily, if unthinkingly, between one kind of image and the other. Whatever differences there were would disappear when the institution set about treating each inmate, when, in Gill's words, prisons "abandon the idea of uniformity . . . to get down to casework, and the individualization and socialization of the criminal."[21] But conflict could not be disposed of so easily. In the hospital model, the doctor ruled and ruled quite arbitrarily; he diagnosed and prescribed, and the patient accepted and swallowed. In the community model, on the other hand, authority was to be shared and responsibility, divided—the goal was partnership, not docile obedience. In other words, in the hospital model the patient was sick and pathological and needed a cure to be imposed upon him; in the community model, the person was more of a misfit or a nonconformist who had to learn new habits and behavior and needed an internal conversion. Furthermore, suppose that the medicine prescribed was bitter. How far could one go in violating the precepts of "normal living" in order to administer it? Pain for the sake of cure was and still is commonplace in a hospital, but was it just as appropriate within a community—was there such a thing as cruel and unusual rehabilitation? Or what if the patient said, "No thank you." Under a community model, could his wishes be disregarded and his compliance coerced?

All these questions are intrinsic to the models. What if one asks prior questions? Were doctors or caseworkers able to understand the "illness" from which criminals suffered, or, even more important, did they have the medicines with which to treat them? Was the state of criminology at all equivalent to the state of medicine? Was it only the

[20]Commons, *Manual*, p. 3; Diary, 1 May 1933, p. 447, 6 July 1932, p. 183.
[21]Diary, 6 July 1932, p. 183.

height of conceit, or a sign of desperation, that prison reformers picked up a medical model? And could one ever really expect to recreate a normal society behind walls? But now we are shifting, appropriately, from assumptions to programs, and from principles to implementation, so let us move directly to consider how Norfolk translated its ideology into a prison routine.

* * *

Since at the Norfolk penitentiary form was inextricably linked to content, we must look at the institution's physical design. The dominant architectural feature, visually and structurally, was the wall that enclosed some 35 acres. The decision to erect it, to be sure, preceded Gill's appointment. However, Gill not only supervised its construction and completed its design but also staunchly defended its appropriateness. The wall was in every respect a prison wall, rising 19 feet above ground and going below it from 4 to 18 feet, equipped with floodlights and searchlights, and topped, at Gill's suggestion, with four strands of barbed wire that carried 2,300 volts of electricity. Five towers with bulletproof glass jutted out, each holding, again to Gill's specifications, an arsenal of machine guns, rifles, and tear gas. Sellin found all this a discordant note at Norfolk and regretted the presence of machine guns and other weapons.[22] Gill was without any ambivalence, accepting the wall not only as a necessary fact of prison life but also as an asset. The principle that custody did not infringe upon rehabilitation was no less valid in architecture than in social work. The wall provided the measure of external security that enlarged the inmates' liberties. "Objections have been raised by visitors," Gill acknowledged, "to the 'bristling' wall." But their opposition was mistaken. "If we make our wall impregnable... we not only reduce the danger to life, but we also make possible a fairly free community within the wall.... Places without a wall have to maintain such a stringent, strict system that psychological conditions are worse than with a wall."[23]

True to this claim, an observer who went behind the wall to enter the enclosure would have the distinct impression of being inside a reformatory as opposed to a prison. Norfolk did not repeat the standard state penitentiary design—an imposing administration building with radiating wings made up of cell blocks—but instead grouped a series of two- and three-story buildings around an open rectangular space. The major-

[22]Sellin to Dunham, 23 October 1930, p. 8.
[23]Ibid., Diary, 21 August 1932, pp. 265–266; 3 August 1933, pp. 513–514.

ity of inmates lived in these dormitories, in single rooms or in four-to-seven-bed cubicles; in some of the dorms, the interior space was open so that the men could move about freely; in others, locked doors and wire mesh sealed off particular sections. Still, Norfolk did not depart altogether from a prison plan. In keeping with the idea that the colony could simultaneously serve the ends of custody and rehabilitation, or, to use another kind of language, could be at once a minimum (open dorm), medium (closed dorm), and maximum security institution, Norfolk had a Receiving Building, which inmates and staff alike referred to as its "jail." Gill intended this structure to house newly arrived prisoners and all disciplinary cases and fitted it with 105 regular cells, using the best steel and the latest in locking devices ("tool proof" was the manufacturer's term). And Gill defended the jail just as he had the wall: The isolation of the few would enable him to treat the many.[24]

The organization of Norfolk's staff followed with remarkable consistency from its guiding principles and physical design. Gill divided the personnel into two separate groups: the custodians and the guards on the one hand, and the caseworkers and the House Officers on the other. Once again, security considerations would be dealt with separately to allow for the implementation of a rehabilitative program. "In most prisons," Gill explained, there prevails "a peculiar mixture of personal relationship and custodial function. . . . A prison guard is at one moment an officer, but at another he is sympathizing with the inmate as a person. The results are sometimes disastrous." Security could be weakened by an overindulgent or too friendly guard, and at the same time, an inmate could be hassled by a meddlesome one. Accordingly, Norfolk "set up a very sharp line of demarcation between the two." Guards were forbidden to fraternize with the inmates, "not even to check them up unless they are creating a disturbance." In keeping with a community model, "they are like the policeman on the beat. He doesn't interfere or accost persons who are going about their business." Guards were to concern themselves exclusively with "escape, contraband, and disturbances. . . . In nothing else do they enter into the institution's life." The ideal recruits to these positions were "young unmarried men who wish to be trained for the State Police." And Gill so treated them: They wore uniforms, carried arms when on duty atop the wall, and lived and slept in barracks just outside the wall, all in "semi-military organization." In both a literal and figurative sense, they were to be at the perimeter of the institution.[25]

[24]*Ibid.*, 21 August 1932, pp. 262–263; Commons, *Manual*, pp. 6–7.
[25]Diary, 3 August 1933, p. 515; 21 August 1932, p. 266.

At the core were the house officers, those who lived with the men in the dormitories and implemented the casework, educational, and vocational assignments. Their function was

> to make the ideal and the program of individual treatment effective in the daily routine of the institution. . . . These House Officers instead of being typical prison guards, are essentially caseworkers, charged with the difficult and responsible task of trying to understand the problems and needs of the inmate, and through the medium of scientific friendship to help them.

Unlike the guards, they did not wear uniforms (by regulation, they were to dress in "clean and tidy ordinary civilian clothes"), and they carried no weapons (except, by regulation, "common sense, good judgment, alertness, fair dealing, firmness, tact, good will").[26] Thus Norfolk's design did have an internal coherence: border patrol along a defensible line that was to allow for therapeutic encounters everywhere else.

This brings us to the most critical and, not surprisingly, most difficult issue confronting Norfolk: how to arrange for the therapeutic encounter and how to bring a commitment to treatment into the daily life of the institution. Where to begin? Gill and all his Progressive colleagues knew the answer, which came directly from the hospital model—with a system of classification. Just as it was absurd for a hospital to think of prescribing the same medicine to every patient whatever his ailment, so it was absurd for a prison to think of administering the same program to every inmate whatever his problem. "Our general hospitals are divided," declared one reformer, "according to the individual nature of each case. . . . Specialization in our penal institutions must not be delayed if we desire to make progress."[27]

But what type of classification system should operate within a prison? The model, unfortunately, did not supply categories; the taxonomy that existed for diseases did not help to distinguish among criminals. Nor was there any inherited wisdom to draw upon. The military organization of the Auburn-type prison or the 24-hour-a-day isolation of the Philadelphia system seemed to the Progressives the very antithesis of individual treatment or a therapeutic environment. The situation did not, however, appear altogether bleak. The disciplines of sociology and psychology, themselves dominated in this period by medical approaches, were struggling with this same problem. Still, the state of the

---

[26]Commons, *Manual*, pp. 8–9, 32–33; Diary, 21 August 1932, p. 267.
[27]United States Attorney General, *Survey of Release Procedures*, Vol. 5, *Prisons* (Leavenworth, Kansas, 1940), p. 293; Diary, 21 August 1932, p. 267.

art was not advanced. The categories lacked coherence and could not make the delivery of treatment effective.

To analyze closely exactly what these classification systems consisted of is to expose the underlying conceptual problems that plagued all (and I do not exaggerate here) Progressive efforts at rehabilitation. The scheme that Gill brought to Norfolk represented the best thinking on the subject. In light of his own background (business school, prison industries, working with Hoover), he found himself most comfortable, personally and intellectually, with Harvard Business School professor, Elton Mayo, who was at this moment conducting his well-known experiments with worker adjustment at the General Electric plant at Hawthorne. There was little that differentiated Mayo's categories from half a dozen other systems. Change a term or two and all of them divided inmates into one of the following five Norfolk categories, the SCAMP plan:[28]

1. *Situational cases.* "Presenting little or no personality problems... domestic, vocational, financial, educational or other... the man whose circumstances and situation are at the bottom of his difficulties.... Clear up the situation... and he no longer tends to be a criminal."

2. *Custodial cases.* "They are the subnormal, the very abnormal, the old, the senile, the unfit... beyond treatment who will always need supervision... low grade mentalities, inadequate personalities, the senile, the hardened criminal."

3. *Asocial cases.* "They have a philosophy which is antisocial.... That group of professional criminals who need to develop a new philosophy... those in which... gangster activities, racketeering, professional criminal practices seem to be the chief factors.... The men who believe in belonging to the gang, who are going to get theirs by hook or crook."

4. *Medical cases.* "Men who are primarily criminals because they are physically unable to make the grade.... These are the handicapped, deformed, tuberculor... who have become criminals mainly by reason of their afflictions."

5. *Personality cases.* "In this class come the psychotics, neurotics, peculiar personalities, who have fallen into crime... all cases where personality difficulties play the major part in leading the

[28]The definitions are a composite of the various definitions that were issued over 1932. See Commons, *Manual*, p. 30; Diary, 12 July 1932, pp. 135–139, 17 May 1932, pp. 119–120, cf. Diary, 15 May 1932, pp. 159–160, and Massachusetts Department of Corrections, *Annual Report... 1932*, p. 19.

man into crime... in which the man's personal problem had
tended to get him crosswire with other people."

Gill was perfectly clear on what SCAMP was not. It was not involved
with the seriousness of the crime or the severity of the punishment.
"Certainly the murderer, the robber and the rapist may be found in all
groups." Second, it was not meant to serve as a prison housing
classification; Gill did not intend to put all the asocial cases into one
dorm and all the personality cases into another. Most schemes, he argued, were too ambitious, attempting to "work out a single classification
which will cover all needs. As a result, the classification is apt to become
a hodge podge of administrative psychology and miscellaneous data."
Nor were these categories to be predictive of eventual adjustment or
success on parole. Finally, and this is most critical: "*It is not a classification
for causation or motivation;* the cause of a crime may lie back in the environment of the individual and yet his present diagnosis may be asocial."[29]

What then were these categories? "First and foremost this is a *treatment* classification and designed primarily to indicate what is to be done
at the moment about any case and by whom." With SCAMP, casework
became "a significant, specific thing," and Gill comfortably returned to a
medical analogy: It allowed the prison reformers "to build up a
therapeutic practice, just as a doctor builds up a practice.... We have a
situational case, a situational disease, and we find that certain things
have helped in treating the cases." Thus, in conceptual terms, the design solved the problem of making the prison into a hospital by identifying what the counterpart for pneumonia was in the criminal. In practical
terms, it indicated who was to do the actual treating.

> These five groupings more or less will be the five techniques to be developed
> for dealing with human problems and their relations. The situational case
> rates the technique of the social worker, the medical case is obviously a
> problem for the doctor, the personality case is a problem for the psychiatrist,
> the asocial case is for education, and the custodial case for the supervisor, the
> police, the caretaker."[30]

Yet as soon as one examines the claims that are being advanced, it
becomes apparent that something of an intellectual shell game is being
played; the categories are both more and less than they first appear. Gill
insisted that SCAMP was a classification not for causation but for
treatment—in other words, one could rehabilitate the deviant without

---

[29]Yahkub, *History of State Prison,* p. 138; *Annual Report... 1932,* p. 19.
[30]Yahkub, *History of State Prison,* pp. 137–138.

first understanding the origins of the behavior. Commissioner Stearns made the point explicitly: "If we are in the dark as to the real underlying *cause* of the crime itself, yet we are confronted with any or all of these [SCAMP] conditions as a *result* of the crime, and can treat them if we will."[31] But in fact, the argument was spurious. The categories incorporated the very kinds of assumptions that Gill and Stearns denied that they were making. SCAMP was based finally not on results but directly on causes, and one needs only to look back to the definitions to confirm the point. The "situational" problem was "at the bottom" of the criminal activity; the "medical" condition was "mainly the reason" for it; the "personality" make-up "plays the major part in leading" men into crime. These categories were explanations not conditions.

Furthermore, Gill proposed that rehabilitation at the Norfolk penitentiary proceed on many fronts, using the skills of psychiatrists, teachers, doctors, and social workers. Norfolk was not going to do all things to all men (a patently impossible task) but was going to make its medicine specific to the disease. To use SCAMP in this way, however, is once again to make clear that these were causational categories. If personality is not at the root of the inmate's problems, then why would a psychiatric intervention prove effective? If the medical ailment was not the cause of the crime, why would a doctor's skills be relevant? Norfolk's assertion that treatment could be independent of explanation had only a superficial plausibility.

I stress this contradiction because, first, it was not unique to Norfolk but was a central problem for many Progressives. William Healy's *The Individual Delinquent* presented the most tangled efforts to understand causality. His summary of "causative factors" in crime was notable only in that it omitted nothing; everything seemed pertinent, from mental conflict to bad companions to defective interests. Those working in the field of mental illness did little better. Adolf Meyer, probably the most influential American psychiatrist of the period, tried to solve the problem of causality by avoiding it, as though the compilation of fact upon fact in a case history could compensate for the deficiencies of theory.

Perhaps even more important, the fallacies in the Norfolk approach point not so much to poor powers of reasoning or the inadequacy of social science concepts but rather to an eagerness to do good that would not be thwarted by an ignorance of how to do good. Thus, Stearns concluded his remarks on treating results, not causes, with the injunction: "Only when we can do nothing, may we regard a man as merely a

[31]Stearns's memorandum on this point was sent by Sellin to Mrs. Florence Taylor, 15 February 1933; filed by the Bureau of Social Hygiene in Box 33, folder 455 (quotation is from p. 2).

custodial problem." Whatever our lack of understanding, we must be doing something.

Oddly, Norfolk's classifications and general design were never questioned closely. Perhaps it was because all of the programs had the ultimate justification of being part of an "experiment." In this sense, the Bureau of Social Hygiene's grant gave Gill not only funds to carry out his work; it gave him a critical source of legitimation. The medical model also helped to spare Norfolk from attack. Just as doctors tried one kind of medicine and then another, so Norfolk too would "build up" a therapeutic practice. The record of the institution—its diary—like the record of the patient's progress—his chart—would reveal which interventions succeeded and which did not. Finally, and most significantly, those who might have been Gill's critics were his collaborators. Thus, so prestigious and innovative a sociologist as W. I. Thomas, whose own work explored the problem of adjustment (from Polish peasants to school children), visited the colony and made a few queries about the categories (why were situational cases in prison at all?) but did not doubt their essential viability or usefulness.[32] Norfolk's wisdom, or, put another way, the contradictions and ambiguities that underlay its design, escaped a fundamental critique because it was so essentially Progressive.

Although most of Gill's energies went into implementing the hospital-treatment model, he did in several ways attempt to realize the ideal of prison as community. Inmates dressed in pants and shirts, not special uniforms; the colony encouraged visits and letter writing. Gill also instituted inmate self-government, modeled on Osborne's Mutual Welfare League. The Inmate Council was to be more than a grievance committee although less than a governing body. The most critical and revealing of all these arrangements was Gill's scheme for housing the inmates. It was almost as elaborate as the classification plan and was no less caught up in a web of contradictions.

Norfolk's system for assigning men to the dormitories was a way both "to facilitate the treatment objectives of the institution" (according to the *Manual*, this was its "primary purpose") and to make the prison into a normal community. Men were to be grouped "upon the basis of their attitude and cooperation in carrying out their *individual programs*, and the extent to which they can be relied upon to take active part in the *community program*." Those who fulfilled the criteria were graded A–1, "entirely cooperative and trustworthy," or A–2, those "who are getting something out of Norfolk and supporting the community program,"

[32]Diary, 25 May 1932, p. 148.

and they enjoyed the greatest privileges (lights out at ten, not nine, the choice of rooms, more visits, and so on). In more traditional language, which Gill also used, they were the minimum-security inmates. Next in rank were the medium-security inmates: B–1, who did not give "full cooperation," and B–2, "not carrying out and not supporting the program, and who cannot be trusted in the dormitory units, or for whom there is no room in the dormitory units." They were locked in their rooms at six, not allowed to participate in the Inmate Council, and limited to writing one letter and receiving one visit weekly. At the bottom of the ladder was the "C group," the "disciplinary problems and who need custodial supervision." These maximum-security inmates were confined to the steel cells in the Receiving Building, "under severe restrictions."[33]

To Gill, this scheme would reward men not for mere good conduct, for doing their time, but for receptivity to treatment, or, in his favorite phrase, for "what the man is getting out of the institution as the result of conscious endeavor." In addition, it made treatment voluntary. All inmates (except the C's) would enjoy a decent minimum of comforts; those who took advantage of Norfolk's opportunities would enjoy special privileges. The housing plan was also designed to emphasize "the constructive forces in each man"; the dormitories would encourage "self-respect, trust, privacy, that is freedom from the stigma of forced restraint... with various types of rooms covering individual needs." Lastly, it promoted an intelligent allocation of resources. Norfolk would devote its energies to those eager to make fullest use of them.[34]

Again, all is not so simple as it first appears. Indeed, more is at stake here than hyperbolic rhetoric (how could dormitories ever reduce the stigma of incarceration imposed by an outside public?) or vague concepts (just what does "getting the most" from Norfolk mean?). A housing system whose "primary purpose" ostensibly was "to facilitate treatment" in fact was a system designed primarily to fulfill custodial needs. The discrepancy between the rhetoric of rehabilitation and the reality of the ABC ranking is apparent as soon as one asks why Gill did not employ the SCAMP divisions for housing the inmates. Why were the treatment categories not used for making dormitory assignments? Why at just this point did Gill abandon the hospital model—which does not divide its wards by patient behavior, one for the cooperative type, another for the less cooperative—and adopt what was a far more conventional scheme—to separate inmates by minimum, medium, and

[33]Commons, *Manual*, pp. 30–31; Diary, 15 June 1932, p. 162.
[34]Diary, 17 May 1932, p. 120, 10 March 1932, p. 37, 18 May 1933, p. 443, 11 May 1933, p. 448. See also Yahkub, *History of State Prison*, pp. 140–141.

maximum designations? Gill himself supplied the answer: The ABC categories took into account the inmates "general attitude which will be based upon previous record and reputation and institutional history." Therapy aside, some men were more dangerous and more troublesome than others, and to ignore this fact would undermine the good order of the institution. The housing classification would protect "the safety and security of the institution."[35]

Had Gill been queried about the discrepancy (of course, he was not), his answer would have been quick: The housing system was to resolve custodial questions to permit therapy. But his response, however Progressive, cannot pass. Security at Norfolk was supposed to be only at the perimeters of the institution, at the wall, with the guards, but we find it to the core, internal to the design. In effect, Gill was bringing in through the back door all the considerations that he had claimed to be abandoning.

Gill's housing scheme also indicated that when not rhetoric but reality counted, treatment took second place to institutional needs. In the end, therapy was the luxury, that which would "also" be done, that which was grafted onto the institutional program. Norfolk's organization did not balance security and rehabilitation. The priorities were clearer than that: *Norfolk by design was first and foremost a prison that delivered some treatment, not a hospital whose patients happened to be criminal offenders.*[36] And turning the definition around is to make more than a stylistic revision; it puts the entire enterprise in a different context.

* * *

In the most obvious ways, and by all accounts, Norfolk's effort to administer treatment was a total failure. The grand design turned into an empty reality. The attempt to implement therapy through casework bordered on the farcical. By mid-1933, one disappointed staff member informed Commissioner Stearns:

> There is a vast difference between what Norfolk is on paper and what it actually is in practice. . . . No social casework has been applied at Norfolk which could be acceptable to any authorities on casework practice. Fundamentally there is no set-up to carry on casework method. The few gestures . . . represent . . . the flounderings of experimenters who have found a free field for expression.[37]

[35]Diary, 17 May 1932, p. 120.
[36]Cf. the comments of Mark Roser, head social worker at Norfolk, *ibid.*, 18 April 1932, p. 78; Powers, *Individualization of Treatment*, p. 240.
[37]Julius Hadley to Stearns, 28 March 1933, p. 5.

At the same time, Louis Balsam, one of Gill's oldest and strongest supporters, put the matter in unmistakably authentic terms: "The House Officers are making 'prefunctory passes' at casework. For the most part they are bored and indifferent about it. Casework days are devoted in fair part to discussions about salary increases, baseball games, swimming, women, and other delightful institutions."[38]

Yet the least interesting aspect of the Norfolk experiment is the final outcome. That it failed is not nearly as intriguing as that it failed in interesting ways. Some of the causes were predictable, which is another way of saying that they are recurring, and so we ought to pay all the more attention to them. And some were surprising and could not be anticipated, alerting us to more covert but critical considerations that innovative efforts in this field need to understand.

An analysis of the dynamics that shaped events at Norfolk begins with the staff. It was at all levels ill equipped to implement a treatment program. Gill himself had no special training in psychology or casework, and perhaps his very faith in the approach was built upon his ignorance. The rest of the staff had no more suitable credentials. The "Officers in Charge of the House Staff" were custodial types. As one staff member reported to Stearns, the deputy superintendent was a former cook and night watchman at the Concord Reformatory; the OIC's were a former taxi driver, a male nurse, a shoe salesman, and a former officer from the boy's reformatory. And as for the house officers themselves, one story will suffice. At the first casework conference, one of them was heard to exclaim that "he did not know what all this casework was about. He was a plumber."[39]

The reasons why Gill compiled such a dismal record at recruitment are not difficult to locate. For one, he felt compelled to recruit OIC's from the officers who had first managed the inmates during the building time; no experiment, it would seem, ever begins totally from scratch. Moreover, Gill was obliged to recruit staff from those who passed civil service exams—and few of these would have graduated social-work school. Then too, whatever the officer's sense of the job, in terms of salary and prerequisites the post was identical to custodial positions in other institutions. "Their real position," as one observer noted, "is comparable to that of attendants in a mental hospital."[40]

But how to reconcile plumbers, shoe salesmen, and attendants with

[38]Diary, 28 July 1933, p. 506; Powers, *Individualization of Treatment*, p. 240.

[39]Sellin to Dunham, 23 October 1930, pp. 3–5; cf. Sellin to Dunham, 16 March 1931, p. 1; Julian Hadley to Stearns, 28 March 1933, pp. 6–7; Diary, 2 January 1932, p. 1.

[40]Diary, 9 May 1932, pp. 100–101; Sellin to Dunham, 22 October 1930, pp. 2–3; Hadley to Stearns, 28 March 1933, p. 7.

such an ambitious design? What kept Gill, or all the others who visited Norfolk, from abandoning the whole project from the outset as absurd? One common hope was that the House Officers could be trained to their position. The Bureau funds, in fact, enabled Gill to hire two men with credentials in the field to head the social-work division. But the better-trained staff simply could not communicate in intelligent fashion with the house officers. Their jargon was unfamiliar to a group of men who lacked college degrees. The house officers were also suspicious and critical of the professionals, calling them "theoretical" and "pedantic"; their explanations for the behavior of the men with whom the officers were in daily contact seemed either too general or too vague to be help ful in any practical ways. A diagnostic label did not give a house officer much guidance in solving immediate problems.[41]

Not surprisingly, the friction between the house officers and their social-worker superiors was intense. The social workers complained that house officers asked the men the wrong questions at the wrong times and thereby ruined their own attempts to compile a meaningful case record; the officers for their part turned casework conferences into the occasion to vent their frustration, creating a dialogue where the two parties regularly spoke past each other.

HOUSE OFFICER: We should be careful not to let the Research Department ... submerge the offspring... by its lengthy case histories.

PSYCHOLOGIST: There was an inappropriate display of emotion, and the attitude of the House Officers seemed to border on antagonism.... A high emotional pitch was maintained.... It seemed that resentment arising out of low wages, long hours... had been vented upon a substitute object.[42]

However acute the division between these two groups, it was mild compared with the split between house officers and the custodial staff. The antagonisms were continuous and pervasive, each certain that the other was engaged in sabotage. The petty quality of most of the incidents points to how emotionally charged the issue was. Since the house staff was articulate and, therefore, more comfortable with the diary, their side is recorded more often. It takes little imagination, however, to see the same incident from the guards' perspective. Thus, the house officers complained that the guards did not open locked doors quickly enough for them, that the guards searched the dorms, and confiscated goods that the house officer had explicitly allowed, or that the guards, against all orders and regulations, insisted on locking the doors of men

[41]Diary, 3 August 1933, pp. 511–512, 12 July 1932, p. 136.
[42]Ibid., 18 April 1932, p. 78, 28 March 1932, p. 46, 1 August 1933, p. 508.

classified A–1 and A–2. As one would expect, the house officers frequently had the support of their social-work superiors, who also were
convinced that the custodians were "tearing down the philosophy" of
Norfolk and that a campaign constantly had to be mounted against "the
advocates who seek to have us move back to the old principles of penology."[43] For their part, the guards complained among themselves
("Casework never did anybody any good. What they need is strict discipline. They are no damn good") and leaked whatever scandalous stories
they could to the press. They released their frustrations in the daily
newspapers instead of in the diary. So it did not take long for Norfolk to
gain the reputation of being poorly administered and unable to keep its
own staff in line. It is not claiming too much to assert that Norfolk was
the scene of a fierce war between custodians and therapists, and Gill
proved to be an inept peacekeeper between the two. He would himself,
of course, be the ultimate victim of the conflict, toppled from his position
at the start of 1934 in part as a result of it. But clearly Norfolk's staff could
not balance custody and rehabilitation.[44]

Norfolk's treatment ambitions also depended to a large degree upon
the cooperation of the inmates. The medicine that was casework demanded their active participation, but in many ways, and for good reasons, it was not forthcoming. In the first instance, inmates were remarkably adept at playing off one staff member against another. Fully aware
of the division among administrators, prisoners skillfully manipulated
the system for their own ends. "If you tell an inmate he can't do a certain
thing," complained one house officer, "he goes around to everyone else
and gets permission."[45]

More important, Norfolk's prisoners proved to be particularly reluctant to confide in those who claimed to be their therapists. Part of the
reluctance undoubtedly reflected their sense that such encounters were
appropriate only for the mentally ill; the inmates, in their words, would
not consent to be "psychoed."[46] Indeed, there was a general ranking of
institutions among inmates that was sensitive to different gradations of
stigma: The prison was preferable to the workhouse—it was more hon-
orable to be a criminal than to be one of the unworthy poor—and the
prison and the workhouse were both preferable to the state hospital—
better to be sane than insane.

[43]*Ibid.*, 5 May 1932, p. 136, 15 January 1933, p. 383, 9 March 1932, p. 43, 17 May 1932, p.
99, 22 July 1932, pp. 219–220.
[44]*Ibid.*, 20 May 1932, p. 137, 4 January 1933, p. 356; Sellin to Dunham, 19 December 1931,
pp. 1–2, 16 March 1931, p. 2.
[45]Diary, 20 May 1932, p. 136, 16 November 1933, p. 613.
[46]*Ibid.*, 23 November 1932, p. 304.

Still stronger reasons prompted inmates to distrust the caseworker. From their experience, he seemed to be only the latest in a long line of officials who pried them for information and wanted them to talk and tell all. Mark Roser, head of social work at Norfolk, complained a few months after his arrival that "the men . . . look upon the casework investigation with an attitude similar as they look upon a police investigation." In his phrase, "They must somehow realize the therapeutic value of frankness, and that the information about themselves which they give to caseworkers will not be used as such information is used by the police."[47] The inmates rejected this contention, as they were certain that whatever they disclosed would be held against them by both the staff and, in even more damaging ways, the parole board. To talk openly about one's actions and attitudes might well, to use the Norfolk jargon, reveal that he was not getting all that he should from the program, and the penalties might be of B or C classification. Worse yet, Norfolk was only one part of the larger criminal justice system, and staff assurances were no guarantee that the information divulged would not ruin their chances for parole. For all the institution's claims to the contrary, the inmates clearly understood that in one basic and critical way the caseworker did not approximate the doctor in a hospital: He did not hold the key to release.

This problem, endemic to all such situations, was exacerbated at Norfolk by the staff's unwillingness to open up the files to inmates. From a caseworker's perspective, no client ever examined his dossier. As Roser told an inmate: "These records were written for use by professional people and like professional medical records they are liable to misinterpretation if read by non-professional men." To the inmates, the officers were compiling a secret dossier, and the less they cooperated with the venture, the better. The inmates interpreted the closing of the records as a sure sign that practically "all of the reports are unfavorable and . . . that casework consists of just that incriminating feature." Accordingly, cooperation seemed positively foolish. "It is generally conceded among them," concluded one caseworker, "that the good things which they do while in the Colony are not recorded to their credit, but that all bum raps, lock ups, etc., go on record and spoil their chances for parole."[48]

Curiously, when Roser himself first arrived at Norfolk, he was particularly sensitive to the problem of therapist as double agent, that is, the caseworker who was supposed to serve both the institution and the

---

[47]*Ibid.*, 11 May 1932, p. 116.
[48]*Ibid.*, 12 December 1933, pp. 645–646, 2 November 1932, p. 291, 29 March 1932, p. 54.

inmate. In one of the first entries in the diary in January 1932, he noted that Norfolk was going to test "how far is one in an official capacity in the Institution able to gain the confidence of the men, and what use should be made of such confidence." This issue, Roser recognized, "has not yet been satisfactorily answered." Could casework take place within an incarcerative setting?

> It involves a question as to whether or not, if ever, the psychological analysis of an individual connected with an Institution will be successful. Talking with such an individual will be quite hard, because he knows [and Roser here does not deny it] the information will be used both for and against him in securing a parole, and in his life here.

He went on to suggest ever so casually that perhaps counseling should be carried on "by an individual who has no official capacity."[49] Whether because the administrative difficulties seemed insuperable (if the institution did not pay him, who would?), or because this was no answer at all (the double-agent bind was not avoided merely by getting the caseworker a grant), or because the very statement of the problem was so anti-Progressive in its assumptions (this kind of conflict of interest could not be pursued), Roser soon dropped the matter. But the inmates, for their part, did not. For them, a caseworker remained a cop.

(A brief aside for those with an interest in parole board proceedings. The men's fears that the board would use the caseworkers' material against them was exaggerated, for the all too obvious reason that the board was too busy to examine the parole dossiers closely and the caseworkers had difficulty in summarizing their reports. The Massachusetts board, like all others, focused far more intently on past criminal record than on institutional behavior or responsiveness to programs. In this sense, the inmates took Norfolk's plans too seriously. Perhaps they could not fathom that all this bother was irrelevant, insofar as release was concerned.)

Inmates' distrust of casework was part of their distrust of the entire Progressive thrust in penology. To them, discretion and indeterminacy meant discrimination and unpredictability. Gill, for example, reported an "interesting talk" with an exconvict who showed "a true 'con' attitude.... Mr. Brown thought the only thing was uniformity, that is, treating everybody alike, and that this was the only system to use." Gill, of course, rejected this notion out of hand; if anything, he was pleased by inmate objections. Gill went on to expound Norfolk's treatment phi-

[49]*Ibid.*, January–March 1932 (as yet unnumbered in its initial pages), Box 33, folder 459, first entry of Mark Roser.

losophy; Mr. Brown, however, would have none of it. His conclusion, as reported by Gill, stood for his fellow inmates as well: "He just could not understand it all."[50]

But what of the treatment program itself? What did the commitment to the SCAMP system amount to in practice? Given the theoretical confusions that underlay the categories, as well as the incompetence of the staff and the suspicions of the inmates, we need not belabor the point of how inept and ineffective rehabilitation actually was at Norfolk. Several points do warrant attention. For one, the all-inclusive character of the SCAMP classifications made it well-nigh impossible to compile a dossier; the social worker had no idea of what to omit. Every detail was seemingly relevant; it was necessary to know the inmate's occupational history (was his a situational case?), the nature of his relationships (was he asocial?), his psychic make-up (did he fit into the grab-bag category of personality?). The system, however, did not provide any way of differentiating the trivial from the important. "There is nothing too small to make note of," the head of research lectured the staff.[51] Consequently, at Norfolk one administrative rearrangement followed another. An initial division between a fieldworker (who went out to interview friends and relatives) and an institution worker (who interviewed the inmate) gave way to one caseworker doing both jobs, which in turn gave way to abandoning fieldwork altogether (the overload of information was staggering, and only one or two cases a week were being completed), which in turn gave way to creating a diagnostic division separate from a treatment division. But shuffling about the staff was a symptom of the deficiencies in the plan itself, not a cure for them.[52]

Nor did SCAMP provide any help in designing treatment strategies. Just as it instructed caseworkers to know everything about an inmate's history, so it told them to do everything to cure him, which was no advice at all. Take, for example, the not atypical recommendations for Lee Sauls, a "personality" case: "Successful treatment . . . will depend upon intensive casework." The man "must be convinced that . . . 'crime does not pay.' In order to get this across to him his H. O. must gain his respect and confidence. . . . If the personality problems are discussed with him the man will be in a better position to adjust himself." In effect, the message amounted to an exhortation to convince him that crime does not pay, not guidance in how to treat him. This case was typical of many. "On the whole," reported one staff member, "programs are

---

[50]*Ibid.*, 10 March 1932, pp. 37–38, and cf. 28 October 1932, p. 289. Here as throughout the essay, I have altered the name of the inmate but have retained the correct initials.

[51]*Ibid.*, 26 July 1932, p. 232.

[52]*Ibid.*, 18 August 1933, pp. 438–40, 15 April 1932, p. 75.

vague, they suggest rather than specify. . . . Programs are made in mass production, and men have been termed worthless or worse as a result of a half-hour interview." With this as the usual situation, it is not surprising to find Gill periodically exclaiming: "We must develop what I have come to call 'significant case work' as contrasted with just case work." To change the jargon from casework to significant casework was another symptom of the problem, not a response to it.[53]

The staff at Norfolk knew exactly how grim the situation was. One caseworker who set out to investigate treatment returned with the dismal verdict that "programs have been inadequate and that—fortunately almost—they have been very partially carried out." Not only were the house officers continuously protesting that the day-to-day tasks of running the units left them little time to talk with the men, but also educational and vocational training and available employment was pitifully inadequate. In all too many instances, the Norfolk program amounted to unskilled construction work, in essence ditchdigging. "The jobs for the majority," conceded Mark Roser in November 1932, "are limited to pick and shovel work, which doesn't involve much trade training." Gill, in an especially telling moment, suggested that ditchdigging had its virtues. "It may be good experience for the men to dig in a ditch who have had vocational training, as it will help to teach them to meet emergencies that are bound to arise in their life outside when their term of incarceration is over. . . . It may well be that we have put too much emphasis on education."[54] That these words were written at the onset of the Great Depression does not make them persuasive, for Progressive reformers had surely taken a long and complicated route to get to a system that equated ditchdigging with treatment.

*   *   *

Whatever Howard Gill or Leonard Dunham or Thorsten Sellin expected from Norfolk, they, and everyone else associated with the experiment, expected that the colony would be administered fairly and humanely. It might not be able to rehabilitate all its inmates, but its failures would be instructive and the amount of harm that it would do would be minimal. No one anticipated that Norfolk would breed its own kind of horror stories, that it would end up as one more miserable prison. In retrospect, it is important to know whether a commitment to treatment, regardless of its success, was in itself useful in making condi-

[53]*Ibid.*, 1 May 1933, p. 577, 13 April 1932, p. 69, 2 November 1933, p. 584.
[54]*Ibid.*, 26 September 1933, p. 561, 15 January 1932, p. 12, 4 March 1932, p. 34.

tions of confinement exemplary, or, to make this point directly relevant to current policy concerns: Is the goal of rehabilitation worth pursuing not because it is realizable but because such an orientation avoids all sorts of other evils? Should the notion of treatment be kept alive as a kind of noble lie?

The Norfolk story does not support such a conclusion. The commitment to rehabilitation did not substantially reduce coercion. Treatment did not temper custody but fell victim to it. Norfolk did not represent the worst evils in the American penitentiary system; the amount of physical brutality was low, and inmates' lives were not in constant jeopardy. Nevertheless, the threat of substantial punishment was central to the administration of the program and for a sizable minority of the inmates (around 15%), a reality. For all the rhetorical allegiance to a medical model, Norfolk remained much more of a prison than a hospital. Worse yet, the process by which custody took precedence over treatment had an inevitable and unavoidable quality.

Not only did Norfolk have its own jail but also Gill was not uncomfortable about the use of solitary confinement within it as punishment. He devised some schoollike penalties, such as keeping inmates on the bench outside his office during recreation periods, but he was not averse to using the lockup. "Segregation in itself," he insisted, "is valuable in calming down a man." Norfolk's use of segregation was not like that of other institutions: "The punitive attitude involves tying him up, which," Gill noted, "may be good for a few, perhaps, but certainly not as a rule"; for its part, Norfolk would confine men to a normal cell without cuffs and keep them on a regular diet.[55] To a number of visitors, such as sociology professor Conrad Taeuber, the arguments were not persuasive. "Somehow, there seems to me to be an anachronism in the use of the lock-up as a means of punishment by an institution that denies the value of imprisonment per se. I admit I have no suggestion. . . . It may be that in some cases no other language is understood by the inmate." Nevertheless, "our whole system of imprisonment seems to have grown up because it is such a simple solution to problems from the standpoint of the individual confronted with them."[56] But Gill did not share his worries. His final answer, which we shall hear again and again, was that Norfolk was being run for the 90% who "can be won back to society," not the 10% who need "punitive measures."

Gill was no less certain that sentences to the lockup at Norfolk, like sentences in the outside society to prison, should be indeterminate. He

[55]*Ibid.*, 26 October 1932, p. 294.
[56]*Ibid.*, 28 August 1933, p. 528.

admitted that "the inmates do not like this type of individual treatment. It demands more of them than a definite sentence which they can fulfill and then be done with." Nevertheless, Norfolk's indeterminate sentence "gives treatment to fit the criminal rather than a punishment for the crime.... Release is controlled by a change in attitude," and "the change in attitude should not be confused with lip service."[57] Gill's consistency here is perhaps not as unexpected as is the staff's disagreement (and the dialogue between them is so evocative of the current debate as to tempt the conclusion that occasionally history does repeat itself). To some of the social workers, the indeterminacy of punishment at the colony was unfair and counterproductive. "We need some deterministic basis for applying punishment," insisted Roser. "The application of punishment should involve a due consideration for the seriousness of the offense.... The inmate should feel that his punishment comes almost automatically when he has transgressed a rule." Norfolk's chief psychologist agreed: "Our task is to avoid antagonism by having a few definite rules, the infractions of which are immediately and automatically met with by punishments which tend to be definite.... It is only by a system of definite and automatic punishments that the men can be convinced that there is justice at Norfolk and in the world." As for Gill's claims that he was linking punishment with treatment, it was better to use other occasions to rehabilitate the offender. Where punishment was concerned, the focus should be on "individual deserts... to convince men that we have been fair," to be "satisfied with the benefits of a universal confidence in justice."[58]

The resolution of these disagreements (which is all too suggestive of what may be the outcome of the present debates) was less a compromise than a hardening of the rules. Gill established a fixed minimum term in the lockup, but not a fixed maximum. The principle of indeterminacy was sacrificed to set a floor for punishment without a ceiling. All sentences to the Norfolk jail were for no less than 80 days, with release allowed only after a change of heart, certified by the disciplinary committee and the superintendent himself. In defense of this procedure, Gill announced that those in the lockup "are to be considered as special problem cases for the casework department. It is the responsibility of the casework department to see that no opportunity for rehabilitation is overlooked for this group."[59] Not for the last time would discretion coupled with severity be cloaked in the garb of treatment opportunities.

The conflict over the duration of punishment within Norfolk was only

[57]*Ibid.*, 26 October 1932, p. 294.
[58]*Ibid.*, 22 November 1932, p. 303, 27 November 1932, pp. 311–314.
[59]*Ibid.*, 25 January 1933, pp. 374–376.

one part of the larger controversy over placing inmates in the ABC categories and implementing the dormitory classific•tions. Once again Gill was at odds with some of his staff, and once again the outcome moved Norfolk closer to an outright prison. The problem became acute in the closing months of 1932 with two particular developments. First, Norfolk's population was becoming more and more typical of an ordinary prison. During the "building time," Gill had taken in only the best of Charlestown's inmates: first offenders and most cooperative workers. By the fall of 1930, he had skimmed off the cream of Charlestown, and by the fall of 1932, with construction just about completed, Norfolk was about to expand its size. The decision, as had always been assumed by Gill and the State Corrections Department, was to admit more and more inmates from Charlestown (throughout these years, Norfolk did not receive any prisoners directly from the courts). The population climbed, from 300 at the end of 1931 to 540 by the end of 1933, and the "quality" dropped. Complaints were now heard of the gangs that came down to Norfolk or of one MacRaughry (of whom more later), who was "undisciplined, intemperate, a sexually promiscuous, boisterous, and thoughtless individual" and who "shows little desire or effort to change."[60]

Simultaneously, the completion of its facilities meant that Norfolk had to go about filling its Receiving Building, putting some inmates into the steel cells. Those who had heretofore been living in the dormitories, more or less on a first-come-first-served basis, were to be reassigned in accordance with their ABC ratings; those graded A would have their pick of rooms, and those graded B or C, who had been enjoying the freedom of the dorms, would now come under a restricted regimen. In effect, this procedure meant, first, that the men labeled B, who had not committed major infractions, had obeyed the rules, but were ostensibly not "getting anything" out of Norfolk, were to be seriously penalized. They not only lost their choice of rooms but also were locked up after 5 o'clock on weekdays, weekends, and holidays. Not surprisingly, they protested vehemently, and Norfolk almost had a riot. Gill's response was uncompromising; men not getting anything out of Norfolk should not enjoy what he defined as privileges. Treatment, he insisted, was voluntary, yet those who did not take advantage of it could not expect rewards.[61] To others, the procedures not only belied the notion of voluntary treatment but also were patently unfair. "For men who have up to the present time been living similar lives to all others, it is quite impossible suddenly to comprehend why they should often arbitrarily

[60]Sellin to Dunham, 23 October 1930, pp. 2, 9; Diary, 27 July 1933, p. 503, 25 September 1933, p. 538.
[61]Diary, 18 May 1933, p. 443.

be denuded of privilege and placed in a lower classification." And the classifications themselves were not so accurate. Could one really differentiate between those who were and were not making progress at Norfolk?[62]

The protests did lead to some changes. A few of the B men were reassigned to A groups, and a new category, A–3, was devised so that men who had been obedient to the rules would not be locked up after work. It was increasingly evident, however, just how heavy a hand Norfolk was laying on its inmates. Gill was now defending his procedures with phrases that came dangerously close to double-talk: "A man is not under punishment because he doesn't have any privileges." The inmates were being subjected to arbitrary judgments. "I am afraid," reported Conrad Taeuber, "that very few of the House Officers and hardly any of the inmates understand the differences among the three A classes.... I will admit, that I had some difficulty in learning what the difference... was, and would hardly be able to stand questioning on it now."[63] And finally, the staff itself was recording its own sense of the growing degree of coercion within the institution. "The emphasis," argued one of Norfolk's most loyal workers, "should be upon making institution programs sufficiently attractive, not upon locking-up participants. This latter is a sad retrogression, and singularly out of place in the Norfolk regime."[64]

No sooner did the controversy over the A and B categories quiet down than another erupted over the C classification. Thirteen inmates were moved from the dorms to the steel cells of the Reception Building, to be confined there whenever they were not at work. In this instance, at least, there was something of a record to go on: Each had a history of major disciplinary infractions. The caseworker, assigned to the C men, Hans Weiss, was soon protesting that this classification constituted bad therapy, as it created a stigmatized class and thereby exacerbated the very problem it was to solve. He recommended that the C category be eliminated, that disciplinary cases be adjudicated quickly, and that those found guilty be confined for short periods of time. "A clear distinction should be made between punishment and housing classification.... A brief, stiff lock-up is more effective and more desirable as a method of dealing with behavior problems than prolonged segregation in a group."[65]

Gill held firm, not only arguing against "set rules of punishment" but

[62]*Ibid.*, 20 January 1933, p. 367, 6 February 1933, pp. 384–385.
[63]*Ibid.*, 18 May 1933, p. 444, 28 August 1933, p. 528.
[64]*Ibid.*, 20 January 1933, p. 367.
[65]*Ibid.*, 16 March 1933, pp. 409–412.

also bluntly insisting that "we don't care what happens to the 10 percent." The minority of troublemakers "does not mean a great deal to us." Practical political considerations were also relevant. "If we can have some successes with fifty or seventy-five percent of our men, we will be allowed to go on. . . . We must insure popular support, because in the last analysis, the public are running this." Then, with a confidence that bordered on arrogance, he concluded that if reform did not take place, "the fault is not with Norfolk but with the men." His response only provoked more criticism. Harvard professor Carl Doering, a member of the casework advisory committee, observed, ever so properly: "It seems that if a man breaks down at Charlestown it is the fault of the system, but if he breaks down at Norfolk it is his fault." Moreover, "the analogy in medicine is that the sick ones are the very fellows who are in need of medical attention—your C class or problem cases."[66]

Gill was a victim not only of reformers' pride but also of the architectual consequences of his willingness that Norfolk have a jail. The Receiving Building counted as part of Norfolk's capacity; the cells had to be filled with inmates. Weiss's successful efforts to reduce the antagonisms of some of the C men and get them back into the general population only made the problem more acute—for who, then, was to go to the Receiving Building? In April 1933, Gill ordered each of the house officers to select three or four of their men who were not getting all that they should from Norfolk (even, he told them, if it was necessary to choose A–2 types) to be housed in the Receiving Building; in this way, dormitory space would be freed for new inmates who had been waiting in the building for reassignment for several months. Staff objected: Architecture was now determining treatment; men were being fitted to the facility, not the facility to the men; and rehabilitation was once again being coerced.[67]

In the diary's lengthy reports on this latest controversy, it becomes acutely obvious that it was impossible for Norfolk to carry out its dual mandate to treat and to punish. In a very real and tangible way, the jail was taking over the institution. The spector of confinement in the steel cells now pervaded the colony. If Gill was prepared to lock up A–2 men (who were supposedly making some, if not full, progress), then clearly any inmate might find himself in confinement. Norfolk's staff was fully aware of this. "The question is," one of the house officers asked in the diary, "Shall Norfolk become a 'penal opportunity school' (with emphasis at least as much on the 'penal' as on the 'opportunity'), or shall it

[66]*Ibid.*, 16 March 1933, pp. 409, 412, 413, 29 March 1933, pp. 424, 426.
[67]*Ibid.*, 17 April 1933, pp. 433–436.

develop into a *treatment institution,"* and a growing number were beginning to suspect how Norfolk would answer it.[68]

All the challenges and debates finally began to wear Gill himself. On June 23 he wrote in the diary:

> It seems impossible that prisons will ever serve as an adequate means of handling the problems of crime. We think of them now as places in which criminals should be confined for reformation. . . . I wonder if we shall not come to another concept. . . . Reliance will be had upon supervision within the community itself as the real corrective. . . . The thought that we can build a community prison which approximates the normal is faint hope.[69]

The designer was starting to abandon hope in his project and, incidentally, to discover the next movement.

Within a week of Gill's disheartened comments, Norfolk began the most tumultuous and chaotic 6-month period in its history. One near escape by a group of inmates attempting to tunnel under the walls, followed by a successful escape by two other inmates going over the walls, set off a chain of events that culminated in Gill's removal as superintendent. It was almost as if he recognized the victory of custody over treatment and began to will his own destruction. More substantively, the disciplinary problems that provoked his despair became so much more acute, and the colony grew so preoccupied with punishment, that Gill's dismissal is almost incidental to the larger point that Norfolk had become a full-fledged prison. One architectural change confirms this. By January 1934, the windows of 12 cells had been boarded up, the cells' plumbing stripped, and their beds removed. Norfolk had its hole.

The final act in the Norfolk drama began on 28 June 1933, when, acting on a tip from some inmates, the guards discovered a tunnel dug toward the prison walls. Although no evidence could be found implicating any particular inmates, the staff did not concern itself with procedural niceties or even elementary fairness. Twenty-three inmates were rounded up and put under 24-hour lockup in the Receiving Building. As one of the OIC's explained, whether they were guilty or not of the attempted escape, their confinement afforded the opportunity to discipline those "with a negative attitude toward Norfolk treatment. . . . By picking up this group of aggressive non-cooperators, it was felt that we would be getting a good portion of the men implicated, and at the same

[68]*Ibid.*, 17 April 1933, p. 437.
[69]*Ibid.*, 23 June 1933, p. 467.

time we would be decreasing our behavior problem in the community."[70] Incidentally, their shift to the Receiving Building did free space in the dormitories, and before the day was up, their beds had been given to other inmates. Not unexpectedly, the 23 men set up a clamor, banging on their cells, shouting, and destroying whatever property they could. The administration responded by preparing tear gas, depriving them of all smoking and reading materials, and forbidding all corrspondence or visits. "They would want to write to all sorts of people," Gill explained, "and people would be given an unfair picture of the while situation. . . . He would be swamped with politicians asking questions."[71]

Cooler heads did prevail, and a bargain was struck between the men and the staff. The institution's sense of itself as something other than an Attica-like prison did encourage both sides to reach compromises; some of the men confessed, and Gill was easy on them. Nevertheless, something critical had happened. The earlier doubts of whether Norfolk would be a penal or a treatment institution were giving way to a clear recognition that, "with all the comforts of Norfolk, its own limited freedom, its humane approach, its modern living conditions, etc., we have realized with something of a shock that it is still a prison."[72] The guards now pushed for stricter regulations over the men, and Gill more and more frequently offered explanations for the failure of his experiment. "It is evident," he declared, "that in a prison community, as in the outside community, minorities govern." That troublesome 10% could not be isolated; sooner or later the institution, whatever its hopes, would organize its entire regimen to handle them. Gill also began to sense the inevitability of the conflict between custody and rehabilitation, the full price that one paid for having a jail. "I am interested that the most serious trouble at Norfolk," he observed, "has come with the opening of the Receiving Building, but in part, I wonder if it is not due to the very nature of the building itself as a repressive agency. It seems that the more bars and locks we have, the more of a reaction against them is engendered." He concluded in a non-Progressive fashion: "A little restriction and a little freedom do not mix." The inmates' "need is for a great deal of freedom or a great deal of repression." Norfolk (or any other institution?) could not have it both ways.[73]

Three months later, in September 1933, two inmates (one of them MacRaughry) who were known to be troublesome went over the wall.

[70]Ibid., 9 July 1933, pp. 477–478.
[71]Ibid., 25 July 1933, p. 493.
[72]Ibid., 13 July 1933, pp. 493–501, 7 July 1933, p. 470.
[73]Ibid., 12 July 1933, p. 472, 9 July 1933, p. 481.

Their escape prompted many staff members to insist along with Roser that "men with long terms and vicious anti-social traits should not be sent to Norfolk." Moreover, they were now prepared to get tough with the hard core, to bring into Norfolk the kinds of punishments and disciplinary practices used in other prisons. To observe these changes is to have the feeling of watching a puppet show, with Norfolk captive of a force quite outside itself. The dynamic of incarceration took them from treatment to mild discipline to brutal discipline. Thus, one of the colony's house officers who had consistently been a treatment enthusiast now suggested:

> We need a stronger discipline than we are giving at the present time. I would suggest that a separate cell block be built for the worse cases. . . . I would suggest that this type of 'bastile' building should have the minimum of comforts and should be the most undesirable place for any human being to inhabit. . . . Only when we show them that we have fire to fight fire with will they be less inclined to play with fire.[74]

He had moved quite a distance from a rehabilitative rationale, and so had the institution. Norfolk has "changed its standards of sending men back to the Receiving Building," Mark Roser was soon explaining. "The criterion now is not so much 'What is the man doing on his program?' as 'How much of a risk is he to the security of the institution?'" Past record and reputation, not receptivity to reform, had become the guiding principle.[75]

Both men justified the new measures with the case of one inmate, Seelington. This hapless fellow, who objected to being moved from the dorms into the Receiving Building for a disciplinary infraction, started throwing furniture around and broke a glass door; he refused to quiet down, even after being placed in the steel cell. "It seemed evident," recounted Roser, "that there was no alternative but to try to change the man's opinion by placing him in a situation in which, as long as his attitude continued, he actually felt physical discomfort, and more physical discomfort than he would normally feel when locked in a cell on the top floor of the Receiving Building." Accordingly, Seelington was handcuffed, locked in a basement cell with a mattress and two blankets, and put on a bread and water diet. After 4 days of this he begged to be released, and was, in Roser's view, a changed man—indeed, a change that seemingly testified to the wisdom and efficacy of solitary on bread and water. Not only was Norfolk breaking the hard case through cruel

---

[74]*Ibid.*, 25 September 1933, p. 537.
[75]*Ibid.*, 25 September 1933, p. 538, 30 October 1933, pp. 580–581.

punishment, and not only was Gill's earlier discrimination between locking up and tying up an inmate gone, but also the process by which this declension took place was all too apparent. Few phrases out of Norfolk's history are more grim than Roser's final comments on the episode: "It is rather evident that once the men get into the Receiving Building they do not feel the discipline of merely remaining in their cells and we are more or less forced, for the morale of the group, to inaugurate a more rigid system of discipline." If anyone needs another reminder of how caretakers can legitimate almost any action, let him ponder Roser's phrase "for the morale of the group."[76]

At this point, Gill was fully prepared to maintain control at Norfolk by applying "some strong force and deprivation." The various schemes that had looked to treatment or to a normal community life within the institution gave way to an overriding concern for security. Thus Gill insisted that "grading according to social attitude be made equal to grading according to casework achievement," which was another way of saying that disciplinary considerations were to become the critical measure for all inmate classifications. Accordingly, prisoner Joseph Hadley was to be confined to the Receiving Building "because he has so much anti-administration influence, plus his general characteristics of clever anti-social individual. This classification is made despite evidence of superficial institutional adjustment."[77]

In light of these developments, it is less of a shock to learn that in November 1933 Norfolk remodeled 12 cells into the hole, or to discover that in January 1934 12 cells were no longer considered enough.[78] The report in the diary on this change offers one last poignant text to examine. The entry, written by the inmate editor of the prison newspaper, described a novel meeting at Norfolk. The inmates and the staff were joined by the state commissioner of corrections to discuss the issue of discipline. "The Superintendent pointed out that this meeting with the Commissioner probably had never been duplicated in the history of penology." However unprecedented the session, the outcome was all too familiar in the history of penology. "It was agreed that secure solitary cells should be installed in which bread and water punishment would be meted out in place of regular rations." The inmate noted that "there was considerable discussion as to which cells should be used as punishment cells. The top floor of the Receiving Building was suggested, also basement punishment cells, to which the Superintendent objected, because so many disgraceful things have happened in

[76]Ibid., 25 September 1933, pp. 540–541.
[77]Ibid., 2 November 1933, p. 585, 30 October 1933, p. 581(b).
[78]Ibid., 2 November 1933, pp. 586–587.

underground places of that sort and he didn't like it." But the reporter knew well how to frame this point: "This was, of course, incidental detail in the discussion and agreement that there was a need for more secure cells and the facilities for solitary confinement which we do not have at present."[79] In the end what was left of Gill's ambitions and the Norfolk experiment was a last pathetic gesture, an incidental detail: In the Norfolk prison the hole would not be in the basement.

*   *   *

The closing events in Gill's administration need not detain us for long. Inmates became less tractable, as evidenced by a drunken Christmas Eve party and a food strike 2 weeks later. The press played up all of Norfolk's problems, as relayed to them by disgruntled guards, and one eager Massachusetts politician set out to advance his career by "exposing" Norfolk. At the end of January 1934, Gill was "withdrawn" as superintendent pending investigations and several months later the withdrawal turned into a dismissal. Gill's replacement did for a time maintain a rhetorical commitment to treatment, but successive annual reports conceded that Norfolk had become just another penal institution, difficult to distinguish from Charlestown. By the end of 1936, the new superintendent conceded that "the State Prison Colony cannot be operated (as it was first intended) purely as a 'rehabilitative' institution, but must be administered to a very great extent as a 'custodial' prison."[80]

Despite the external interventions and that Gill was finally a victim of state politics, the critical elements in the Norfolk story remained the internal ones. Once it had the hole, the experiment was over. That Gill left the scene when he did was probably to his good fortune. It could then appear, however mistakenly, that the final decline took place under another's authority; indeed, that Gill was removed may even have helped to blur the genuine significance of the events and made it seem that reform had fallen victim to politics, not to its own dynamic. The scapegoat could be Massachusetts, and the most vital considerations, the nature of Progressive assumptions and the reasons why they were incapable of successful application, could be ignored.

Perhaps the Norfolk story as I have attempted to reconstruct it is clear enough not to need a final gloss. The text may well speak for itself. Let me draw out, however, at least in summary fashion, some of the impli-

---

[79] Ibid., 6 January 1934, pp. 680–681.
[80] Massachusetts Department of Corrections, Annual Report . . . 1936, p. 16.

cations that I find most compelling. First, insofar as the discipline of history is concerned, there is little doubt that the record of past efforts at social engineering is often explicit and detailed enough to allow for a whole series of case studies that illuminate not only the end result of interventions but also the processes that brought them about. Historians can work at the microlevel. There are other Norfolk-like diaries to be uncovered and analyzed, and the contributions that can be made from such an approach are only beginning to become apparent.

Second, and more particularly to the general issue of social reform, the Norfolk story reallocates the burden of responsibility and justification from those who would be prepared to trust the benevolent impulses of the reformer to those who would regard him with an acute suspicion. The novelist George Eliot insisted that it would be ignorant unkindness to be angry with ignorant kindness; I would maintain that if anger is not the appropriate response, then extraordinary caution surely is. The problem with ignorant kindness is that we tend to let down our guard, to trust to it too much. We are ready to suspend belief, to grant indulgences on the wrongheaded notion that the resulting cruelties will necessarily be less severe, that the pledge to do good will somehow offer protection against disastrous results.

Third, and still more important, the events at Norfolk raise many troubling points about anyone's ability to deliver effective treatment within an institution. The narrative points to a series of particular questions that would demand solution. How will a trained staff be recruited? How will therapists live with caretakers? Do we have a conceptual framework that will produce meaningful treatment techniques? Are classifications merely descriptive statements or are they relevant to treatment? And even more important, Norfolk reveals the difficulty, dare I say the impossibility, of any program that would mix reform with custody. I am persuaded that Norfolk's fate speaks clearly to the larger issues of probation, parole, and the juvenile court within the criminal justice system and that to join assistance to surveillance is to create a tension that cannot persist and will be far more likely to be resolved on the side of surveillance. Indeed, the implications of such a finding to the fields of mental health and social welfare are probably no less compelling. The most mischievous of all Progressive assumptions was embodied in Norfolk's first principle, that it could "guard securely" and return "better men."

Finally, the Norfolk experience does raise the complex issue of whether the difficulties of administering a humane prison *system* are not insurmountable. An account of any one institution, or, indeed, of many institutions, cannot resolve the point. Too many contingencies will inevitably remain, no matter how extensive the inquiry. In the instance of Norfolk, one can at least imagine a series of different circumstances producing different outcomes. What if the custodial staff had been recruited from outside the system so as to share a greater affinity with a rehabilitative ethic? Or perhaps another chief administrator at Norfolk would have been much more successful than was Gill in settling intrastaff disputes. And, of course, Norfolk's ultimate significance rests in its highly unusual character, for taking itself and the Progressive ideology so seriously. All of this means that it would be inappropriate to make major claims for settling so critical a question as the compatibility of custody with decency on the basis of the Norfolk case.

Yet, the matter need not rest there. In the end, Norfolk is a text that should be interpreted with an eye to its "meaning" in the way that an anthropologist will find meaning in an immolation ceremony or in a cock fight. Such an interpretation will not be substantiated by the methodology of the social sciences—by the broadness of the sample or the typicality of the test case—but, nevertheless, it may have its own validity. In this spirit, let me suggest (and I would not use a stronger term than that) the following reading.

In corrections we all too often come up against the need for one more sanction. Not that we cannot here or there run one decent institution; rather, the decency of any one place rests ultimately upon a more coercive back-up, and that back-up in turn rests upon the presence of a still more coercive back-up. If the inmate will not behave at Allenwood, we have the threat of Lewisburg, and if he will not behave at Lewisburg, we have the threat of administrative segregation, and if that will not do, solitary, and if that does not break him, bread and water, or physical punishment. Is there any point short of brutality where the system can stop? It is with this sense of things that I become uneasy when I hear about plans for a strictly custodial arrangement for incarceration; it may be a cleaner and more honest rationale than a rehabilitative one, but it lends an impression that one can hold an inmate and not do harm, that confinement and decency throughout *all* sectors of an incarcerative system can be achieved.

I am not about to propose an answer to the problem of punishment. In fact, to come back to my experience with the Committee for the Study of Incarceration, we did not come up with an alternative to the prison either.[81] But let me say that as an historian I am more and more dismayed by such a bankruptcy of imagination.

---

[81]Andrew von Hirsch, *Doing Justice* (New York, 1976); see also Norval Morris, *The Future of Imprisonment* (Chicago, 1974).

Accordingly, I applaud and join in the efforts to reduce the number of offenders whose acts would be deemed serious enough to warrant the severity of an incarcerative penalty and to cut dramatically the sentence time that would be served. Perhaps a frankly custodial model tied to a determinate sentence will promote such ends. But reformers may want to speak in a whisper. The new proposals still keep us very much in the business of confinement, and that seems to be nightmarish business. For me, in the end, Norfolk is a parable. Its fall, its degeneration to the hole with bread and water, is the indictment of the system.

II

THE HISTORY OF SOCIAL PROBLEMS

5

THE MORASS:
AN ESSAY ON THE
PUBLIC EMPLOYEE PENSION PROBLEM[1]

ROBERT M. FOGELSON

"We've got into a deeper and deeper morass," M. Lewis Thompson, manager of the Los Angeles Fire and Police Pension System (LAFPPS), told a reporter in 1972, "and there's no cheap way out."[2] Thompson knew what he was talking about. At the time the LAFPPS, which covered the city's 10,187 firemen and policemen, had on its rolls 6358 retired officers and their survivors, roughly two beneficiaries for every three officers, to whom it paid $41 million in benefits, about $24 million more than in 1962. To meet the system's current expenses and amortize its prior obligations, the city council appropriated $63 million, which was 45% of the fire and police departments' payrolls, 32% of the city's property taxes, and 11% of its total expenditures. With $63 million going to the LAFPPS and another $18 million going to the City Employees' Retirement System, which covered 19,786 of the city's nonuniformed employees, Los Angeles spent more on pensions than on anything else except for schools and police. The LAFPPS's revenues, which included member contributions and investment earnings, as well as appropriations by the council, exceeded its expenditures by $46 million in 1972. But the system's obligations grew by even more, and its unfunded liabil-

[1]A grant, No. 5–ROI–MH25292–03, from the Center for Studies of Metropolitan Problems, National Institute of Mental Health, supported some of the research on which this chapter is based.
[2]Los Angeles Times, 13 March 1972.

ity climbed from $722 million to $861 million, roughly $80,000 for each fireman and policeman and about six times the annual payroll of the two departments. Two years later the unfunded liability reached $1.2 billion, or about one-seventh the assessed value of the city.[3]

The situation was as bad, if not worse, in many other cities. With 1316 active firemen and policemen and 1128 retired firemen and policemen (and their survivors), Minneapolis was supporting two fire and two police departments in 1972. New Orleans, which had 2546 active firemen and policemen and 2181 retired firemen and policemen (and their survivors), was in much the same bind, as were Oakland, New York, Seattle, Indianapolis, and Washington, D.C. For every dollar that Detroit spent on policemen's and firemen's salaries in 1972, it put more than 50 cents into policemen's and firemen's pensions. The situation was not quite as bad in San Francisco, but it was worse in Oakland, where an actuarial firm reported in 1976 that in order for the city's fire and police pension system to fulfill its present and future obligations the municipal authorities would have to raise their contributions from a modest 18% of payroll to a mind-boggling 129%. The Law Enforcement Officers and Fire Fighters pension system, which covers all uniformed officers in the state of Washington, had in 1973 an unfunded liability of $443 million, roughly $50,000 for each policeman and fireman. The Pittsburgh policemen's pension system had in 1975 an unfunded liability of $95 million, roughly $60,000 for each policeman and about six times the annual payroll of the Pittsburgh police department.[4]

Under these circumstances it is not surprising that public employee pension systems, of which firemen's and policemen's pension systems are an integral part, have aroused widespread concern in recent years. According to Congresswoman Martha W. Griffiths of Michigan, these pensions are like "time bombs ticking away in every major American city." According to Jackson Phillips, a vice-president of Moody's Investors Service, they are "the darkest cloud hanging over the cities." Alfred Parker, executive director of the Tax Foundation, has compared public employee pensions to an "iceberg." Dean Lund, executive secretary of

[3]City of Los Angeles, Board of Pension Commissioners, *Annual Report: 1972*, pp. 5, 9, 32, 39; Los Angeles City Controller, *Annual Report: 1972*, p. 104, Schedule C-3; City of Los Angeles, Department of Pensions, "Fire and Police Pension System" (1975), p. 8, Department of Pensions Files, Los Angeles.

[4]U.S., Bureau of the Census, *Census of Governments, 1972: Volume 6, Topical Studies: Number 1, Employee Retirement Systems of State and Local Governments* (Washington, D.C., 1973), pp. 30–53; U.S., Congress, House of Representatives, Committee on Education and Labor, Subcommittee on Labor Standards, *Hearings on the Public Service Employee Retirement Income Security Act of 1975*, 94th Cong., 2d sess., pp. 23, 84, 98; *Oakland Tribune*, 15 January 1976; *Washington Journal of Commerce*, 13 November 1976.

the League of Minnesota Municipalities, has likened them to an "albatross." A Boston *Globe* reporter has referred to them as a "tapeworm"— "the more it grows the more it eats." A Los Angeles *Times* reporter has called the city's pension plans a "bottomless morass." Another *Times* reporter has described them as the public's "Achilles heel." Conrad M. Siegel, a well-known actuary, has said that many pension plans in Pennsylvania are "just, plain and simply, a disaster." The *Institutional Investor* has asked, "Will pension costs push America's cities over the brink?" The Massachusetts Taxpayers Foundation has raised the question, "Will a day come when the money runs out?" The *Nation's Business* has suggested that pension costs "may break the cities." And the *Wall Street Journal* has warned that a "Day of Reckoning" is at hand.[5]

The authorities have not been unmindful of the warnings. The Pennsylvania Department of Community Affairs, the New York State Permanent Commission on Public Employee Pension and Retirement Systems, and the Minnesota State Planning Agency have done studies of the problem. The House of Representatives Subcommittee on Labor Standards has held hearings on pension reform, and the House Task Force on Public Pensions has made a comprehensive survey of state and local pension systems.[6] These studies are invaluable. Along with the publications of the Census Bureau and Social Security Administration, they provide a mine of information about the membership, coverage, benefits, eligibility requirements, and investment policies of public pension systems. By applying standard actuarial techniques, they calculate the current obligations of these systems, project their future liabilities, and evaluate alternative ways of putting these systems on a sound financial basis. So far as I know, however, none of these studies has attempted to figure out how and why so many public employee pension systems have gotten into such precarious conditions. None of these studies has tried to find out how and why these pension systems have become such a drain on the cities' resources that they now threaten the financial viability of urban America.

I would like to explore this issue by looking at the history of the Los

[5]U.S., Congress, House of Representatives, Committee on Ways and Means, *Hearings on General Revenue Sharing*, 92d Cong., 1st sess., p. 290; Barbara A. Patocka, "Will Pension Costs Push America's Cities Over the Brink?" *Institutional Investor*, June 1975, pp. 55, 57; "The Hidden Costs That May Break the Cities," *Nation's Business*, September 1971, p. 31; Dean Lund, "Fire and Police Pension Funds: An Agonizing Reappraisal," *Minnesota Municipalities*, September 1971, p. 270; *Boston Globe*, 17 October 1976; *Los Angeles Times*, 13 March 1972, 27 November 1975; Massachusetts Taxpayers Foundation, *Paying for Public Pensions: Will a Day Come When the Money Runs Out?* (1976); *Wall Street Journal*, 25 June 1973.
[6]U.S., Congress, House of Representatives, Committee on Education and Labor, *Pension Task Force Report on Public Employee Retirement Systems*, 95th Cong., 2d sess.

Angeles Fire and Police Pension System. I have picked a fire and police pension system because in every city I have studied, the public employee pension problem turns out to be largely a firemen's and policemen's pension problem. Los Angeles is a case in point. In 1972 the LAFPPS had slightly more than half as many active members as the City Employees' Retirement System. Yet the LAFPPS had nearly twice as many retired members as the LACERS; it paid out almost three times as much in benefits, consumed more than three times as much in property taxes, and carried close to four times as large an unfunded liability.[7] The pattern was much the same in San Francisco, Oakland, Portland, and Seattle, but it was by no means a Pacific Coast phenomenon. In 1972 New Orleans had 112 retired firemen for every 100 active firemen, 65 retired policemen for every 100 active policemen, and 17 retired nonuniformed employees for every 100 active nonuniformed employees. In 1972 Detroit put $6400 into the policemen's and firemen's pension fund for each uniformed officer and $2000 into the city employees' pension fund for each nonuniformed employee. In 1976 Minneapolis reported that its pension systems had unfunded liabilities of more than $140,000 for each fireman, nearly $100,000 for each policeman, and less than $30,000 for each nonuniformed employee.[8]

I have chosen the LAFPPS not so much because it is a fairly typical municipal fire and police pension system as because its fiscal plight cannot be explained by mismanagement or skulduggery. The system's staff is extremely capable, and its actuaries are highly qualified. Its records are well kept, its reports are informative, and its funds are invested in a prudent manner. The system has been free of scandal since the early 1940s, when it became enmeshed in a scheme to purge the Los Angeles police department of dozens of high-ranking officers.[9] It has shunned as well many of the questionable practices which have discredited other public employee pension systems in recent years. The LAFPPS has not encouraged officers to retire in order to escape disciplinary proceedings, a practice that was commonplace in Philadelphia in the early 1970s, according to the Pennsylvania Crime Commission. Nor has the system rubber-stamped applications for disability pensions, a practice that was

[7]*Los Angeles Times*, 13 March 1972; Census Bureau, *Employee Retirement Systems of State and Local Governments*, pp. 30–31.

[8]Census Bureau, *Employee Retirement Systems of State and Local Governments*, pp. 38–39, 42–43; State Planning Agency, Office of Local and Urban Affairs, "Minneapolis–St. Paul Study. Part II: Report on Pensions" (1978), p. 32. Figures for New Orleans include widows and other survivors.

[9]Roy Hampton and E. L. Thrasher to Los Angeles City Council, 9 March 1942, and Norris J. Nelson to Los Angeles City Council, 12 March 1942, Los Angeles City Council Files, No. 10380, Municipal Records Center, Los Angeles (hereafter cited as LACC Files).

so widespread in Washington, D.C., in the late 1960s that Chief of Police Jerry V. Wilson called it "scandalous." And neither has the LAFFPS added in overtime when computing benefits, a practice that enabled one celebrated New York City bus driver who earned $13,000 a year to retire on an annual pension of $15,600.[10]

I intend to look at the history of the LAFPPS because the system has been in financial difficulty from almost the very beginning. The problem came to the surface in the late 1910s, when the Municipal League of Los Angeles, one of the principal monuments of the Progressive movement, warned that the fire and police pension systems—at that time two separate systems—were heading for serious trouble and urged the city council to put them on a sound financial footing. The problem also generated a furor in the early 1930s, when an actuary reported that the LAFPPS's unfunded liability had grown to $19 million and, at a time when hard-pressed property owners were demanding cutbacks in municipal spending, recommended that the authorities put an additional 44% a year into the system. The problem created an uproar in the early 1950s as well, when another actuary revealed that the unfunded liability had risen to $169 million and added that it would continue to rise unless the city council increased its annual appropriations from $4 million to $13 million.[11] In view of this long record of financial difficulty, it seems to me that the only way to find the sources of the pension problem in Los Angeles is to delve into the history of the LAFPPS, from its founding in the 1890s to the efforts to change the system in the 1960s.

Underlying this inquiry are a few distinct though closely related questions, the answers to which should enhance our understanding of the pension problem not only in Los Angeles but also in other cities. First, why did Los Angeles and other cities decide to provide pensions for firemen and policemen in the late nineteenth and early twentieth centuries? How did the sponsors overcome the long-standing and deep-seated opposition to pensions, especially to service pensions, for public employees? Second, why did the LAFPPS become so expensive? Why did the number of retired officers rise so steadily, not only in absolute terms but also relative to the number of active officers? Why, in short, did Los Angeles end up with two fire departments and two police departments? Third, why did the system's revenues fall so far short of its

[10]Pennsylvania Crime Commission, *Report on Police Corruption and the Quality of Law Enforcement in Philadelphia* (1974), pp. 538–582; *Washington Post*, 14 March 1971; *New York Times*, 27 July 1975.
[11]Municipal League of Los Angeles, *Bulletin*, 12 November 1917, pp. 5–6; *Los Angeles Times*, 30 August 1931, 15 February 1932; *Los Angeles Examiner*, 28 January 1954; M. M. Devore to Norris Poulson, 24 January 1957, LACC Files, No. 77868.

obligations? Why were the municipal authorities unwilling to raise the
members' contributions, increase the tax levies, or take other steps to
hold down the system's mounting unfunded liability? Fourth, why have
the system's many critics been unable to change it in ways which would
ease its fiscal plight? Why have they failed in one effort after another to
tighten the eligibility requirements? What, in other words, are the constraints on pension reform in Los Angeles?

The origins of the LAFPPS go back to 1889, when the California legislature passed an act enabling the cities and counties to set up pension
systems for firemen and policemen. Under this act, the local authorities
could retire an officer who had served for 20 years and reached the age
of 60 on a pension of one-half the salary attached to the rank he had held
for 1 year preceding retirement. They could also retire an officer who
had been disabled in the line of duty, regardless of age, on a pension of
one-half the salary attached to his rank at the time of retirement. If an
officer died in the line of duty, they could give his widow and dependent children a pension of one-third the salary attached to his rank at the
time of death. To pay for these pensions—which were known, respectively, as service, disability, and dependents pensions—the local authorities were empowered to deduct two dollars a month from the salary
of each fireman and policeman, as well as to appropriate funds from a
bewildering array of other sources. These included proceeds from the
sale of unclaimed property, revenues from the licensing of saloons, pool
halls, pawnbrokers, and junk stores, and fines levied on officers who
broke departmental regulations and citizens who violated municipal ordinances. Incorporating the cardinal provisions of this act into local ordinances, the Los Angeles city council formed a policemen's pension
system in 1899 and a firemen's pension system 2 years later. [12]

The council's action generated little controversy, because by the turn
of the century most big cities had come to believe that firemen and
policemen were entitled to pensions. [13] To understand why, it is necessary to bear in mind several things which were happening in urban
America at the time. During the nineteenth century police and fire departments were adjuncts of the political machines, prime sources of jobs
for party stalwarts. The jobs were quite attractive, especially to Irish
Americans and other first- and second-generation newcomers, but they

[12]Los Angeles Fire and Police Protective League, *History of the Department of Pensions of
the City of Los Angeles* (1939), p. 1.
[13]Charles P. Neill, *Pension Funds for Municipal Employees and Railroad Pension Systems in
the United States,* U.S. Senate Documents, 61st Cong., 2d sess., No. 427, 1910, pp. 36–85;
George Austin Ketcham, "Municipal Police Reform" (Ph.D. diss., University of Missouri),
pp. 218–221.

were also extremely insecure. The politicians who appointed the rank and file could also dismiss them, and a change of administration usually meant a purge of the municipal payroll. As a result few firemen and policemen grew old or incapacitated on the job. If they did—if they survived the periodic purges or if they suffered serious injury—their superiors were reluctant, in the words of one police chief, to "put them out onto the world." Instead, they employed these officers in "some light capacity" in Washington, D.C., gave them "desk jobs" in Boston, and assigned them to "soft snaps" in Chicago. This practice was so common in Chicago that a former New York official who investigated the police department there at the turn of the century found "old and incapacitated men tucked away in every corner."[14]

Things began to change in the late nineteenth century. In an effort to weaken the power of the political machines, the Progressives, a group of upper-middle- and upper-class reformers, exerted pressure on the authorities to put firemen and policemen under civil service. The reformers also brought pressure on the fire chiefs and police chiefs to make sure that their men spent the day fighting fires and chasing criminals rather than doing favors for ward bosses. These reforms ran into tremendous resistance in most cities, but after a while they were put into practice in enough cities so that for the first time many firemen and policemen grew old and disabled on the job. The reformers also exerted pressure on the authorities to abolish the traditional way of dealing with superannuated and incapacitated officers. How, they argued, could a fire or police department do its job if some of its officers were in their 60s or 70s and others were physically unfit for duty—if, in the words of a former police official, the force was "an asylum for old and decrepit men." The "dead-wood" would have to go.[15] Uncertain that their superiors could withstand the reform pressure, many firemen and policemen concluded they they needed a more formal device to protect them and their families against the hazards of old age and injury, that, in other words, they needed a pension system.

Many of their fellow Americans were unenthusiastic about the idea. If a policeman is disabled while on duty, a Boston alderman remarked in 1892, "the city certainly should take care of him and his family." But why, he asked, should it pay an able-bodied man $600 to $1200 a year for

[14]*Police and Firemen's Pension Fund*, U.S. Senate Documents, 63d Cong., 1st sess., No. 10, 1913, p. 47; Roger Lane, *Policing the City* (Cambridge, Mass., 1967), p. 183; Alexander R. Piper, *Report of an Investigation of the Discipline and Administration of the Police Department of the City of Chicago* (Chicago, 1904), p. 11. See also Robert M. Fogelson, *Big-City Police* (Cambridge, Mass., 1977), chap. 1.

[15]Piper, *Investigation of the Discipline*, p. 14; William McAdoo, *Guarding a Great City* (New York, 1906), p. 64; Fogelson, *Big-City Police*, chap. 2.

the rest of his life "for [doing] nothing" just because he has served the city for 20 or 30 years and reached the age of 65? It should not, insisted another alderman who strongly objected not only to the idea of pensions but also to the concept of retirement. Since the country was founded, he argued, it has adhered to the principle that every man should put aside a part of his wages so that "when he arrives at the age of fifty or sixty he will have something laid by with which to support himself and his family." Drawing on a deep-seated tradition, he declared that "if a man is well and strong, or reasonably so, even if he has reached the age of sixty or sixty-five, there is no reason why he should not work so long as he is able to."[16] To give pensions to policemen would be a serious mistake, a Rochester alderman warned in 1886, because "we would soon have the teachers, the firemen and all city employees asking the same thing." Since policemen had no stronger claims to pensions than other public employees, another alderman insisted, the authorities would be hard put to turn down these requests, which would place an intolerable burden on the taxpayers.[17]

These objections were groundless, the firemen and policemen responded. Walking the beat for 10 or 12 hours a day, 6 or 7 days a week, often in rain, snow, and numbing cold, policemen cannot go on working indefinitely. Most patrolmen are unfit for duty after 20 or 25 years of service, Providence Police Chief Benjamin H. Child told the city council in 1892. According to Providence Fire Chief George A. Steere, the same held true for firemen, who were on call at the station house for 24 hours a day 51 weeks a year.[18] Nor can firemen and policemen prepare for the future in the same way as other municipal employees with less hazardous jobs. In constant danger from the time the alarm rings until, to quote Chief Steere, "the order is given to 'pack up'," the fireman can never know when he will be struck down in the line of duty. Neither can the policeman. The risks are so great that the insurance companies rarely cover firemen and policemen, and then only at prohibitive rates. Firemen and policemen should be treated not like other municipal employees, their spokesmen claimed, but like soldiers or sailors who were engaged in a "war against fire" and a "war on crime." They protect their fellow citizens in peacetime just as soldiers defend them in wartime. As Commissioner Rhinelander Waldo told the International Association of

---

[16]City of Boston, Common Council, *Reports of Proceedings*, 18 July 1892, pp. 704–708, 1 August 1892, pp. 724–727.

[17]City of Rochester, Bureau of Municipal Research, *Municipal Research*, July 1944, p. 411.

[18]*Report of the Joint Special Committee Relative to a Pension Fund for Disabled Policemen and Firemen with Accompanying Resolution*, Providence City Documents, No. 7 (Providence, 1893), pp. 4–6, 11–13.

Chiefs of Police in 1912, they are entitled to pensions from the city as much as soldiers are entitled to pensions from the nation.[19]

In the end the authorities sided with the firemen and policemen for several reasons. The charges that pensions were paternalistic and un-American lost much of their credibility in the late nineteenth century when the American Express Company, Baltimore and Ohio Railroad, and several other corporations established retirement systems for their employees. The argument that the authorities should not treat firemen and policemen in a more favorable way than other municipal employees was not particularly compelling at a time when the military analogy was gradually emerging as the conventional wisdom of the American people. The distinction between disability pensions and service pensions was hard to maintain in the face of testimony by many well-known fire and police chiefs that for uniformed officers 20 or 25 years of service was the functional equivalent of disability. The firemen and policemen were probably backed by a few machine politicians who realized that a pension system could be used to remove incumbent officers and thereby create additional openings for party stalwarts, a fairly common practice in Chicago and New York in the 1890s. The firemen and policemen were also supported by many well-meaning Americans, like the editors of the Oregon *Daily Journal*, who argued in 1913 that a proposed pension system for Portland's firemen would cost the average taxpayer no more than 10 or 15 cents a year.[20]

By the turn of the century, the Progressives, for whom a pension system was an integral feature of the long-term campaign to upgrade the public service, joined forces with the firemen and policemen. So far as the reformers were concerned, a pension system would do more than just eliminate the many superannuated and incapacitated officers who were no longer able to carry their weight and were blocking the advancement of younger and more capable firefighters and patrolmen. A pension system would also attract many highly qualified persons who would not otherwise have considered a career in public service. A de-

[19]*Ibid.*, p. 13; International Association of Fire Engineers, *Proceedings of the Thirty-First Annual Convention* (1903), pp. 69–70; National Firemen's Association of the United States, *Report of the Proceedings of the Twelfth Annual Convention* (1909), pp. 102–103; International Association of Chiefs of Police, *Proceedings of the 19th Annual Convention* (1912), p. 88, and *Proceedings of the Twenty-Second Annual Convention* (1915), p. 36.

[20]David Hackett Fischer, *Growing Old in America* (New York, 1977), pp. 165–167; Fogelson, *Big-City Police*, pp. 53–58; *Police and Firemen's Pension Fund*, pp. 48–49; *Report Relative to a Pension Fund for Disabled Policemen and Firemen*, p. 6; State of Illinois, Senate Committee of Investigation, *Report on the Chicago Police System* (Springfield, 1898), p. 11; State of New York, Senate Committee Appointed to Investigate the Police Department of the City of New York, *Report and Proceedings* (Albany, 1895), 5:4, 737–743; *Oregon Daily Journal*, 27 May 1913.

cent pension would be "the most encouraging inducement that we could offer to the policeman or the fireman," Superintendent Richard Sylvester of Washington, D.C., told a congressional committee in 1913. Provided that the benefits were not vested—provided that unless disabled, an officer could not receive his benefits (or any part thereof) until he completed 20 or 25 years of service—a pension system would discourage veteran officers from quitting after 10 or 15 years. Finally, a pension system might even deter some firemen and policemen from taking payoffs and otherwise violating departmental regulations, because if caught, they stood to lose not only their jobs, which was bad enough, but also their pensions, which for many veteran officers was even worse.[21]

A few skeptics warned that a pension system for firemen and policemen would be a heavy burden on the taxpayers. These warnings were discounted in most cities, and in Los Angeles they seemed particularly farfetched. Between 1899 and 1922, when the fire and police pension systems were merged into one system, the LAFPPS gave out only 218 pensions, of which 117 were for disability, 44 for service, and 57 for dependents. And in 1922 the system had on its rolls only 135 retired officers (and their survivors), or about 1 beneficiary for every 13 officers, to whom it paid about $115,000 in benefits. To cover the cost of the LAFPPS, the city council appropriated $136,000, which was somewhat more than it spent on the city attorney's office and slightly less than it spent on the playground department. This sum came to roughly 4% of the fire and police departments' payrolls, 1% of the city's property taxes, and a fraction of 1% of its total expenditures. The LAFPPS had rolled up an unfunded liability of $6 million by 1922, but that was only $3000 for each fireman and policeman, less than twice the payrolls of the two departments, and under 1% of the assessed value of the city.[22]

These figures were misleading, however. For the Los Angeles city council had recently changed the LAFPPS in a way that did not then show up in the system's statistics but would in time have a profound impact on its financial condition. To be eligible for a pension under the provisions of the original state enabling act, an officer who was not disabled in the line of duty had to do more than just put in 20 years of service. He also had to reach the age of 60. An age requirement, which was incorporated into most service pensions at their inception, served

[21]*Police and Firemen's Pension Fund*, p. 47; Fogelson, *Big-City Police*, p. 59. See also Lewis Meriam, *Principles Governing the Retirement of Public Employees* (New York, 1918), pp. 3–17.

[22]"Pensions Granted: Summary of Number and Yearly Totals of Pensions Granted During the Years Listed Below," LACC Files, No. 21072; untitled actuarial report, 1922, tables 4 and 5, Department of Pensions Files; *Report of the Controller of the City of Los Angeles: 1925*, pp. 56–63; Protective League, *History of the Department of Pensions*, p. 3.

two purposes. First, it prevented an officer who joined the force in his early 20s from retiring in his middle 40s and living off the taxpayers for the next 30 or 40 years. Second, it reinforced the traditional notion that "a pension should not be paid to an able bodied man under any circumstances," to quote the Finance Committee of the Los Angeles city council.[23] In Los Angeles, where the age requirement was 60, a fireman or policeman who was appointed at age 29, which was about average in 1900, would have to put in at least 30 years to be eligible for a pension. At 60 he could expect to live on average another 14 years.[24] Hence even if he did not resign, was not fired, and did not die beforehand, an officer would spend 2 years at work for each year on retirement, an arrangement that kept pension costs down.

Opposition to the age requirement surfaced in Los Angeles in 1911, when the voters approved a charter amendment that empowered the city council to make changes in the fire and police pension systems. Soon after the election, the firemen and policemen, who had sponsored the amendment, pressed the council to adopt a new system that would have eliminated the age requirement and raised the service requirement from 20 to 25 years. Incorporated into two ordinances, the proposal was endorsed by the council's Legislative Committee. But on a recommendation from the Finance Committee, which pointed out that under the proposed system an able-bodied officer could retire at half pay at age 46, the council voted to table the ordinances. Two years later, however, the council yielded to pressure from the firemen and policemen and lowered the age requirement from 60 to 55. Six years later the firemen and policemen again appealed to the council to abolish the age requirement, as well as to make other changes in the pension system. The Municipal League urged the council to defer action until it did a study of the fiscal implications of the proposed changes. After both the Chamber of Commerce and the Merchants and Manufacturers Association endorsed the proposal, however, the council gave firemen and policemen the option to retire after 20 years of service regardless of age.[25]

What prompted the council to reverse its position is hard to say. As the Municipal League later charged, a deal may have been arranged by which the Chamber of Commerce and the Merchants and Manufacturers

[23]Los Angeles City Council, Records, 19 December 1911, p. 545, City Clerk's Office, Los Angeles.
[24]"Service Pensions—Fire and Police," LACC Files, No. 21072; U.S., Department of Health, Education, and Welfare, Public Health Service, *Vital Statistics of the United States, 1973. Volume II - Section 5: Life Tables* (Rockville, Md., 1975), p. 14.
[25]*Los Angeles Express,* 24 February 1911; *Los Angeles Herald,* 1–5 March 1911; *Los Angeles Times,* 7 March 1911, 7, 9, 11, April 1919; Los Angeles City Council, Records, 19 December 1911, pp. 543–545, 1 July 1913, p. 406, 7 July 1913, p. 8, 3 September 1913, p. 347, 4 September 1913, p. 357, 12 September 1913, pp. 383–384.

Association agreed to endorse the abolition of the age requirement if the firemen withdrew from the American Federation of Labor and the policemen halted their attempts to form a union.[26] Champions of the "open shop," who had waged a long and hard campaign against unionization of the private sector, the chamber and the association would probably have gone to almost any lengths to prevent the firemen and policemen from affiliating with organized labor. As the years went by, the council may also have found it harder and harder to uphold a requirement that had already been abandoned in New York, Baltimore, Pittsburgh, Cleveland, New Orleans, and other cities. Following the logic of the military analogy, which was by then widely accepted in Los Angeles, the council may have reached the conclusion that firefighting and policing were too strenuous for anyone over 50.[27] From this conclusion it was a short step to the position that instead of retaining an age requirement, the council should do everything possible to encourage middle-aged officers to make way for younger ones. Whatever the council's motives, the abolition of the age requirement had an adverse impact on the financial condition of the LAFPPS in the years ahead.

In the absence of an age requirement, another change that was underway also had a negative effect on the system's financial condition. During the late nineteenth century, few cities viewed youth as an important criterion for firemen or policemen. A recruit could join the force at 40 in some cities, at 50 in others, and at any age in still others. The reformers strongly objected to this policy on several grounds. For one, it attracted many candidates who had already failed in one line of work or another and had only applied to the fire department or police department when they could do nothing else. For another, it produced many recruits who were already so fixed in their ways, so hostile to new ideas, and so full of misconceptions that they could not be trained to be competent firefighters or policemen. For still another, it filled many positions with officers who were already well into their 30s and 40s and would probably be too old to carry their weight in 10 or 15 years. In order to upgrade firefighting and policing, the reformers reasoned, it was imperative to lower the age at which officers joined the force. Following this reasoning, the reformers exerted intense pressure on the authorities to revise the entrance requirements so that no one who was more than 30 years old could be appointed to the fire or police department.[28]

Most cities gave in to this pressure and lowered the maximum age for

[26]Municipal League of Los Angeles, *Bulletin*, 31 May 1926, pp. 1–3.
[27]*Philadelphia Inquirer*, 23 June 1924.
[28]Leonhard Felix Fuld, *Police Administration* (New York, 1909), pp. 82–83; New York Bureau of Municipal Research, *Report on a Survey of the Government of the City and County of San Francisco* (San Francisco, 1916), p. 172; Cleveland Foundation, *Criminal Justice in Cleve-*

recruits to 30 or 35. Los Angeles was a case in point. Up to 1889, the year in which the state legislature empowered the city to establish a pension system, Los Angeles permitted anyone who was at least 25 and no more than 50 to become a fireman or policeman. But over the next few decades, the authorities gradually tightened the entrance requirements until no one could be appointed to the fire or police department who was less than 21 and more than 30. As a result, the age at which firemen and policemen joined the force dropped. Although the statistics go back only to 1900, the average entry age probably fell from at least 30 in the late nineteenth century to about 28 in the first third of the twentieth century and roughly 25 in the second third.[29] The average age at which firemen and policemen became eligible for pensions declined as well. Until 1913, when the age requirement was lowered to 55, it was 60. After 1919, when the age requirement was abolished, it was 48, except for officers appointed after 1927, when the service requirement was raised from 20 to 25 years. After 1947, when the service requirement was rolled back to 20 years, it was 45.

These changes—the abolition of the age requirement and the decline of the entry age—would have put a strain on the financial condition of the LAFPPS under any circumstances. But the strain would probably not have been too severe were it not for yet another change that was taking place in the Los Angeles fire and police departments. During the late nineteenth century, when firemen and policemen were appointed every 2 years and a change in administration was normally followed by a thorough purge, both departments had a staggering turnover rate.[30] By the late 1920s, however, the rate had fallen to about 10% a year, with 5% from resignation and another 5% from dismissal, though it was probably much higher for policemen than for firemen. The turnover rate continued to drop in the 1930s, reaching a low of about 4% a year in the second half of the decade, and then started to rise during and after World War II. During the 1950s, the rate climbed to close to 10% a year—though the dismissal rate, which had fallen to 3% a year in the 1930s, dropped to slightly less than 2% a year.[31] Thus, as the years

land (Cleveland, 1922), pp. 26–28; August Vollmer, "Police Conditions in the United States," in National Commission on Law Observance and Enforcement, Report on Police (Washington, D.C., 1931), pp. 62–63; Citizens' Police Committee, Chicago Police Problems (Chicago, 1931), pp. 51–52.

[29]Los Angeles Times, 27 June 1889; Second Annual Report of the Civil Service Department of Los Angeles California: 1904; "Service Pensions—Fire and Police." See also the rules and regulations of the Board of Civil Service Commissioners, 1911–1958, and the annual reports of the Board of Pension Commissioners, 1954–1960.

[30]Los Angeles Times, 22,31 March, 6 May 1889; Fogelson, Big-City Police, pp. 27–28.

[31]I have based these figures on statistics in the files of the Department of Pensions, annual reports of the Board of Pension Commissioners, and annual reports of the fire and

passed, there was not only a fall in the age at which most firemen and policemen became eligible to retire but also a rise in the proportion of officers who reached retirement age. Instead of resigning or being dismissed, most officers now retired and went on the pension rolls.

Other than the Great Depression, which drove the resignation rate down to roughly 1% a year during the 1930s, there were two main reasons for the decline of the turnover rate. First, under pressure from the rank and file and the reformers, the authorities took steps that made firefighting and policing more attractive. They raised the starting salary, which went up from $115 a month to $200 a month in the 1920s and, after barely holding its own during the depression, climbed to $575 a month in the late 1950s. They gave similar raises to the superior officers. They also shortened the workday and workweek, lengthened the sick leaves and annual vacations, improved the opportunities for promotion, and increased the pension benefits for widows and other survivors. Second, the voters approved measures that made firefighting and policing more secure. At the insistence of the reformers, who were intent on cutting the ties between the local politicians and public servants, the voters adopted a charter amendment in the early 1900s that provided that firemen and policemen could be removed only for cause. And at the urging of the police officers, who were bent on enhancing the autonomy of the force, the voters approved another amendment 30 years later that turned the disciplinary process over to a departmental trial board and imposed a 1-year statute of limitations on the alleged infractions.[32]

It was not long before the LAFPPS felt the impact of these changes. Between 1926 and 1951, the average fireman and policeman was appointed at age 27, put in 22 or 23 years, retired at age 50, and, according to the United States Life Tables, lived another 22 or 23 years. In other words, he spent 1 year on a pension for each year on the job. Little wonder that the pension rolls swelled. Between 1922 and 1960, the LAFPPS, which had hitherto given out 218 pensions, granted another 5662, of which 3396 (or 60%) were for service, 804 (or 16%) for disability, and 1462 (or 24%) for widows and other dependents. By 1960 the system had on its rolls 3840 beneficiaries, or one beneficiary for every two firemen and policemen. Of this number, 2282 (or roughly 60%) were service pensioners, all of whom had presumably been able bodied at retirement and nearly one-quarter of whom would not yet have been eligible for a

---

police departments. For somewhat different figures, see Protective League, *History of the Department of Pensions*, pp. 5–6. For the Municipal League's reaction to the decline in the turnover rate, see its *Bulletin*, 20 September 1931, pp. 2–3.

[32]Jack Halstead, "Let's Talk Pensions," *Los Angeles Fire and Police Protective League News*, June 1962, pp. 1, 5–7; Fogelson, *Big-City Police*, pp. 79, 184.

pension if the city council had retained the original age requirement. The swelling rolls, plus the rising salaries, drove the total benefits up from $115,000 in 1922 to $580,000 in 1930, $1.7 million in 1940, $4.7 million in 1950, and $13.3 million in 1960. Thus for every dollar Los Angeles spent on fire and police payrolls in 1960, it paid out roughly 25 cents for fire and police pensions, fully 21 cents more than in 1922.[33]

As early as 1917, 4 years after the city council lowered the age requirement to 55, the Municipal League began to voice its concern about the financial condition of the fire and police pension systems. Citing the record of New York City, whose pension systems were much older but no more liberal than Los Angeles', the league warned that the benefits, then only 3% of payroll, might in time climb to as much as 16%. When the firemen and policemen appealed to the council 2 years later to abolish the age requirement and otherwise liberalize the pension systems, the league argued that the changes would weaken the city's fiscal position. Pointing to the history of the London pension system, whose costs had climbed from 1% of payroll to 29%, the league claimed that Los Angeles might later have to put 30 cents into pensions for each dollar it spent on salaries.[34] The league was not opposed to pensions per se, its spokesmen stressed, but it believed that any scheme to change the system should include a detailed estimate of the fiscal implications. It also held that the council should defer action on any legislation until it hired an actuary to do a study of the fire and police pension systems. The study, which was done in 1922, revealed that the two systems had incurred an unfunded liability of $6 million, which was even more than the league had anticipated.

According to the Municipal League, the LAFPPS was heading for trouble largely because it was violating the two cardinal principles of a sound pension system. The first principle was that the system should be contributory, that is, the employees should bear a fair share of the costs, preferably one-half. The other half should be borne by the employer. Underlying this principle was the conviction that a pension system served the interests of both employer and employees. It not only enabled the employer to get rid of superannuated employees but also protected the employees against the hazards of old age. Under a provision of the original enabling act, the city had at first deducted two dollars a

[33]"Service Pensions—Fire and Police"; "Pensions Granted: Summary of Number and Yearly Totals of Pensions Granted During the Years Listed Below"; "Analysis of Pensions," LACC Files, No. 21072; Department of Health, Education, and Welfare, *Life Tables*, p. 14; City of Los Angeles, Board of Pension Commissioners, *Annual Report: 1960*, pp. 6, 35; Department of Pensions, "Fire and Police Pension System," p. 8.
[34]Municipal League of Los Angeles, *Bulletin*, 12 November 1917, pp. 5–6; Anthony Pratt to City Council, 22 April 1919, LACC Files, No. 867.

month from the salary of the firemen and policemen and put it into their pension funds. The council, however, dropped this provision in 1913 and in its place adopted a policy by which the city contributed 2.5% (and 6 years later, 3.5%) of fire and police payrolls to the pension systems. The league sharply criticized the council's position. A noncontributory policy would destroy the "mutuality of interest" between employer and employees and put an intolerable burden on the taxpayers. Citing a letter from the Carnegie Foundation, which had been asked to evaluate the LAFPPS, the league warned that a noncontributory policy would eventually drive the pension system into bankruptcy.[35]

The issue came to a head in 1926, when the Los Angeles Fire and Police Protective League, which had been organized by the firemen and policemen in 1922, mounted a campaign to raise the minimum salary from $170 to $200 a month. The campaign created a splendid opportunity for the Municipal League and other critics of the LAFPPS, who threatened to withhold support for the salary hike unless the firemen and policemen came out in favor of pension reform. Forced on the defensive, the Protective League stated that its members were willing to pay one-half the cost of the service pensions but thought the public should bear the full cost of the disability pensions. To further mollify the critics, who were incensed that many able-bodied officers were retiring in their early and middle 40s, the Protective League declared that its members would not oppose a change in the service requirement. After some negotiation, the council placed a charter amendment on the ballot that required each member to contribute 4% of his wages to the pension system and raised the service requirement from 20 to 25 years. At the urging of the Protective League, Municipal League, and property owners associations, which charged that the LAFPPS "smacked too much of charity," the voters approved the amendment in 1926.[36] It remained in force until 1947, when the voters passed another charter amendment that increased the contribution rate to 6%, rolled back the service requirement to 20 years, and established an off-duty disability pension.

Between 1927 and 1960, the firemen and policemen contributed about $37 million, or just over $1 million a year, to the pension system. And

[35]Anthony Pratt to City Council, 23 June 1922, LACC Files, No. 2404; *Los Angeles Times,* 25 March 1922; Municipal League of Los Angeles, *Bulletin,* 28 August 1925, p. 6; Protective League, *History of the Department of Pensions,* p. 1; Meriam, *Retirement of Public Employees,* pp. 96–97.

[36]Howard T. James to City Council, 25 March 1925, LACC Files, No. 1090; Joseph H. Stace to City Council, 17 September 1926, LACC Files, No. 2661; *Los Angeles Times,* 24 January 1926; Protective League, *History of the Department of Pensions,* pp. 2–3; Harold J. Scott, "The Record of Twenty Successful Years," *The Firemen's Grapevine,* August 1943, p. 21.

yet they bore only a little more than one-quarter of the system's costs, which was much less than the Municipal League had hoped for.[37] To understand why, it is instructive to look at the 61 firemen and policemen who retired on service pensions in 1952. According to the LAFPPS, these officers had served an average of 24 years before retiring, which meant that on average they were appointed in 1928. The base pay in 1928 was $200 a month, and it remained so until 1943, when the council approved the first in a series of raises that brought it up to $395 a month in 1952. Thus for the first 15 years, the 61 officers contributed 4% of $200 a month (or, if they had been promoted, 4% of a salary that was pegged to $200 a month). For the next 9 years, they put in 4% or, after 1947, 6% of from $250 to $395 a month. Yet upon retiring these officers were entitled to roughly one-half of their average salary in the last 3 years, which came to about $370 a month. In point of fact, they drew on average a pension of $210 a month, which was more then they had earned during most of their careers.[38] Incidentally, the 37 firemen and policemen who retired on disability pensions in 1952 (and were therfore entitled to 50–90% of their final salary) received an average of $240 a month.

The second principle of a sound pension system was that the system should be funded. By this the Municipal League meant that the city should put into the pension system each year enough money not only to cover current expenses but also to build up a fund that if prudently invested would produce enough income to meet future obligations. Underlying this principle was the assumption that the taxpayers should pay their full share of the pension costs as the costs were incurred rather than when they came due. The LAFPPS, however, was not funded. It operated on a "pay-as-you-go" basis. The city council simply appropriated enough money annually to make up the difference between the system's revenues and expenses. No funds were put aside for the time, at most 20 or 25 years in the future, when a large and rapidly growing number of newly appointed firemen and policemen would be eligible for a service pension. The Municipal League charged that this arrangement was highly irresponsible. It permitted one generation of taxpayers to ease the eligibility requirements, raise the benefit levels, and otherwise liberalize the system and then to pass the costs on to another generation of taxpayers. If the costs were passed on from gener-

---

[37]"Fire and Police Pension Fund: Revenues," LACC Files, No. 21072; Pension Commissioners, *Annual Report: 1960*, p. 35.

[38]"Service Pensions—Fire and Police"; Jack Halstead, "Let's Talk Salaries," *Los Angeles Fire and Police Protective League News*, June 1962, pp. 1, 5–7; "Pensions Granted: Summary of Number and Yearly Totals of Pensions Granted during the Years Listed Below."

ation to generation, a point would eventually be reached when the taxpayers would be hard put to meet current expenses and the system
would be hard pressed to avoid bankruptcy.[39]

The league's efforts were rewarded in 1922, when the voters adopted
a charter amendment that placed the LAFPPS on a funded basis. But this
success was short-lived. Eight years later, in the depths of the depression, an actuary recommended that the city put an additional 44% a year
into the fund. Unwilling to accept this recommendation, the Protective
League and the Chamber of Commerce financed another actuarial report. Done by the nation's foremost actuary, this report concluded that
the city should put in an additional 100% a year. Well aware that the
hard-strapped taxpayers would not stand for such a hike, the council
submitted a charter amendment that returned the LAFPPS to a "pay-
as-you-go" basis. The voters approved the amendment in 1932.[40] The
issue emerged again in the mid-1950s, when an actuary disclosed that
the system's unfunded liability had gone up to $169 million. Stunned by
this finding, Mayor Norris Poulson appointed a citizens' committee to
look into the problem. The committee, which represented the Protective
League, the Chamber of Commerce, and other groups, disagreed about
eligibility requirements and benefit levels. It agreed, however, that the
city should abandon the "pay-as-you-go" policy. On the committee's
recommendation, the council submitted a charter amendment that put
the system back on a funded basis and directed the city to amortize the
unfunded liability within 50 years. The voters adopted the amendment
in 1959.[41]

Despite the objections of the Municipal League and other civic groups,
the LAFPPS operated on a "pay-as-you-go" basis for all but 10 of its first
60 years. The depression was partly responsible for this turn of events. If
the economy had not collapsed, the voters would probably not have
abandoned the funded system (or at any rate not in the early 1930s). But
the recovery was well underway by the early 1940s and yet it took almost
another 20 years for the voters to return the LAFPPS to a funded basis.
The system stayed on a "pay-as-you-go" basis through the late 1950s for
several reasons. For one, the Protective League opposed a change on the
grounds that a funded system would cost the taxpayers more than a

[39]Anthony Pratt to City Council, 1 August 1921, LACC Files, No. 2146; *Los Angeles
Times*, 25 March 1922; Meriam, *Retirement of Public Employees*, pp. 60–62, 328–337.

[40]*Los Angeles Times*, 31 August, 6 December 1931, 11, 15, 21 February, 25 March, 26 April
1932; Protective League, *History of the Department of Pensions*, pp. 4–8.

[41]*Los Angeles Examiner*, 28 January 1954; Devore to Poulson, 24 January 1957; James
Carbray to Norris Poulson, 16 January 1957, LACC Files, No. 77868; Samuel Leask, Jr., to
Charter and Administrative Code Committee, 1 December 1958, LACC Files, No. 77868,
Supplement No. 3.

"pay-as-you-go" system—a position that had long been discredited by the actuarial profession, the league's critics pointed out.[42] For another, the politicians were reluctant to push for a change if it meant taking on the firemen and policemen, who were a formidable political force, and stirring up the taxpayers, who would have had to pay more in the short run under a funded plan. It was far better to let future politicians deal with the problem. For yet another, the voters were probably too confused by the actuarial jargon to understand fully the fiscal implications of a "pay-as-you-go" system, and even if they had understood them, the voters might well have preferred to pass the costs on to the next generation of taxpayers.

Between 1928 and 1959, when the LAFPPS went back on a funded basis, the city paid about $85 million, or roughly $2.5 million a year, into the system, which was around two and a half times as much as the firemen and policemen contributed. In 1960 the city shelled out $6.3 million more, which was roughly 12% of the fire and police payrolls and about 7% of the city's property taxes. Combining the city's appropriations with the members' contributions and the earnings on investments, the LAFPPS was able to meet its current obligations, which was more than some other fire and police pension systems were able to do so. It was even able to build up a reserve of $14 million, which was about what its expenses came to in 1960. But the system was unable to put aside enough money to help cover its future obligations, much less to amortize its prior obligations. Its unfunded liability skyrocketed. Between 1922 and 1932, when the LAFPPS was on a funded basis, the deficit rose from $6 million to $24 million. From 1932, when the system went back on a "pay-as-you-go" basis, to 1954, when the next actuarial survey was made, it climbed to $169 million. During the next 6 years, it jumped to $315 million. Thus between 1922 and 1960 the system's unfunded liability increased from $3000 to $40,000 for each fireman and policeman, from two to six times the fire and police payrolls, and from 1% to more than 8% of the city's assessed value.[43]

By the early 1960s, shortly after the LAFPPS was put back on a funded basis, the authorities were under pressure to change the system again. The pressure came largely from two groups, the Chamber of Commerce and the Fire and Police Protective League. The chamber, which was the spokesman for the city's commercial and industrial elites and the succes-

---

[42]"Your Pension System," *Los Angeles Fire and Police Protective League News*, 15 February 1954, p. 1.
[43]"Fire and Police Pension Fund: Revenues"; Pension Commissioners, *Annual Report: 1960*, pp. 5, 28, 35; Protective League, *History of the Department of Pensions*, pp. 3–8; *Los Angeles Examiner*, 28 January 1954; Los Angeles City Controller, *Annual Report: 1974*, p. 104.

sor to the Municipal League as the watchdog of the LAFPPS, was concerned about the rising cost of the system. To take the LAFPPS off a "pay-as-you-go" basis was not enough, the chamber pointed out; it was also imperative to cut the system's expenses, either by tightening eligibility requirements or by reducing benefit levels. Along with several taxpayers groups, the chamber had been pushing for such changes for well over a decade, but thus far it had been stymied by the vigorous opposition of the Protective League.[44] The league, which represented the active (and, to a lesser degree, retired) firemen and policemen, was troubled too, but by a different problem. Many of the retired officers (and their widows) were on a fixed pension that was pegged to the salaries of the 1930s and 1940s. With the steady rise in the cost of living, some of them were close to destitute. Although the voters had refused to give a cost-of-living adjustment to disabled firemen and policemen in 1959, the league was determined to win for its members a hedge against inflation in the years ahead.[45]

The city council responded to this pressure by instructing the city administrative officer, C. Erwin Piper, to do a study of the LAFPPS and figure out what if any steps should be taken to revise the system. A former FBI agent with a Ph.D. in public administration and a profound grasp of local politics, Piper was well qualified for this job. Starting in late 1963, Piper and his staff held a series of separate meetings with each of the groups which were vitally interested in the policies of the LAFPPS. The meetings dealt with eligibility requirements, benefit levels, funding arrangements, members' contributions, cost-of-living adjustments, and a wide range of other issues. Two principal points of view emerged out of these meetings. One, which was expressed by the Chamber of Commerce and the California Taxpayers Association, held that the pension system was too liberal. Its advocates suggested that the city reimpose an age requirement, raise the service requirement, lower the disability payments, and retain a fixed pension. The other point of view, which was articulated by the Protective League, Chief William H. Parker, and several retired officers groups, felt that the system was not

---

[44]Los Angeles Chamber of Commerce, "Proposed City of Los Angeles Charter Amendment No. 1," Report of the State and Local Government Committee, 9 February 1959, pp. 1–5; Los Angeles City Administrative Officer, "Review of Fire and Police Pension System," minutes of meetings of 17 and 27 December 1963; all of these reports are in the City Administrative Officer Files, City Hall, Los Angeles (hereafter cited as CAO Files).

[45]Walter C. Peterson to Los Angeles City Attorney, 17 March 1959, Los Angeles Fire and Police Protective League, "Statement of Policy," 9 March 1959, Samuel Leask, Jr., to Personnel Committee of City Council, 9 March 1959, Los Angeles Fire and Police Protective League, "Argument in Favor of Proposed Charter Amendment No. 1," all in LACC Files, No. 88060.

liberal enough. Its supporters proposed that the city maintain the current eligibility requirements and benefit levels and establish fluctuating pensions, which should be pegged either to fire and police salaries or to the cost of living.[46]

Following these meetings, Piper and his staff began to draft a new pension system that would provide at least equivalent benefits to the firemen and policemen and reduce the costs to the taxpayers. He submitted his recommendations to the council in November 1965. Under the proposed system, which would cover new recruits and veteran officers who elected to join, firemen and policemen would have to serve 25 years and reach age 50 to be eligible for a service pension. At age 55 (or, for disabled officers, at 55 or after 5 years on a pension, whichever came first) retired officers (or their survivors) would receive an automatic 1.5% a year increase in their base pension. To pay for the new pension system, the members would contribute 6% of their salaries, plus one-half of the expense of the cost-of-living increase, and the city would put in enough money to meet the entry-age cost and the interest on the unfunded liability. To alleviate the plight of the retirees and their families, whose benefits were pegged to the salary levels of the 1930s and 1940s, the minimum pension would henceforth be $150 a month if the recipient were single and $200 a month if married.[47] The proposed system was an ingenious effort to provide relief for the taxpayers and security for the officers in a way that would be acceptable to the Chamber of Commerce and the Protective League.

But Piper's proposal was not acceptable to the league, whose president called it "a slap in the face to every policeman and fireman."[48] At the core of the league's opposition were its objections to the proposed changes in the eligibility requirements. The league argued that the imposition of an age requirement was inadvisable in policing, firefighting, and other extremely hazardous, quasi-military occupations that needed young men in prime physical condition. The league also claimed that an extension of the service requirement was inappropriate at a time when the fire and police departments were finding it hard to attract qualified recruits. To retain veteran officers the city should not tighten eligibility requirements, the league insisted; instead, it should offer them incen-

[46]Los Angeles City Administrative Officer, "Review of Fire and Police Pension System," minutes of meetings of 3, 4, 5, 10, 15, and 27 December 1963, CAO Files; Piper to City Council, 8 June 1964, app. pp. 1–22, LACC Files, No. 116278.

[47]Piper to City Council, a report on "Proposed New Fire and Police Pension System," 24 November 1965, pp. 3–10, LACC Files, No. 116278. Under no circumstances would the members have to contribute more than 2% of their salaries for the cost-of-living adjustment.

[48]Los Angeles Herald-Examiner, 6 December 1965.

tives to stay on the job. The benefits should be set at 2% of final salary for each of the first 24 years of service, raised to 55% after 25 years, and set at 3% for each additional year, up to a maximum of 70%. The pensions should be pegged to the cost of living, but to hold down expenses, the increases should be restricted to service pensioners (and their survivors), deferred until the twenty-fifth anniversary of their appointments, and limited to 2% a year.[49] These recommendations were incorporated into a plan that the league submitted to the council in June 1966.

Piper opposed the league's plan. It offered the city nothing in return for the cost-of-living adjustment, he pointed out. The city would do better to adopt a modified version of his own plan, which lowered the service requirement to 20 years, raised the cost-of-living adjustment to a maximum of 2% a year, and hiked the minimum benefits to $250 a month for retired officers and $200 for their widows. Also opposed to the Protective League's plan was the Chamber of Commerce, which objected on the grounds that it would cost the taxpayers an additional $5 million per year, permit officers to retire regardless of age, and require the city to pay only the interest on the unfunded liability. Despite the opposition, the league pressed the council to put its plan on the ballot in the November election. Its spokesmen stressed that the plan would not only protect the officers against inflation and help the departments recruit qualified personnel but also reduce the costs of the system by encouraging the veteran officers to remain on the force. The league, which in Piper's opinion probably had "more political clout than any other group in city government" and was prepared to use all it had on this issue, brought strong pressure on the councilmen. And after making some minor revisions, notably one that required the city to continue to amortize the unfunded liability but extended the deadline from 50 to 70 years, the council voted nine to four to submit the league's plan to the voters.[50]

Shortly thereafter the Protective League launched a campaign on behalf of what was officially listed as Proposition P. Following a strategy it

[49]John A. Thompson to City Council, 14 June 1966, LACC Files, No. 130081; "Pension Report," *Los Angeles Fire and Police Protective League News*, March 1966, pp. 1–6.

[50]C. Erwin Piper, "Proposed New Fire and Police Pension System," report to the Police, Fire, and Civil Defense Committee, 13 July 1966, pp. 3–10, LACC Files, No. 116278; Los Angeles Chamber of Commerce, State and Local Government Committee, "Proposed New Fire and Police Pension System," 4 August 1966, pp. 1–3, LACC Files, No. 116278; *Los Angeles Herald-Examiner*, 9 August 1966; *Van Nuys News*, 11 August 1966; *Los Angeles Times*, 13 March 1972. For an analysis of the council's decision, see Ilene G. Greenberg, "Going Through the Motions: A Study of Pension Reform in Los Angeles" (Paper written for the Harvard-MIT Joint Center for Urban Studies' project on municipal employee unions).

had used to promote other charter amendments, the league persuaded a group of distinguished citizens, headed by former governor Goodwin Knight, to come out in favor of Proposition P. It got endorsements from Mayor Sam Yorty, 10 of the 15 councilmen, 14 of 15 members of the fire, police, and pension commissions, and the chiefs of the fire and police departments. The league even prevailed on the Chamber of Commerce and California Taxpayers Association to refrain from including an opposing statement in the Information Pamphlet that was sent to every registered voter. Using broadsides, advertisements, and canvassers, many of whom were off-duty firemen and policemen, the league stressed the same points it had made to the council in August. Besides modernizing an out-dated pension system, Proposition P would help the city to attract qualified recruits, retain veteran officers, and maintain public safety, an argument that probably struck a responsive chord in the wake of the 1965 riots in south-central Los Angeles. It "will not require an increase in taxes!" either, the league declared. Speaking for the opposition, the Property Owners Tax Association of California warned that Proposition P would raise taxes by more than $5 million a year and pleaded with the voters to turn down the amendment. In the end Proposition P carried by a majority of slightly more than 60%.[51]

As a concession to the Chamber of Commerce and taxpayers associations, the league had restricted the cost-of-living adjustment to service pensioners and their survivors and limited it to 2% a year. Once Proposition P was approved, the league moved to eliminate these provisions. In 1969 it asked the council to put on the ballot a charter amendment extending the cost-of-living increase to disability pensioners and their survivors. The council, which had turned down the same request in 1967, agreed. Although the Chamber of Commerce 'and taxpayers groups were far from enthusiastic about the proposed change, they were hard pressed to come up with a good reason why the city should give a cost-of-living increase to some pensioners and not to others. The voters, who had rejected a similar proposal in 1959, adopted the measure by a majority of close to two to one.[52] Two years later the league drafted a charter amendment lifting the ceiling on the cost-of-living adjustment and pegging it point by point to the Consumer Price Index. The

[51]*Los Angeles Times*, 23 August 1966; "Proposition P," *Los Angeles Fire and Police Protective League News*, October 1966, p. 1; Melvin Horton, secretary of Property Owners Tax Association of California, transcript of broadcast on KNXT, 13, 14 October 1966, CAO Files; "Vote Yes on P," Los Angeles Fire and Police Protective League broadside, CAO Files; "Argument in Favor of Proposed Charter Amendment 'P'," Election Division Files, City Clerk's Office, Los Angeles.

[52]Piper to Sam Yorty, 29 January 1969, CAO Files; "Argument in Favor of Proposed Charter Amendment No. 2," Election Division Files.

Chamber of Commerce and taxpayers associations were dismayed by the proposal, the fiscal implications of which were staggering, but they were hard put to explain the logic of a 2% ceiling. In another demonstration of its political clout, the league prevailed on the council to put the proposal on the ballot. After a vigorous campaign, in which the firemen and policemen contributed more than $300,000 to the league's warchest, the amendment carried by a vote of 226,000 to 218,000, slightly less than 2%.[53]

In the meantime, the pension rolls swelled, rising from 3840 in 1960 to 7448 in 1976, by which time there were nearly three beneficiaries for every four firemen and policemen. With salaries pegged to prevailing wages in Los Angeles and, after 1966, benefits pegged to the cost of living, the pension costs soared, climbing from $13 million to $70 million. To cover the current expenses and amortize the unfunded liability, the city put $103 million into the LAFPPS in 1976, which was close to $97 million more than it spent in 1960. This was about seven times as much as the firemen and policemen contributed to the system and four times as much as the system earned on its investments. It was also 49% of the fire and police departments' payrolls, 35% of the city's property taxes, and 8% of its total expenditures. With another $38 million going into the City Employees' Retirement System, Los Angeles spent close to one-half of its property taxes on its pension funds. After 1964 the LAFPPS's revenues exceeded its expenses. But its unfunded liability continued to go up, climbing from $315 million in 1960 to $1.5 billion in 1976. To put it another way, it rose from $40,000 to $150,000 for every fireman and policeman, from six to seven times the fire and police payrolls, and from one-twelfth to one-sixth the assessed value of the city.[54]

As things stand now, the pension rolls will swell in the years ahead, with the number of beneficiaries gradually approaching the number of firemen and policemen. As salaries go up and the cost of living climbs, the pension costs will also increase, probably rising above 50% of fire

[53]Otho R. Allen to City Council, 9 March 1970, LACC Files, No. 70–5576; Milton Harker, secretary of the Property Owners Tax Association of California, transcript of broadcast on KGIB, 2 May 1971, CAO Files; Los Angeles Chamber of Commerce, State and Local Government Committee, "Fire and Police Pension Charter Amendment Proposition 2, May 25, 1971," 6 May 1971, CAO Files; "Argument in Favor of Proposed Charter Amendment No. 2"; Los Angeles Fire and Police Protective League, "Official Audit and Report for the Campaign to Pass Charter Amendment 2," 1971. For an analysis of the league's campaign, see Janet M. Corpus, "Dollar for Dollar: A Study of the Cost of Living Escalator in the Los Angeles Fire and Police Pension System" (Paper written for the Harvard-MIT Joint Center for Urban Studies' project on municipal employee unions).

[54]Pension Commissioners, *Annual Report: 1960*, pp. 6, 35; City of Los Angeles, Board of Pension Commissioners, *Annual Report: 1976*, pp. 7, 11, 35, 36; Los Angeles City Controller, *Annual Report: 1976*, Schedule C–3.

and police payrolls. The LAFPPS (and to a lesser degree the CERS) will need more and more money from the city. Barring an economic catastrophe of the magnitude of the Great Depression, Los Angeles will be able to honor its obligations to the retired officers and their dependents. It is not Hamtramck, the small rundown industrial city adjacent to Detroit whose mounting pension bills drove it to the brink of bankruptcy in the early 1970s.[55] Los Angeles is a great metropolis, with a healthy and diversified economy, a modern physical plant, and a large and growing tax base, which has not yet been fully tapped. It has ample resources to weather the fiscal storms that have beset New York, Cleveland, and other eastern and midwestern cities in recent years. But if the LAFPPS will not drive Los Angeles to the brink of bankruptcy (or even force it, like New York City, into de facto receivership), the system will impose a heavy burden on the taxpayers. Perhaps even more important, it will compel Los Angeles to allocate its resources in the years ahead in a way that will exacerbate some of its pressing social problems.

Two of these problems are worth spelling out. For some time many residents have appealed to the municipal authorities to stop the rising crime rate and the apparent breakdown of public order. Unshackle the police department, they have proposed; abolish plea bargaining, impose mandatory sentencing, and eliminate the parole board. At the same time other residents have pleaded with municipal authorities to help blacks and other minorities to gain access to the fire and police forces and other public agencies which are overwhelmingly white. Start recruiting in the ghettos, they have recommended; rewrite the civil service tests, downgrade the character checks, and impose a residency requirement.[56] Both groups have favored an expansion of the fire and police forces: one on the grounds that it would raise the level of public order, the other on the grounds that it would increase the opportunities for minority groups. There is much to be said for this proposal, especially because Los Angeles has relatively few officers for a city of its size. In 1970 its police department had 6103 officers, or 1 for every 461 residents, and its fire department had 3162 officers, or 1 for every 891 residents, both of which were much less than most other big-city departments. Of the nation's 10 largest cities in 1970, only Dallas and Houston, the 2 southern cities in the group, had fewer firemen and policemen per capita than Los Angeles.[57]

---

[55]*Wall Street Journal*, 24 November 1975; D. Smith, "Hamtramck: Waiting for Pilsudsky," *The Nation*, 10 January 1972, pp. 41–43.
[56]Fogelson, *Big-City Police*, chap. 11.
[57]International City Management Association, *The Municipal Year Book* (Washington, D.C., 1970), pp. 407, 451.

Thus far the council has not greatly enlarged the fire and police departments, which now have about as many uniformed officers per capita as they had in 1950. And it will probably not do so in the years ahead. The average fireman and policeman now costs Los Angeles well over $30,000 a year, more than $20,000 for salaries and benefits and more than $10,000 for pensions, which is a lot of money even for a well-to-do city. The council has little control over salaries, which are linked by charter provision to prevailing wages in greater Los Angeles. Indeed until 1978 it had to use a formula to compute raises for uniformed officers.[58] The council has even less control over pensions, which are pegged by charter amendment to the Consumer Price Index. To hold down the cost of firefighting and policing, the council has therefore only one option: to hold down the size of the fire and police departments. It is a trade-off: the city gives its firemen and policemen handsome wages and generous pensions and in return expects two officers to do what it takes three officers to do in New York, Chicago, and Philadelphia. The trade-off is satisfactory to the firemen and policemen. But for the many residents who believe that the two departments should be enlarged, either to improve the quality of public safety or to enhance the opportunities for minority groups, the trade-off leaves much to be desired.

Other than to close the fire and police pension system and to force the recruits to join the state retirement system, which is what Oakland did a few years ago, Los Angeles can deal with the pension problem in two ways. First, the city can attempt to raise the system's revenues. The authorities can urge the Board of Pension Commissioners to invest more heavily in corporate stocks, which are supposed to bring a higher rate of return than government bonds to tax-exempt organizations. This is an appealing idea, because the system's assets are now so large that if the board managed to hike the rate of return by just 1%, it would increase earnings by more than $6 million a year. But the board has already invested over one-quarter of its funds in stocks, which are by no means free of risk, and under the city charter it cannot put more than 50% of its assets into the market.[59] The authorities can also call on the firemen and policemen, who do not bear anything approaching one-half the cost of their pensions, to contribute more than 7% of their salaries to the system. If the officers paid one-half of the entry-age cost, which is supposed to cover the basic benefits and the cost-of-living adjustments, the LAFPPS

[58]New York Times, 1 January 1978; David Lewin, "Wage Determination in Local Government Employment" (Ph.D. diss., University of California, Los Angeles, 1971), pp. 123–125.
[59]Pension Commissioners, Annual Report: 1976, p. 35.

would receive an additional $10 million or so per year. But the firemen and policemen would not go along with a scheme that would close to double the contribution rate, and neither would most of their fellow citizens.

Second, the city can attempt to lower the system's expenses. The authorities can try to reduce the benefit levels, perhaps by basing the pensions not on final salary but on average salary in the last 3 years, which was the practice from 1927 to 1962. The authorities can also try to reimpose a ceiling on the cost-of-living adjustment, either 2 or 3%, which was the policy in Boston, St. Louis, Detroit, and other cities in 1974.[60] But these changes might not be acceptable to the voters, who have traditionally been quite solicitous of the firemen and policemen. Even if the voters approved, these changes would not go to the core of the pension problem, which is the large and growing number of beneficiaries. To deal with this issue, the authorities can try to induce the firemen and policemen to postpone retirement, perhaps by giving them more of a voice in assignments and other matters after they have put in 20 years. The chiefs of the fire and police departments would doubtless object to such a proposal as an unwarranted encroachment on managerial prerogatives, and most of the superior officers would probably agree with them. The authorities are therefore left with only one alternative, to appeal to the voters to reimpose an age requirement, perhaps 50 or 55, or to increase the service requirement, perhaps to 25 or 30 years, or to do both.

The firemen and policemen will strongly oppose any attempt to change the eligibility requirements, and if the past is indicative, they will probably get their way. During the mid-1920s the Municipal League, which was distressed that many able-bodied officers were retiring in "the prime of life," called on the council to impose an age requirement of 50. The Board of Pension Commissioners endorsed the proposal, but the Protective League strongly objected, and the council yielded to the league's objections. Several years later the Los Angeles Realty Board, which regarded the current system as "impractical," urged the council to put a charter amendment on the ballot setting an age requirement of 60. Although the Los Angeles *Times* and other influential bodies sympathized with the board's position, the council refused to go along with its request. During the mid-1950s Mayor Poulson's citizens' committee issued a majority report recommending an age requirement of 55. The Protective League, whose representatives drafted a minority report, op-

[60]Martin E. Segal Company, "Boston Police Department: Special Report on Retirement" (1974), p. 16. See also Robert Tilove, *Public Employee Pension Funds* (New York, 1976), pp. 231–232.

posed the recommendation, and though the mayor and the Chamber of Commerce favored it, the council declined to give the residents a chance to vote on it. Less than a decade later the city administrative officer came up with his plan to impose an age requirement of 50 and raise the service requirement to 25 years. But the league submitted an alternative plan that retained the existing requirements, and, as I pointed out earlier, the council put the league's plan on the ballot.[61]

Moreover, it is not clear that the reimposition of an age requirement would greatly reduce the costs of the LAFPPS. Let me explain why. Under the present system, which allows firemen and policemen to retire after 20 years regardless of age and requires a careful screening of all disability claims, only one out of four officers has retired on a disability pension. Los Angeles has done much better than San Francisco, where more then 40% of the retired officers receive disability pensions, and Washington, D.C., where disabled officers make up more than 80% of the fire and police pension rolls. Since disabled pensioners normally retire 5–10 years earlier than service pensioners in Los Angeles—and therefore not only contribute less to the system but also collect more from it—this has saved the LAFPPS a lot of money. Early in the 1970s, however, a growing number of Los Angeles policemen and firemen started to apply for disability pensions, probably because they became aware that a sizable portion of the benefits were exempt from federal income taxes. The number of disability pensions rose sharply.[62] If Los Angeles reimposes an age requirement, some officers will wait an extra 5 or 10 years for a service pension, but many others, some of whom will have a legitimate case, will apply for a disability pension instead. And the increased costs of the disability pensions may well offset the projected savings on the service pensions.

Another campaign to reimpose an age requirement is now underway. Whether it will succeed remains to be seen, but even if it does, it will be some time before the change has much of an impact on the financial condition of the LAFPPS. The reason lies in the legal status of public employee pensions in California. During the late nineteenth and early twentieth centuries, a pension was considered a reward or a gratuity,

[61]Pension Commissioners, *Annual Report: 1976*, pp. 11–17; *San Francisco Examiner*, 25 August 1976; San Francisco City and County Employees' Retirement System, *Annual Report: 1975–1976*, p. 14; *Washington Post*, 14 March 1974; U.S., Congress, Senate, Committee on the District of Columbia, *Hearings on Fiscal Pressure on the District of Columbia. Part 3: Pension Systems*, 94th Cong., 1st sess., p. 7.

[62]Municipal League of Los Angeles, *Bulletin*, 28 August 1925, pp. 5–6; Tom Ingersall to Board of Pension Commissioners, 30 November 1931, Department of Pensions Files; *Los Angeles Times*, 6 December 1931, 25 March 1932; Chamber of Commerce, "Proposed City of Los Angeles Charter Amendment No. 1," pp. 4–5.

which could be reduced or even withheld at the pleasure of the authorities. The original enabling act even included a provision by which a pensioner could lose his benefits if he were convicted of a felony, became an habitual drunkard, moved out of the state, or disobeyed the rules of the pension board. But in a series of landmark cases, notably *Allen* v. *City of Long Beach*, the California Supreme Court after World War II redefined a pension as a contractual obligation. According to the court, the authorities cannot impair the value of a pension; they may change the pension, but they cannot take something from the employees unless they give them something of comparable value in return.[63] Hence if the authorities reimpose an age requirement (or raise the service requirement), the change would apply only to new employees. It would not reduce the current expenses, at least not in the near future; nor would it lower the unfunded liability. An age requirement might cut costs in the long run, but in the short run, as Thompson said in 1972, "there's no cheap way out."[64]

ACKNOWLEDGMENTS

In addition to the Russell Sage Foundation, the author would like to thank Mr. M. Lewis Thompson, former Manager of the Los Angeles Fire and Police Pension System, and Dr. C. Erwin Piper, former City Administrative Officer of Los Angeles, for their exemplary cooperation.

[63]Summary of provisions of Los Angeles Fire and Police Pension System, 13 May 1954, pp. 7–8, Department of Pensions Files; Allen v. City of Long Beach, 45 Cal. 2d 128 (1955). On the legal status of public employee pensions, see Rubin G. Cohen, "Public Employee Retirement Plans—The Nature of the Employees' Rights," *University of Illinois Law Forum,* Spring 1968, pp. 32–62.

[64]*Los Angeles Times,* 13 March 1972. Shortly after correcting the page proofs for this essay, I learned that, in spite of strong opposition by the firemen and policemen, the reform effort had succeeded. On November 4, 1980, the voters approved a charter amendment that set up a separate pension plan for new recruits, a plan that not only imposed an age requirement of 50 but also put a 3% ceiling on the cost-of-living adjustment. (Conversation with Mr. William S. Hutchison, Assistant Manager, Los Angeles Fire and Police Pension System, November 17, 1980.)

6

WOMEN'S CLINICS OR DOCTORS' OFFICES: THE SHEPPARD–TOWNER ACT AND THE PROMOTION OF PREVENTIVE HEALTH CARE[1]

SHEILA M. ROTHMAN

Through the action of educated women, I look confidently to see the new spirit of democray test the conventional in every direction, with the result of making women and therefore the whole race very much healthier, happier and more useful than they are at present.

—Emily James Putnam
At the fiftieth anniversary
of Vassar College, 1915

The quality of medical care is an index of a civilization.

—Dr. Ray Lyman Wilbur
In the *Final Report* of the
Committee on the Costs of
Medical Care, Chicago, 1932

To examine social policy in the field of health care today is to be immediately overwhelmed by a series of fundamental disagreements. Nothing seems settled any more—not the ethics that should underlie the patient–doctor relationship, not the limits that should define medical intervention, and not the principles that should determine health insurance. In some cases, it seems we have too much doctoring, so the physician intrudes with his advice, in others too little, so the poor lack necessary services. For years doctors ranked at the top of public opinion surveys as the most trusted of all professionals, but they are now beginning to rank as the most frequently sued professionals. In 1966 a public opinion survey found that 73% of Americans polled had a "great deal" of confidence in the medical profession; by 1977 the number had drop-

[1]The material in this chapter is adapted from Chapter 4 of *Woman's Proper Place: A History of Changing Ideals and Practices, 1870 to the Present* by Sheila M. Rothman (New York: Basic Books, 1978). Copyright © 1978 by Sheila M. Rothman. Adapted by permission.

ped to 43%.[2] In short, wherever one looks there is a widespread sense of crisis, or, to make this same point in more positive fashion, for the first time in decades, new and alternative models for the delivery of health care are receiving serious and surprisingly widespread attention.

I intend to examine the origins of this crisis from a special vantage point, an interest in American social policy toward women and children. I have been brought into the field of health care because this field traditionally has involved women to an extraordinary degree—just how extraordinary will emerge in this chapter. Furthermore, the women's rights movement of the 1960s and 1970s, appropriately enough in light of this record, made health care a major point in its reform agenda. Thus, an analysis of past social policies toward women and children can inform the current confrontations between women and doctors, children and doctors, and the state and doctors.

Moreover I come to these issues as a historian, curious to understand how present-day arrangements for delivery of services and divisions of responsibility first developed. Specifically, when did it become the task of the doctor engaged in private practice to give routine health examinations to children? When did the doctor begin to offer preventive health care to women? When did it become clear that such tasks would be carried out privately, not at public expense? These developments, in fact, are quite recent. In the Progressive era, the task of maintaining health and preventing illness was a woman's task. Only in the 1920s and 1930s did the medical profession take over these traditional female responsibilities, and the causes and implications of the take-over are at the heart of this chapter.

One major event illustrates and clarifies the dynamics: the passage, the implementation, and then the defeat over the course of the 1920s, of the Sheppard–Towner Act. The Sheppard–Towner Act grew out of Progressive reform efforts by women. It assumed that the tasks of maintaining the health of women and children belonged to women. And it looked to the state to expand this role by setting up a national network of clinics in which women trained in maternal and infant hygiene would teach, especially the poor and ignorant, the best methods to prevent ill health. Clinics, in effect, were bridges across the social gap. In Sheppard–Towner, the results bore little relation to the original design. In their efforts to implement these highly ambitious programs, women reformers turned over to private physicians, and private physicians eagerly sought and accepted, the tasks initially set out for women and the

[2]The current dilemmas in the field of health emerge vividly in John H. Knowles, ed., *Doing Better and Feeling Worse: Health in the United States* (New York, 1977). The survey appears in the *New York Times*, 12 June 1977, p. 55.

state. In effect, the women and the doctors in the 1920s created the system, and the problems, with which we are struggling today.

In 1921 Congress passed the Sheppard–Towner Act, the first federally funded health care program to be implemented in this country. Its mandate was clear—to reduce the infant and maternal mortality rate—and so was its strategy—to provide states with matching federal funds to establish prenatal and child health centers. In these centers, women trained in the scientific care of children would teach expectant mothers the rules of personal hygiene and offer the parent advice on how to maintain and improve the health of her children. The effort to reduce mortality was to be essentially instructive. Advances in health care were not to come from the construction of hospitals, from medical research, from the training of medical specialists, or even from new cures for disease. Rather, educated women were to instill in other women a broad knowledge of the rules of bodily hygiene and in this way to prevent the onset of disease.

Sheppard–Towner was a stunning victory for women reformers, who saw in its passage the first result of female suffrage.[3] Here was compelling evidence that women could translate their political power into a special kind of effort to raise levels of health and welfare. For one, the act gave women a primary, although not exclusive, role in the field of community health and welfare. For another, it expanded the responsibility of the state; the act assumed that it was the obligation of the state to guard the health of its citizens. Finally, Sheppard–Towner saw itself as offering a type of service that would not conflict with the practice of private physicians. The field of preventive health care was open; private doctors would cooperate with public clinics to improve the health of women and children. These three assumptions reflected the ideas and experiences that women reformers had already learned and tested in their clubs and settlement houses during the heyday of Progressivism. Since these assumptions were critical to the structure of the program, and they are all problematic today, it is important to understand how each of them became established in health policies.

The role that Sheppard–Towner assigned to women reflected the special relationship between women and health whose origins go back to the nineteenth century. Current then was the notion that women were excessively frail, a frailty that exceptional intellectual activity would

---

[3]U.S. Congress, House of Representatives, Committee on Interstate and Foreign Commerce, *Public Protection of Maternity and Infancy*, 66th Cong., 3d sess., 1921, and Senate, Committee on Education and Labor, *Protection of Maternity*, 67th Cong., 1st sess., 1921. James Stanley Lemons, *The Woman Citizen* (Urbana, Ill., 1972), gives a detailed account of the political history of the act.

exacerbate. This judgment, perpetuated especially by male physicians, became a matter of open and vociferous debate when educators sought to establish female colleges. The doctors contended that inherent female biological disabilities did not allow girls to pursue an education and remain healthy. Women entered the classroom at their peril. In order, then, to counteract this stereotypic view, the founders of female colleges felt compelled to design a curriculum that would provide education and at the same time not prove debilitating.

They found their answer in an ordered routine, in the precepts of "preventive gynecology." The regimen, not so dissimilar from the "moral treatment" that the Jacksonian asylum prescribed to cure the insane, demanded that fixed hours for study alternate with fixed times for physical exercise. Vassar College, the first of the women's colleges, established a schedule that demanded early and punctual rising and retiring, regular eating, and daily physical exercise. The female college graduate would be physically robust and intellectually accomplished. She would not require drugs, rest cures, or surgical intervention. College training liberated women not only from the tyranny of medical dicta but also from the treatments that had dominated the lives of their mothers.[4] "College for girls," insisted Alice Freeman Palmer, Wellesley's president, "are pledged by their very constitution to make a persistent war on the water cure, the nervine retreat, the insane asylum, the hospital—those bitter fruits of the emotional lives of thousands of women." By 1900, the college had won the war. "We know," declared M. Carey Thomas, president of Bryn Mawr College, "that college women are not only not invalids, but that they are better physically than other women in their own class of life."[5] Instead of ruining the health of middle-class women, a college education guaranteed it.

The college graduate became the model that transformed the public lives of women. If virtuous habits had given nineteenth-century mothers the right to lead crusades to elevate the morality of the community, hygienic rules gave their twentieth-century daughters the right to lead campaigns to elevate the health of the community.

Educated women did not doubt their right to exercise leadership in the field of health. They had led the campaigns in their local communities and cities to establish municipal bureaus of child hygiene and

---

[4]John H. Raymond, *Vassar College, Its Foundation, Aims, Resources and Course of Study* (1873), pp. 13, 17, 76; Vassar Female College, *Report on Organization* (n.d.), p. 7. Annie G. Howe, *Health Statistics of Women College Graduates: Report of a Special Committee of the Association of Collegiate Alumnae* (Boston, 1885), was intended to provide statistical data to demonstrate that college did not ruin female health.

[5]Alice Freeman Palmer, *Why Go to College?* (Boston, 1897), p. 11; M. Carey Thomas, "Present Tendencies in Women's Education," *Educational Review*, January 1908, p. 69.

baby health stations to educate parents in the rules of hygiene. Sheppard–Towner incorporated this goal into its programs. Part of its funds would go to sending public health nurses into the home to teach better health practices. At the same time, Sheppard–Towner looked to establish public clinics where mothers would bring children for physical examinations; they would be informed not only about special deficiencies that the child might have but also about the importance of maintaining a clean home, buying pure milk, and keeping the child in the school and out of the factory. Thus, Sheppard–Towner aimed to provide specific health services while promoting all the child-welfare reforms.

Second, once women assumed that the prevention of illness had both a public and a private dimension, that infant mortality was not an immutable vital statistic but an index to the level of child welfare, they helped to establish the protection of health as a duty of the state. Sheppard–Towner incorporated this judgment. The Sheppard–Towner clinics were at one with the enlarged public school, the municipal bureaus of hygiene, and the playgrounds.

"Well-baby clinics," declared Dr. Josephine Baker, the chief of the New York City Bureau of Child Hygiene, "should be as free as the public schools, in either case the reservation being left to the parents to take their babies or children to private schools or private physicians. . . . Public health is not a special privilege but a birthright. . . . The infant welfare station is as much a part of the public function as the public baths, public playgrounds, libraries and schools."[6] Health was another of the state's obligations to its citizens.

Finally, the sponsors of Sheppard–Towner assumed that no rival in the private sector had already claimed the field of preventive health. In assigning this task to women and the state, they assumed that physicians engaged in private practice were generally unwilling and often unable to offer this type of preventive health care to their individual patients. In fact, private doctors in 1920 used their skills to try to cure those already sick; medical schools were not training physicians to conduct preventive health examinations. The Sheppard–Towner Act respected their domain. Its intervention was to the end of *preventing* illness; it would not offer remedial medical services. "It is not the purpose of the child health conference to hold examinations or consultations for the obviously ill child or baby," reported the Children's Bureau, the federal agency in charge of overseeing the act. "Sick children, if brought

---

[6]S. Josephine Baker, "Problems in Connection with the Administration of Well Baby Clinics," *The Public Health Nurse* 18 (June 1926): 330.

to the conference are referred to the family physician or other agencies for care and treatment."[7] By rigidly separating the role of the private doctor from the role of the public clinic, Sheppard–Towner proponents believed they could expand the responsibility of the state without antagonizing the doctor or infringing on his territory. No conflict of interest seemed to impede the program's promise.

It was in another way as well a reasonable expectation. The medical profession had already conceded to states and municipalities the right to intervene in the name of public health. Private physicians did not challenge the practice of doctors working from municipal or state departments of public health to control communicable disease by purifying water, milk, and sewerage supplies. They were generally disinterested in public health campaigns, defining them as charitable and humanitarian, not a part of their workaday concern.

The depth of societal acknowledgment of this division of public and private roles is best illustrated by the apathy that the most conservative elements of the medical profession encountered when trying to defeat Sheppard–Towner in 1921. Wary of any state expansion in the field of health care, the American Medical Association effort to prevent the enactment of the measure did not get far. Part of the reason for their failure may well reflect congressional fear of the new, and therefore unknown, power of female voters. Perhaps more important, the AMA found little interest within the profession. Private physicians did not vigorously support the organization because they did not believe that the programs offered by Sheppard–Towner would in any way compete with the services they offered to their private patients.[8] This was a public health program that belonged to women and the state and hence was not their concern.

Women reformers were convinced that these conservative physicians could not defeat their program. To the staff of the Children's Bureau, they were a "reactionary group of medical men who are not progressive and have no public health point of view." As such, they were that part of the citizenry that opposes "all public health which aims to make an enlightened community" and had no special antagonism to Sheppard–Towner. They simply objected to everything. Clearly, as Progressive reforms took hold in more and more communities, narrow and self-

[7]Fred L. Adair, *Obstetric Education* (New York, 1931); American Child Hygiene Association, Transactions, 1919. p. 79; U.S. Children's Bureau, *Bulletin* no. 203, p. 11.

[8]Lemons, *Woman Citizen*, pp. 163–167, describes the American Medical Association efforts in detail. The Illinois State Medical Association and its *Journal* led the fight to support the AMA effotts, but few other state associations copied their passionate rhetoric.

interested groups like the American Medical Association would lose credibility.[9]

For all this, the reformers did remain respectful of medical skills and territory. In setting up public child health and prenatal care centers, they insisted again and again that the state was supplying an essential service that could not and would not be delivered by private doctors. "When this prophylactic health service can be offered by private physicians to any extent," Dr. Baker even went so far as to say, "there is little doubt that people who can afford to pay for such service will avail themselves of the opportunity." But this was not the case; reformers were operating in an open field. The problem, as Dr. Baker explained, was not "how can we eliminate from our well baby clinic those parents who could afford to pay for this service, but rather, how can we induce them to take advantage of this opportunity for the continued health of their babies?"[10]

Moreover, the child health center defined its intervention as different than that of the average general practitioner. It would examine healthy children; the doctor treated sick ones. Rather than focus on the symptoms of disease already found in the child, the examiner in the center would measure the general physical condition of the well child. Instead of offering prescriptions or performing surgery to cure a defined illness or physical defect, the center staff was offering educational advice on how to improve or to maintain health. It was to be as familiar with the developmental patterns of healthy children as the general practitioner was with the symptoms of disease.

The professionals who embodied this new attitude and generally staffed the centers were public health nurses and female physicians. In daily practice, the public health nurse was a combination of nurse and social welfare worker, combining bedside care with hygienic advice. Appropriately enough, her training frequently came from courses offered in schools of social welfare. Then too, she was usually on the staff of a settlement house, a municipal department of child hygiene, or a public school, not a part of a hospital setting. By virtue of her work in education and disease prevention, the public health nurse became the ideal staff member for the Sheppard–Towner programs.

In translating these assumptions into practice, the Sheppard–Towner program drew heavily on the experience of the New York City Bureau of Child Hygiene. The bureau was founded in 1908 through the efforts of settlement-house workers and child-welfare reformers. Its chief, Dr.

[9]Anne E. Rude, director, Division of Hygiene, Children's Bureau, to Morris Sheppard, 7 July 1922, Files of the U.S. Children's Bureau, National Archives, Washington, D.C.
[10]Baker, "Problems of Well Baby Clinics," p. 331.

Baker, like other specialists in child hygiene, was convinced that "control of child life is more of a socio-economic than a medical problem; more a question of environmental adjustment, industrial opportunities, living wage, civic cooperation, than of medical and nursing care per se." Consistent with this orientation, the New York bureau worked to promote the health of children by educating mothers, reforming socioeconomic conditions, using the public school to detect health defects, and by referring the sick for medical treatment. In short, its slogan went, "Better mothers, better babies and better homes."[11]

Public health nurses conducted most of the activities of the department, usually at baby health stations. First set up as milk depots, where women from tenement-house districts could receive pasteurized Grade A milk at prices cheaper than those of the neighborhood stores, these stations soon were also offering hygienic advice on the care of babies and preschoolers and teaching rules of personal hygiene to expectant mothers. No one before had linked the distribution of pure milk with counseling. But to Dr. Baker, the 68 Baby Health Stations were "educational preventoria or prophylactic centers dedicated to [the] policy of keeping well babies and children well, and emphasizing the preventive rather than the curative side of child hygiene work."[12]

Public health nurses also visited the homes of expectant mothers before, during, and after childbirth; the more these women understood about hygienic care of infants, the greater were their children's chances for survival and the lower were their own risks of serious complications or death in pregnancy and delivery. The nurses offered "advice and instruction in diet, hygiene, clothing, fresh air, exercise, rest, care of the breasts, skin and teeth." They also administered urinary examinations, made appointments at dispensaries for tuberculin and venereal disease tests and at hospitals for those with serious medical problems. They referred women in need of relief to social welfare agencies—this too was part of their function. Finally, the public health nurses referred a few women to hospitals for delivery—those presenting "suspicious signs and symptoms and histories of previous prolonged and complicated labor."[13] They recognized that medical intervention was sometimes necessary to prevent death during childbirth, but these were the exceptional cases.

The bureau staff typically linked the "normal" to the "natural" in its attitude toward not only childbirth but also breast-feeding. Despite the

[11]New York City Department of Health, *Annual Report 1920*, pp. 76, 150.
[12]*Ibid.*, pp. 147, 149.
[13]In 1920, 3157 mothers received this type of care from public health nurses.

availability of pure milk from the Baby Health Stations, the nurses encouraged mothers to breast-feed their babies. Pasteurized milk was for older children; the infant deserved the breast. Breast-feeding at once promoted and demonstrated a close maternal tie between mother and child. In this way, a woman would train herself to meet the infant's needs, and later, the child's needs.[14]

The feeding of children played a large role in the bureau's activities. Fat babies were healthy babies, and the bureau taught mothers to share this judgment. Fat babies were scheduled to come to the baby health station for checkups less frequently than puny, undernourished ones came. A fat baby seemingly required less oversight. The bureau conducted "better baby" contests to educate the public in the importance of food, rest, and exercise. Fat babies also symbolized, at least to the bureau, the Americanization of the immigrant mother. Here was a sign that she had become sensitive to the precepts of preventive health care.

The bureau intended that all its program fulfill a new model for the delivery of health services. An alliance of social and medical interventions would prevent illness and cure disease; social interventions were as vital to maintaining health as medical ones were to restoring health. Thus, when the bureau initiated periodic examinations of preschoolers in its baby health centers, and of school children in the public schools, they employed both social and medical skills. The medical knowledge of the physician had to be combined with the social hygienic understanding of the public health nurse. To diagnose a defect and make a referral was only one part of preventive health care; to train the mother and the child to good health habits was no less critical.

The commitment of the New York City Bureau of Child Hygiene to illness prevention made it judge success in a novel way. It measured the effectiveness of its programs not by the number of children sent to the dispensary for treatment but by the number who did not require remedial medical care because of their programs. In effect, the absence of disease among a segment of the population prone to ill health and mortality marked progress. The bureau noted with pride a decrease in the amount of contagious disease in the schools once the public health nurses visited the institutions. So too, the bureau established "open air classes" in the public schools for the puny and undernourished child and then measured the results not by the number of children who at-

[14]New York City Department of Health, *Annual Report 1920*, pp. 159–160. The department reported that in 1913 only 54 percent of babies attending the health stations were breast fed; by 1920 the number had risen to 67 percent. In 1925, for reasons that will become clear later, the number began to drop again.

tended these classes but, rather, by the number whose health was sufficiently improved to return to the regular program.[15]

The Sheppard–Towner Act enlarged and expanded these original
programs of the New York Bureau of Child Hygiene to fit the needs of all
children in all types of communities, small towns and rural areas, as well
as large cities.[16] The very size of the task compelled Sheppard–Towner
to assign priorities. Whereas the Bureau of Child Hygiene had focused
primarily on providing services to immigrants and tenement-house
dwellers, the Sheppard–Towner programs decided to focus first on
families living in rural areas and second on those in small towns.[17]

The Sheppard–Towner program, ever conscious of its national scope,
sought to create a series of permanent governmental units that would
promote child-welfare reforms. To receive federal funds, a state had not
only to approve matching funds but also to establish a state agency that
would coordinate its health programs with the Children's Bureau. This
agency was required to be a separate unit, a bureau of child hygiene or
division of child welfare, within the state department of health. Its
concern for children could not be diluted with any other responsibility. Furthermore, this agency had to spawn county agencies—mini-
departments of child hygiene—to administer the funds. All of this
was intended to bring into being a powerful and pervasive network of
governmental bodies whose *exclusive* concern was with child welfare.
The reformers here had a firm grasp on how administrative organization
was to further social reforms.[18]

Sheppard–Towner also intended to rely upon and encourage the
promotional activities of educated women. Before a local community
would establish a Sheppard–Towner clinic, its members had to be sen-
sitized to the need for preventive health care. The availability of federal
funding would supply the impetus to begin the work. Urban women
had already campaigned on this platform; now their more rural counter-

---

[15]*Ibid.*, pp. 184–190, 211.

[16]The federal government allocated $1.24 million for Sheppard–Towner for 5 years. It was
a modest stipend for a program that intended to purchase expensive professional services,
but not for one that was primarily educative. As a result, its supporters did not find the
budget too meager for their programs. See, for example, Grace Abbott, "The Federal
Government in Relation to Maternity and Infancy," *Annals of the American Academy of
Political and Social Science* 151 (September 1930): 100. Between 1924 and 1929, there were
2978 prenatal and child health centers established in the country that used in part
Sheppard–Towner funds.

[17]Before the passage of the act in 1919, the Children's Bureau conducted a "Children's
Year," in which it tried to adapt the programs of large cities to fit the needs of rural areas
and small towns. For an example of the novel types of programs they devised, see Janet
Geister, "The Child Welfare Special," American Child Hygiene Association, *Transactions*,
1919, pp. 214–222.

parts would agitate against polluted water, inadequate sewerage, un-
purified milk, and child labor. It was their turn to promote compulsory
schooling laws, kindergartens, and playgrounds.[19]

The administration of the Sheppard–Towner program also followed
the precedents set by the New York Bureau of Child Hygiene. The
public health nurses remained the mainstay of the program, far out-
numbering the physicians.[20] They were the ones who gave hygienic
advice, encouraged breast-feeding, gave routine care to expectant
mothers. In Sheppard–Towner, too, the education of mothers was the
keynote of the enterprise. Just as the bureau's public health nurses had
entered the public schools to teach immigrant girls the rules of preventive gynecology, the Sheppard–Towner nurse taught the same lessons
to their rural and small-town counterparts. Under the administration of
Sheppard–Towner, the "better baby" contests took place at county fairs,
and health clinics were frequently held in specially equipped mobile
trucks named "the Child Welfare Special." Again, the skills of the
physician, while not ignored, were not central to the program. A few
full-time physicians assumed administrative responsibilities, generally
heading a state program, and part-time and even volunteer physicians
conducted the health conferences. But Sheppard–Towner essentially relied on the skills of women trained in the scientific care of children and
female-led community reform campaigns to reduce infant and maternal
mortality.

The federal government set up a federal Board of Maternity and Infant

[18]Abbott, "Federal Government," pp. 92–94. Abbott notes that previous to 1920, 28
states had established bureaus of child hygiene or divisions of child welfare. Of this
number, 16 were organized in 1919. She believed that this was a result of the intensive
efforts of the bureau and the educated citizens of the various states during the Children's
Year. It was the ability of this type of pressure to restructure the Department of Health that
led the supporters of the act to set these funding stipulations. Under the terms of the act,
each state received $5000 outright, and an additional $5000 was available if the state
matched the funds. The balance of the appropriation was to be distributed among the
states, if matched, on the basis of population. In 1927 only five states did not take matched
funds. Only two states, Massachusetts and Connecticut, did not participate in the program. U.S., Children's Bureau, *Bulletin*, No. 186, *The Promotion of the Welfare and Hygiene of
Maternity and Infancy*, pp. 22–23.

[19]The organizers of the Children's Year relied on the clubs of women to publicize their
efforts. See Giester, "Child Welfare," and also yearly reports on the administration of the
act. These reports continually credit women's clubs for aiding their efforts. See especially,
U.S., Children's Bureau, *Bulletin*, No. 137, pp. 24–25, No. 146, p. 19, No. 178, pp. 21–24,
No. 194, pp. 24–25. In the files of the Children's Bureau are references to the extensive
support given by the various chapters of the W.C.T.U., the Y.W.C.A.'s, and the Women's
Auxiliary of the Protestant Episcopal Church.

[20]In 1926, there were 812 nurses employed by the program. The nurses conducted
"Little Mother's Classes." The bureau estimates that there were 1365 classes held under
the program in which 22,207 girls were given instruction. U.S., Children's Bureau, *Bulletin*, No. 178, p. 20.

Hygiene to oversee Sheppard–Towner activities. The three government officials who exercised this oversight were the surgeon general of the United States Public Health Service, the United States commissioner of education, and the chief of the Children's Bureau. It was their expertise in public health, education, and child welfare that underlay the new program.

Finally, the act respected the division of labor between the private physician and the clinic that the New York bureau had established. "The principles to be adopted in administering these laws," announced the Children's Bureau, "are largely in the social and economic fields, and it is not a health measure in the sense which the prevention or cure or treatment of disease is a health measure. . . . It belongs in its health aspect to that field of hygiene which doctors have long since discovered and turned over to the laity to practice."[21] When critics persisted in asking why a nonmedical organization had any responsibility in the field, reformers responded that health maintenance demanded more than medical skills alone could provide.

> Prenatal and maternity care means more than good obstetrics; it means normal family life, freedom of the mother from industrial labor before and after childbirth, ability to nurse the child, above all, education in standards of care so that women and their husbands will demand good obstetrics and will no longer voluntarily run the risk of unnecessary child bed fever and similar preventable tragedies.[22]

Good medicine, in other words, was only a small part of a program for health. More vital were the reform campaigns launched by educated women and the hygienic skills practiced by others.

Is there any convincing way to measure the actual impact of Sheppard–Towner on the health and well-being of women and children? Some evidence demonstrates that both the infant and maternal death rates did in fact decline during the period of legislation. In 1921 the infant death rate was 75.6 per 1000 live births; by 1927 it had fallen to 64.6 per 1000. So too the maternal mortality rate was 6.7 per 1000 in 1921 and 6.5 in 1927. The gross figures, however, were not as important to the women who administered the act as was that, to them, the decline in mortality occurred in just the ways that demonstrated the critical importance of Sheppard–Towner. Grace Abbott noted that the major decline in infant mortality occurred in the lessening of infant deaths from "gastrointestinal conditions." This decrease pointed to both the importance

[21]Anne Rude to Gertrude Lane, 25 June 1921, Files of the U.S. Children's Bureau.
[22]*Memorandum* of the Child Welfare Committee of the National League of Women Voters (n.d.), *ibid.*

of better knowledge about child hygiene and the availability of whole milk at cheap prices. She also contended that the major reduction in the maternal death rate demonstrated the effectiveness of prenatal care because fewer women were dying from "puerperal albuminuria and convulsions, a cause influenced by prenatal care." At the same time, Abbott did concede that better prenatal care had little effect on some causes of maternal mortality; for example, decreases occurred in "accidents of pregnancy, other accidents of labor, or puerperal septicaemia." In fact, deaths from "puerperal hemorrhage had a tendency to increase." In short, in areas where lay education mattered, as in nutrition or good physical hygiene, Sheppard–Towner reduced mortality. In areas where the quality of medical skills were critical, Sheppard–Towner had no impact. Overall, the indicators did point to the success of the act, but physicians noted correctly that education would not be effective in all instances. But rather than to divide responsibility, to ask for medical training in addition to lay training, the doctors proposed policies that would promote medical training at the expense of lay training.[23]

For all the enthusiasm, successes, and political influence of its proponents, Sheppard–Towner was not destined to be the model under which generations of Americans would receive health services. By 1929, the medical profession had mounted a highly effective campaign that not only defeated the act but also made obsolete its assumptions about the proper methods of delivering health care. The defeat of Sheppard–Towner marked the end of female expertise in the field of health care and, at the same time, shifted the provision of preventive health services from the public to the private sector. Women trained in hygiene working in state-supported clinics gave way to physicians engaged in private practice.

Leaders of the medical profession successfully worked to expand the domain of the private doctor so as to take over the role of women and the responsibility of the state. In essence, they helped to incorporate the services offered by the public clinics into the practice of the private physician. Over the course of the 1920s, it became for the first time appropriate and desirable for a private doctor to offer preventive health services and to give advice on personal hygiene. "Unquestionably, the greatest possibilities of usefulness of the physician to the public lie in the field of preventive medicine," John M. Dodson told his colleagues of the American Medical Association in 1923. "The family physician who seeks to render to his patients the service which will do them the most good is bound to enter the field of preventive medicine: to become in other

---

[23]Abbott, "Federal Government," pp. 98–100.

words, the family health advisor as well as the family physician."[24] And his remarks were well heeded. By the end of the decade, not only children but also adults went to family doctors for periodic health examinations. General practitioners now judged both the progress of disease in the sick and the level of health in the normal. Just as easily as these doctors dispensed drugs or recommended surgery, they gave advice on personal habits.

The downfall of Sheppard–Towner directly reflected the willingness of physicians to assume these novel tasks. By incorporating preventive health care into the services of the general practitioner, the AMA was able to persuade the federal government in 1927, as they had not been able to do in 1921, that private doctors were the appropriate and the exclusive guardians of *all* matters of health, including, of course, the reduction of infant and maternal mortality rates. What is so startling, in retrospect, is how quickly even a modest program in preventive health service transformed the practice and image of the private physician.

By 1930 the average general practitioner had, in fact, shifted the locus of his services from the sickroom to the office, from a reliance on emergency calls and bedroom care to a system of advance appointments and routine examinations of the healthy. The doctor equipped and reorganized his office to provide patients with not only remedial medical treatment but also advice on the proper ways to maintain good health. For the first time, physicians began to keep detailed records of the past history and current state of health of their individual patients, to include charts on height and weight, and to measure each individual developmental change in light of the patient's past medical and social history. They began to investigate minor ailments and to encourage the correction of physical defects before incapacitation occurred. In brief, they expanded their private practices to include the functions reformers had established for the team working in a publicly funded clinic.

This shift does not reflect scientific advances. General practitioners did not suddenly discover new techniques that dramatically increased their diagnostic abilities. Nor did they obtain novel equipment that justified this change. Rather, the private doctor's assumption of public health services was a social not a medical phenomenon. It reflected, as its timing makes clear, a medical response to a political innovation.

It was the nationwide Sheppard–Towner program that was the catalyst in transforming private medical practice. In fact, by funding a Sheppard–Towner program, a community often took the first step to-

[24]John M. Dodson, "The Growing Importance of Preventive Medicine to the General Practitioner," *Journal of the American Medical Association* 81 (1923): 1428.

ward altering the private practice of its local doctors. Sheppard–Towner programs were set up only in communities that specifically asked for the service, and the request itself revealed that at least some influential citizens were committed to preventive health care. "The local support of a center," reported the Children's Bureau, "indicates that the community desires the health of the mothers and babies conserved." But the establishment of Sheppard–Towner programs required the support not only of the lay community but also of the resident medical professionals. Frequently, the state agency would not permit a local community to act without the endorsement of its local medical society. This stipulation was to prevent later conflict. It also had the immediate effect of forcing local doctors to take an open stand on a public health issue; they could not remain neutral bystanders, as they had in earlier public health campaigns. If doctors resisted the establishment of a program that promised to save babies and mothers and to improve the health of children, they were cast in an unattractive light. If they accepted the program, they agreed to the importance of preventive health care. Furthermore, the Sheppard–Towner clinics, particularly in small towns and isolated areas, had to rely on local physicians to conduct preventive health examinations—unlike the New York bureau, these areas did not have a preexisting core of physicians already active in the field of public health. Therefore, the local doctor who gave verbal approval to Sheppard–Towner had, in fact, to be at least in part responsible for its administration. Once local doctors began to offer a popular service within a public clinic, they soon transferred preventive health care to their own offices.[25]

The ambitious nature of Sheppard–Towner contributed to private doctors' incorporation of its services. The demonstration prenatal conferences that they established, for example, extended beyond the giving of hygienic advice; they were to become a model for an ideal type of full health care. The bureau did try to remain scrupulous in its relationship with the private doctors. In Minnesota, for example, before a woman could be examined at a demonstration prenatal conference, the nurse had to ask her private physician, if she had one, for permission, and after the conference a record of the examination was sent to him.[26] Similar procedures were followed in other states, and all of them had the effect of placing the family doctor in a peculiar position. From his perspective, his patients were getting a medical service from a public

[25]U.S., Children's Bureau, *Bulletin*, No. 156, p. 6, No. 137, p. 25.
[26]Report on the Sheppard–Towner program in Minnesota during 1923, Files of the U.S. Children's Bureau. Reports for Michigan and New York indicate a variation of this type of procedure.

clinic that they could be receiving from him. No wonder, then, that many of them brought Sheppard–Towner techniques into their own practices.

General practitioners were also encouraged to alter their delivery of medical services by an open and active campaign of the American Medical Association to defeat Sheppard–Towner. Beginning precisely in 1922, the first year that Sheppard–Towner operated, the AMA and local medical societies urged physicians to transform their practices, and that this encouragement followed so immediately after the passage of Sheppard–Towner that it points to its major motivation: to remove the government from the business of health care. The drive was successful. Local medical societies offered instruction to all physicians (members or not) on the techniques of well-child and well-adult examinations and on the importance of routine prenatal care for expectant mothers. Medical schools also offered instructions to encourage physicians already engaged in private practice to acquire these techniques.[27] The physicians took the time to learn the lessons.

[27]Alec N. Thomson, "Periodic Health Examinations, What a County Medical Society Can Do in the Campaign," *American Journal of Public Health* 16 (1926): 592; B. L. Bryant, "Organization of County Medical Societies for Promoting Periodic Medical Examinations," American Medical Association, *Bulletin* 19 (March 1924); Elliott B. Edie, "Health Examinations Past and Present and Their Promotion in Pennsylvania," *American Journal of Public Health 15 (June 1925): 604–605;* American Child Health Association, *Transactions,* 1927, gives examples of how medical schools conducted this work; see especially in this volume, Bordon S. Veeder, "Washington University Medical School and Child Health," pp. 281–282. I recognize that the periodic health examinations preceded the Sheppard–Towner Act. At the same time that the New York City Bureau of Child Hygiene was conducting routine examinations of infants in the baby health stations and of school children in the public schools, insurance companies were recommending periodic health examinations for their policyholders, and the U.S. Army was conducting them for its officers. Even a few industrial companies had begun to encourage their employees to undergo periodic examinations. But then, since the movement preceded Sheppard–Towner, why did the AMA wait until 1922 to endorse periodic health examinations, if not for the threat they perceived in Sheppard–Towner? Moreover, the overt links between the AMA campaign and Sheppard–Towner were not to be explicitly and openly announced, and yet there are references to the seriousness of the threat. "Thus far the medical profession has not attempted to correct the situation which caused the Sheppard–Towner legislation," Carl Henry Davis told the American Child Health Association in 1928. "What have we to offer as a substitute?" (Carl Henry Davis, "Report of the Section of Obstetrics, Gynecology, and Abdominal Surgery of the American Medical Association," American Child Health Association, *Transactions,* 1928, p. 36.) I am suggesting that the AMA is just one part of the story. I have explored earlier how the personal experience of the physician can make him/her responsive to the changeover. Sheppard–Towner itself was not the only threat. During the 1920s, commercial companies began to hire doctors to conduct these examinations. "There are springing up all over the country," the AMA warned its members in 1924, "commercial companies engaging physicians as employees to conduct periodic health examinations, anticipating a profitable business for their stockholders. It would be a reproach to the profession for a commercial company . . . to make a success in a field that is peculiarly professional." (Editorial, "About Several Things," American Medical Association *Bulletin,* 19 [June 1924]: 167.)

The official journal of the AMA published instructions for carrying out a preventive health examination and made available printed forms to help doctors take on these new tasks. Not until 1922 did the American Medical Association authorize its Council on Health and Public Instruction to "prepare forms suitable for use by private practitioners of medicine in carrying out the purposes of the periodic health examination." In a lengthy and specific article the next year, Haven Emerson, the chairman of the council, described record-keeping techniques and the equipment necessary for the examination. "The methods employed are those used in the diagnosis of disease," Emerson assured the doctors who found all this new. "The attitude of mind, the point of view of physician and patient, is the chief distinguishing feature which makes the health examination sufficiently novel and important . . . to justify the following suggestions." First, the physician was to take a lengthy and highly detailed history of his patient. Filling out the forms already in use in public clinics demonstrated a private physician's commitment to health maintenance. "Even though inquiry as to the past illnesses of the patient and his ancestors," conceded Emerson, "does not directly contribute to the exact knowledge of his present bodily function and structure, the past personal and family history must be obtained because of the light they often throw on the patient's health."[28] Still, Emerson assured physicians, if their schedules were too crowded, they could ask the patients themselves to fill out the sheets before the examination.

Emerson also encouraged doctors to restructure the style of their medical practices so as to offer preventive health services. "Health examinations," he insisted, "should be arranged for on an appointment basis and not merely as incidental to service for the sick at crowded office hours." He argued that "an appointment is in every way desirable for both patient and physician, because of the necessity of spending not less than from three quarters of an hour to an hour with each patient." Unlike the patient with a specific complaint or symptom, the healthy patient required a head-to-toe examination. Yet the new type of examination did not demand the purchase of costly equipment. Physicians usually possessed most of the tools needed for the examination; they simply had to use their old equipment in a new way: "The tape measure, tongue depressors, spot light, stethoscope, blood pressure instrument, otoscope, laryngeal mirror, nose speculum, vision chart, rubber gloves, vaginal speculum, weight scales, simple urine test and a thermometer" were the necessary tools, and all doctors had them.

The health examination, to be sure, did require a novel kind of skill

[28]Haven Emerson, "Periodic Medical Examinations of Apparently Healthy Persons," *Journal of the American Medical Association* 80 (1923): 1376, 1377, 1378.

and hygienic knowledge. "Physicians whose training and attention have been devoted almost exclusively to the treatment of serious or long-established disease processes," Emerson cautioned, "will not find themselves at once prepared to guide applicants for health service in the practices of personal hygiene." Hence, he encouraged them to review "the physiology of digestion and nutrition, and the effect and uses of physical exercise and development on the muscular, nervous, circulatory and respiratory system." But sensing the formidability of this assignment, he told his colleagues that the task was not really so difficult. There were five common disorders to be detected among people in apparent good health: "sleeplessness, constipation, overweight, underweight and arterial hypertension." To alleviate these difficulties, "the physician should be prepared to give special instruction as to hygiene, manner of life, diet, etc. according to his own opinion in helping people, who think themselves quite well."[29] In other words, by assuming the task of preventive health examinations, the doctor made his own understanding of the rules of hygiene, the model for the patients. The doctor's idea of a good diet and of proper exercise would prevail. The "opinion" of the average physician now took precedence over the judgments of educated women and, as we shall see, the consequences of this change were far reaching.

The AMA's instructions to physicians reappeard in many state journals of medicine, and state associations also mailed sample forms and lengthy instructions for conducting health examinations to their members. Indeed, this proliferation of advice, forms, and directives protected the average doctor from charges that he was starting to offer these services solely for private gain. "If it is sponsored by state, county, or district societies," Dr. Frank Billings told a meeting of the AMA, "it relieves the family physician of any accusation that he is pushing this thing for his own benefit, because it is pushed by all organized medicine."[30] The association's endorsement of periodic health examinations gave a legitimacy to this new medical role. The physician was offering a public health service and reorganizing his practice to offer modern care.

General practitioners were facing other pressure that further encouraged their incorporation of this new role. Even before the passage of Sheppard–Towner, family doctors had begun to sense a loss of confidence among patients and the general public. First, they were not identified with public health measures; many doctors did not even offer their patients immunizations against disease. Second, as E. S. Levy, the president of the American Public Health Association, noted in 1923: "In spite of the fact that regular medical practice today is comparably superior to what it has ever been, there has never been a time when the people had less confidence in it."[31] Moreover, the growing importance of medical specialists compounded the problems of the general practitioner. The specialists were becoming a dominant force within the profession during the 1920s. The rise of obstetricians and pediatricians represented the critical development.[32] The specialists appeared to be the most scientific of doctors, and they were usually more comfortable with the type of health care that Sheppard–Towner advocated. These specialists were convinced of the significance of periodic examinations for good health. "One of the most important measures to be developed is systematic periodical physical examinations," Dr. L. Emmett Holt told the American Pediatric Association. "This is fast becoming one of the most significant departments of public health. It makes possible the early recognition and correction of physical defects, the supervision of diet and inauguration of proper hygiene."[33] Given this judgment, some specialists allied with Sheppard–Towner, lending their approval to its efforts to educate the public in preventive care.

The specialists' dedication to preventive health reflected not only their concern for public welfare but also narrower professional interests. For one, their own identification with preventive medical care allowed them to set themselves apart from general practitioners. Whereas family doctors relied on remedial medical treatment, specialists would focus on the importance of diagnostic skills. General practitioners could intervene only once illness occurred, but specialists' skills in many cases obviated the need for intervention. The specialists, then, were not only offering

[31]Harry H. Moore, *American Medicine and the People's Health* (New York, 1927), p. 140. This volume also provides an excellent understanding of the crisis facing the medical profession during the 1920s. Dodson confirms it.

[32]For an account of the mounting tensions between the general practitioners and the specialists, see Rosemary Stevens, *American Medicine and the Public Interest* (New York, 1971), pp. 148 and passim. Stevens states in addition that the Sheppard–Towner program provided substantial assistance to the pediatricians and the obstetricians in their campaign to publicize their specialties (p. 200). For other discussions of these issues, see Bernhard J. Stern, *Social Factors in Medical Progress* (New York, 1927), and throughout the various *Reports* of the Committee on the Costs of Medical Care (Chicago, 1931–1932).

[33]L. Emmett Holt, "American Pediatrics, a Retrospect and a Forecast," American Pediatric Association, *Transactions* 35 (1923): 15. Earlier Holt was an ardent supporter of training women for this important task. He frequently spoke to women's clubs on this subject. See, for example, L. Emmett Holt, "Physical Care of Children," *Third National Congress of Mothers* (1899), p. 233. After the enactment of Sheppard–Towner, he wanted physicians to assume these tasks. To this end he urged medical schools to begin teaching personal health and the hygiene and care of healthy children.

the public a "preventive" model for medical services but also expanding the demand for their own special skills.

Without this shift to preventive health care, it is also doubtful whether the new specialists would have attracted sufficient patients to maintain a practice. Few obstetricians could earn a living only by delivering babies; few pediatricians could keep a practice by treating only sick children. By normalizing preventive care, the specialists expanded the opportunities for a private practice devoted solely to obstetrical or pediatric services. The specialist easily justified the assuming of these new tasks. "The duty of the pediatrician," Holt insisted, "is not only to advance knowledge in all subjects related to the growth and health of children but to see that such knowledge is applied, for of what value is our knowledge unless it is used?"[34]

The Children's Bureau, as might be expected, was eager to ally itself with the specialists to promote preventive health care. It appointed them lecturers and consultants to the program; the bureau also used them to conduct demonstration health examinations, to encourage a county or town to accept a new program, to assist in writing pamphlets for nationwide distribution, and to instruct general practitioners on the best way to conduct a health examination. At the annual bureau–Sheppard–Towner conferences, the specialists played a major role, encouraging state directors to publicize the importance of periodic medical examinations for children and expectant mothers.

The specialists did help to legitimate the programs in many communities. Sheppard–Towner in Minnesota, for example, not only employed obstetricians to conduct prenatal examinations but also gave local doctors the opportunity to consult with a prominent specialist. These encounters offered something to everyone in the community. The obstetrician received an opportunity to demonstrate to women "what constitutes a good obstetric examination" and to give a general talk about hygiene of pregnancy to which all the women of the community were invited. The general practitioner had the opportunity "to bring a complicated case for consultation to the specialist." And Sheppard–Towner programs gained prestige through this association. As the director of the Minnesota program told the Children's Bureau, "The success of the conferences is due to the effective advance work of the nurse and the fact that the conferences are conducted by well known obstetricians."[35]

The initial cordiality between child-welfare reformers and pediatri-

[34]Holt, "American Pediatrics," p. 15.
[35]Report on the Sheppard–Towner program in Minnesota during 1923.

cians was apparent at the 1922 annual meeting of the American Medical Association. The Pediatric Section approved a resolution supporting the newly passed Sheppard–Towner Act, while at the same convention, the organization's House of Delegates condemned it. A highly emotional confrontation followed. "A committee of wrath was sent by the House of Delegates to reprimand the Pediatric section," reported one physi-cian. "They were met with unrepentance and jeers."[36] Clearly, the pediatricians, if not the AMA, were comfortable allying with a program that promoted preventive health care, despite its nonmedical sponsor-ship. (Following this event, the AMA prohibited sections from making their own recommendations.)

The alliance between the specialists and the Children's Bureau played a critical role in the defeat of Sheppard–Towner. Within a short time, the Children's Bureau began to value not only the assistance of physicians but also their diagnostic expertise. Once it assumed that a high degree of medical skill guaranteed good health, the importance of the type of services offered in the clinics declined. Thus, when physicians aggres-sively set out to capture leadership in the field, to take responsibility not only for medical diagnosis but also for all types of preventive health services, they encountered little public protest. The Children's Bureau, to choose one example, did not challenge the propriety of Dr. Holt's claims that pediatricians "must be teachers and leaders of the public in all these matters. This field we have neglected in the past; we have left the subject of popular health education too much to the nurse, the social worker and the nutrition teacher, and some of these groups largely owing to our neglect, have gotten somewhat out of hand."[37]

Over the course of the 1920s, the specialist was able to establish an alternate model for health delivery that shifted responsibility for the reduction of the infant and maternal mortality rate from public health nurses to the medical profession and their institutions. First, they con-verted the supervision of pregnancy into a physician's preferably an obstetrician's, job. They minimized the significance of general rules of hygiene. The bodily processes of every woman were different, they maintained, so whereas good diet or adequate sleep might be useful for some, it could not guarantee an uneventful pregnancy in others. "We all appreciate that pregnancy is a physiological condition," Dr. Robert L. de Normandie told the directors of the Sheppard–Towner program, "but because of the fact that it may quickly become pathological, it is neces-sary to instruct each patient at her first visit to report to the physician

---

[36]Marshall Carlton Pease, *American Academy of Pediatrics, 1930–1951* (New York, 1952), p. 17.
[37]Holt, "American Pediatrics," p. 16.

any untoward symptoms."[38] The possibility of abnormality in a pregnancy was so great that the advice of public health nurses was almost irrelevant. Only a doctor who understood the complex physical functioning of the individual pregnant woman could determine what health instruction each patient required, and these instructions were not even necessarily consistent throughout a single pregnancy. "Prenatal care," Dr. de Normandie went on, "means medical supervision of the pregnant woman."[39] It now became vital for women to visit the physician's office frequently throughout the prenatal period. Instead of one examination by a physician (as initially recommended by Sheppard–Towner) for the "suspicious cases," the specialist demanded monthly visits at first, then biweekly, and finally weekly visits. The obstetrician was not only to discover gross abnormality but also to guard against any unforeseeable complications, which were, they insisted, ever so likely to occur.

As intensive medical supervision during pregnancy became appropriate, the nurse who gave hygienic instruction, whereas not removed from the office, lost all independent authority. "A properly qualified nurse may work in conjunction with the physician in the observation of a patient," declared Dr. de Normandie. "The nurse, however, must not assume any responsibility for her medical supervision; and her visits do not take the place of visits to the physician."[40] She could carry out a physician's instructions, but they were hardly a team. The total supervision of all aspects of prenatal care had become the task of the medical profession.

So powerful was their rhetoric and so compelling were their credentials that beginning in the mid-1920s, the Children's Bureau listened to the specialists and spread their doctrines. They began to urge the appropriateness of the physicians' judgment in setting standards for prenatal care. "Only by careful study of each case," reported the bureau, "is it possible to determine whether a patient should be allowed to stay at home or be sent to a hospital."[41] As the protection of the health of the individual became identified with the level of training of their physicians, the judgment of a mother dedicated to the principles of child hygiene shrank in importance; neither the specialist nor any longer the

[38]Robert L. De Normandie, "Standards of Prenatal Care," in U. S., Children's Bureau, Bulletin, No. 157, Proceedings of the Third Annual Conference of State Directors in Charge of the Local Administration of the Maternity and Infancy Act, 1926, pp. 18, 19.
[39]Ibid., p. 19.
[40]Ibid., p. 17.
[41]U.S., Children's Bureau, Bulletin, No. 153, Standards of Prenatal Care; An Outline for the Use of Physicians, p. 5.

Children's Bureau granted her a centrality in promoting child health. Regardless of the amount of maternal dedication, they insisted, each child required intensive medical supervision. Thus, while still preferring breast-feeding to bottle-feeding of infants, they did not endow it with its earlier significance. "It is important," stated the Children's Bureau's new 1926 pamphlet on standards for child health examinations, "that the feeding of normal infants whether breast or artificially fed, be supervised regularly in order that serious disturbances may be prevented by remedying minor ones. Mothers who are nursing their infants often need simple advice quite as much as those whose infants are artificially fed."[42] Now the fat baby had to come as often to the clinic as did the undernourished one. College training did not give women the complex medical understanding of child development now believed essential to raise healthy children.

These judgments came to the fore as the specialists in the late 1920s, for all the shift in Children's Bureau views, threw their weight against the continuation of the Sheppard–Towner program. They pervaded, for example, the testimony of Dr. George Kosmak, a prominent obstetrician active in the New York Academy of Medicine. Kosmak defined pregnancy as a "medical problem" and therefore objected to a "strictly medical problem being turned over to lay organizations for a solution."[43] The proper and the best method for reducing maternal mortality was to improve the training and facilities of obstetricians. Kosmak did not intend to eliminate the role of government in reducing maternal mortality but to alter it. He told the House of Representatives committee hearings on extending Sheppard–Towner that he was "not opposed to the federal government participating in any movement to improve the care of pregnant women and their offspring"; rather, he believed these patients would be best served through federal support of medical training and research.[44] Pregnant women, he argued, died primarily from sepsis infection and the toxemias of pregnancy. By understanding the etiology of these infections, which originated in individual pathology and not in

[42]U.S., Children's Bureau, *Bulletin*, No. 154, *Standards for Physicians Conducting Conferences in Child Health Centers*, p. 5. There is evidence to suggest that the number of infants bottle-fed rose just this time. See New York City Department of Health, *Annual Report, 1925*, pp. 76–77.

[43]U.S., Congress, House of Representatives, Committee on Interstate and Foreign Commerce, *Child Welfare Extention Service*, 70th Cong., 2d sess., 1929, p. 126. I have not gone into detail on the efforts of the Children's Bureau to keep the program going. They did point to a reduction in infant mortality over the decade they had served the cause. In a sense they had achieved their goal, and their arguments for continuation therefore did not seem powerful any longer.

[44]*Ibid.*, p. 125.

social or economic environment, the physician could cure them. "Research is an entirely different matter," Kosmak contended,

> from matching state appropriations to be expended in more or less unessential activities leaving the great problem untouched, namely the actual improved care of the pregnant woman. This cannot be accomplished by visiting nurses and social welfare workers—it depends on better medical attention. We are deluding ourselves as doctors as well as the public if we depend for relief on measures such as those deployed by the Sheppard–Towner and similar Acts.[45]

Sheppard–Towner was now the "unessential activity." By emphasizing the medical pathology of pregnancy and the potential ability of medical oversight, research, and institutions to eliminate this pathology, the specialists made a convincing argument. With it, they not only defeated Sheppard–Towner in 1929 but also channeled federal funds to suit their own priorities.

The defeat of the measure was not the exclusive work of the specialists. Not only did the skills of women have to be denigrated but also their efforts to deliver services with public funds had to be repudiated. The doctors had to sell the government on their superior training and the effectiveness of their institutions and to persuade them of the illegitimacy of community clinics. Whereas the specialists discredited the abilities of women, the American Medical Association along with other "liberty-minded" organizations discredited their politics. The AMA engaged in a vicious smear campaign: Florence Kelley, one of the most ardent supporters of the measure, was "the ablest legislative general communism had produced," and Sheppard–Towner was a "Bolshevik plot" inspired in Moscow. As reprehensible as the rhetoric was, so it was effective. Sheppard–Towner went down, the victim of the general practitioner's new style, the specialist's new authority, and the American Medical Association's new political power.[46]

The 1930 White House Conference on the Health and Protection of Children highlighted all these changes. The prominent role given to child-welfare reformers and educated women in earlier White House conferences on children now went to the medical specialists. Grace Abbott, who had been in charge of the administration of Sheppard–Towner, took only a minor part. The specialists who had lectured for her were in the lead, and the value of specialized medical skill as the guarantor of health was prompted throughout the proceedings.

[45]*Ibid.*, p. 125.
[46]For a complete coverage of this campaign, see Lemons, *Woman Citizen*, pp. 172–176.

Child-welfare reformers had organized and dominated the first White House conference in 1909 and expanded their role in the subsequent conference in 1919. Throughout the 1909 conference ran an optimism about the ability of educated women to devise and to execute social policies to uplift the lower classes.[47] The rhetoric of the 1930 conference was remarkably different. "Our country has a vast majority of competent mothers," President Herbert Hoover told the delegates, "but *what we are concerned with here are things that are beyond her power. . . .* She cannot count the bacteria in the milk; she cannot detect the typhoid which comes from the faucet, or the mumps that pass round the playground. . . . The questions of child health and protection are a complicated problem requiring much learning and much action." Yet it was just a decade earlier that Hoover had delivered a different message. Then, he told the American Association of Child Hygiene, "I am one of those who hope much for these problems [of child care] from the enfranchisement of women. The major part of the progress to date has been due to the insistence of our women." Within just this period, as Hoover's shift reflected, the educated mother had come obsolete. The world, it seemed, had moved beyond her skills.[48]

The 1930 conference broke with its predecessors in yet another way. The earlier conferences had focused on the dependent and deviant child; the 1930 one took as its mandate the needs of *all* children, regardless of social class. This change too reflects the obsolescence of female knowledge. Expert insight was as relevant to the children of the middle class as to the children of the poor. Regardless of a mother's social class or education, she had to consult a pediatrician in order to raise a healthy child and, concomitantly, to go to an obstetrician in order to protect her own well-being during pregnancy. The expert had assumed the functions of an educated mother.

In light of these changes, we can now appreciate two related and

---

[47]Conference on the Care of Dependent Children, *Proceedings* (Washington, D.C., 1909); U.S., Children's Bureau, *Bulletin*, No. 60, *Conference on Child Welfare Standards.*

[48]White House Conference on Child Health and Protection, 1930, *Proceedings* (New York, 1931), p. vi (italics added); American Child Hygiene Association, *Transactions*, 1920. Hoover's statements fit well with the shift he witnessed during the decade. In 1920 he was an active member of the American Child Hygiene Association, whose president was Dr. S. Josephine Baker and whose membership endorsed the efforts of child-welfare reformers. By 1923 the association incorporated the American Child Health Association and took its name. Its board became increasingly composed of physicians; its policy towards Sheppard–Towner in particular and child-welfare reform in general became more circumspect. The change in title is therefore significant. As a child hygiene association, the group assumed that problems of child care would be solved by the improvement of personal and communal hygiene—by child-welfare reform. As a child health organization, it looked to the skills of physicians, to the individual relationship between doctor and

critical developments in the field of health in the 1930s. First, this decade witnessed an expansion of federal support to research. Second, a revival of Sheppard–Towner did occur, but it was under the domain of welfare, in the Social Security Act. And the thrust of these two decisions would set the direction of social policy for the next 30–40 years at least. Beginning in the 1930s, the federal government began to fund universities and hospitals to conduct scientific research into the origins of disease; at the same time, federal responsibility for the direct health care of its citizens would be considered a welfare rather than a health appropriation. Thus, in 1930, the government established the National Institute of Health and in 1935 set up the National Cancer Institute with a $700,000 appropriation. This commitment expanded during World War II.[49] Indeed, it has been claimed by some researchers that the major expansion of federal funding for medical research in the post–World War II era followed much on the groundwork of the 1930s.

The Social Security Act in 1935 revived Sheppard–Towner, providing federal funds once again for maternal and child health services. The new program followed along the lines of the 1920s measure and even enlarged its budget.[50] But there were several critical differences in the revival, beyond its classification as a welfare rather than as a health measure. For one, the funds were specifically set aside for rural and economically distressed areas. This provision made it clear that the programs were to become not a model for health delivery services for all citizens, but a stopgap measure for those who could not afford the best type of care, the care of the specialist. Second, although public health nurses continued to provide the basic services and receive one-half of the funds, a far larger percentage of the sums than in the earlier programs went to physicians. The Social Security program paid homage to the medical profession in still another way. As much as one-third of its funds now went to funding postgraduate courses to give already practicing physicians additional training in obstetrics and pediatrics.[51]

---

patient, for the solution. A discussion of the changing nature of this organization can be found in Phillip Van Ingen, *The Story of the American Child Health Association* (New York, 1935).

[49]John E. Dietrick and Robert C. Brown, *Medical Schools in the United States at Midcentury* (New York, 1953), pp. 97–101; Stephen R. Strickland, *Politics, Science and Dread Disease* (Boston, 1972); also Stevens, *American Medicine*, pp. 279, 274–277. The government had funded research earlier through the institutions of the U.S. Public Health Service. What is novel here is research funded by the federal government in nonfederal agencies.

[50]Gilbert Y. Steiner, *The Children's Cause* (Washington, D.C., 1976), pp. 210–211.

[51]For an interpretation of the program's goals, see Edwin F. Daily to Robert D. Mussey, 27 April 1936, Files of the U.S. Children's Bureau. In the program itself most state directors were not merely physicians but those with special training in obstetrics, pediatrics, or public health administration. See also *Report of the Program for the Fiscal Year Ending June 30, 1938, ibid.*

The 1930s, then, showed a pattern of federal support that would evolve more clearly over the next several decades: Medical training and research became the core of the health program. In its name, national expenditures now looked to promote the level of training of physicians and to expand their knowledge of and their investigations into the etiology of illness. Delivery of services, as done under Sheppard–Towner, was now a part of the welfare system. What the Progressive reformers had kept together, the professionals broke apart.

When one moves from the decisions taken in the 1920s and 1930s to the issues that are so problematic in the field of health care today, an understanding of the historical processes assume a relevance that is as obvious as it is significant. In the first instance, the analysis clarifies exactly what it is that protest groups are disturbed about, whether they join under a women's rights, patients' rights, or welfare rights banner. Indeed, to a rather astonishing degree, and without any self-conscious historical sense, these groups are looking behind the medical practices that prevailed over the period 1930–1970 and back to the years 1900–1920. In ways that continue to surprise me, much of the contemporary rhetoric sounds surprisingly familiar to a historian, as though there were direct links between the reformers of the Progressive era and the reformers of today.

Links there are, but they are not so much personal as they are conceptual. The feminists of 1900 and of 1970 were both eager to use health care to advance social ends, and were both, for different reasons of course, not deferential to expertise. (If the Progressives operated in a preprofessional era, the feminists now operate in an antiprofessional one.) And a sense of the intended and unintended effects of the first reform makes its successor movement seem all the more reasonable and may well heighten our empathy for it. The practice of medicine, as we seem to need to be reminded again and again, often responds at least as much (I would be ready to argue more) to social determinants as to scientific ones. Not that a historical analysis should breed or encourage a simple-minded antiprofessionalism. Rather, by explaining how it is that doctors assumed these contemporary roles, we are brought back to an understanding that there is nothing fixed, inevitable, or inherently useful in the traditional system; that gynecologists ended up as sex counselors, or that doctors became health advisors, is not testimony to the suitability of their training or the relevance of their credentials to these tasks. In this way, then, history becomes not a debunking but a demystifying discipline—and we find ourselves better able to hear the claims of protest groups and to take seriously their calls for change.

7

HISTORY, SOCIAL POLICY, AND CRIMINAL JUSTICE[1]

LAWRENCE M. FRIEDMAN

This chapter deals with a few aspects of the history of criminal justice in the United States. It is written, however, with something of a special slant, a slant toward policy. Can society get any help in solving problems of crime and punishment from what we know or can guess about the past?

Crime, especially crime on the streets, is one of the major issues of today.[2] Since the criminal justice system has the job of catching and punishing criminals, it is not surprising that it takes some of the criticism. Some people feel that we treat criminals too gently; others feel that the system has failed for the opposite reason: because it is inhuman, corrupt, chaotic, and inconsistent, breeds cynicism and disgust, and creates a climate that produces the very evil it is supposed to prevent.

[1]My research on the history of criminal justice, and in particular the study of crime and punishment in Alameda County, California, was supported by LEAA Grant No. 75 NI-99-0086 and by National Science Foundation Grant No. SOC 76-24217.

[2]According to a poll taken in 1976, crime was number two on the list of American worries. *New York Times*, 4 June 1976, p. 12; see also John E. Conklin, *The Impact of Crime* (New York, 1975), p. 76-77. Most people in a national survey carried out in 1975 thought that the government was spending too little on "halting the rising crime rate," *National Data Program for the Social Sciences, Spring 1975 General Social Survey* (Ann Arbor, 1975), p. 98. But James Q. Wilson thinks the fuss is less than it should be; he feels the issue has been "neglected," except by conservatives (*Thinking about\Crime* ([New York, 1975]), pp. 71-86.

SOCIAL HISTORY AND SOCIAL POLICY

We can call the two views *hard-line* and *soft-line*.[3] The voices are jarring and discordant, but they oddly enough often point to a single set of issues. Sometimes, both sides agree that something is wrong, and they even (surprisingly) agree on what in general should be done about it. Both, for example, attack plea bargaining, although for different reasons.

We have, then, a system in crisis, attacked from all sides. How did it get that way? Can we learn something from the past? We will examine three specific issues. The first, *discretion* in the handling of felons, is a general procedural problem. The second, *plea bargaining*, is a specific practice. The third, *victimless crime*, is an issue of substance, an issue about the way society defines the nature of crime.[4]

HANDLE WITH CARE:
DISCRETION AND THE DANGEROUS OFFENDER

The core of any system of criminal justice is the problem of the dangerous offender, the man or woman who is charged with serious crime (murder, armed robbery, burglary, arson, rape). At the core of current debate is the question of *discretion* in the handling of such offenders. This issue is involved even in the endless quarrel over capital punishment. The country is deeply divided and confused on this issue; the United States Supreme Court itself cannot make up its mind. First, in a landmark case, the court declared capital punishment unconstitutional, partly because it was too discretionary;[5] then the Court reversed

[3]See Herbert L. Packer's distinction between the "Crime Control Model" and the "Due Process Model" of criminal justice, in *The Limits of the Criminal Sanction* (Stanford, 1968), chap. 8.

[4]Generally speaking, the history of criminal justice has been badly neglected by scholars, and many issues that might be illuminated by historical study remain in the dark. For instance, the growing literature of deterrence—for overviews, see Franklin E. Zimring and Gordon J. Hawkins, *Deterrence: The Legal Threat in Crime Control* (Chicago, 1973); Jack P. Gibbs, *Crime, Punishment and Deterrence* (New York, 1974)—would probably benefit a great deal from studies of trends over time. Careful studies of historical crime rates are beginning to appear. They include Ted Robert Gurr, *Rogues, Rebels and Reformers: A Political History of Urban Crime and Conflict* (Beverly Hills, Calif., 1976); Roger Lane, "Urbanization and Criminal Violence in the 19th Century: Massachusetts as a Test Case," in *Violence in America: Historical and Comparative Perspectives*, ed. H. D. Graham and Ted R. Gurr (Washington, D.C., 1969); and Theodore N. Ferdinand, "The Criminal Patterns of Boston Since 1849," *American Journal of Sociology* 73 (1967): 688; cf. also David Philips, *Crime and Authority in Victorian England: The Black Country 1835–1860* (London, 1977).

[5]Furman v. Georgia, 408 U.S. 238 (1972).

itself and decided that mandatory death sentences were unconstitutional, but discretionary ones (of a sort) maybe not.[6] Exactly what the state of the law is at this writing is quite unclear.

Discretion was crucial to the argument in these cases. Indeed, it is crucial to many arguments about criminal justice. Both hard-liners and soft-liners agree that there is too much "discretion" in the system. To hard-liners, discretion makes the system ineffective; to soft-liners, it makes it unjust. The indeterminate sentence is under fire, as is plea bargaining. The hard-line view is, of course, afraid of letting dangerous people loose, or loose prematurely. The soft-line stresses injustice. Under the indeterminate sentence, a man or woman's life is at the mercy of a board or agency that can imprison for many years—or life—without recourse of law. Both sides thus want to wring discretion out of the system, as much as one can.

Discretion: It is curious to note the rise and fall of this simple English word. Its old-fashioned meanings include tact, good taste, delicacy in handling. Practically speaking, discretion refers to a kind of power, power to choose between alternates, power that cannot be effectively challenged. In government and law, a person who exercises discretion has power to use his own judgment to make final, hard-and-fast determinations. The word tends to take on a sinister cast. We hear more and more about bloated, monstrous government power intruding on our lives. Discretion now means uncontrolled power more often than it means sound judgment.[7]

Discretion is difficult to quantify or even to identify. It is found throughout government and law, at every level. The president has wide discretion; so does the policeman on the beat. In the criminal justice system, discretion is everywhere: The police have discretion, and so do judges, jurors, prosecutors, and parole boards. And, after all, so do defendants and their lawyers. There is discretion in decisions to arrest or not, to prosecute or not, to charge with murder or manslaughter, to grant probation or not. The sentencing power is particularly striking. Like cases are not treated alike, and sentencing can be a matter of whim—even a matter of the judge's digestion.[8]

Probation, indeterminate sentence, and parole are key instruments of

---

[6]Woodson v. North Carolina, 428 U.S. 280 (1976); Gregg v. Georgia, 428 U.S. 153 (1976).

[7]Kenneth C. Davis, *Discretionary Justice: A Preliminary Inquiry* (Baton Rouge, 1969).

[8]"It is reported that one judge ate his breakfast near the court building; the lawyers who had cases in his court made a practice of going into the restaurant to observe him, for his sentences would vary by years with the state of his digestion; they secured continuances on the days they observed he had indigestion." Edwin H. Sutherland, *Criminology* (Philadelphia, 1924), p. 279.

discretion. All were innovations that took hold in the late nineteenth and early twentieth centuries. At the time, they were supposed to make criminal process more humane, more exact, and at the same time more effective. Probation is usually traced to Boston, in the period before the Civil War.[9] But probation was actually not much used until the very end of the nineteenth century; in some states probation began even later. California established an adult probation system in 1903. An amendment to the penal code allowed adult probation, after conviction, if there were facts "in mitigation of punishment" (either in the "circumstances" of the case, or in the record developed by the probation officer), or if probation would serve the "ends of justice."[10] This was certainly a vague grant of power.

Probation was a step on the road to progress—at least in the judgment of most contemporaries. It gave the defendant a second chance, a chance to walk the straight and narrow path. Of course, probation had to be intensely individual. In each case, someone had to sift the facts carefully, to see whether the defendant was a proper candidate. In this way, probation *heightened* discretion, which was already part of the sentencing process. But emphasis shifted to the *offender*, rather than to the offense—in theory at least.

From the very start, the probation officer's report was the key to probation. This almost always determined whether a man or woman went to prison or jail, or went home. Judges tended to defer to probation officers. The probation officer was *the* expert on the case; he had gone over the facts minutely. Probation officers were not bound by any particular rules. They used their judgment. As one officer put it, in 1904, "I investigate their record thoroughly.... I trace men back as far as I can.... They come into my office.... I am always glad to talk to them.... I talk to them, and sometimes I talk to their employer. Sometimes the employers know why I am there and sometimes they do

[9]Charles L. Chute, "Development of Probation in the United States," in *Probation and Criminal Justice*, Sheldon Glueck, ed. (New York, 1933), p. 225. On the themes developed in this section, see also, in general, David Rothman, "Behavior Modification in Total Institutions: An Historical Overview," *Hastings Center Report* 5 (February 1975): 17.

[10]California Penal Code, § 1203, as amended. Probation officers were to be appointed from among officers of some "charity organization, society, associated charities, or . . . strictly nonsectarian charitable association," or from among "citizens, either men or women." California Code of Civil Procedure, §131. A network of unpaid volunteers, drawn from settlement house workers and staffs of charities, was intended. This was criticized on the grounds that "volunteer workers" were "well-meaning" but "not . . . very efficient." The work ought to be done "by men and women who have special criminological and penological training, and who are employed by the state." Maurice Parmelee, *Criminology* (New York, 1918), p. 403. This, of course, later came to pass. See Bernard J. Fagan, "Selection and Training of Probation Officers," in *Probation and Criminal Justice*, Sheldon Glueck, ed. (New York, 1933), p. 70.

not."[11] The reports were, or could be, based on hearsay, prejudice, rumor, or investigation, uncontrolled by any canons of evidence. Yet, for a defendant who pleaded guilty, or who was convicted (and this was the lot of most defendants), the probation officer determined the defendant's fate. The question of prison or probation was as important, practically speaking, as guilt or innocence.

Early probation reports in Alameda County, California, tell a tale of great, almost unbridled, discretion. No one passed a statute—no one could—stating that of two people guilty of the same crime, one would go to prison, and one would not, depending on family background, personal habits, and the mind and heart of the probation officer. But this is exactly what happened. It was like a jury system—without rules of evidence. What we read in these reports is, to put it mildly, legally irrelevant: that, for example, a 16-year-old boy, in 1907, smokes about 10 cigarettes a day but does not drink, "has masturbated since about 14 and still has not mastered himself altogether," "has been to houses of prostitution three times," "does not gamble" but is "fond of theatre, going weekly," and "reads magazines" but "has no library card."[12]

Probation became more and more common in the county over the years. A probation report was filed in 89% of the felony cases between 1950 and 1974 that resulted in conviction, and more than 3 out of 10 convicted defendants were put on probation.[13] It has also become, in some places, a matter of routine, of rules of thumb. In one midwestern town, defense attorneys felt they could predict what the probation officer would recommend 95% of the time. This is because they knew the patterns: All first offenders accused of property crimes qualified for probation (for example); fourth offenders charged with violent crimes did not. The judge almost always took the probation officer's recommendations. So much for probation as a careful, individual process.[14]

There were tendencies toward rules of thumb in Alameda County as well. A plea of guilty was almost a prerequisite for probation—out of 63 men referred to probation in 1909–1910 in the court of Judge Everett Brown, 62 had pleaded guilty![15] Still, there was no way for a lawyer to

[11]Ezra Decoto, in *Proceedings of the Third California State Conference of Charities and Corrections* (1904), pp. 125, 128.

[12]Report and Recommendation of Probation Office, People v. Charles H., Superior Court, Alameda County, California, Criminal Casefile No. 4347 (1907).

[13]This and other facts about dispositions in Superior Court, Alameda County, come from a sample of such cases drawn by the author and Robert V. Percival, for the period 1880–1910, with a smaller sample for the years 1910–1970.

[14]David W. Neubauer, *Criminal Justice in Middle America* (Morristown, N.J., 1974), pp. 241–243.

[15]Report, *In the Matter of Applicants for Probation*, 8 June 1910 (Criminal Files, Superior Court, Alameda County).

predict outcomes 95% of the time, or anything close to this. True, first offenders were often recommended for probation, but this was hardly a rigid rule. L. Howard Mendell, convicted of forgery in 1908 (Superior Court, Alameda County, Cal., Criminal Casefile No. 4296), had never been arrested before. But the probation officer found out that Mendell had a bad reputation. Mendell had been in trouble in the army. An old doctor, back home in Missouri, said that Mendell was a fraud, a forger, and a thief and "would have been prosecuted but for the respect in which his father, mother and brother are held. I am of the opinion that he is a very dangerous criminal." The report came out against probation, because of Mendell's "general history and character." Probation was denied.

The indeterminate sentence was another invention of the late nineteenth century. One of its founding fathers was Zebulon Brockway, who described the "Ideal Prison System for a State" in 1870: Prisoners should be "wards of the state," under the "custody and control" of prison officials; they should stay in prison until, in the judgment of those officials, there was a "reasonable probability" that the prisoner possessed a "sincere purpose to become a good citizen" and had the strength of character to live a law-abiding life.[16]

This was an idea, it seems, whose time had come. Under a New York law of 1877, courts were no longer to "fix or limit the duration" of sentences, for those sent to the reformatory at Elmira. Instead, the Board of Managers of Elmira would grade the prisoners, like so many school-children. When the prisoners had enough "marks or credits" and seemed able to "live and remain at liberty without violating the law," the board could set the prisoner free.[17] At first, the indeterminate sentence was discretionary, and rare. But in 1901, it became mandatory in New York for first offenders.[18] Other states adopted indeterminate systems of their own. The typical statute provided for a minimum sentence, often 1 year. The judge did not set a maximum—the statutes did this— while the prison board at the end of the minimum term would fix a sentence, presumably based on the way the prisoner had behaved. The Illinois statute, passed in 1899, set out a list of facts about the prisoner for the warden to note including "early social influences" that bore on the prisoner's "constitutional and acquired defects and tendencies." The

[16]Zebulon R. Brockway, *Fifty Years of Prison Service* (1912; reprint ed., Montclair, N.J., 1969), pp. 126–133; see also Edward Lindsey, "Historical Sketch of the Indeterminate Sentence and Parole System," *Journal of the American Institute of Criminal Law and Criminology* 16 (1925): 9.

[17]Laws N.Y. 1877, ch. 173, p. 186.

[18]Sutherland, *Criminology*, p. 512.

warden was also "from time to time" to take "minutes of observed improvement or deterioration of character." Meanwhile, the state's attorney and the convicting judge had the "duty" to furnish the board with more facts—whatever they knew about the convict's "habits, associates, disposition and reputation" and whatever facts would "tend to throw any light on the question as to whether such prisoner is capable of again becoming a law-abiding citizen.[19]

The theory of the indeterminate sentence was simple. No judge, not even a Solomon, could really tell when a criminal was "cured and fit to be set at liberty." Only "careful officials" who had the man "in their continuous charge" and who might "study and observe him for months and years" could do this job.[20] Prison, which would "prepare" the prisoner for life outside, must last as long as the prisoner is "unfit to be free." The prisoner must be "the arbiter of his own fate. He carries the key of his prison in his own pocket."[21] August Vollmer thought sentences should be totally indeterminate: "from zero to life... regardless of the offense committed." There were people who "should be permanently detained the very first time they are apprehended." It was as senseless to let these people go "as it is to release persons suffering from leprosy."[22]

In one regard at least, the indeterminate sentence resembled probation; it replaced some of the judge's power and discretion and shifted it elsewhere, at first to amateurs, later to professionals. And, once more, it made punishment depend on factors that were not strictly "legal" in the conventional sense. A judge's sentence, to be sure, had always been cut to the particular case, but the judge was ordinarily limited to what was presented in evidence. Under the indeterminate sentence law, punishment depended on the prison board, which fixed the real sentence. Theory, as in probation, centered on the *criminal:* was he capable of reformation? Such a judgment could hardly be made by flat rules, or in the courtroom setting. The old sentencing system had been "happy-go-lucky" and, worse, "utterly unscientific." Under the indeterminate sentence, the offender earns his liberty by his own efforts. The decision is made not by a "judge who has to guess on the spur of the moment" but by a "regularly organized board," acting "with deliberation and justice" and with "full data as to the prisoner's conduct."[23]

From the very start, of course, voices were raised against the indeter-

[19]Laws Ill. 1899, p. 142.

[20]John C. Taylor, "The Need for a 'Sure Enough' Indeterminate Sentence," *Charities*, 17 September 1904, Vol. 12, No. 38.

[21]Charlton T. Lewis, "The Indeterminate Sentence," *Yale Law Journal* 9 (1899): 17, 19.

[22]*Report of the California Crime Commission, 1929* (Sacramento, 1924) p. 65; see also "The Indeterminate Sentence," by "A Prisoner," in *Atlantic Monthly* 108 (1911): 330.

[23]Prison Reform League, *Crime and Criminals* (Los Angeles, 1910), pp. 244–245.

minate sentence. Some people were afraid that dangerous criminals might be released too soon. But at least in the early years, sentences probably became longer, not shorter. This happened, apparently, in Indiana, Illinois, and California. Those sentenced after passage of the law served more years than did those sentenced before. In California, it was claimed, some of the differences were dramatic: The penalty for rape more than *doubled*, from 9 years and 11 months, on the average, to 20 years and 6 months. [24]

Another reform of the late nineteenth century was *parole*. England developed a "ticket-of-leave" system early in the nineteenth century, but American parole really begins with the New York reforms of 1869 establishing the Elmira Reformatory. By 1910, 20 states had parole laws. [25] Parole meant early release from prison; the prisoner served the rest of the sentence outside, but under a parole officer's supervision. Parole was, in a way, a combination of probation and the indeterminate sentence: The fate of the prisoner depended on a board *and* on an officer much like the probation officer. Parole was, also, another way to give a second chance. If the defendant failed to win probation and failed to convince prison authorities to fix a short sentence, he might yet convince a parole board to release him, because of good behavior. Parole, too, focused on the offender, not on the offense.

A fourth reform is worth noting: *juvenile justice.* Juvenile courts grew up, in part, to sidestep the use of criminal process and jails for young offenders. The idea was to take young people out of the system altogether—to provide an alternate process. Juvenile probation preceded adult probation; in some states, convicted juveniles were sent to special institutions—"reform schools." [26] But children were still tried by regular courts. The first true juvenile court was set up in Chicago at the end of the nineteenth century. Here, in theory, proceedings were not "criminal" at all; children under a certain age could not (in theory) commit any crimes. But the juvenile court did not deal only with "crime" in the adult sense. The pioneer Illinois law, significantly, was a law to "regulate the treatment and control of dependent, neglected and

---

[24]See Robert H. Gault, "The Indeterminate Sentence Law a Success," *Journal of the American Institute of Criminal Law and Criminology* 12 (1921): 5. The differences were smaller for other crimes (2 months for burglary, for example), but almost invariably sentences *after* the passage of the law were more severe.

[25]Lindsey, "The Indeterminate Sentence and Parole System," p. 9. A federal parole law was passed in 1910, 36 Stat. 819 (act of 25 June 1910, ch. 387); see *Annual Report of the Attorney General of the United States, 1911* (Washington, D.C., 1911), pp. 73, 396–398.

[26]In California, for example, a statute passed in 1889 set up a state reform school. This was the Preston School of Industry, which opened in 1894. See Preston School of Industry, *2nd Biennial Report* (Sacramento, 1896).

delinquent children." It covered children who were "destitute or homeless or abandoned; or dependent on the public for support," or were beggars, "lacked proper parental care," lived in a "house of ill-fame or with any vicious or disreputable person," or whose homes were unfit by reason of "neglect, cruelty or depravity on the part of... parents." The law applied as well to those who were under the age of 8 and were found "peddling or selling any article, or singing or playing any musical instrument upon the street or giving any public entertainment."[27]

Whether children were dependent or delinquent, the court had a great deal of discretion. The judge could send a child to an institution, put a child on probation in his or her own home, or assign a child to a foster home. The idea was, as one scholar put it, to create "a new adjudicating mechanism, a chancery or non-criminal court of equity," for the special use of children. The court would not concern itself with legal "rights." Reform schools had long "enjoyed" paternal and parental powers; now these were "extended to the entire legal process as it touched the delinquent. By emphasizing probation, the juvenile court was to be considered a place of aid and education, not punishment."[28] The idea caught on like wildfire. In Denver, Judge Ben Lindsey's campaign led to the passage of a juvenile law in 1903.[29] By 1909, 10 states and the District of Columbia had passed laws authorizing juvenile courts; 12 states followed in the next 3 years. By 1925, all states but 2 had juvenile court laws, and in 1945 it was unanimous.[30]

The very idea of the juvenile court gave tremendous leeway to judges, social workers, and others in and around the court. The whole baggage of rules and rights was done away with. Here too, the emphasis was on the individual child—who he or she was, not what he or she had done. Juvenile justice was to the minor what probation was to the adult, except that the juvenile was never formally convicted of a crime.

Probation, indeterminate sentencing, and parole were all parts of a single burst of reform. All shifted emphasis from the offense to the offender. All looked to sift out those capable of rehabilitation from those who were not, those fit for life in decent society from those who were not. Even juvenile justice centered on the offender, not the offense. The

---

[27]Laws Ill. 1899, p. 131.

[28]Robert M. Mennell, *Thorns and Thistles: Juvenile Delinquents in the United States, 1825–1940* (Hanover, N.H., 1973), pp. 131–132; see also Sanford Fox, "Juvenile Justice Reform," *Stanford Law Review* 20 (1970): 1191; Anthony M. Platt, *The Childsavers: The Invention of Delinquency* (Chicago, 1969).

[29]D'Ann Campbell, "Judge Ben Lindsey and the Juvenile Court Movement, 1901–1904," *Arizona and the West* 18 (1976): 5.

[30]Mennell, *Thorns and Thistles*. See also Herbert H. Lou, *Juvenile Courts in the United States* (Chapel Hill, N.C., 1924).

reforms were primarily concerned with saving the savable, but they were concerned with the unsavable as well, who were locked up as long as possible—forever perhaps—for the good of society. Roughly at the same time, concern grew over "born criminals," eugenics, the feeble-minded, and the awful danger that society might be "swamped with incompetence." The phrase comes from the notable case of *Buck* v. *Bell* (1927), in which the Supreme Court upheld a Virginia law for sterilizing the feebleminded. In this case, Oliver Wendell Holmes, Jr., delivered his famous line: "Three generations of imbeciles are enough."[31] In 1909, California had passed a law to "asexualize" prisoners. A prisoner who was convicted twice or more of sex crimes, or three times for "any other crime" if there was "evidence" that he was "a moral or sexual pervert," was eligible for this treatment.[32] Laws against recidivists, too, were generally tightened. Some were downright savage. California's Habitual Criminal Act of 1923 provided life sentences for three-time offenders.[33] In *Graham* v. *West Virginia* (1912), the Supreme Court upheld a law under which a man sentenced to the penitentiary three times in succession could be imprisoned for life.[34]

Penal reforms reached a kind of compromise in the late nineteenth and early twentieth centuries—a sort of trade-off between hard-liners and soft-liners. This bargain sold the souls and bodies of incorrigibles in exchange for better breaks for the redeemable. Discretion was a feature of the *meliorating* reforms, as, indeed, of any system that focuses on the individual offender.

Recent trends, however, seem to be turning back the clock. Most of the nineteenth-century reforms have fallen into disrepute. The indeterminate sentence is out of favor with both sides. Reformers feel it is arbitrary, harsh, and discriminatory. Prisoners complain of the "constant mental torture of never really knowing how long you'll be here."[35]

[31]Buck v. Bell, 274 U.S. 200, 207 (1927); on the eugenics movement, see Mark H. Haller, *Eugenics: Hereditarian Attitudes in American Thought* (New Brunswick, N.J., 1963); see also David M. Kennedy, *Birth Control in America: The Career of Margaret Sanger* (New Haven, 1970), pp. 113–122; J. H. Landman, "The Human Sterilization Movement," *Journal of the American Institute of Criminal Law and Criminology* 24 (1933): 400.

[32]Laws Cal. 1909, ch. 720. A life prisoner could also be "asexualized." The statute did state that the operation could not be performed unless in the judgment of the medical superintendent it would be "conducive to the benefit of the physical, mental or moral condition of the inmate." California passed a more elaborate statute on the subject in 1913, Laws Cal. 1913, ch. 364, §2.

[33]Laws Cal. 1923, 111 (Penal Code §644). See the harsh so-called Baumes Law of New York, Laws N.Y. 1926, ch. 457, §2.

[34]Graham v. West Virginia, 224 U.S. 616 (1912).

[35]This was said by a woman prisoner in California and quoted in John Kaplan, *Criminal Justice: Introductory Cases and Materials* (Mineola, N.Y., 1973), p. 569.

The hard-liners, in turn, are afraid that it holds out too much hope for the criminal; they want definite (and harsh) punishments. California abolished indeterminate sentencing effective 1 July 1977 (California Penal Code, §1170) and replaced it with a system of flat sentences. For habitual criminals, or those who commit crimes under "aggravating" circumstances, the sentences can be very severe. How the new law will work out remains to be seen.

Parole, too, is increasingly under attack. Hard-liners contend that parole is a "compromise" with "the thug, the gangster, the killer and racketeer," who win "cut-rate penitentiary sentences."[36] In practice, the parole board never functioned as ideally pictured; it never made calm, precise, individual decisions. On the one hand, it developed "guidelines" and rules of thumb. The inmate's hearing was nasty, brutish, and short. And, on the other hand, decisions were influenced (it was said) by "ignorance, pure caprice, bigotry, and other abuses of discretion." If parole boards can not or will not distinguish between inmates who reform and those who do not, then the parole system has lost its premises and should not survive.[37] At least one state, indeed, has abolished it.

For juvenile justice, too, disillusionment has set in. By the 1960s, we hear that the child receives, as the Supreme Court put it, the "worst of both worlds"; he gets "neither the protections accorded to adults nor the solicitous care and regenerative treatment postulated for children."[38] Juvenile homes (it was said) were no better than (or different from) prisons. In the landmark case of *In re Gault* (1967), the Supreme Court held that juveniles were entitled to a battery of procedural rights: the right to counsel, the privilege against self-incrimination, the right to confront and cross-examine witnesses.[39] *Gault* aimed to destroy the (unjust) informality of juvenile court, but there is a question what impact it actually had. The impact, perhaps, was less than intended. New formal requirements merely gave rise to "informal arrangements," among intake officers and others, to get around the formal procedures.[40] What-

---

[36]Martin Mooney, *The Parole Scandal* (Los Angeles, 1939), pp. 135–136.

[37]Anne M. Heinz, John P. Heinz, Stephen J. Senderowitz, and Mary Anne Vance, "Sentencing by Parole Board: An Evaluation," *Journal of Criminal Law and Criminology* 67 (1976): 1.

[38]Kent v. United States, 383 U.S. 541, 566 (1966).

[39]387 U.S. 1 (1967). Donald L. Horowitz, *The Courts and Social Policy* (Washington, D.C., 1977), chap. 5; see also Edwin M. Lemert, *Social Action and Legal Change: Revolution within the Juvenile Court* (Chicago, 1970), on juvenile court reform in California, which took place 6 years before *In re Gault*.

[40]Horowitz, *Courts and Social Policy*, pp. 218–219.

ever its impact, *Gault* was meant to be part of the war against discretion, a corrective to arbitrary power.

Once again, the emphasis has shifted, this time back to the offense itself. Neither hard-liners nor soft-liners have much faith in rehabilitation, in treating the individual. James Q. Wilson speaks for many when he says we can do nothing about the "roots" of crime (that is, their social origins) or change warped minds. But we can deal with crime itself—we can lock people up.[41]

Yet discretion is a pervasive and illusive beast; smoked out of one lair, it finds itself another. There is discretion in the legal system, because discretion is useful, even necessary. First of all, it makes it possible to handle cases one at a time. However angry people may become about crime and criminals, they do not give up the idea of justice; justice implies treating people as individuals, one by one, which excludes flat rules, even if one could agree on the content of the rules. Any "reform" is likely to embody a compromise, since there is no general agreement about the functions and goals of criminal justice, or about how criminals should be handled. Moreover, the system is complex and cumbersome—tugged now this way, now that, by social forces. In such a system, discretion flourishes, either openly or in secret cracks and flaws.

Discretion did not begin with parole, indeterminate sentence, and probation. What could be more discretionary than a jury? Before parole, there was the governor's pardoning power. It is clear that some governors used this power pretty freely.[42] "Experts" on parole boards replaced the governor's grace and favor, but this merely meant exchanging one kind of discretion for another. In Missouri, for example, as late as 1889–1890, the governor pardoned 130 prisoners. After 1905, in the parole era, pardons dropped dramatically—there were only 2 in 1921–1922.[43]

What went wrong with all the successive waves of reform? There is a deep desire to blame problems on form. Reforming becomes possible precisely because both hard-liners and soft-liners agree (to scrap the indeterminate sentence, for example). But by the same token, one or both sides is bound to be disappointed. If different parts of society expect radically different results from criminal justice, they cannot all be satisfied; *no* formal change can work this magic. And the historical re-

[41]Wilson, *Thinking about Crime.*

[42]Barry L. Salkin, "The Pardoning Power in Antebellum Pennsylvania," *Pennsylvania Magazine of History and Biography* 100 (1976): 507.

[43]A. J. Kuhlman, "Pardons, Paroles and Commutations," in *The Missouri Crime Survey* (New York, 1926), p. 488.

cord suggests that both sides mistake cause and effect. Recent disillusionment came about partly because society is so troubled about serious crime, hence the shift to an emphasis on the offense itself. The old policies, however, were not to blame. Rising (or falling) crime rates *make* policies, and not the other way around. The crime wave is real, but its causes and cures are obscure, to say the least. Nobody has ever shown whether and how much the criminal justice system contributes to crime rates—not with any precision.

PLEA BARGAINING: ITS CAUSE AND CURE

Plea bargaining is currently one of the most controversial practices in the criminal justice system. It is a notorious fact that few people arrested for serious crimes go to trial; many cases are dismissed. Of those that are not dismissed, most—in some jurisdictions up to 90%—are resolved by a guilty plea and a bargain. Only a tiny minority undergo the drama of the 12-man jury.

Plea bargaining is a term that covers a number of practices. What they have in common is a guilty plea and a bargain. Typically, the defendant agrees to plead guilty because of a deal struck between the prosecutor and the defendant or, more usually, his lawyer. (In some places the judge may play a role). In return, the defendant will face a less serious charge, or some charges will be dropped altogether, or the sentence will be reduced. For the last decade or so, demands have been heard on all sides to do something about the practice; an enormous literature has grown up.[44]

The fuss is recent, but plea bargaining is older than most people realize. Its popularity has gone up and down over the years. Plea bargaining first attracted attention from scholars and specialists in the 1920s, and opinions were decidedly mixed. The Chicago Crime Com-

[44]See, for example, Arthur Rosett and Donald R. Cressey, *Justice by Consent: Plea Bargains in the American Courthouse* (Philadelphia, 1976); Donald J. Newman, *Conviction: The Determination of Guilt or Innocence without Trial* (Boston, 1966); John Kaplan, "American Merchandising and the Guilty Plea: Replacing the Bazaar with the Department Store," *American Journal of Criminal Law* 5 (1977): 215; John F. Klein, *Let's Make a Deal: Negotiating Justice* (Lexington, Mass., 1976) (dealing with Canadian data). On the judge's role, see Albert W. Alschuler, "The Trial Judge's Role in Plea-Bargaining," *Columbia Law Review* 76 (1976): 1059. Among the studies that show plea bargaining in action today are James Eisenstein and Herbert Jacob, *Felony Justice: An Organizational Analysis of Criminal Courts* (Boston, 1977); Martin A. Levin, *Urban Politics and the Criminal Courts* (Chicago, 1977); Malcolm Feeley, *The Punishment Is the Process* (New York, 1979). A special issue of the *Law and Society Review* (Vol. 13 [Winter 1979]) was devoted to plea bargaining.

mission, for example, felt that plea bargaining was essentially corrupt.[45] The Morse–Beattie report, in Oregon, on the other hand, felt that bargaining was good for both sides. The state saved money, while plea bargaining made the defendant "more receptive to individualized treatment which seeks to change his attitude toward society and awaken in him a realization of his present maladjustment to life."[46]

The practice has been receiving an increasingly negative press. Both hard-liners and soft-liners attack it. In theory, plea bargaining is a compromise; it therefore tends to overpunish the innocent and underpunish the guilty. One study claims that up to one-third of the people who plead guilty would escape conviction if they went to trial.[47] (Whether this mean they were "innocent" is another question.) Others deny that the "bargains" are bargains at all. Prosecutors overcharge; that is, they pile on absurd numbers of "counts," everything "down to and including spitting on the sidewalk."[48] Then, they offer to drop some charges if the defendant will plead guilty to the charges that were meant all along. Plea bargaining, others say, makes a mockery of justice. Bargaining does away with trials and reinforces a "corrupt view of the world." Bargained sentences are unjust, and unjust punishment "cannot deter."[49] Soft-liners in general see plea bargaining as proof that society has given up on fairness and due process. In the event, the poor and weak come off the worst.

From the other side, the attack has been just as shrill. Plea bargaining shows softness and rot. "Vicious criminals" wriggle their way out of punishment; dangerous felons get off with a rap on the knuckles. Hard-liners want absolute—and harsher—sentences. Since both sides attack plea bargaining, it is no surprise to find serious efforts to get rid of it, or at least control it. There is an obvious parallel to the attack on the indeterminate sentence.

The origins of plea bargaining are murky, to say the least. It is usual to connect plea bargaining with crowded dockets, with modern big-city

[45]The commission in 1928 demanded the removal from office of judges who allowed plea bargaining. Mark H. Haller, "Urban Crime and Criminal Justice: The Chicago Case," *Journal of American History* 57 (1971): 619, 732–733.

[46]Wayne L. Morse and Ronald H. Beattie, *Survey of the Administration of Criminal Justice in Oregon* (Eugene, Oreg., 1932), p. 138; Raymond Moley, *Politics and Criminal Prosecution* (New York, 1929), pp. 156–158.

[47]Michael O. Finkelstein, "A Statistical Study of Guilty Plea Practices in the Federal Courts," *Harvard Law Review* 89 (1975): 293.

[48]Albert W. Alschuler, "The Prosecutor's Role in Plea-Bargaining," *University of Chicago Law Review* 36 (1968): 50, 85.

[49]Irving R. Kaufman, "The Injustices of Plea-Bargaining," *New York Times*, 13 December 1976, p. 37; see also Jonathan D. Casper, *American Criminal Justice: The Defendant's Perspective* (Englewood Cliffs, N.J., 1972), p. 81.

courts. Plea bargaining, in other words, is a response to pressures. The squeeze on money, people, and time makes shortcuts necessary. Alschuler talks about "an administrative crisis of major proportions in our criminal courts." Resources are "seriously inadequate"; only the "guilty plea system has enabled the courts to process their case loads." If so, we expect to find a relationship between urbanization and plea bargaining. And the problem could be attacked by adding more judges, courtrooms, and staff.

Past data, however, suggest another story. Plea bargaining is much older than the 1920s. A few reported cases from the nineteenth century touch on plea bargaining or related practices. These are cases where a defendant agreed to plead guilty because someone, usually the prosecutor, promised lighter treatment in return. These cases were rare; a defendant would appeal only when the promise was broken, which could not have been common.[50] Such scattered cases do not, of course, prove that there was a *system* of plea bargaining anywhere. But plea bargaining becomes possible—even probable—in any system that allows defendants to plead guilty. This leads us to expect it in the nineteenth century, and certainly in the late nineteenth century.[51] The cases confirm this suggestion, as does a chance document here and there. In New York City, according to one study, around the time of the Civil War, the district attorney encouraged defendants to plead guilty to lesser offenses. Such bargains were "always under the table."[52] There are hints of a similar practice in England.[53]

---

[50]One clear case was Myers v. State, 115 Ind. 554, 18 N.E. 42 (1888). Myers pleaded guilty to larceny, after a promise that he would get no more than 2 years in prison. The judge gave him 10, and Myers appealed. The court reversed; the defendant could withdraw his guilty plea and start over. In Camron v. State, 32 Tex. Crim. 180, 22 S.W. 682 (1893), the defendant had turned state's evidence but was prosecuted anyway. The appeal court reversed his conviction, mentioning how useful it was to reward people like Camron, who helped "convict their confederates." Jay Wishingrad, "The Plea-Bargain in Historical Perspective," *Buffalo Law Review* 23 (1974): 499, reviews the cases, but most cases he cited are not really relevant. The history of the cases is also reviewed in Albert W. Alschuler, "Plea Bargaining and Its History," *Law and Society Review* 13 (1979): 211. A fuller version of the findings reported in this chapter is in Lawrence M. Friedman, "Plea Bargaining in Historical Perspective," *Law and Society Review* 13 (1979): 247.

[51]See Milton Heumann, "A Note on Plea-Bargaining and Case Pressure," *Law and Society Review* 9 (1975): 515.

[52]Wilbur E. Miller, *Cops and Bobbies: Police Authority in New York and London, 1830–1870* (Chicago, 1977), p. 80.

[53]H. Waddington to T. B. Burcham, 16 September 1862, H.O. 60/7/57 Public Record Office, in which Waddington, of the Home Office, complains to a magistrate in Southwark that offenders eagerly grasped at the "privilege" of pleading guilty to "stealing from the person" to avoid the heavy sentence for robbery, a more serious crime. Waddington felt that "permission to plead guilty, followed by a trifling sentence," was no way to deter crime.

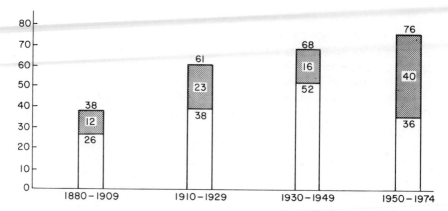

Figure 7.1. Initial and changed pleas of guilty as percentage of all pleas, Superior Court, Alameda County, 1880–1974. Shaded areas indicate pleas of innocent, later changed to guilty; white areas indicate initial guilty pleas. $N = 1487$.

We studied the records of the Superior Court of Alameda County, California, organized in 1880. From the very first, there is blatant, naked evidence of plea bargaining. For example, a certain Albert McKenzie was charged with embezzlement in 1880. McKenzie, an agent for a sewing machine company, was accused of pocketing $52.50 in gold coin, which had been paid to the company. On 15 December 1880, McKenzie appeared in court and pleaded not guilty. The judge set a trial date, 7 February 1881. On that date, McKenzie asked permission to withdraw his plea and plead guilty to the crime of embezzling less than $50. This new plea, "with the consent of the District Attorney," was allowed by the court. The judge gave McKenzie a 6-month sentence.[54]

McKenzie's case was far from unique. Plea bargaining was not dominant in Alameda County, but it was by no means rare. Figure 7.1 shows pleas of guilty to reduced charges as percentages of all pleas in the county, between 1880 and 1974. The percentage has been growing remarkably, but even in the earliest period, it amounted to a reasonable number of cases. It is not always clear why. If the prosecutor had a weak case, he might try to persuade the defendant (through his lawyer in the main) to plead guilty to *something*. William McCormick, a horse trainer, was charged with murder in 1902 after he shot and killed a groom on a ranch. McCormick had been dead drunk at the time. The assistant dis-

[54]People v. McKenzie, Superior Court, Alameda County, California, Criminal Casefile No. 51 (1880). Note that judge and prosecutor accepted a plea to a crime that McKenzie could not possibly have committed: He had embezzled either more than $50, or nothing at all.

trict attorney moved to reduce the charge to manslaughter: "No malice could be shown," he admitted. The court granted the motion; then McCormick pleaded guilty.[55] A case from San Mateo County (another Bay Area county) shows the same process at work. The crime was robbery, and the defendants, Frank Williams and George Brown, pleaded not guilty. Then, "in open court," they admitted they were "guilty of a battery . . . and desired to plead guilty then and there to said offense." The district attorney was agreeable. He told the court that he had no evidence on the robbery charge except the testimony of a complaining witness. This was "uncorroborated," and "a conviction would be doubtful." The court went along.[56]

Judges, as we can see, plainly accepted the practice. It was rare indeed for them to turn down a guilty plea.[57] They winked at the irrationalities and inconsistencies of the system. They accepted pleas of petty larceny, for example, even when the evidence plainly showed grand larceny or nothing. In one incident, in 1888, three defendants were charged with breaking into a railway car. The court let one defendant, John Feno, plead guilty to second-degree burglary (defined as burglary by day) (Case No. 840), even though his companion, E. H. Howard, had already been convicted of first-degree burglary (burglary by night).

Besides the evidence of open plea bargaining, the records suggest an important but unspoken deal as well. The defendant understands that it will go better for him if he pleads guilty. He pleads guilty, then, hoping or expecting a lenient sentence. We can call this *implicit* plea bargaining, borrowing the phrase from Milton Heumann.[58] Implicit plea bargaining is hard to show directly. For one thing, it depends in part on the state of mind of judges and the scuttlebutt among defendants. Both are hard to show *systematically* for the past. Occasionally, the curtain lifts a bit. In 1910, a defendant in Alameda County pleaded guilty to grand larceny; the judge (Everett Brown) told him: "I am going to be lenient now and give you the full benefit . . . for the plea of guilty. . . . You can rest assured if you had gone on the witness stand and told some perjured tale about this affair, you would have received a heavier sentence. . . . You are entitled to the credit, and I am going to give you the credit for having

[55]*Oakland Tribune*, 15 May 1902, p. 1.
[56]People v. Williams and Brown, Superior Court, San Mateo County, California, Criminal Casefile No. 711 (1886). I am indebted to Michael Rosiello, for this example (Term Paper, "Plea Bargaining in San Mateo County," Stanford Law School, June 1976).
[57]People v. Ah Young, Superior Court, Alameda County, California, Criminal Casefile No. 756 (1887), was one of the rare unfortunates. He offered to plead guilty to petty larceny if the court forgot about a prior conviction. But the judge refused and sent him to Folsom Prison for 18 months.
[58]Heumann, "A Note on Plea-Bargaining."

entered a plea of guilty."[59] There were other benefits from the guilty plea in Judge Brown's court. In this same year, Judge Brown granted probation to 42 adults. All but one of them had pleaded guilty; defendants stubborn enough to plead not guilty and demand a trial were almost never rewarded with probation. Perhaps there were *some* differences between cases that went to trial and those that did not; still, the word that got around to defendants and their lawyers must have been unmistakable: For a chance at probation, plead guilty.[60]

It is sometimes possible to show implicit plea bargaining statistically. According to the Missouri Crime Survey, an urban defendant who pleaded guilty reduced the chance of going to prison by about half.[61] In any event, implicit bargaining has undoubtedly influenced defendants and prosecutors for a century or more. It has continued to exercise enormous influence up to the present. In the 1950s, the *Yale Law Journal* sent out a questionaire to all federal district judges. Two-thirds of the judges who answered said that the defendant's plea was "a relevant factor in . . . sentencing procedure." The relevance was all in one direction: A defendant who pleaded guilty earned "a more lenient punishment than the defendant who pleaded not guilty."[62]

In general, a high rate of guilty pleas is an indicator of implicit plea bargaining. After all, why would a person plead guilty, giving up the chance for acquittal, unless he expects to get something for his plea? Some defendants plead guilty out of remorse, self-hate, to get things over with, or because of sheer hopelessness. But this hardly explains the behavior of great masses of defendants.

In 1929, Raymond Moley summed up the data: Far more people, all over the country, were convicted on guilty pleas than were convicted by judges or juries. This was true of 88 out of every 100 in New York City, 85 out of every 100 in Chicago, 70 out of every 100 in Dallas, 86 out of

---

[59]Proceedings upon Sentence, pp. 5–10, People v. Louis Schroeder, Superior Court, Alameda County, California, Criminal Casefile No. 4825 (1910).

[60]Neubauer, in his study of "Prairie City," remarks that "The court system in Prairie City penalizes those who demand a jury trial. . . . One type of penalty is the denial of probation. Of the seventeen defendants found guilty at trial during 1968, only one received probation. Significantly, the lone exception involved a bench trial, not a jury trial. Otherwise the system operates under an iron-clad rule: defendants convicted by a jury trial will not receive probation." *Criminal Justice in Middle America*, p. 240.

[61]*Missouri Crime Survey*, p. 317. Rural data did not show a comparable effect, but there was some *explicit* plea bargaining in city and rural counties alike. Of 1158 pleas in urban counties, 121 were pleas of not guilty later changed to pleas of guilty to a lesser offense; 163 withdrew a plea of "not guilty and pleaded guilty as charged." Of 1522 pleas in rural counties, 192 withdraw not guilty pleas, either to plead guilty "on the nose" or to lesser charges (p. 315).

[62]"Comment: The Influence of the Defendant's Plea on Judicial Determination of Sentence," *Yale Law Journal* 66 (1956): 204, 206–207.

every 100 in Cleveland, and 79 out of every 100 in Des Moines. In rural counties, too, the guilty plea predominated: 91% in New York, 79% in California, and 58% in Georgia. And the guilty plea was not a recent growth. In 1839, in New York State, one-quarter of the cases ended in guilty pleas. A decade later, guilty pleas disposed of half, and the percentage mounted steadily from then on.[63] In Franklin County, Ohio, in the 1930s, 84.7% of the convictions were the result of guilty pleas. Most defendants pleaded guilty as charged; only about 7% pleaded guilty to lesser offenses (a sign of *explicit* plea bargaining).[64]

To sum up, plea bargaining is at least a century old; implicit plea bargaining may be even older. Studies suggest that implicit plea bargaining was, in most places, more common than explicit plea bargaining until after the Second World War. In Alameda County, the percentage of guilty pleas rose steadily until the 1930s. It then leveled off and began a rapid decline. More than half of the defendants today plead not guilty at first, then plea bargain (through their lawyers).

For at least a century, full-scale trial by jury has *not* been the norm in Alameda County. There is reason to believe that patterns of disposition were similar in many parts of the country in the late nineteenth century. In other places, "trials" were still common. But what kind of trial? Trial by jury is conventionally and romantically pictured as a full-scale elaborate test of the prosecution's case, stoutly resisted by a full-scale elaborate defense. This picture is highly inaccurate. In the central criminal courts of London in the early nineteenth century, for example, trial by jury was virtually universal. But it was not "trial by jury" in the sense of Patricia Hearst's case, or Lizzie Borden's. Elaborate trials were confined to very serious cases, such as murder. For a shopkeeper's boy who stole a ham, for a pickpocket, for a servant girl who took a spoon, the normal case was cut-and-dried. "Trials" lasted a short time—perhaps half an hour at the most. Proceedings were perfunctory. A jury was selected quickly. The complaining witness stated his case; if there was a constable, he stated his case; the defendant sometimes brought in a witness or made a statement; verdict followed almost immediately; then the court went into the next case on its list.[65]

---

[63]Moley, *Politics and Criminal Prosecution*, pp. 159–164.

[64]William J. Blackburn, *The Administration of Criminal Justice in Franklin County, Ohio* (Baltimore, 1935), pp. 77–79. Many defendants were already in jail; the prosecutor promised to bring up their cases quickly—but only if they pleaded guilty. Defense lawyers (usually assigned counsel who earned small fees) helped to persuade prisoners to plead guilty, to save time and effort all around.

[65]Data on the Central Criminal Courts of London, housed in the Public Record Office, London, were gathered by Lawrence M. Friedman, Robert V. Percival, and Jane E. Friedman.

Perhaps there never was a golden age of trials. If there was, it came before the rise of professional police forces, full-time prosecutors, and scientific crime fighting (fingerprinting, blood tests, and the rest). In a system run completely by amateurs, or by part-time officials, and without modern techniques of crime detection and proof, the trial may be as good a way as any to filter out the innocent from the guilty. No doubt, trial by jury worked roughly but accurately enough in preprofessional days.

But when criminal justice turns professional, a better filtering system develops. Inevitably, the center of gravity shifts from amateurs and part-timers, to professionals. The new system developed rather slowly in the nineteenth century. As it grew, the *presumption* shifted away from trial by jury. There were other ways to handle defendants. After all, a person accused of crime has already been "tried" by police and prosecutors (in some places also by grand jury) before he ever reaches judge and jury. Nobody, perhaps, said out loud that this second stage was a waste of time and money. But there is evidence in social behavior. It is one of the ideas lying behind vigilante outbursts, for example. Everywhere the police had power to get around some of the fripperies of due process. People winked at "police brutality"; the "crime control model"[66] was popular in the late nineteenth century. Whatever the official dogma, people knew that trials took place in the streets, in the station house, in prosecutors' offices, and they approved. Trial by jury in the romantic sense was the exception, not the rule.

It is also important to ask: Who were the defendants, and how did society regard them? Trial by jury is supposed to be trial by one's peers. But people do not think of "criminals" as peers. They consider them trash, defectives, inferior beings, "fiends," "brutes," and so on. A trial for such people, especially when they are "obviously guilty," is a waste of time. This is particularly true if trials increase the danger that the accused may slip free through some loophole in the law.

The twentieth century did not invent routine or short-cuts—or plea bargaining. Enough is known of the history of plea bargaining to cast doubt on modern attempts to "abolish" the practice.[67] Plea bargaining is not as intimately connected with "crowded urban courts" as people think it is; rather, it is a way to save time and effort that gained currency because the alternatives seemed costly and unnecessary. It cannot be disentangled from the guilty-plea system, the professionalization of criminal justice, the discretion of prosecutors (and defense attorneys),

[66]Packer, *Limits of the Criminal Sanction.*
[67]See Thomas W. Church, Jr., "Plea Bargains, Concessions and the Courts: Analysis of a Quasi-Experiment," *Law and Society Review* 10 (1976): 377.

the costs of full trials, and, most important of all, public attitudes toward crime, punishment, and criminals.

If we try to abolish plea bargaining, by fiat, chopping off its head, so to speak, it will probably survive or, more likely, change its form. In any case, implicit bargaining is devilishly hard to get rid of—even assuming we want to. This is so because the alternative—full "due process" trials for everybody accused of crime—is costly and unpopular and probably unnecessary. It has been this way for at least a century. Outright abolition of plea bargaining goes too much against the grain.

It might be better to admit that full-scale trials are no solution to the problem of criminal justice. Elaborate trials are no way to decide the fate of the ordinary defendant. Society needs to reform the operating system, but it cannot resurrect a dead system or bring back a golden age that was perhaps always a fairy tale. If most "trials" take place outside of court, and must, the question is where are they held, how are they held, and what precisely is wrong with them? What are the real costs to the defendant's rights, or to the health of society? How can *this* system be reformed? Exactly what is it about plea bargaining that is obnoxious, and how can it *realistically* be changed?

Again, as with indeterminate sentence, parole, and juvenile justice, we suspect that the drift of modern policy flows from a false diagnosis of cause and effect. And we suggest that historical evidence can play at least a modest role in uncovering this misdiagnosis.

HANDS OFF:
THE RISE AND FALL OF VICTIMLESS CRIME

Nobody doubts that murder, robbery, arson, and rape are dangerous and deplorable; hard-liners and soft-liners disagree about tactics, but hardly about ends. The issue of victimless crime is rather different. The same factions spar with each other, but hard-liners want to strengthen enforcement, and soft-liners would like to wipe these "crimes" off the books. The acts, it is said, are not crimes at all; it is enforcement and its consequences that are evil. Reformers can point to some solid accomplishments: Sex practices of various stripes "between consenting adults" are legal in some states, some states have softened their marijuana laws, and legislatures seem willing to look change in the face, in a way that was once unthinkable.

The concept of a "victimless crime" is distinctly modern. The phrase, which is probably about a generation old, in a way prejudges the issue. If there is no victim, why prosecute? Why punish people for harmless sin? Mere vice is arguably "not the law's business."[68] But the good citizen in colonial Massachusetts, and probably most people in the nineteenth century, would have had trouble grasping the idea. For the Puritan, sins punished as crimes were not victimless at all. There were plenty of victims: the sinner himself, his family, and, indeed, the whole society. Did not God wipe Sodom and Gomorrah off the face of the earth because of "victimless crime" (among other things)? Throughout legal history, people have generally accepted the role of the state in enforcing the moral code. If the state falls down on the job, the whole social fabric may disintegrate.

Whether a victimless crime lacks a "victim," it typically lacks a complainant. Neither the sellers of vice nor their customers usually complain. By common consent, victimless crimes include prostitution, gambling, sexual deviance, drug addiction, and drunkenness. Such conduct has been found in luxuriant profusion from the dawn of history. In colonial America, the leaders of society took a dim view of sin, and many such acts—for example, fornication—were frequently and vigorously punished. By the nineteenth century, the wheel had turned, and laws were less rigorously enforced. The legal system shifted emphasis from transgressions against the moral law to property crimes (mostly stealing).[69] The major concern of criminal justice in the early nineteenth century was theft.

We looked at a sample of nineteenth-century prosecutions in the central criminal courts of London (records housed in the Public Record Office). In 1800, it was a capital offense to steal anything worth more than five pounds. The death penalty for theft was not usual, but theft was the crime most commonly prosecuted, and punishment could be severe. A 63-year-old man, Thomas Vaughan, was sent for 2 years to the house of correction in 1806 for stealing a bed sheet; a 12-year-old boy

---

[68]Gilbert Geis, Not the Law's Business? (Washington, D.C., 1972); Edwin Schur, Crimes without Victims (Englewood Cliffs, N.J., 1965); Packer, Limits of the Criminal Sanction, chap. 16.

[69]On the rise and fall of (colonial and postcolonial) enforcement of laws against victimless crime, see William E. Nelson, "Emerging Notions of Modern Criminal Law in the Revolutionary Era: An Historical Perspective," New York University Law Review 42 (1967): 450; Lawrence M. Friedman, "Notes toward a History of American Justice," Buffalo Law Review 24 (1974): 111; Michael S. Hindus, "The Countours of Crime and Justice in Massachusetts and South Carolina, 1767–1878," American Journal of Legal History 21 (1977): 212.

Hendrik Hartog, in "The Public Law of a County Court: Judicial Government in Eighteenth-Century Massachusetts," American Journal of Legal History 20 (1976): 282, 299–308, argues (with regard to fornication) that the shift away from "moralistic purposes" had occurred by the eighteenth century. Fornication law had become a "way of allocating the costs of legitimacy." The county, generally speaking, only prosecuted when a child was born and was likely to be a drain on county funds.

who stole a cheese was sentenced to 7 years on a convict ship in 1840.[70] The typical defendant was a man accused of theft, shoplifting, or taking money from an employer—men like William Humphreys, 30 years old, accused in 1806 of taking sheets from the room he rented and pledging them to a pawnbroker.[71] Crimes of violence made a small showing in the records, and victimless crimes, at the felony level, were very rare. A few notorious or scandalous cases occurred—a bishop was arrested in 1822 for attempted sodomy[72]—but nothing suggests systematic enforcement.

Of course, we know that crimes of violence *did* occur and that thousands of violations of the moral laws took place every day. In England, a big literature now deals with the darker side of Victorian life; when scholars turn over the stones, all kinds of debauchery crawl out.[73] But society in the first half of the century, as far as one can tell, was not terribly interested in prosecuting moral offenses. It was in hot pursuit of property crime. In the United States, the situation was roughly the same; public drunkenness was the only victimless crime that produced much work for the criminal courts, as far as we can tell.[74]

Unfortunately, we know only a little about the day-to-day work of ordinary criminal courts, and almost nothing about justice courts and police courts. Almost certainly, enforcement of morality took a back seat to control of dangerous behavior—and to public discipline as well. Victimless crimes were left alone, behind drawn curtains and shutters. Of course, this was at least partly a matter of necessity. The colonists relied on a network of gossips and informers. Among transient populations, the "crime" of fornication or adultery is much harder to detect. But this was surely not the whole story. The emphasis was on *public*, not private, behavior. Drunkenness was punished because, like blatant prostitution, it was a public, open offense. Harvey Graff examined jail registers from Middlesex County, Ontario, for 1867–1868. There were 535 entries; drunkenness and prostitution were well represented, but fornication, adultery, and sodomy were completely absent.[75]

[70]Lawrence M. Friedman, "The Devil Is Not Dead: Exploring the History of Criminal Justice," *Georgia Law Review* 11 (1977): 257, 264.

[71]P. Com. 1/3/446, Public Record Office. Humphreys was sentenced to 7 years transportation.

[72]Arthur N. Gilbert, "Sexual Deviance and the Law in Eighteenth and Early Nineteenth Century England" (Paper presented at the Annual Meeting of the American Society for Legal History, Philadelphia, October 1976).

[73]See Kellow Chesney, *The Victorian Underworld* (New York, 1972); Ronald Pearsall, *The Worm in the Bud: The World of Victorian Sexuality* (London, 1969).

[74]On this point, see Lane, "Urbanization and Criminal Violence," p. 359.

[75]Harvey J. Graff, "Crime and Punishment in the Nineteenth Century: A New Look at the Criminal," *Journal of Interdisciplinary History* 7 (1977): 477, 486–487.

Of course, we do not really know what "society" (meaning, respectable, well-off, articulate people) thought. But we can make a kind of educated guess, based on inferences from the behavior of social institutions. If we want to explain what the legal system *did*, the easiest way is to assume that it responded more or less to a kind of public opinion and that this public opinion did not care about indecency as *sin* but did care about indecency when it threatened order and discipline in society. Respectable society did not expect people to be angels and, as far as the lower orders were concerned, did not much care. But behavior and discipline in public, this was something else again. Immorality, pornography, and prostitution could hardly be abolished, but they were not to be legitimated. Drunkenness was a crime when it spilled over into the streets. Adultery was a crime, but mostly when it flaunted itself. In Ohio, for instance, it was a crime to desert husband or wife "and live and cohabit with another... in the state of adultery," or for a married man to "keep any other woman, and notoriously cohabit with her."[76] The enemy, in short, was disorder and *open* immorality, not secret sin.

This, very generally, is what we think we see in the first half or so of the nineteenth century. Toward the end of the century, the picture changes, and there develops a new, intense concern with victimless crime. We will mention a few milestones. In the 1870s, societies "for the suppression of vice" were formed all over the country. The most famous was the Boston group, later called the Watch and Ward Society. In 1873, Congress passed the so-called Comstock Law, which imposed severe penalties on anyone who mailed an "obscene, lewd, or lascivious" book, or "any article or thing designed for the prevention of conception or procuring of abortion."[77] In 1895, Congress, by law, prohibited the sale of lottery tickets across state lines. This was a crushing blow to the lottery business and drove it underground for about 70 years.[78] In 1910, the famous (or infamous) Mann Act was passed.[79] The idea was that evil men lured innocent women into lives of prostitution. The campaign was first directed against foreign prostitutes, with their exotic perversions, but the law as passed covered any woman dragged into vice (across state lines, that is); the Mann Act made it a crime to transport women across

---

[76]Ohio Stats. 1841, pp. 244–245. Illinois Criminal Code of 1845, ch. 38, §11, speaks of an "open state of adultery, or fornication"; California (1872, Penal Code §269a), of "open and notorious cohabitation and adultery."

[77]17 Stats. 598 (act of 3 March 1873); see Paul S. Boyer, *Purity in Print: Book Censorship in America* (New York, 1968); generally, on the moral reform movement, see David J. Pivar, *Purity Crusade, Sexual Morality and Social Control, 1868–1900* (Westport, Conn., 1973).

[78]28 Stats. 963 (act of 2 March 1895, ch. 191); see J. Ezell, *Fortune's Merry Wheel: the Lottery in America* (Cambridge, Mass., 1960).

[79]36 Stats. 825 (act of 25 June 1910).

state lines "for the purpose of prostitution or debauchery, or for any other immoral purpose."

It is interesting to track another crime, once called "statutory rape" and now known as "unlawful sexual intercourse" in California. A man commits this crime by having sex with a girl who, in the eyes of the law, is too young for that sort of thing. The offense was never widely prosecuted. Sex with a child outrages most people; normally such a crime, if discovered, would be vigorously prosecuted. But where the girl is legally underage yet old enough to know what she is doing (she may look and act even older), this is a "victimless" crime in the more conventional sense. The "crime," then, depends on the age of consent. From the late nineteenth century on, the age of consent rose dramatically. The age of consent in California before 1889 was 10! The age was raised from 10 to 14 in 1889, to 16 in 1897, and finally, in 1913, to 18.[80] Punishment was the same as that for forcible rape: "imprisonment ... for not less than five years." After 1913, then, it was a felony to have sex with a girl of 17. This would not have been a crime in the nineteenth century.

The so-called Red Light Abatement Movement also flourished about the time of World War I. "Red light districts" were part of an old, comfortable system. Prostitution was illegal, of course, but, in the words of a Chicago vice report, "custom and precedent" made the laws against houses of prostitution "practically inoperative."[81] In 1866, there were said to be 615 houses of prostitution in New York City, along with 99 "houses of assignation, seventy-five concert saloons of bad repute, two thousand six hundred and ninety prostitutes, six hundred and twenty waiter girls of ... bad character, and one hundred and twenty-seven bar-maids" who were "vile." Bishop Simpson of the Methodist church, in a rather hysterical speech at Cooper Institute, claimed there were as many prostitutes as Methodists in the city. Keepers of houses had no reason to hide themselves and their trade. The police left them alone, unless they were "noisy," disturbed the peace, or became a "public nuisance.... All the public houses of prostitution are known to the authorities."[82]

This system continued into the twentieth century. The police closed their eyes to red light districts (or opened them only long enough to take bribes). Then a crusade against vice burst on the cities like a rocket—

[80]California Penal Code 1872, §261; Laws Cal. 1889, ch. 191, p. 223; Laws Cal. 1897, ch. 139, p. 201; Laws Cal. 1913, ch. 122, p. 212.

[81]Vice Commission of Chicago, *The Social Evil in Chicago* (Chicago, 1911), p. 160.

[82]Matthew Hale Smith, *Sunshine and Shadow in New York* (Hartford 1880), pp. 371–372. See George T. Kneeland, *Commercialized Prostitution in New York City* (1913; reprint ed., Montclair, N.J., 1969), especially chap. 7.

"more dramatic," in some ways, than the crusade "which closed the saloon." Early rumblings of this moral volcano were heard in Chicago, of all places. On 12 October 1909, an evangelist, Rodney Smith (called "Gipsy"), led "a band of 12,000 Christian men and women" through the red light district on Twenty-second Street, "in an attempt, like the crusaders of old, to reclaim the region to Christianity." In 1912, 10,000 people paraded in the rain, demanding a "clean Chicago." Finally, in that year, the law took action and closed the district—at least for a time.[83]

Stern new laws, so-called Red Light Abatement laws, now swept the country. Michigan's law, passed in 1915, authorized the attorney general, "or any citizen," to bring action in chancery to abate any house of prostitution as a "nuisance." Since "any citizen" could start the ball rolling, it was possible to sidestep a corrupt or unwilling police force.[84] In any event, the movement carried a message: Flabby moral compromises were unacceptable. Vice must be destroyed, once and for all. The law—so said Edith Hooker—must not permit fornication: the fount of "venereal disease, prostitution and many other ills." The "ill results of vice" should be brought home to the young.[85] Of course, the movement did not wipe out vice; what it did destroy was a historic compromise.[86]

Society took another fateful step when it made drug addiction a crime. This was new. Sherlock Holmes himself had been described as addicted to cocaine. In the nineteenth century, addiction was considered a vice, like strong drink, but it did not make men criminals. The first steps in the war on drugs were small ones. In Illinois in 1879, for example,

[83]Walter C. Reckless, *Vice in Chicago* (1933; reprint ed., Montclair, N.J., 1969), pp. 1–3. There had been, of course, earlier campaigns against prostitution, although rarely as a "movement." See, for example, the account of Virginia City, Nevada, in Marion Goldman, "Prostitution and Virtue in Nevada," *Society* 10 (November–December 1972): 32.

[84]Laws Mich. 1915, No. 272, p. 481. Under section 3 of this law, "evidence of the general reputation of the place shall be admissible for the purpose of proving the existing [sic] of the said nuisance."

In some cities, the police did join in, responding to public outcries. In 1917, the police blockaded the famous Barbary Coast in San Francisco. They closed 83 brothels and drove 1073 women out of the quarter. Herbert Asbury, *The Barbary Coast: An Informal History of the San Francisco Underworld* (New York, 1933), pp. 312–313. By 1917, red lights had dimmed in every major and many minor cities, and the movement had swept from New York to Honolulu.

[85]Edith Hooker, "The Case Against Prophylaxis," *Social Hygiene* 5 (April 1919): 163, 183. Hooker argued *against* prophylactic clinics and *for* vigorous enforcement of laws punishing fornication and prostitution: "The prophylactic station necessarily brings fornication within the law, for any statute forbidding fornication must be a dead letter if the station is to continue openly in operation" (p. 182).

[86]It is interesting to see that the *idea* of a vice district—Boston's "Combat Zone," for example—is back in fashion.

druggists were told not to sell cocaine without a prescription.[87] A New York law of 1905 treated cocaine, morphine, and opium as "poisons"; they could not be sold at retail without a proper label.[88] California tried to stamp out its "opium dens" and "joints," which it associated with Chinese laborers. Private use of opium, however, was never forbidden.[89] But in 1914, Congress passed the Harrison Act, under which no one could buy narcotics without a prescription.[90] In 1919, in *Webb* v. *U.S.*,[91] the Supreme Court took a further step. A doctor could prescribe drugs only for "medical" reasons; an addict's need for a fix was not such a reason. This meant the end of any *legal* sale of drugs.

Some states went even further. Arkansas in 1907 made it a crime to make, sell, or give away cigarettes.[92] And the most striking monument of the movement was, of course, Prohibition—a total, national ban on the saloon and liquor trade. The Eighteenth Amendment was ratified in 1919. This was the climax of an old, strong, persistent movement, but Prohibition, preceded by a great deal of state legislation, was its finest hour, its brief but heady triumph.[93]

The law exploded, then, after 1870—creating new victimless crimes and revitalizing old ones. Were these laws actually enforced? Information, even about Prohibition, is scanty at best; scraps here and there suggest that police and prosecutors did become at least somewhat more serious about victimless crime. There were some obvious crackdowns, and more people were arrested, proportionately, for victimless crimes than before. In most cities, however, the percentage of such arrests probably did not add up to much. There was no doubt great local variation; one writer claims that Washington, D.C., and Cincinnati prosecuted 1000 cases of fornication in 1916 and 131 cases of adultery; in New

[87]Laws Ill. 1897, p. 138. A Missouri law of 1887 outlawed "opium dens" (Laws Mo. 1887, p. 175); the act also covered "hasheesh." On the history of drug laws, see Troy Duster, *The Legislation of Morality* (New York, 1970); David F. Musto, *The American Disease: Origins of Narcotics Control* (New Haven, 1973).

[88]Laws N.Y. 1905, ch. 442, p. 977.

[89]California Penal Code, §307 (originally passed 1874); see In re Sic, 73 Cal. 142, 14 P. 405 (1887).

[90]38 Stat. 785 (act of 17 December 1914). The act covered "opium or coca leaves" and all their various derivatives.

[91]249 U.S. 96 (1918). In form, the Harrison Act was a tax law; in U.S. v. Doremus, 249 U.S. 86 (1918), the Supreme Court sustained the law, against the argument that "it was not a revenue measure, and was an invasion of the police power reserved for the States."

[92]Acts of Ark., 1907, no. 55, p. 134.

[93]The literature on Prohibition is vast. See especially Jospeh R. Gusfield, *Symbolic Crusade: Status Politics and the American Temperance Movement* (Urbana, Ill., 1963); Andrew Sinclair, *Era of Excess: A Social History of the Prohibition Movement* (Boston, 1964). On the movement in the states there is also a sizable literature; see, on Michigan for example, Larry Engelmann, "Dry Renaissance: The Local Option Years, 1889–1917," *Michigan History* 59 (1975): 69.

York City, on the other hand, a mere 10 cases of adultery made it to court.[94] Between 1872 and 1910, morals arrests, excluding gambling and drunkenness, made up less than 1% of total arrests in Oakland, California. But there were *some* scattered prosecutions, especially for unlawful intercourse—enough to pose real risk to a man with too young a partner.

No doubt, some story other than routine police work lay behind each prosecution: an outraged mother, an angry lover, an unwanted pregnancy. Yet the state pursued some cases with considerable ardor. Trials of statutory rape were among the most sensational of the day in Alameda County. One such was the trial of A. C. Webb, Jr., in 1906. A 13-year-old girl, Flossie Cook, was his accuser. In his closing statement, the prosecutor hammered away against the crime. California, he said, has chosen to throw its "protection" around a girl, until she is 16; she cannot legally consent to "an act that is going to forever and always determine her future existence." She is too young to choose "the life of a beast" over "the life of mankind." When we dip into early records of juvenile court, we find that a taste for sex (or at least experience) was enough to label a girl "delinquent." English records are also revealing: There was a real upsurge in morals prosecutions at the end of the nineteenth century. Men were arrested for "carnally knowing" girls of 14 and 15, or older. England, too, had raised its age of consent. Sexual deviance was also more frequently punished.[95] Red Light Abatement was itself an example of enforcement of moral laws, and Prohibition was all too real. It is often said, somewhat glibly, that Prohibition failed utterly, that enforcement was a farce. Prohibition was certainly a *political* failure, and drinking did not stop. But the jails were crowded with violators, and the effect on drinking habits was far from zero.[96]

The question remains: What brought about the great resurgence of morality? It is tempting to see a kind of moral class struggle, a struggle for moral hegemony, between the old WASP elite and the new waves of immigrants. This is Joseph Gusfield's thesis,[97] and it has something of the ring of truth. There were also new, practical reasons to worry about immorality. People understood more about venereal diseases; prostitution and promiscuity were problems of public health, not matters of

[94]Howard B. Woolston, *Prostitution in the United States, prior to the Entrance of the United States into the World War* (1921; reprint ed., Montclair, N.J., 1919), pp. 229–230.

[95]Edwin Q. Coles, for example, was arrested in 1890 for trying to induce one Henry Piper to "commit an act of indecency." 5 May 1890, P. Com. 1/137/243, P.R.O. Coles was acquitted. See also H. Montgomery Hyde, *The Cleveland Street Scandal* (London, 1976).

[96]See J. C. Burnham, "New Perspectives on the Prohibition 'Experiment' of the 1920's," *Journal of Social History* 2 (1968): 58.

[97]For this thesis, see Joseph Gusfield, "Moral Passage: The Symbolic Process of Public Designations of Deviance," *Social Problems* 15 (1967): 175.

mere morals or taste. The drug problem became, perhaps, objectively more serious; heroin was a brand-new product in 1900.

Still, none of these factors seems to capture all of the force behind the outbreak of morals. I would like to suggest one more factor. Criminal justice over the years had become more democratic. "Democratic" may seem an odd word to use for moral rigidity, but the social base of power had broadened in the nineteenth century. All adult white males, for example, gained the vote. Power flowed to a large, compact, middle-class mass, and with it came the new morality.

Earlier in the century, criminal justice was perhaps a more elite affair—rules imposed from above on a subject population. Why bother about what common people, farm hands, factory workers, and people in city slums did to and with each other? These people were, after all, "animals." It was absurd to punish a carpenter's apprentice for sleeping with a 16-year-old servant girl and equally absurd to punish slaves for fornication. (*Legal* marriage was not allowed to slaves at all.) No one expected these people to have high standards. Nineteenth-century elites, unlike the Puritan elders, did not care deeply about the morals of the lower orders. By 1900, the middle class ruled morally as well as politically. High-minded people believed in one society, one community, and one universal code, moral and legal. It was not a return to Puritan theology, but rather a return to the idea of stern and uniform norms. This brought with it once more the attempt to enforce conventional morality.

The idea was utopian even in the seventeenth century, and in 1880 or 1910, it was the height of foolishness. The one society did not exist. There had been, perhaps, a rough consensus about order and discipline and implicit treaties on enforcement and moral hegemony. Everyone gave honor and respect to certain well-known rules of conduct, which "nice" people followed. Other behavior was tolerated—provided it was discreet, or segregated, in red light districts, for example. After 1870, the armies of the righteous brutally broke the unspoken truce, declaring war on secret vice.

The results were, in the long run, disastrous. Order and discipline—in the nineteenth-century sense—were losing their grip. The righteous now faced a new spirit of individual assertion, social, economic, and political. Those who were members of minorities (including life-style minorities) began to demand first toleration, then equality, then, beyond that, a deeper and stronger legitimacy. They too rejected old compromises. They wanted their "crimes" wiped off the books. They wanted "decriminalization"—repeal of the laws against victimless crime. This is the situation today.

What do we learn from the historical record? For one thing, the sequence of events is enlightening. There is no unbroken tradition of punishing victimless crime. Campaigns against immorality have ebbed and flowed. To tamper with such laws does not undermine pillars on which society rests. The laws are products of specific times and places; their foundations in the culture are weaker than we think and are eroding before our very eyes.

The story has another side as well. At times, huge numbers of people have supported these laws, with great energy. They seem to derive immense psychological satisfaction from these laws. Perhaps they need to feel that *their* habits and ideals make up official morality. Such people, foot soldiers of the righteous, still exist in enormous numbers; "alternative life-styles" fill them with horror. A social upheaval underlay the revolution of morality; it may not yet have run its course.

If only one could reach these citizens with a message and a lesson or two from the past! But hard-liners do not listen, least of all to squeaky little voices from the ivory tower. Social scientists have battered away in vain at laws about abortion, gun control, drugs, and pornography. Historians do not add very much, to be frank.

Not very much—even assuming we knew what the "lesson of history" is. A process is going on in the country redefining the meaning of "freedom." People have learned to tolerate a high level of control—in the way they drive their cars, in heavy taxation, in massive red tape. At the same time, the zone of personal privacy and autonomy may be expanding. Laws against victimless crime stand in the way. There is a vigorous debate over issues of victimless crime. It might be helpful to understand that many of these laws are the residue of the misguided moral explosion—an explosion so disastrous that much of it (Prohibition for example) had to be long ago abandoned. Unlike plea bargaining, which is older than people think it is, laws against victimless crime are in an important sense much younger than we think.

CONCLUSION

We have discussed a few aspects of criminal justice in the recent past. What, one may ask, does it add up to? How much has relevance to debates over what to do *now*?

In one sense, very little. But this is an infant field; historical research on criminal justice, in any quantity, has only just begun. New information may turn up that policymakers find more immediate, more compelling. On the whole, I tend to be skeptical, but it is certainly possible.

Scholarship—and this includes historical scholarship—is valuable when it shows us social systems as they are and were, rigorously, with all their shadings and depths, their roots in the past and their dynamics in the present. When we beam the searchlight of scholarship on criminal justice, what do we see? We see incredible complexity. The system is large and unwieldy. It is worse than decentralized; it is not so much a system as an exploded system; little bits and pieces lie around in every state, city, county, town, and police station. It has been that way for generations. Coherence cannot be imposed on such a system. There are too many people with a finger in the pot. Legislatures grind out rules, police and detectives find and arrest criminals, prosecutors prosecute them, defense attorneys defend them, judges, juries, probation officers, prison officials, parole boards, and others all have parts to play, not to mention the defendants and their families—and the victims and theirs. Everybody has his own viewpoint and interests. Everybody can veto everyone else. The police can make nonsense of the work of the judges; the judges can throw a monkey wrench into the work of the police. Probation officers and prison guards can destroy the plans of the legislature. The jury can make a mockery of rules. Any root-and-branch reform has to take all these roles and processes into account. The people who scream for harsher sentences forget the system is like a leaky hose: If you turn pressure up at one end, more water may or may not run out at the other.[98] This does not mean, of course, that nothing can be changed or that nothing can be changed unless everything is changed. But, historically, a system has developed which is extraordinarily gangly and loose-jointed. This kind of system is not easy to change from above—or below.

Reforms old and new usually fail to attack problems of the system as a whole. If we bring lawyers (a formality) into juvenile court, are we also bringing in plea bargaining (an informality)? Long, fixed sentences encourage dickering and negotiating before the courtroom phase. Will the determinate sentence have much impact on the system in operation? Reformers (on both sides) ignore the leaky hose. Processes and procedures are largely secondary. What matters is power: who calls the tune in some little corner of the system. Professionals (police, judges, lawyers) run the system, within limits set by public pressures and demands. Reformers have a say, too, because they are active, busy, and exert what influence they can. Defendants, too, have a voice. How much depends on their proxies (civil liberties groups, for example) and on

[98]Lawrence M. Friedman, *The Legal System: A Social Science Perspective* (New York, 1975), p. 90.

whether they make effective use of their bargaining power (prosecutors are willing to pay *something* for cooperation). The war on "discretion" is clearly affected by rights consciousness and militance. But no one can distinguish between changes in criminal justice that are direct results of militance and those created by *legal* change (which militance in turn brought about).

Paradoxically, the law itself is sometimes a stumbling block to reform. Over the years, the legal system has become more sensitive to the formal rights of defendants. There were sensational advances in the generation of the Warren Court. The changes have been, on the whole, on the side of the angels. Court decisions gave leverage to defendants and their lawyers and helped in the war against police brutality, race prejudice, and assembly-line justice.

Hard-liners insist that reforms "coddle" criminals, that they swaddle dangerous thugs in a thick, warm blanket of "rights." They blame "liberal courts" for the outburst of violent crime. There is no evidence for this at all. The truth is much more complicated. Nobody would seriously argue that the right to counsel, for example, helps to *prevent* crime or deter the criminal. The reforms tend to work against speed and efficiency, but speed and efficiency are often what the defendant wants and needs. Take, for example, the exclusionary rule, which shuts out evidence gathered illegally by the police (found, for example, in an illegal search). In California, today, defense lawyers routinely enter motions to suppress the evidence (on the grounds of illegality). The courts just as routinely deny the motion. (Very occasionally, they allow it.) In either case, a step has been added to the process, and each step takes time.

Reformers are lawyers; lawyers think in procedural terms. It seemed only natural to work for reform by fighting battles over procedure all the way up to the Supreme Court in Washington. At times, this was the only *practical* way to attack injustice. Local courts were vicious, corrupt, or indifferent. The police laughed at soft-liners. The Supreme Court listened and acted. But high-court doctrines are brittle, unrealistic *rules* about rights; they are all-or-nothing rules, rules far from the working reality of justice and alien to the thinking of the ordinary man and woman. These people believe that the police only arrest the guilty; they want something done, and quickly, about the menace of crime.

Hence, reformers never succeed in imposing their will on the system. They win short-run victories, but they never humanize criminal justice as much as they would like to. The hard-liners are little better off. They too are unable to mold the system as much as they would like. Their draconian solutions are also impossible, either to achieve or to carry out. The problems are tough and resistant to solutions. The *system* is tough and resistant to change.

This should come as no surprise, There are too many clashing viewpoints and interests. In the United States, a more or less open society, nobody can impose a clean, "rational" solution on a problem when there is no hope of social consensus.

Historical research is policy oriented in one primitive sense: it raises (to use current jargon) people's consciousness. Professionals in the study of crime and criminal justice are, like most of us, profoundly ignorant of history. But knowledge without a sense of the past is peculiarly orphaned and rootless. If we do not know where we come from, we can not know where we are, or where we are going. We have argued that current policy rests, at least in part, on misdiagnosis of the past. Historical knowledge, at the very least, can expose these fallacies and raise important questions. The typical person arrested in Oakland, California, in the late nineteenth century was a white laborer, native born and 33 years old; one person out of three prosecuted for serious crime in London in 1810 was a woman. To know these things leads us to wonder why the situation today should be so different. What has happened in the world and why? Which situation is "normal," and why?

Of course, history itself is not static. Every generation redefines the past in its own image. Current social concern always affects fashions in history. It changes what historians write about. The revolt of the the minorities has had a major impact on the way history is written. This in turn seeps into textbooks, feeds other channels of communication, and helps build another revision of history and conventional wisdom.

People caught in the web of criminal justice—victims, defendants, and their families—are a kind of minority in America. Policy battles rage all about them, but their interests are mostly represented by proxies. They rarely speak themselves, and hardly anybody listens. The policy debates are sometimes hysterical, sometimes ignorant. These dark caves of social order badly need new explorers.

Major changes in policy rarely, if ever, take place simply because somebody writes a book. *Pressure* brings policy, but pressure comes from people and groups who demand their rights or interests, and this in turn depends on how they (and others) look at the world. The education or miseducation of the public is part of politics, and the public mind is built up bit by bit, stone by stone. A sense of the past is at the least one part of this building process.

ACKNOWLEDGMENTS

Many students have helped me with the work, in particular Robert V. Percival, and I would like to express my gratitude to him and to the others.

III

THE USES OF HISTORY IN
THE MAKING OF SOCIAL POLICY

8

MIRRORS OF HARD, DISTORTED GLASS: AN EXAMINATION OF SOME INFLUENTIAL HISTORICAL ASSUMPTIONS ABOUT THE AFRO-AMERICAN FAMILY AND THE SHAPING OF PUBLIC POLICIES, 1861–1965

HERBERT G. GUTMAN

The controversy over the relationship between public policy, the "black family," and the desperate condition of the urban black poor in the 1960s was neither the first nor the last such dispute. It centered around Daniel P. Moynihan's *The Negro Family in America: The Case for National Action* (1965). Like earlier controversies about the black family and public policy, the 1960s dispute rested upon fixed assumptions about the *history* of the black family. But it differed in two important ways from the earlier disputes. Its subjects were the urban—not the rural—black poor, those millions of black Americans who had made their way from the rural South to the urban North between 1940 and 1965. Moreover, a single historical work—E. Franklin Frazier's *The Negro Family in the United States* (1939), a pathbreaking study—hovered over the entire controversy. Its author was no longer alive, but that work survived him and was accepted by most historians and social scientists as the definitive study of the subject. "We have the great study of E. Franklin Frazier," Nathan Glazer wrote in 1963, and "aside from that precious little." Glazer was right. Neither Moynihan nor his critics disputed Frazier's writings about the family. Although they debated the relevance of Frazier's arguments about the slave family to the condition of poor, urban Afro-Americans in the 1960s, they accepted its accuracy.[1]

[1]The mid-1960s dispute over the black family is well documented in Leo Rainwater and William L. Yancey, *The Moynihan Report and the Politics of Controversy* (Cambridge, 1967). Glazer's comment is found in his "Introduction" to Stanley M. Elkins, *Slavery: A Problem in American Institutional and Intellectual Life* (Chicago, 1963), p. xv.

Parts of this chapter appeared in *Historical Reflections* 6(Summer 1979): 183–199, and in Michael Craton, ed., *Roots and Branches: Current Directions in Slave Studies* (Toronto: Pergamon, 1979).

239

Subsequent scholarship has shown that Frazier's work contains serious historical limitations, especially in examining the slave family and lower-class black families after slavery. The reasons are examined far into this chapter, but it is useful at the start to summarize his essential arguments. Scattered evidence allowed him to argue that enslavement had destroyed all African family and kinship beliefs and practices and that the harshness of Anglo-American slavery meant that only "privileged slaves" (artisans, drivers, and house servants) had access to the mainstream cultures and could sustain "normal" families. For the rest, the "maternal family" prevailed. "Under slavery," Frazier insisted near his career's end, "the Negro family was essentially an amorphous group gathered around the mother or some female on the plantation. The father was a visitor to the household without any legal or recognized status in family relations." The "maternal (or "matriarchal") family accompanied most ordinary slaves into legal freedom and rural poverty and traveled with their migrant children and grandchildren to northern cities and urban poverty. Segregation and caste status isolated the great majority of them from the mainstream national culture and bred among them what the anthropologist Charles Valentine scornfully characterizes as a "deficit culture." Particular historical developments meant that disorganized and unstable family life—the product of slavery—were at its core.[2]

Examples of how Frazier's historical synthesis shaped the thinking of policy-oriented social scientists and government officials, among others, in the 1960s abound. Three are selected merely to illustrate that influence. In 1963, Nathan Glazer and Daniel P. Moynihan explained in *Beyond the Melting Pot: The Negroes, Puerto Ricans, Jews, Italians, and Irish of New York City*:

> Migration, uprooting, urbanization always create problems. Even the best organized and best integrated groups suffer under such circumstances. But when the fundamental core of organization, the family, is weak, the magnitude of these problems may be staggering. The experience of slavery left as its most serious heritage a steady weakness in the Negro family.

"Family disorganization and unstable family life among Negro Americans," the sociologist and demographer Philip M. Hauser wrote 2 years later, "is a product of their history and caste status in the United States. During slavery and for at least the first half century after the emancipation, the Negro never had the opportunity to acquire the patterns of sexual behavior and family living which characterize middle-class white

[2]E. Franklin Frazier, *The Negro Church in America* (New York, 1963), pp. 31-33.

society." The absence of opportunity and discriminatory practices toward black males "perpetuated and reinforced the matriarchal Negro
family structure created by slavery." That same year, the controversial
Moynihan "Case for National Action" appeared. Its author did not
create a fictive black family history to justify particular policy recommendations. Instead, he accepted conventional academic historical wisdom, concluding, "There is no one Negro community. There is no one
Negro problem. There is no one solution. Nevertheless, at the center of
the tangle of pathology is the weakness of the family structure. . . . It
was by destroying the Negro family under slavery that white Americans
broke the will of the Negro people."[3]

This chapter does not examine the controversy that followed the publication of what came to be called the Moynihan Report. Nor does it deal
with the Afro-American family and what is newly known about its history. Important aspects of that subject (a few of them briefly summarized further in the chapter) have been detailed at length by this
author in *The Black Family in Slavery and Freedom, 1750–1925* (1976). A
very different but nevertheless closely related portion of "black family
history" is explored in this chapter. Two moments in time—the Civil
War and the early postbellum years and then the last 2 decades of the
nineteenth century and the early years of the twentieth century—are
studied to show how shifting public policies toward black Americans
rested in part upon particular misperceptions of the Afro-American family and its history and how, in turn, particular misperceptions of the
Afro-American family and its history affected different public policies.
In the first of these time periods, Yankee Civil War reformers sought to
integrate the newly liberated slaves into the bourgeois civic order. But
later, Cavalier New South repressers sought to protect the civic order
from the liberated slaves. Both groups affected immediate public
policies, and each group made important but different mistaken assumptions about the Afro-American family and its history. This is
learned by examining the speeches and writings of little-known
nineteenth-century white Americans such as Clinton B. Fisk, Mansfield
French, J. L. Tucker, and Philip A. Bruce. They illustrate a pattern that
continued into the twentieth century, causing the novelist Ralph Ellison
to complain in our time, "Prefabricated Negroes are sketched on sheets
of paper and superimposed upon the Negro community; then when

---

[3]Nathan Glazer and Daniel P. Moynihan, *Beyond the Melting Pot: The Negroes, Puerto
Ricans, Jews, Italians, and Irish of New York City* (Cambridge, 1963), p. 52; Philip M. Hauser,
"Demographic Factors in the Integration of the Negro," *Daedalus* 94 (1965): 854; Daniel
P. Moynihan, "The Negro Family in America . . . ," in *Moynihan Report*, ed. Rainwater and
Yancey, pp. 75–76.

someone thrusts his head through the pages and yells, 'Watch out there, Jack, there's people living under here,' they are all shocked and indignant."

Much more is involved in studying these earlier moments in time than a mere academic exercise that once again examines the historic functions of social, racial, and class myths. We learn that the policymakers in the 1960s were not the first to use "history" as a way of framing a "social problem." But, more significantly, we also learn a great deal about the "history" that they used. By examining what was said and written about the black family in these two earlier historical moments, it is possible to comprehend why E. Franklin Frazier's *Negro Family in the United States* can no longer serve—as it did between 1940 and the mid-1970s—as a "useful" history of either the slave family or the family of the poor rural and urban descendants of exslaves. But we shall also understand why this same book transcends its many servere limitations as *history* and survives as an intellectual effort of paramount importance. This is because Frazier's book, and the ways in which he constructed historical arguments and used historical data, began to free early twentieth-century American social science and historiography of some of its many racial preconceptions.

It is useful at the start to illustrate how recent scholarship on the Afro-American family has altered Frazier's earlier historical paradigm. Some of the new evidence is summarized later in this chapter and should be contrasted with the common historical assumptions policymakers made in the 1960s.[4] It should be emphasized, of course, that this new scholarship does not minimize the distinctive adverse circumstances that affected Afro-Americans, such as the breakup of slave families and marriages by sale and gift, the rural poverty and segregation following Emancipation, and the urban poverty following northward migration. Instead, it shows that poor blacks, even as slaves, were not simply the victims of an oppressive and exploitative circumstance. Durable Afro-American domestic arrangements and norms developed among them in the century and a half preceding the general emancipation despite the severe constraints imposed upon slaves, the frequent involuntary breakup of marriages and families, and the absence of any legal protection for slave families. These norms emerged because the slaves—mostly field hands and laborers—forged a widespread, adaptive, and distinctive family and kinship system out of their African

---

[4]The summary draws from some of the evidence found in Herbert G. Gutman, *The Black Family in Slavery and Freedom, 1750–1925* (New York, 1976), *passim*, especially chaps. 1–6, 9, 10, and app. A.

and American experiences, a process that started well before the nation's independence and was recreated after 1800 by slave men and women sold from the Upper South to the Lower South. Slaves valued families and ties to more distant kin mostly because of what one slave generation learned from an older slave generation and then passed on to a new slave generation. Generational ties served as the underpinning of an adaptive Afro-American culture that sustained cumulative slave traditions and survived the sale of individual slaves and even the breakup of entire slave families. Enlarged kin and quasi-kin networks accompanied slaves into legal freedom. How they served poor blacks between 1865 and the great northward twentieth-century migrations remains a subject for much detailed study. But enough is known about the slave and poor black free family and household to make it clear that most lower-class black households—during and after slavery—were composed of two parents. A brief summary of some of the new evidence follows.

1. The typical slave family between 1830 and 1860—and I mean here the plantation slave family composed of field hands and laborers—was in intact family. Sometimes husbands and wives had different owners. Most adult slaves married, and unless broken by an owner, usually by sale or following estate division (that happened in about one in six or seven marriages), most slave marriages lasted until the death of a spouse. That was important because slave divorce existed, and marriages could be ended voluntarily. Most slave children, including the hundreds of thousands sold as older teenagers and young adults, grew up knowing a slave mother and a slave father. Prenuptial intercourse and childbirth occurred often, but most unmarried slave mothers later took husbands and remained with them until death. Some slave mothers never married but retained close ties to an enlarged blood kin group. A slave father often had a son named for him, but it rarely happened that a slave daughter was given her mother's name. Slave blood cousins rarely married. Slave exogamy indicated a profound awareness of kin relations. Not surprisingly, slave children—at least 40% in the third and fourth generations—were named for kin, usually blood kin (paternal and maternal aunts and uncles, grandparents, and even great-grandparents). The slave surname usually served to connect a slave to his or slave family of origin, not to an immediate owner.

2. Emancipation did not shatter the fragile family connections formed by Afro-Americans during their enslavement. Evidence left by thousands of exslaves in 1865 and 1855 shows that about five-sixths of exslave households contained either a married couple or two parents

and their children. An 1866 North Carolina law required that exslaves legalize their marriages and pay a 25-cent fee, and records surviving for slightly more than one-third of North Carolina's counties show that between one-half and two-thirds of exslave couples registered their marriages. Among the 18,000 mostly illiterate couples registering marriages, about 1 in 4 had lived with the same mate for 10–19 years and another 1 in 5 for 20 or more years. These were not the experiences of "privileged" exslaves. About 9 in 10 of those reporting such domestic arrangements were field hands and common laborers. Their children also valued legal marriage, which is shown in North Carolina white and black marriage registration in seven counties between 1867 and 1890. It cost one dollar to register a new marriage. Most of the black registrants were sharecroppers, tenants, and ordinary laborers. In all, 12,458 white and black marriage licenses were studied. Blacks purchased 61% of them, and blacks made up exactly that percentage of the population. Legal marriage was just as highly prized among them as it was among better-off North Carolina whites. Similar but far less complete Mississippi records for these same years confirm the North Carolina evidence.

3. Occupational and household data from the 1880 federal manuscript census—an examination of the composition of nearly 15,000 rural and urban Virginia, South Carolina, Mississippi, and Alabama black households—indicates the extreme poverty of most of these former slaves and their children. Few owned land, had skills, or held middle-class occupations. Despite their poverty, more than 9 in 10 lived in households with an immediate family at the core. Moreover, a husband or father was present in most southern Afro-American households in 1880, more so in rural than in urban settings. Most poor households contained just an immediate family. Sometimes a lodger, but rarely more than two, lived in the household. So did blood kin, often older women but more usually grandchildren, nephews and nieces, and brothers and sisters of adult family heads. Some unmarried mothers everywhere headed households, but most poor black women did not. They lived in households as grown daughters, wives, or widowed parents.

4. Early twentieth-century migrants to northern cities—at first, mostly single young adults and married couples—came from poor rural and urban southern black families. They were often the grandchildren of men and women emancipated in 1865. They did not carry a disorganized domestic life with them to the urban North, which is learned by reconstructing poor Afro-American households in New York City in 1925. The occupations and household status of nearly 60,000 Manhattan blacks that year—mostly central Harlem residents and totaling about one-third

of the island's blacks—are now known. About 9 in 10 were day laborers, service workers, and skilled wage earners. They were far poorer than other working-class New Yorkers. They lived in about 14,000 households, mostly between 125th and 140th streets, and their domestic arrangements indicate that migration and urbanization in the first 3 decades of this century did not cause widespread family disorganization about poor urban blacks.

Four "indicators" show why. First, enlarged households, often containing two or more families along with kin and unmarried lodgers, were far more common in 1925 than in 1860 in either the rural or the urban South. But these adaptive responses to migration and northern urban poverty did not entail widespread family disorganization. About 6 in 7 of these households had at their core either a husband and wife or two parents and their children. Second, households in which a husband was absent—especially those headed by younger women—were relatively insignificant. Far fewer such households existed in Harlem in 1925 than in the rural and urban South in 1880 and 1900. Women under the age of 30 headed 3% of all these 1925 households. And just 32 households among these nearly 60,000 black New Yorkers were headed by a woman under 30 and contained three or more children. Third, older working-class black men held their own as fathers. Three in four men aged 45 and older were unskilled workers, and 3 in 4 households headed by black men that old were headed by men with unskilled occupations. Fourth, five in six central Harlem children under the age of 6 lived with both parents. The obstacles to decent living and family life encountered by poor Harlem blacks in the 1920s are well known, but a "pathological" family life was not one of these obstacles. Their behavior makes that clear. On the eve of the Great Depression, the emerging black ghetto was not filled with broken and disorganized poor black families.

The slave family and that of its poor southern and northern descendants between 1865 and 1925 differed from the one described by E. Franklin Frazier in *The Negro Family in the United States*. This is suggested by this brief summary, but the reader should constantly keep this data in mind while reading what Clinton B. Fisk, Mansfield French, J. L. Tucker, and Philip A. Bruce, among others, said about the Afro-American family during and after slavery. Their views of its *history* shaped the public policies that they advocated. History framed the debate over the policies they proposed. It was no different then than in the 1960s. What differed was the history itself that policymakers drew upon in defining "social problems." A new scholarship makes it clear that all three groups misunderstood—and for different reasons—the history of the slave family and of those poor men and women descended from Afro-American slaves.

"ROOT, HOG, OR DIE!"

Yankee "family policy" during and just after the Civil War—if such "policy" existed—rested upon deeply held beliefs about nineteenth-century American society, the slave South, and the slaves themselves. Two sets of independent but complementary beliefs shaped private and public Yankee social policies meant to transform the liberated slaves into legally free men and women. One was proscriptive, and the other was prescriptive. The first emphasized the ways in which enslavement had systematically denied Afro-Americans access to the rules of civil society and had bred beliefs and behavior dysfunctional with that society. To one or another degree, most of the men and women who made and enforced policies affecting southern blacks shared these beliefs. No persons better illustrated their complementarity than Clinton Fisk and Mansfield French. In speeches and pamphlets aimed at integrating the exslaves into civil society, Fisk and French illustrated how the marriage between evangelical Protestantism and free market ideology affected regionwide public social policies. Fisk headed the Kentucky and Tennessee Freedmen's Bureau, and French played a lesser but nevertheless significant role among the wartime and early postwar South Carolina and other Atlantic Coast blacks. Their mission was to undo generations of "chattelization" and bring southern blacks into the mainstream of American life.

Our interest in Fisk focuses upon his 72-page pamphlet *Plain Counsels for Freedmen in Sixteen Brief Lectures* (1866). The American Tract Society's decision to publish it delighted Fisk, who had earlier given these talks and believed them "useful in quieting discontentment" among Kentucky and Tennessee freedmen. So did O. O. Howard, who sent copies to the Mississippi Freedmen's Bureau with instructions that *Plain Counsels* be circulated and "read to plantation negroes." The pamphlet was either sold at a low price or given away. Bound in a green cover, *Plain Counsels* gave the appearance of a bank deposit book. A belief that the exslaves knew little if anything about the rules of civil society informed every page in Fisk's pamphlet.[5] The exslaves' particular history had denied them any such awareness, and legal freedom therefore required

---

[5]Clinton B. Fisk, *Plain Counsels for Freedmen in Sixteen Brief Lectures* (Boston, 1866), *passim*, especially pp. 14-17, 23, 28, 31-34, 40-44, 47, 53-54.

simple instructions about these rules. The arguments and even the illustrations in *Plain Counsels* could have been published with little change in early nineteenth-century England. Fisk and others like him descended directly from British moralists like Hannah More, who had preached and propagandized to "modernize" the emerging British working class by convincing it that Time-Thrift and Contracts had divine sanction. The pamphlet's illustrations explained to illiterate exslaves what could not be read. The black Paul Thrifty decorated the frontispiece. He dug the ground with a shovel while a small child watched with awe. Paul Thrifty's cabin was neat and well appointed. An inside-page illustration showed a three-generation black family seated in its living room, with a fireplace decorated with two busts, a painting on the wall, and an interested cat watching a grandfather read to attentive children. Paul Thrifty had his exslave adversaries, Dick Slack among them. Seated near a shabby cabin, Dick Slack wasted time talking with a dog. Peter Puff and Betty Simple shared injurous habits with him. They danced, "hopping around the ballroom like a monkey."

Fisk instructed the exslaves about the "civic economy," Paul Thrifty serving as his implicit model. In detailing the "dos and don'ts" necessary for wordly success by the black poor, Fisk directed particular messages to "young men," "married folks," and the "little folks" and devoted entire lectures to such themes as "work," "religion," "free labor," "crime," "receipts and expenditures," and "contracts." "White men," exslaves learned, "are very much influenced by a man's success in making a good living. . . . They make very polite bows to Frank P. and Mr. S. because they have money in the bank." Concise maxims dotted *Plain Counsels.* "A leak in the kitchen will drain good fortunes." "Earn money and save it. Do not spend it at suppers, parties, and dances." Commercial metaphors sustained God's will in everyday noneconomic relations such as marriage and love. Marriage was "a partnership—sanctioned by heaven, cemented by love." "Listen," the enthused Fisk wrote, "the very first verse of the Holy Bible tells us that God is a worker—that in six days he made all this great world on which we dwell, and the sun and moon and stars. All the holy angels in heaven are very busy." Fisk gave a new meaning to the oldest story: "Why, when God placed Adam and Eve in the garden of Eden, before either of them had ever done a wrong thing, and while they were as pure as the angles, he made gardeners of them." Contracts, including the marriage contract, deserved special attention:

> You have all heard a great deal about contracts, have you not, since you have been free? A contract is something which binds two or more parties. For

example, John and Mary agree to get married. John promises Mary and Mary
accepts John. That is a marriage contract. Again: John Doe agrees to give
Richard Roe fifty dollars for a month's work. That is a contract for labor; and,
if Richard Roe performs the labor, John Doe must pay him. Contracts are
very numerous; numerous as the leaves on the trees almost.

"The world," Fisk admonished, "could not get along without them."
Perhaps unconsciously but nevertheless significantly, others than the
exslaves surfaced in Fisk's lecturers. That became clear in his admoni-
tions concerning Time-Thrift:

You can not afford to smoke fine cigars. I say nothing of the wrong, but of the
cost.... You can not afford to spend money for useless dress and ornaments.
... Dress well, but in cheap, plain apparel.... You have no time to spend in
kicking up your heels. I speak of time, not of the right or wrong of danc-
ing....

The exslaves served Fisk as surrogates for the mid-nineteenth-century
urban lower-class whites. Enslaved Afro-Americans had more than
their share of lower-class vices but did not smoke cigars and purchase
watch-chains. In his hints to exslave husbands, Fisk again illustrated his
confusion:

Husbands must provide for their families.... Some men have a way of going to
saloons, shows, groceries, concerts, and theaters, and leaving their wives
and children night after night alone. This is mean and bad.

Just what plantation blacks could be expected to make of such advice
escapes understanding. Shows, concerts, theaters, and saloons were
just as alien to rural Tennessee, Kentucky, and Mississippi Afro-
American culture as were fine cigars and costly rings. Fisk had done
much more than idealize northern middle-class family sociability and
warmth. He had confused the exslave with the urban white poor and
caricatured the beliefs and behavior of both groups. Contemporary
documents do not record how the exslaves responded to Fisk's many
suggestions, but according to his 1888 campaign biographer, *Plain Counsels* gave them "a new consciousness of value" because it had been
printed "for them alone." Indeed, the advice it offered had "the worth
of gold."

Whereas Mansfield French had not worked in the same areas of the
South that Fisk had, French shared Fisk's beliefs about the slave's past
and the exslave's future. His *Address to Masters and Freedmen*, delivered
"at several points in the Southern States" and published in Macon,
Georgia, in 1865, summed up his prescription to restore the exslaves to

civic health.[6] He emphasized the "Chastity Ideal," which subordinated sexual intercourse to marriage. "The marriage relation among you," said French, "must be as sacred as among the whites." Every woman wanted "a good husband and a good home," but the exslave wife had to "try to be worthy" of her husband's love: "Be more loving and agreeable than any other woman can be, then he will not seek the company of any other woman. Men love quiet, tidy, happy homes, and smiling, loving wives." French especially worried that Emancipation would liberate—not transform—slave habits, encouraging men to "indulge their lusts" and women to "throw their womanhood to the commons." "I beg you, I beseech you," French pleaded, "to leave not only your chains, but your vices behind. Come into freedom with clean hands and clean lips. Your freedom must, in no case, be used as a license to do wrong."

French's prescription for black health mixed the Chastity Ideal with a heavy dose of free market medicine. Justifying federal unwillingness to distribute land to them, French told the exslaves: "All that is left to your masters is their plantations and their manly character. . . . Some of you may think Providence has dealt more generously with them than with you. But look at it again." The Civil War had cost the planters their sons, their money, and "all their negroes." The goverment, he told them, "leaves the land and stock with your masters, while to you it gives simply your freedom. This seems to place you out in the cold; but be not discouraged. The Government has really complimented you in this. It has faith in you, too." How the "old hen" managed with "her family" had much to teach the exslaves. After the "little chicks" learned how to "scratch" from her, the old hen "takes a last look at them, and off she runs, clucking as she goes, 'Now, little chicks, scratch or die!' Did you ever see a little chick that did not scratch a living?" French compared the federal government to the old hen. The authorities promised to help the exslaves until they could "take care" of themselves. Then, "Uncle Sam will say to all his black children, Now scratch or die." Emancipation tested the old slaves in new ways: "Freedom allows you to work, allows you to play, and allows you to starve if you wish. . . ."

French and Fisk retain a commanding importance because their world view is essential to understanding the successes and the failures associated with public and private policies meant to elevate the exslave. The two typified the outlook of mainstream Yankee evangelists and entrepreneurs pressing for positive social reform aimed at the freed

[6]Mansfield French, *Address to Masters and Freedmen by Rev. M. French, With Marriage Code for Freedmen, Instituted by the Freedmen's Bureau* (Macon, Ga., 1865), *passim* (facsimile copy in Mansfield Joseph French, *Ancestors and Descendants of Samuel French the Joiner of Stratford, Connecticut* (Ann Arbor, Mich., 1940).

population. French's insistence that the exslaves had to "scratch or die" may have been inelegantly phrased, but his advice rested on the belief that the compulsion associated with chattel slavery would, and had to be, replaced by the compulsion associated with the free market. Others like Horace Greeley developed the same point. In a celebrated *New York Tribune* editoral published on 25 May 1865 and entitled "Root, Hog, or Die," Greeley explained:

> Freedom and opportunity—these are all that the best Government can secure to White or Black. Give every man a chance, and let his behavior control his fate. If negroes will not work, they must starve or steal; and if they steal, they must be shut up like other thieves. If there be any among them who fancy that they, being free, can live in comfort without work, they have entered a school in which they will certainly and speadily be taught better.

Once "the wreck of slavery" had been cleared away, the federal government would "break up our Freedmen's Bureaus and all manner of coddling devices and let the negroes take care of themselves."[7]

Licentiousness and immorality ranked as high as laziness and idleness on the check list of notorious and damaging vices bred among enslaved Afro-Americans and deserving special attention from Yankee reformers. Family policy linked these distinct vices together. "A man," the *Nation* insisted, "is morally ruined, in the eyes of the economist, when he runs about whoremongering, instead of working at his calling and supporting his wife and child." Two other early postwar *Nation* editorials that mentioned neither slaves nor Afro-Americans but fretted over the "Future of the Family" illuminate the underlying beliefs that spurred Yankee black-family reform. "Real permanence and strength" in marriage could "never be looked for amongst average men and women in the absence of a high moral and religious culture, unless it has a 'home' as a basis." The "great mass ... in all countries" had "only been slenderly influenced by "moral and religious ideas." No more than "habit and custom" sustained marriage among the masses: "the custom of living with one wife," "the female custom of submission," and "the male custom of enforcing obedience by blows and abuse." The great migrations that accompanied the transition to modern society had dangerously unsettled such traditional restraints and caused the decline of the "sacredness of the marriage tie." Custom and habit restrained passion and instinct. The *Nation* censured advocates of liberal divorce laws because such persons either ignored the "sexual passion" or treated it

---

[7]*New York Tribune*, 25 May 1865, quoted in George Fredrickson, *The Black Image in the White Mind* (New York, 1971), pp. 182–183.

"simply as 'lust'—that is, a depraved appetite, only found among vile men," and no different from the "love of alcoholic drinks or cockfighting":

> The sexual passion—the animal, brute passion—through which God, apparently in ignorance of the laws of "moral progress," has provided for the perpetuation of the human species—is the most untamable of all passions.... Its regulation ... was the very first step in civilization. The founding of the family was the first attempt to regulate it. The first object of marriage is still to regulate it.

Civil marriage and the patriarchal family tamed male sexual passions, but at some cost. Both allowed some men to hold "extravagent" notions of their authority, causing frequently just complaint but not justifying liberal divorce laws. The reason was simple. Codified sexual repression (the repression of "passions" through the civil law) had removed from man "the mark of the beast" and encouraged him to gratify "certain propensities which he is sure to gratify somehow ... like a human being." The *Nation* identified sexual restraint, civil marriage, and family stability with "civilization" itself.[8]

Such mid nineteenth-century class and sexual beliefs applied in special ways to enslaved Afro-Americans. As slaves, their marriages had not been sanctioned by the civil law, and therefore "the sexual passion"—the vice of "licentiousness"—went unrestrained. Most emancipated blacks, moreover, were very poor and consequently without "high moral and religious culture." "High culture" could not quickly be imposed upon the exslaves, but the restraints associated with legal marriage could. The concept of moral and social obligation rooted in "contract," moreover, promised to develop out of such ritual. In itself, the formal marriage ritual signified entry into civil society, and Yankee "family policy" focused on the marriage ritual and little else. Exslaves, illiterate plantation blacks prominent among them, legalized their old marriages in significant numbers over the entire South. Sometimes, Yankee reformers pressed legal marriage upon them. But the typical exslaves who legalized old marriages did so without any assistance from either northern or southern whites, which is striking evidence that the civic norms associated with legal marriage were known to Afro-American slaves. They simply could not act upon those norms. That, however, was not evidence that they had "herded" together

[8]*The Nation*, 3 December 1868, pp. 453–454, 26 May 1870, pp. 332–333, 10 June 1870, p. 367. See also Peter Cominois, "Late Victorian Sexual Responsibility and the Social System," *International Review of Social History* 8 (1963). 18–48, 216–250.

as men and women. Moreover, the flurry of legal marriages that
accompanied the emancipation was not a fleeting fancy. In the decades
following the Emancipation, southern blacks, illiterate plantation
workers prominent among them, registered new marriages exactly
in proportion to their place in the population.[9]

UP FROM BARBARISM

Wartime and early postwar Yankee policymakers, such as Mansfield
French and Clinton B. Fisk, defined their mission toward the exslaves as
teaching them the rules of civil society. That mission depended upon a
perception of how enslavement had distorted the Afro-American social
character. Ingrained antibourgeois, or nonbourgeois, habits toward sex,
marriage, and the family, as well as toward work, wealth, and property,
had to be transformed. But an important reversal in public policy objectives occurred in the 1880s and the 1890s. Civil society now had to be
protected from the exslaves and their immediate descendants. The
ideology sustaining that radical shift assumed that a social debacle had
followed a premature emancipation, and its proponents promised to
protect the civic order from that grave mistake. Distinctive racial, class,
and sexual beliefs merged to argue that the Afro-American social
condition—particularly black family and sexual life but also the black
material circumstance—had deteriorated following the emancipation.
White critics of black capacities called it *retrogression*. Emancipation had
removed the social restraints imposed upon "African" slaves. Yankee
innocents had spread falsely optimistic views about their social
capacities. Southern Bourbons promised to redeem the South and the
nation by reimposing their historical dominance over an inert population that had revealed an incurable incapacity to conform decently to the
rules of civil society. The clergyman J. L. Tucker and the lawyer-
journalist–historian Philip A. Bruce served late nineteenth-century
policymakers as Fisk and French had served an earlier generation of
Yankee reformers. But Tucker and Bruce viewed the Afro-American
historical experience very differently.

J. L. Tucker made a secure reputation for himself in a single speech.
The son of an upstate New York Baptist preacher, Tucker and a brother
fought in the Confederate army. After the war, Tucker and his mother
settled in Columbus, Mississippi, where he planted cotton without suc-

---

[9]Gutman, *Black Family in Slavery and Freedom, 1750–1925* (New York, 1976) pp. 14–17,
412–418.

cess ard worked briefly as a bank clerk. Upon recovery from a near fatal illness, Tucker became an Episcopal clergyman. Before moving to Jackson, he was secretary to the Episcopal Board of Missions in New York City. Tucker was not an insular southern cleric. He received national attention because of a speech at the October 1882 Eighth Congress of the Episcopal Church in Richmond, Virginia.

Tucker's talk deserves notice because of its national ramifications and its policy objectives. He wanted the northern clergy to quit the South and leave all missionary work to southern whites. Tucker favored expanded black industrial education and separate black parishes but insisted that southern whites own all black church properties. Only the southern clergy could "lead poor Africa to the Throne of God," because Yankee clerics "barely know a negro when they see him." Tucker's policy objectives required that he demonstrate that northern whites did not understand southern blacks and that southern blacks could neither manage their everyday lives nor produce a capable clerical leadership. He did so by examining the behavior of blacks as slaves and as free men and women. "The negro is retrograding morally," he said of the exslaves. They professed "a form of Christianity without its substance" and deceived those who had little historical familiarity with Africans and their Afro-American descendants. Travelers to Africa, for example, mistakenly used "the terminology of civilization" in their published accounts, causing a "confusion of thought . . . as great as if a geologist" described "the formation of rocks in the phraseology of a prayer meeting." Africans had come to the New World as "absolute barbarians," and enslavement had imposed nothing more than "outward restraint." Culture change could not occur. By "precept and punishment," some owners had enforced "marriage, truthfulness, and honesty," but the great majority of slaves had "no preceptor but the driver's whip" and believed that "those who had so wronged them . . . could not be sincere guides in any minor matters." Slaves conformed outwardly but remained inwardly unchanged: "Being punished for transgression. . . . they quickly learned to conceal the transgression." Tucker explained: "They accepted the outward form but refused the inward substance of the new ideas. They seemed to believe and obey, but really disbelieved and disobeyed."

Emancipation allowed the exslaves to act on their inward beliefs, and "a relapse into many practices of African barbarism" naturally followed. "Their present moral condition," Tucker said, "is but the natural outgrowth of the training in slavery upon the habits of the native Africans." The exslaves deceived innocent Yankee whites by an "outward form of Christianity with an inner substance of full license to all desires and passions." That was "the key to much that puzzles one in the negroes to-day." Tucker characterized the meaning of emancipation for "the great mass": "Hundreds and thousands of marriages were at once dissolved without formaility, and new ones formed also without formality." Yankee dollars supported new black churches that "sprang up everywhere" but had "no religion" in them. And "underneath the surface," "a seething mass of new sins of a character indescribable— unnameable—" thrived.

It was worst in localities where blacks outnumbered whites. There, Tucker said, "we have Africa over again, only partially restrained." Plantation blacks lived "in an open abandonment of even the semblance of morality, and had lost "almost the idea of marriage." In a Black Belt county he knew well, 300 white couples and 3 black couples had purchased marriage licenses from the county clerk.[10] "I know of whole neighborhoods including hundreds of negro families, where there is not one single legally married couple. . . . This statement will hold true for millions of colored people; and these things are but hints." Tucker could not "tell the full truth before a mixed audience," but defined the problem posed for whites: "The Colored people are among us for all time. . . . They touch us at all points." "Self-preservation" required that the "children of disobedience" be disciplined. Yankee clergymen had to join Yankee soldiers in quitting the South, and southern white clerics had to own southern black church properties and thereby guide black moral and social behavior.[11]

Tucker also had his critics, and the two most prominent among them were the white Mississippi Methodist clergyman Charles K. Marshall, described by historian Vernon Wharton as that state's "wealthiest" and one of its "most learned preachers," and the black Episcopal clergyman Alexander Crummell, described by historian August Meier as "the leading nineteenth-century Negro intellectual." Marshall and Crummell disputed Tucker's insistence that the slaves and then the free descendants of Africans had been unaffected by their American experiences and

---

[10]Tucker was mistaken in his numerical assertion. His evidence came from Hinds County, Mississippi. In that county's first district, however, 684 marriage licenses were issued between January 1879 and January 1883. Three in four went to blacks. The percentage of licenses issued to blacks (75.3%) equaled the percentage of blacks aged 15–45 (74.5%) living in Hinds County in 1880. As in other southern places for which comparable evidence exists, blacks purchased marriage licenses in proportion to their numbers in the population.

[11]J. L. Tucker, *The Relation of the Church to the Colored People* (Jackson, Miss., 1893), pp. 1–87. See also *New York Times*, 28 October 1882; Louis Tucker, *Clerical Errors* (New York, 1943), pp. 1–15.

therefore threatened to pollute the civic order. But their arguments found little resonance in the public debates that accompanied the coming of segregation and disfranchisement. Tucker's reputation was firmly fixed when the Ninth Edition of the *Encylopedia Britannica* (1884) confirmed his argument. Its essay on the "Negro" described the African as holding the "lowest position in the evolutionary scale," giving as the most important reason "the premature ossification of the skull, preventing all further development of the brain" so that "lateral pressure from the frontal bone . . . clouded" the "intellect." The article admitted that "interested advocates" disputed over the Negro's "mental temperament," but it was "fixed by heredity," so that "any attempt to suddenly transform the negro mind by foreign culture must be, as it has proved to be, . . . futile." And what of the Negro's "moral status"? It was just as hopeless. A single piece of evidence backed that judgment: the "lurid light . . . cast by the report of the Rev. Dr. Tucker at the American Church Congress for 1883." The *Britannica* misdated the Richmond meeting but quoted Tucker accurately. Blacks did not remain "faithful to each other beyond a few weeks." They stole from one another at prayer meetings. Their clergy lived "in open concubinage, addicted to thievery, lying, and every imaginary crime." "It is more correct to say of the negro," concluded the *Britannica*, "that he is non-moral [rather] than immoral." A northern-born Mississippi clergyman anxious to chase Yankee missionaries from the South and to subvert black church independence had become an international expert on the Afro-American.[12]

Tucker's ideas were not original, and his individual importance should not be exaggerated. They deserve emphasis because they—and not the writings of men like Marshall and Crummell—typified a vast outpouring of printed material that shrouded the realities of everyday Afro-American life in the 1880s and 1890s. That literature had several social and public functions. It increasingly allowed adherents to celebrate the Civil War but to bemoan the ill-timed and hasty emancipation of the enslaved. It permitted believers to turn the poverty and difficult social circumstance of most rural and urban southern blacks inward and to fix the blame on the victims themselves. It served, as George Fredrickson has written, to "justify a policy of repression and neglect." The stress on Afro-American familial instability and sexual immorality,

---

[12]Charles K. Marshall, *The Colored Race Weighed in Balance*, 2d ed. (Nashville, 1883), pp. 1–64; Alexander Crummell, *A Defence of the Negro Race in America from the Assaults and Charges of Rev. J. L. Tucker, D. D., of Jackson, Mississippi*, reprinted in Crummell, *Africa and America, Addresses and Discourses* (Springfield, Mass., 1891), pp. 83–125; *Encyclopedia Britannica*, 9th ed. (New York, 1884), 18:316–318.

moreover, strengthened arguments calling for new forms of external control over black life and contributed powerfully to the justification of disfranchisement and increasingly rigorous legal separation.[13]

Published in 1889, Philip A. Bruce's *The Plantation Negro as Freeman* supported Tucker's argument and most fully expounded the retrogressionist view of the Afro-American experience. The author, the book, and its reception therefore deserve close attention. Only recently, and in a strikingly original way in George Fredrickson's *The Black Image in the White Mind*, has this neglected work been given needed notice. According to Fredrickson, Bruce (who had not yet become the highly regarded historian of colonial Virginia) "put the case for a 'black peril' in the South on a firmer foundation" than had any social analyst to that time. Bruce, who was 33 years old when the book appeared, had grown up in Charlotte County, Virginia, and his life experiences bridged the Old South and the New South. His father had owned a 5000-acre tobacco plantation and more than 500 slaves. An uncle served as the Confederacy's secretary of war. Thomas Nelson Page, the popular novelist whose racial views echoed Bruce's, was his brother-in-law. Even more than Tucker, Bruce was not an insular southerner. His education was the best formal schooling available to late nineteenth-century Americans. A graduate of the University of Virginia, he attended the Harvard Law School, worked for a time as a Baltimore lawyer, grew tired of the legal profession, and in 1887 joined a brother to manage the Richmond, Virginia, Vulcan Iron Works. An uncle headed one of Birmingham's new iron and steel mills, a firm later absorbed by the United States Steel Corporation. Posing as a "traveler," Bruce published a series of articles in the *New York Evening Post* in 1884 that told northern readers that Virginia blacks in their "social, economic, and sanitary ways" were "much superior to... the lowest class of those who in our principal [northern] cities work in the unwholesome atmosphere of factories." He tried unsuccessfully to publish the articles as a book, but several northern publishers, unhappy with its arguments, rejected it. Bruce reworked the manuscript, and G. P. Putnam's published *Plantation Negro* in its popular series "Questions of the Day," along with such authors as the English social and political theorists Walter Bagehot and Thorold Rogers, the *grande dame* of New York philanthropy Josephine Shaw Lowell, the high tariff advocate F. W. Taussig, the brilliant economist David A. Wells, and the aristocratic New York politician and civic reformer Theodore Roosevelt. R. L. Dugdale's influential *The Jukes: A Study in Crime, Pauperism, Disease, and Heredity* appeared in the same series, too. Warning readers that his

---

[13]Fredrickson, *Black Image in the White Mind*, pp. 244–282.

study "might seem gloomy and repelling in its moral aspects," Bruce insisted that he had examined southeastern Virginia's blacks impartially and dispassionately to see how they lived when free of any influences "except those that emanate from themselves." He feared only that he had erred in applying to Afro-Americans "the common ethical standard by which members of the white community are judged."[14]

Bruce's retrogressionist analysis rested on his characterization of black family and sexual belief and behavior. The first two chapters in *Plantation Negro*, entitled "Parent and Child" and "Husband and Wife," emphasized the same point: blacks could not manage their family lives themselves, and emancipation had resulted in a severe and increasingly menacing deterioration in their social and moral condition. Unaware of the difference "between a virtue and a vice," slave parents could not instruct "their children in the simplest moral principles." The "discipline of slavery" therefore had been "advantageous in a repressive way to the child, selfish and ruthless as it was too often." Because emancipation had transformed owners into employers, whites no longer exercised traditional authority. Black parents could not replace "the discipline . . . enforced by the slaveholder," because they acted merely "upon all the impulses of their nature":

> It is too much to expect that parents, trained as negroes have been, will be deeply interested in the moral condition of their children. . . . The children have come into the world by the operation of an instinct, and the burden which their rearing imposes is borne as thoughtlessly as that instinct itself was indulged.

Young girls learned the wrong lessons from their parents: "Chastity is a virtue which the parents do not seem anxious to foster and guard in their daughter." Bruce did not mince words in describing black sexual behavior. "The plantation negro is as much a child of nature now, however civilizing the influences that surround him," Bruce wrote, "as if he had just been transported from the shores of his original continent." "In the sexual relations," Bruce argued, "this insensibility and want of control are exhibited to a very remarkable degree, for the procreative instinct being the most passionate that nature has implanted in his body, it is unscrupulous in proportion." The plantation black "saw no immorality in doing what nature prompts him to do."

[14]Philip. A. Bruce, *The Plantation Negro as Freeman* (New York, 1889), pp. v–ix; Darrett B. Rutman, "Philip Alexander Bruce: A Divided Mind of the South," *Virginia Magazine of History and Biography* 68 (1960): 388–406; L. Moody Simms, "Philip A. Bruce and the Negro Problem," *ibid.* 75 (1967): 348–362; Fredrickson, *Black Image in the White Mind*, pp. 244–282.

Unrestrained sexual abandon doomed the black and endangered the white. Even so harsh a social institution as slavery had been unable to "moderate this instinct." Settled family life was the only "fortification against promiscuous intercourse." "Marriage," Bruce explained, "under the old regime was very like unlawful cohabitation under the new, only that the master, by the power he had, compelled the nominal husband and wife to live together." Slavery therefore made "true marriage impossible," and that condition regularly tempted "both sexes to revert to the natural relations of mere temporary impulse and convenience." Emancipation unleashed these impulses. "Lasciviousness," said Bruce,

> has done more than all the other vices of the plantation negro united to degrade the character of their social life since they were invested with citizenship.... The truth is that neither the men nor the women as a mass look upon lasciviousness as impurity.... Marriage, however solemnly contracted and however public the religious ceremony sanctioning it, does not hamper the sexual liberties of either of the parties.

Like Tucker, Bruce inveighed against the black clergy (who "offend the sacredness of their own marriages"), but he believed black women to be the main cause of Afro-American sexual depravity. The black male, moreover, found "something strangely alluring and seductive . . . in the appearance of a white woman" because of the "wantonness of the women of his own race." The absence of complaints by black women of being raped served as "strong proof of the sexual laxness of plantation women as a class." The black woman acted more directly on her racial instincts than did the black man because she was "altogether removed . . . from any repressive influence which whites might exercise over her on close association."

Bruce's description of black family and sexual behavior served to sustain his essential warning that "their original spirit as a race has not been modified." He wrote:

> In short, we find precisely the same weaknesses in the delegate who sits in the legislature, the teacher who had graduated from college, the preacher who has studied the Bible . . . and the common laborer who toils from morning until night with his hoe or spade.

Racial realities were far more important than were class differences among blacks. The most serious error that could be made was to view the Afro-American as "merely a white man in disposition whom the Creator has endowed with a black skin." If blacks shared "a common attribute with whites," it was "only with white *children*," and that was "a common immaturity of nature":

There are few essential differences between a colored parent and his children... father and mother, son and daughter, are remarkable for the same inability to control themselves owing to common peculiarities of temper, for the same dulness of the power of retrospection, and [the] same lack of foresight.... As long as life itself lasts, he retains the spirit of childhood.

"As a race," said this son of the Old South and the New South, blacks "bear the same moral relation to the Caucasian as a child does to an adult." Emancipation had cut off black children from their white parents, and a necessary retrogression resulted. The Afro-American "character" in the late 1880s therefore "approximates... more closely to the original African type than the character of their fathers who once were slaves.... The further development of these traits means the further departure of the negroes from the standards of the Anglo-Saxon." Emancipation had cut the black off from "the spirit of white society" and given "greater vigor" to his "distinctive social habits."

A prophet of doom, Bruce did not flinch from the policy implications that flowed from his assumptions and arguments. He predicted "intellectual reversion" and "further moral decadence." Further separation from "the tradition of slavery" and the "spirit of subservience which they still feel in their association with the ruling class" promised increased social disorder. In "a few generations," moreover, "formal and legal marriage will be less frequent than now... and the promiscuous intercourse between the sexes will grow more open and unreserved." Such were the consequences of a hasty emancipation that had removed blacks from direct social control by well-bred whites. Bruce favored harsh remedies. Immediate disfranchisement was essential to forestall "anarchy and barbarism." Because the South could not "permanently remain half black and half white," Bruce urged that blacks be shipped out of the country, "even... so suddenly as to wholly blight, for a time, the material interests of the South." The South would be "relegated to its primeval condition" and "settled again exclusively by a white population, just as if it were virgin territory."[15]

Reactions to *The Plantation Negro as Freeman* penetrate the late-nineteenth-century "public mind" and make clear that many contempo-

[15]Bruce, *Plantation Negro as Freeman*, pp. 1–28, 83–85, 126–129, 136–141, 242–261.) See also Philip A. Bruce, "Evolution of the Negro Problem," *Sewanee Review* 19 (October 1911): 385–399, in which Bruce commended the "notable achievements" of "constructive local (Southern) statesmanship" and emphasized especially "the practical disfranchisement of the negro, the prohibition of the intermarriage of the races, the interdiction of their co-education, their separation in all public conveyances, and their domiciliary segregation in the cities." Bruce felt such legislation to be "absolutely necessary to the preservation of Southern society."

rary readers viewed Bruce's policy perspective as a welcome one. Reading the reviews makes it difficult to believe that only a quarter of a century separated Appomatox and their publication. The book did not sell well, but the quality of its readers made up for its narrow readership. Southern editors praised it, and so did northerners who described it as detached, objective, and well informed. *Popular Science Monthly* said it would "dispel any too ideal view of the black race which the reader may hold." The *Hartford Times* found it an accurate portrait of "the shiftless, tumbledown, animal, good-for-nothing life of most of these people in the rural parts of the South." It was "unprejudiced and impartial," said the *Princetonian*, "a book every American should read." The *Boston Daily Advertiser* described Bruce's methods as "impersonal as a scientist's analysis of some Antediluvian animal." "An intelligent Southerner . . . apparently free of prejudice," Bruce had demonstrated that "freedom, instead of bettering" the black, had "perverted him." "Offered freedom," the liberated slaves had "accepted license." Bruce's book convinced the *Philadelphia Evening News* that "the struggle to free the negro" had ended as "a failure." Others praised Bruce. A personal letter of congratulations came from the eminent nothern editor George William Curtis. And in separate but equal letters, Jefferson Davis and Grover Cleveland commended the author of *The Plantation Negro as Freeman*. [16]

The celebration of Bruce's vivid volume suggests the congeniality of its central assertion that unchanging "Africans" hardly had been affected by more than two and a half centuries of changing American experience. Educational policymakers like J. L. M. Curry and Amory Dwight Mayo, for example, shared this belief. A prominent northern Unitarian, early an abolitionist, and later an incessant propagandist for the New South materialist credo, Mayo found "as many grades of natives, intellectual, moral, and executive force" among southern black as among white women. But even the "accomplished teachers" among them shared "one abyss of perdition" with their less fortunate sisters ("brutes"): "the slough of unchastity in which, as a race, they still flounder, half unconscious that it is a slough—the double inheritance of savage Africa and slavery." Curry, a prewar Alabama congressman and a postwar agent for the influential Peabody Fund, believed that the removal of the interest and authority of owners" had caused southern blacks to fall "rapidly from what had been attained in slavery to a state of original fetishism." The behavior among many of "the younger genera-

[16]Rutman, "Bruce: A Divided Mind," pp. 388–406; Frederick Ludwig Hoffman, *Race Traits and Tendencies of the American Negro*, (New York, 1973), pp. 194, 202, 228, 231–232; S. P. Fullinwinder, *The Mind and Mood of Black America* (Homewood, Ill., 1969), pp. 49–50.

tion of both sexes gave proof of what degeneracy can accomplish in a quarter of a century." A *Charleston News and Courier* editorial similarly observed, "Everybody knows that when freed from the compelling influence of the white man he reverts by a law of nature to the natural barbarism in which he was created in the jungles of Africa." Enslavement had not transformed Africans into Afro-Americans. Charles Marshall and Alexander Crummell had viewed that historical process differently. Both had been mistaken in even daring to view it as an historical process. Slave owners had done their best but could do no more than police unchanging "Africans." And emancipation followed by Yankee benevolence had been even more futile. The southern black social and moral condition had worsened between 1865 and the century's last decade; hence the modern "Negro problem," more properly defined as the "African problem."[17]

Influential early twentieth-century historical and social science writings implicitly or explicitly shared assumptions with Bruce. One significant work illustrates the potency of these beliefs: Howard Odum's 1910 Columbia University dissertation *The Social and Mental Traits of the Negro*. Years before Odum won a well-deserved reputation as a pioneering and perceptive student of southern regionalism, he sought to "contribute something toward a scientific knowledge of the negro." Southern blacks deserved "sympathy" and had to be encouraged to find "simple success and happiness," but the mainstream culture had "no place for a black white man." Odum focused on the family: "If the home, which Ribot has called the atom of the social structure is bad, it needs no logic to see that the total organism is bad." Among southern blacks, "their first and crying need is for home life and training":

> The negro has little home conscience or love of home, no local attachments of the better sort. . . . He has no pride of ancestry, and he is not influenced by the lives of great men. . . . He has little conception of the meaning of virtue, truth, honor, manhood, integrity. . . . he does not know the value or the meaning of words in general. . . . They sneer at the idea of work. . . . Their moral natures are miserably perverted. Such a statement should not be interpreted as abusing the negro; for, considering the putrid moral air he breathes, . . . there could be no other outcome.

"No people," Odum believed, "can live above their home life." And "in his home life the negro is filthy, careless, and indecent. He is as destitute

[17]Mayo, quoted in Anna Julia Cooper, *A Voice from the South by a Black Woman* (Xenia, Ohio, 1892), p. 204; Curry, quoted in Fredrickson, *Black Image in the White Mind*, pp. 260–261; *Charleston News and Courier*, 11 January 1898, quoted in George Tindall, *South Carolina Negroes, 1877–1890* (Columbia, S.C., 1952), p. 260.

of morals as any of the lower animals. He does not even know the meaning of the word." Tucker and Bruce surfaced as Odum explained
why this condition existed. The "utter lack of restraint," he claimed,
"deadens any moral sensibilities that might be present." Blacks had a
powerful sensuous capacity" and acted on "little more than impulses."
The Afro-American "social self" therefore had "not developed the love
of home and family nor the desire to accumulate property." No solution
to this problem was possible until it was realized that "the negro
differs from the white not only in development but also in kind."
That was "the first essential to a satisfactory discussion of the problem."
It had been different decades earlier. The "oversight of the white man in
slavery days" had "kept the home of the negro in a more organized
state." Apparently," Odum was convinced, "nothing will restrain the
negro in his present state except the law."[18]

Early-twentieth-century retrogressionist ideology affected far more than
the definition of the "Negro Problem" and the public policies meant to
deal with it. It had a lasting influence on the conceptualization of the
Afro-American historical experience that, in turn, affected the definition
of the "Problem" itself, as well as public policy. The racial and social myth
of Afro-American retrogression concided in time with the initial professionalization of historical writing and became reified in monographic
historical writings about black enslavement and black emancipation and
legal freedom. In restoring the historian Ulrich B. Phillips to the mainstream of Progressive historiography, Daniel J. Singal has demonstrated
that Phillips interpreted the "antebellum period... within the framework of New South values," that he "did not see the plantation as a
latterday version of the feudal manor but rather as a highly efficient
economic unit," and that "the old regime in his hands turned into the
embodiment of traditional Yankee virtues." But Phillips, whose academic
writings on slavery as well as on the South, delved deeply into source
materials and set the dominant pattern for 4 decades of early twentieth-
century scholarship, also was influenced by retrogressionist ideology.[19]

That ideology shaped Phillips's conception of the Afro-American as
distinct from the southern historical experience. "A century or two
ago," explained Phillips in 1904, "the negroes were savages in the wilds
of Africa. Those who were brought to America, and their descendents,
have acquired a certain amount of civilization... in very large measure

---

[18]Howard Odum, *Social and Mental Traits of the Negro: Research into the Condition of the
Negro Race in Southern Towns* (New York, 1910), *passim,* especially pp. 36–42, 150–176,
213–237.

[19]Daniel Joseph Singel, "U. B. Phillips; The Old South as the New," *Journal of American
History* 63 (1977): 871–891.

the result of their association with civilized white people." Phillips para-
phrased Bruce: "Several keen-sighted students have already detected a
tendency of the negroes, where segregated in the black belt, to lapse
back toward barbarism. Of course, if its prevention is possible, such
retrogression must not be allowed to continue." Early in his career (and
in greater detail in his later works), Phillips, living in the age of Jane
Addams, sought to show that slave owners ("the better element of the
white people") "did what we call, in the modern phase, social settlement work." Phillips associated the patriarchal feature of the plantation
system with its racial function, as contrasted with its economic function,
made "necessary" because "the average negro has many of the characteristics of a child, and must be guided and governed, and often
guarded against himself, by a sympathetic hand." Dominance by well-
bred, upper-class whites—not "whites" but "the planter and his wife
and children and his neighbors"—was essential "for example and
precept among the negroes." Phillips explained in 1905:

> It is mistaken to apply the general philosophy of slavery to the American
> situation without very serious modification. A slave among the Greeks or
> Romans was a relatively civilized person, whose voluntary labor would have
> been far more productive than his labor under compulsion. But the negro
> slave was a negro first, last, and always, and a slave incidentally.

More than a decade later in *American Negro Slavery*, Phillips would describe "typical negroes" as "creatures of the moment, with hazy pasts
and reckless futures." As slaves, Africans had been "profoundly modified but hardly transformed by the requirements of European civilization." So began an influential strain in American historical writing that
would view enslavement as beneficial to Africans and their Afro-
American descendants and that would view the decades following the
Emancipation as providing little more than proof of the essential civic,
social, familial, and moral incapacities of the Afro-American descendants of African slaves. The central theme of Afro-American history
became the study of the presence or absence of artificial and external
"restraint."[20]

A fixed and increasingly professional conception of an historical process defined the early twentieth-century "Negro Problem." The im-

[20]U. B. Phillips, "The Plantation as a Civilizing Factor" (1904) and "The Economic Cost
of Slaveholding in the Cotton Belt" (1905), reprinted in Phillips, *Slave Economy of the Old
South*, ed. Eugene D. Genovese (Baton Rouge, 1968), pp. 83–89, 117–135; Phillips, *American Negro Slavery* (Baton Rouge, 1969), pp. vvii–ix, 8, 291.

mediate post-Emancipation years were seen as the start of a modern social debacle. A critical moment in American social history became instead the beginning of a new "natural history." Walter L. Fleming insisted in *The Civil War and Reconstruction in Alabama* that "during 1865 and 1866 the fickle negroes, male and female, made various experiments with new partners, and the result was that in 1867 thousands of negroes had forsaken the husband and wife of slavery times and 'taken up' with others." Or, "many negro men seized the opportunity to desert their wives and children and get new wives. It was considered a relic of slavery to remain tied to an ugly old wife, married in slavery." Or, "now the children were running wild, in want, neglected, becoming criminals and vagabonds. Negro fathers ran off when freedom came.... The negro mother, left alone, often incapable and without judgment, could not support her children. Or, "foeticide and child-murder were common crimes." Or, "upon the negro woman fell the burden of supporting the children. Her husband or husbands had other duties." Or, "negro women began to flock to towns; how they lived no one can tell; immorality was general among them. The conditions of Reconstruction were unfavorable to honesty and immorality among the negroes, both male and female." Not one of these general historical descriptions rested (or rests) upon any historical evidence. Instead, they followed from the retrogressionist belief that the half-savage–half-infant exslaves could not manage decent but difficult lower-class private and public lives. "A black skin," explained John Burgess in *Reconstruction and the Constitution*, "means membership in a race of men which has never of itself succeeded in subjecting passion to reason, has never, therefore, created any civilization of any kind."[21]

THE FAVORED FEW AND THE VICTIM CLASS

We shift forward in time from the retrogressionist historians and social scientists to examine briefly the significant and influential writings of the sociologist E. Franklin Frazier. Despite recent and often severe criticisms of his historical writings, Frazier and his major works—such as the pioneering essay "The Negro Slave Family" published in the *Journal of Negro History* (1930) and his books *The Negro Family in Chicago* (1932), *The Negro Family in the United States* (1939), and *The Negro in the United States*

[21]Walter L. Fleming, *The Civil War and Reconstruction in Alabama* (New York, 1949), pp. 271, 381, 523, 763–764; John Burgess, *Reconstruction and the Constitution* (New York, 1905), p. 133.

(1949 and 1957)—retain and will continue to have great importance. Although his work on the black family shaped bitter public policy debates in the middle 1960s, its importance transcends that episode. In his Preface to *The Negro Family in the United States* (1939), the sociologist Ernest Burgess called it "indispensable" and correctly observed, "it explodes completely, and it may be hoped once and for all, the popular misconception of the uniformity of behavior among Negroes. It shows dramatically the wide variation in conduct and family life by social classes." That was and remains Frazier's enduring contribution. His historical work, moreover, significantly influenced the rewriting of Afro-American history by antiracist scholars as different as Gunnar Myrdal, Kenneth Stampp, and Stanley Elkins.[22]

Surprisingly, the corpus of Frazier's work had very little influence on public policy during his lifetime. His most important books, indeed, contain little explicit discussion of public policy and its relationship to the Afro-American family. In his Introduction to the second edition of *The Negro in the United States* (1957), the sociologist Louis Wirth shrewdly assessed that encyclopedic volume:

> The emphasis in this study is not upon the formulation of broad social policies, but upon the meticulous analysis of social processes. The choice of approach is not due to the author's disinterestedness in policies, but rather rests upon the belief that only through the understanding of the complicated processes of interaction of the various elements with one another can we arrive at a critical evaluation of policies and a realistic view of what is possible and what is desirable.

Wirth's characterization of Frazier's commitment to studying "social processes" applies as much to his works on the Afro-American family as to his more wide-ranging scholarship. In the revised and abridged edition of *The Negro Family in the United States* (1948), Frazier described that book as dealing "with social processes rather than historical events."[23]

Frazier's constant concern with "social processes" resulted from much more than his close association with the Department of Sociology at the University of Chicago in the 1920s and the 1930s. What he learned there (particularly the influence of Robert E. Park's four-stage historical race relations "cycle") served his underlying purpose in writing a detailed and, by contemporary academic standards, empirically rich history of

---

[22]E. W. Burgess, "Preface," in E. Franklin Frazier, *The Negro Family in the United States* (Chicago, 1939), pp. ix–xvii.

[23]Louis Wirth, "Introduction," in E. Franklin Frazier, *The Negro in the United States* (New York, 1957), p. viii; E. Franklin Frazier, *The Negro Family in the United States*, rev. ed. (Chicago, 1966), p. xx.

the Afro-American family. But what Frazier learned at the University of Chicago did not define its underlying purpose. Frazier was deeply concerned with the condition of the urban black poor, most of whom had migrated from the rural South between 1910 and 1930. But neither *The Negro Family in Chicago* nor *The Negro Family in the United States* was a book that read their condition "backward" in order to "explain" it. Instead, those books are best understood as historical works that conceptually challenged the retrogressionist assumptions that dominated so much early twentieth-century academic social science and historiography and that shrouded the behavior of poor rural southern black migrants. This is one reason why it is so important to understand the retrogressionists; otherwise, Frazier's work cannot be understood. He knew their writings well, organized historical evidence to refute them, and studded his earliest and most mature works with harsh references to them.[24]

The strategy Frazier used to dispute their dominance can best be characterized as an "opportunity model," which allowed him to define the history of the Afro-American family in a way that directly challenged and exposed retrogressionist beliefs in the "unchanging Africans." Time and again, but especially in Part Three ("In the House of the Father") of *The Negro Family in the United States,* he used concrete historical example to illustrate how the social processes associated with the opportunity model worked. Privileged slaves (usually servants and artisans), antebellum free blacks, property-owning rural Reconstruction and New South "Black Puritans," and the urban black middle and upper class demonstrated that when given access ("opportunity") the descendants of Africans adapted to and internalized mainstream ("white") social and cultural family mores. In Frazier's model, opportunity was closely but not exclusively associated with skill and property. "Economic conditions," he wrote of rural New South black property owners, "have permitted the germs of culture, which have been picked up by Negro families, to take root and grow." What mattered most to him, however, was that he had defined a genuine social process by which the African could and often had been transformed into an American, finding "within the patterns of the white man's culture, a purpose in life.[25]

Frazier rested his opportunity model on harsh environmentalist assumptions, essential in his effort to discredit retrogressionist history and social science and thereby turn the "Negro Problem" on its head. "Af-

---

[24]An excellent account of Park's work, its antiempirical weaknesses, and its formative influence on Frazier is found in Stanford M. Lyman, *The Black in American Sociological Thought: A Failure of Perspective* (New York, 1972), pp. 22–70.

[25]Frazier, *Negro Family in the United States,* p. 259.

rica" could have no place in defining that problem. Frazier's classic work assumed that initial enslavement radically transformed the African and nowhere more decisively than in family and kin matters:

> Probably never before in history has a people been so nearly completely stripped of its social heritage as the Negroes who were brought to America. Other conquered races have continued to worship their household gods within the intimate circle of their kinsmen. But American slavery destroyed household gods and dissolved the bonds of sympathy and affection between men of the same blood and household.... Through force of circumstances, they had to acquire a new language, adopt new habits of labor, and take over, however imperfectly, the folkways of the American environment.

Frazier held to this view throughout his life. Years after the publication of *The Negro Family in the United States*, he tersely wrote, "The mating or sexual associations which Negroes formed on American soil were largely in response to their natural impulses and the conditions of the new environment." Far more was involved in this formulation than the mere denial of so-called African survivals. The retrogressionists could best be answered by demonstrating that *only* their New World experiences shaped the development of *diverse* Afro-American social institutions and patterns of belief and behavior. These diverse developments, in turn, depended entirely upon differential access to "the folkways of the American environment." Family organization (much less function) was determined by the position of the slaves and their descendants in the changing American social and class structure. Imperfect adaptation resulted from incomplete access.[26]

The opportunity model and its harsh environmentalist assumptions served Frazier well and won him deserved recognition. He had identified a social process that accurately described the *historical* development of family arrangements among those blacks whom he accurately described as the "favored few," those who had "escaped from the isolation of the black folk." The retrogressionists, moreover, had been routed. Frazier's model had successfully transformed the "Negro Problem" into an "American Problem" and turned the unsolvable "race question" into a difficult but solvable "class question." He could truthfully write in 1949:

> During the past fifteen years, American sociologists have abandoned biological explanations of the sex behavior of Negroes and have rejected the attempt

[26]*Ibid.*, pp. 21–33; Frazier, *Negro in the United States*, pp. 8–21, 623–627; E. Franklin Frazier, "The Negro Family in America," in *The Family: Its Function and Destiny*, ed. Ruth Nanda Ashen, rev. ed. (New York, 1959), pp. 65–84.

to ascribe such behavior to the influences of African culture. They have analyzed the sex and family behavior in terms of historical and social factors which have molded the Negro family in the American environment.

Frazier deserved nearly all the credit for this radical shift in focus. "The character of the Negro family during the various stages of its development," Frazier wrote in describing the transformation of a "victim race" into a "victim class," "has been affected by the isolation of Negroes in American society. The lack of opportunity for the Negro male to participate freely in the economic organization and his subordination to whites... have all affected the organization and functioning of the Negro family."[27]

But the opportunity model contained significant historical deficiencies. It could not explain the development of family arrangements among those slaves and exslaves who were denied access to the mainstream culture. The social process so crucial to Frazier's dispute with the retrogressionists excluded the great majority of slaves and exslaves. The victim class remained isolated from the changing civic order. It was, so to speak, a class without a social history and would remain so until drawn into mainstream social processes by external structural changes and enlarged opportunities.

The "maternal family" supplemented Frazier's opportunity model and also flowed from its harsh environmentalist assumptions. It served Frazier significantly in his ongoing critique of the public policies associated with retrogressionist beliefs. The key to its emergence and survival among "the vast majority of slaves" and on "a fairly large scale" in the rural South before and after Emancipation was the static, ahistorical, and mistaken concept of social isolation. Not all slaves experienced that isolation:

> Where the planatation became a settled way of life and a social as well as an economic institution, the integrity of the slave family was generally respected by the masters. Moreover, the social relations which grew up facilitated the process by which the Negro took over the culture of the whites.... The white man's ideas and sentiments in regard to sex and family relations were communicated to the slaves.... These cultural advantages were restricted mainly to the house servant.

But these developments occurred only "under the most favorable conditions." Relatively few slaves benefited from them. Among those denied such access, the maternal family "developed out of the exigencies of life

[27]Frazier, Negro in the United States, p. 627, and "Negro Family in America."

in the new environment." Having no historical antecedents, it was merely a reactive social formation. It had its origins in "maternal feeling . . . dependent largely upon the physiological and emotional responses of the mother to her child" and became "the essential social bond in the family." It was a "natural organization." Concrete historical examples filled those pages of *The Negro Family in the United States* devoted to the "House of the Father." But the several chapters in that work dealing with the "House of the Mother," not surprisingly, were nearly barren of contemporary historical evidence.[28]

That hardly mattered, for Frazier's ahistorical maternal slave family served two important historical functions for him. It allowed him to retrieve the slave woman from retrogressionist abuse and slander, the "tradition" that "has represented her as a devoted foster-parent to her master's children and indifferent to her own." The elderly matriarch ("Granny, the Guardian of Generations"), moreover, became Frazier's substitute for the aged loyal "mammy." Just as significantly, the maternal slave family allowed Frazier to attack retrogressionist assertions of postbellum black family and social deterioration.[29]

Postbellum history proved the retrogressionists wrong. Emancipation drew the isolated plantation blacks into mainstream social processes for the first time, but the failure of the Reconstruction isolated them once again. And retrogressionist public policies intensified their isolation:

> As the result of emancipation the Negro was thrown into competition with the poor whites. At the same time he became estranged from the former slaveholding class, and the sympathetic relations which had been built up during slavery were destroyed. Since the nature of the contacts between whites and blacks was changed, the character of acculturation was changed. If the democratic aims set up during the Reconstruction had been achieved, this estrangement would not have occurred.

Instead, retrogressionist public policies triumphed and denied access to the isolated blacks. "When race was made the basis of status," Frazier said of such legislation, "the Negroes in defense . . . withdrew from the whites." Retrogressionist public policies restored the old isolation. But black deterioration—as the retrogressionists claimed—did not follow. Instead, "there came into existence two separate worlds and, as far as spatial separation permitted, two separate communities." The social processes unleashed by the Emancipation were reversed:

[28]Frazier, *Negro Family in the United States*, p. 47, *Negro in the United States*, p. 14, and "Negro Family in America."

[29]Frazier, *Negro Family in the United States*, chap. 8.

> Since the Negro's personal life was oriented toward the separete Negro world, he derived his values from that world. The patterns of behavior and ideals which he took from the white man were acquired generally through formal imitation of people outside his social world. In their social isolation, the majority of Negroes were forced to draw upon their meager social heritage which they had acquired during slavery.

The imposition of renewed isolation, however, differed from that accompanying initial enslavement. Rural blacks fell back on their *American*—not African—experiences, however imperfectly adapted:

> In the world of the Negro folk in the rural areas of the South, there grew up a family system that met the needs of the environment. Many of the ideas concerning sex relations and mating were carried over from slavery. Consequently, the family lacked an institutional character, since legal marriage and family traditions did not exist among a large section of the population.

Such developments were not evidence of retrogression. Frazier defended them as necessary adaptations to a harsh new class and racial order and described them with much sympathy. He explicitly criticized Philip A. Bruce, among others, for failing to "take into account the folkways and mores that had grown up among the rural Negroes."[30]

The analytic categories that Frazier created ("isolation" and "opportunity") to refute the retrogressionists shaped his pioneering examination of early twentieth-century rural black migration to northern cities. Just how that happened and its consequences require separate and careful study. Briefly, Frazier described the painful social disorganization that accompanied the 1900–1930 migration but insisted that migration northward, whatever its cost, finally promised to free the social process unleashed by the Emancipation and then harshly repressed by the political retrogressionists. "The world of the city," Frazier wrote in 1932, "is a destroyer as well as a builder of traditions." Significantly, if somewhat surprisingly from the distance of the late 1970s, *The Negro Family in the United States,* published in 1939, had an optimistic conclusion. That was so even though the Great Depression had damaged poor rural and urban blacks much more severely than it had any other segment in the population. A place of "destruction," the city of the 1920s and the 1930s was also a place of "rebirth" for the migrant black poor. Frazier associated that "rebirth" with the final rejection of old rural folkways, the repudiation of sterile black middle-class opportunity models and the integration of the new black workers into the industrial working class. Expanding industrial production promised to make all of this possible.

[30]Frazier, "Negro Family in America," and *Negro in the United States,* p. 629.

Increasingly influenced by popular front Marxism, Frazier found that the "most significant element in the new social structure is the black industrial proleterit." He believed that "as the isolation of the black worker is gradually broken down, his ideas and patterns of family approximate those of the great body of industrial workers."[31]

Frazier was far too optimistic. The "social process" soon was blocked once again. A long secular trend had begun that saw little more than transformation of the surplus rural black poor into the unemployed and underemployed urban black poor. By the early 1960s, Frazier's harsh environmentalist assumptions about the "isolated" black folk had become the underlying "historical process" that sustained "deficit culture" theories and the so-called culture of poverty. The grandchildren of Mansfield French and Clinton Fisk surfaced to shape public policy. Ironically, Frazier's work encouraged this rebirth, because Frazier had not written a history of the black family. Instead, he had used varieties of historic black family experiences to illustrate how a particular social process worked and to redefine the race question as a class question. But he had not written the history of a changing victim class and its family life. No one in the 1930s knew how to do that. Frazier should not be blamed for illustrating what was a general deficiency in historical conceptualization and historical methodology.

THE FUTURE

We return briefly to the 1960s and the debate over the so-called Moynihan Report and its implications for public policies affecting poor urban blacks and their families.[32] One result of that debate was a new scholarship that radically revised conventional understanding of the slave family and its poor rural and urban descendants. That revision is still underway, but the victim class has entered into the historical mainstream and no longer is seen in isolation. Few suggested more clearly the close connection between this new understanding of the victim class and its history to mid and late twentieth-century public policies affecting the black urban poor than Roger Wilkins. Then a member of the *New York Times* editorial board, Wilkins explained:

[31]E. Franklin Frazier, *Negro Family in Chicago*, (Chicago, 1932), p. 243, and *Negro Family in the United States*, pp. 475, 487.

[32]Some of these conclusions draw upon a presentation made by the author to the Rockefeller Foundation and published in *RF Illustrated* 3 (September 1977): 11. Invaluable evidence of the important uses that poor rural and urban blacks make of kin and quasi-kin networks in the 1950s and 1970s is found in Carol Stack, *All Our Kin* (New York, 1974), and Demitri Shimkin *et al.*, *The Black Extended Family* (The Hague, 1978).

Critics of Mr. Moynihan's family report persisted because of the importance of the lines of policy it suggested. If one concluded that the human
destruction and degradation in black communities resulted from an historical pathology of several centuries' duration, then a certain set of policy
choices tinged with large amounts of despair about black capacities are likely
to follow.

If, on the other hand, one concluded that weakness in black family structure was exceedingly rare until the great migration northward, which started
during World War II and continued after agri-business made millions of rural
blacks economically superfluous, then a very different set of judgments
would follow. They would be based on the assumption that job discrimination and the inability of the Northern urban economy to absorb all those
migrants accounted for most of the damage suffered by the black family and
that job creation and equal opportunity were the most urgent remedial
courses to pursue.

Wilkins made these comments in the early fall of 1976. Three-quarters of
a century earlier, the distinguished historian and social scientist W. E. B.
DuBois disputed retrogressionist historians and social scientists in a different language, but his insight did not differ from that of Wilkins.
Complaining that "sociologists gleefully count bastards," DuBois reminded them that "to be a poor man is hard but to be a poor race in a
land of dollars is the very bottom of hardships."

The new scholarship increasingly demonstrates how poor blacks—
even as slaves—were not crushed by those hardships. The four great
migrations that had cut through their long and tortured American experience had not stripped them of a capacity to create, sustain, and use a
distinctive Afro-American family and kinship system. The first migration from Africa, of course, involved initial enslavement. But by the
mid-eighteenth century, a distinctive Afro-American family and kinship
system had developed, that was new and adaptive—neither African nor
American but Afro-American. The second migration involved the mass
movement of Afro-Americans (not Africans) from the Upper South to
the Lower South in the first half of the nineteenth century. Following
the industrial revolution and the coming of the cotton gin, it involved
more than half a million persons and was probably the largest forced
internal migration in the Western world in that century. The victim class
carried with it conceptions of family and kin function to the Lower South
and in ways as yet little understood reconstructed their slave lives based
upon beliefs and practices similar to those of their parents and
grandparents. At the time of the emancipation, ordinary exslaves in
places as different as Mississippi and Virginia therefore shared much in
common in their family and kin arrangements and in how they used
them. The third great migration involved the decendants of these slaves

leaving the rural and urban South for the northern cities from about 1900 to the Great Depression. That migration involved changes in the composition of the poor urban black household, but these adaptations were not accompanied by widespread family disorganization. Why that did not happen remains unclear, but the answer to that question will be better known after we have studied how the enlarged kin and quasi-kin networks formed by the slaves and sustained by their immediate descendants moved with the victim class from the South to the North.

And then there is the fourth and most recent migration. It began during the Second World War and continued into the 1960s, a migration that was not simply a black migration but involved a vast shift among poor rural whites and blacks to the mid-twentieth-century American city. In that period, about 20 million Americans made their way from the farm to the city. Our understanding of the fourth migration, which is so essential to formulating humane, workable, and socially constructive public policies, has rested upon a grave misunderstanding of the three earlier migrations. Poor rural black migrants did not bring with them a long history of family and kin disorganization into decaying, mid-twentieth-century northern cities. Historians now are slowly reexamining the earlier migrations and seeing how Africans, and especially Afro-Americans—first as slaves and then as destitute, legally free men and women—dealt with those difficult and often painful moments.

The fourth migration, however, commands renewed and indeed fresh study by others than historians. Social scientists and students of public policy must put aside erroneous historical beliefs in examining how rural southern poor blacks in our time have been transformed into urban northern poor blacks and how their family and kin life have been unconscionably strained in the past 3 and a half decades. What is now known about the victim class and its history until 1925 shows that widely held "historical" and "cultural" explanations for their current vulnerability and suffering are spurious. The new scholarship instead directs attention to the recent failings of an economic and social system, not to its victims or their grandparents and great-grandparents. The new scholarship, moreover, suggests that the ways in which poor urban blacks in the 1960s and 1970s rely on kin and quasi-kin networks to sustain them have a long history—one that is as the core of the enduring but changing Afro-American experience. That fact, among others, should be kept in mind as we deal with decaying late-twentieth-century cities and with those Afro-American men, women, and children who have been most directly and indecently ravaged by that decay and the moral insensitivity that has accompanied it.

9

URBAN PASTS AND URBAN POLICIES

SEYMOUR J. MANDELBAUM

INTRODUCTION

For at least a century, urban policy discussions in the United States have been conducted within a national community of senior bureaucrats, planning and social science professionals, elected officials, businessmen, and leaders of other major interest groups. The community has grown in size and internal complexity over the years, but its essential dynamics have been remarkably stable. Community deliberations precede government action and then flow through and around it—legitimating, evaluating, guiding, destroying, and changing.[1]

This chapter explores the manner in which historical assertions have been employed in two community debates. The first debate, in the late 1960s and early 1970s, dealt with the intentional redistribution of the population; the second, which is still very much alive, with the urban implications of regional shifts in people and wealth.

[1] My own conception of the policy community is largely derived from Kenneth Paul Fox, *A Better City Government: Innovation in American Urban Politics, 1850–1937* (Philadelphia, 1977). In a paper dealing with telecommunications issues, I employ a similar concept but a different term, describing a "design" rather than a "policy" community. The terms are intended to be virtually equivalent. See "The Design of the Designing Community," in *Evaluating New Telecommunications Services*, ed. Martin C. J. Elton *et al.* (New York, 1978), pp. 663–679.
An earlier version of this chapter appeared in the *Journal of Urban History* 6(August 1980): 453–483, and is reprinted here by permission from Sage Publications, Inc.

SOCIAL HISTORY AND SOCIAL POLICY   ISBN 0-12-598680-7

I have not tried to present a complete narrative of the substance and political dynamics of these two debates. My concern is with the form and uses of historical statements and not with their particular content or correctness, with history in policy deliberations and not (at least here) with preferred urban policies.

Within the policy community, as in any other group, participants develop a shared memory of how the world has been and how they have acted. In many circumstances, this memory need only be evoked cryptically without full explication. Throughout its history, the policy community has, however, been too diversified, too open, and too dependent upon outside support to rely wholly on cryptic evocation. As new members are socialized and rival positions attacked or justified, personal memories are explicated and formalized. Shared histories become objects of controversy. The community debates not only what it should do but also the protocols for recording what it has done and the adequacy of particular accounts.

This mobilization of memory usually begins with short-term, self-reflective histories of the community's deliberations and the immediate context of a policy debate. Characteristically, however, it is broadened so as to justify or devalue rival positions. The debates over urban congestion at the turn of the century, or, more recently, those over crime, violence, and pollution, all moved outward from an argument over the current state of the world toward the expansion and reorganization of memories of the extended past.[2] Historical accounts and future policies were designed in tandem.

Professionalized inquiry into urban history plays only a modest role in this articulation and design of memories. Far from caring too little about history, all the participants in the policy community care too much about it to leave it to any group of specialists or to wait for the development of a scholarly consensus.

The account in this chapter of the varied forms of this caring is directed to one major prescription. Attempting to change the way the community views the past requires an unusually deep commitment to sustained dialogue. A dialogic effect is destroyed at the outset if the historian assumes that the actors are either ignorant or uncaring or that they are unruly and impatient children who must learn to listen attentively to the knowledgeable adult.

[2]See, for examples of this expansion, Adna Ferrin Weber, *The Growth of Cities in the Nineteenth Century* (Ithaca, 1963 [orig. publ., 1899]); Hugh Davis Graham and Ted Robert Gurr, eds., *The History of Violence in America: A Report to the National Commission on the Causes and Prevention of Violence* (New York, 1969); and Barry Commoner, *The Closing Circle: Nature, Man and Technology* (New York, 1971).

NATIONAL URBAN GROWTH POLICY

A Brief History

Urban policy analysts prior to 1965 rarely imagined that they could or should control the direction of interurban migration or the distribution of growth among cities. Their conversations were dominated by city–suburban differences, the problems of urban-based poverty, and an aging central city infrastructure. After the Watts riots in 1965, policy discussions focused on the threat of pandemic racial warfare.

The term "urban growth" appeared in conversations within the policy community in two contexts. The first included a varied set of issues all directed to the pattern of suburban development and its relationship to the character of central cities. Analysts and advocates debated deconcentration, renewal, sprawl, racial and income barriers in the suburbs, and the efflorescence of governmental units. One group of histories written to address these issues pointed to the tendentiousness of the idea of individual land ownership; another, to the slow and problematic influence of residence upon culture.[3] The 1967–1968 National Commission on Urban Problems, capturing the quality of this discourse, did not deal with a national policy on population distribution as part of its own extensive urban program. The city, the commission stressed, "must be viewed in terms of the entire urban area, in terms of all its functions and in terms of all of its people." It did not propose to view *a city* in the context of the *entire* set of cities and regions and their relations. "Urban growth" was a problem of city–suburban relations and the intrametropolitan political economy.[4]

The idea of "urban growth" was used in a different way in discussions of the role of town and cities in the revitalization of "depressed regions." The debate over regional development contributed an important (although ultimately thin) idea to the conception of a national urban growth policy. After World War II, a vigorous group of American scholars, enlarging upon European theoretical suggestions, had developed a synthetic image of the spatial organization of society and of a comprehensive "regional science." Even the most ambitious proponents of the new science did not imagine that they could adequately forecast, let alone guide, the order they perceived. They believed, however, that

[3]John Delafons, *Land-Use Controls in the United States*, 2d ed. (Cambridge, Mass., 1969), is an example of one body of work; Herbert J. Gans, *The Levittowners: Ways of Life and Politics in a New Suburban Community* (New York, 1967), of the other.

[4]National Commission on Urban Problems, *Building the American City* (New York, 1969), p. ix.

they knew enough to locate and externally cultivate promising small towns so as to stimulate their adjacent regions. It seemed a modest intellectual step from the observation that in the past, spatially concentrated activity had diffused over a broad area to a strategy of encouraging growth centers. Only a few academic members of the policy community argued more broadly that regional theory and international planning practice provided an adequate basis for the development of a national urban growth strategy in the United States. Programs to encourage urban development in lagging regions would complement (without replacing) more conventional attacks on city–suburban and racial issues.[5]

It was not, however, the regional science community or its outposts in the Economic Development Administration that expanded the idea of growth centers into the cornerstone of a broader national policy.[6] The first expansive thrust came from the Department of Agriculture, observed rather warily by suspicious officials at EDA and the Department of Housing and Urban Development. Sprung loose from its scholarly and agency roots, the idea of guiding the distribution of population ran freely through the policy community until it was retamed by its progenitors.

As early as 1966, President Lyndon Johnson had told a small-town audience in Pennsylvania that "the cites will never solve their problems unless we solve the problems of towns and smaller areas.[7] This theme was further advanced by a group centered in the office of Secretary of Agriculture Orville L. Freeman and advised by the Greek architect and planner Constantinos Doxiadis. The agriculture group argued that it was possible simultaneously to address two nagging issues: "Our metropolitan areas have more people and problems than they can cope with. All around us they are exploding with violence. At the same time, many villages, small towns and their surrounding countryside are being

---

[5]See the discussion of growth centers and larger urban policies in Lloyd Rodwin, *Nations and Cities: A Comparison of Strategies for Urban Growth* (Boston, 1970), and the important historical model in Eugene Smolensky and Donald Ratejezak, "The Conception of Cities," *Explorations in Entreprenurial History*, 2d ser. 2 (Winter 1965): 90–131. For a line to USDA concerns, see Brian J. L. Berry, *Strategies, Models and Economic Theories of Development in Rural Regions*, U.S., Department of Agriculture, Economic Research Service, Agricultural Economic Report no. 127 (Washington, D.C., 1967).

[6]I have followed the version of the history of the idea described in the Advisory Commission on Intergovernmental Relations, *Urban and Rural America: Policies for Future Growth* (Washington, D.C., 1968), and extended by Lowdon Wingo, "Issues in a National Urban Development Strategy for the United States," *Urban Studies* 13 (1976): 3–27. The Wingo article is a particularly interesting illustration of the manner in which the policy community generates accounts of its own deliberations.

[7]ACIR, *Urban and Rural America*, p. xv.

drained of people and economic vigor."[8] A program to build "Communities of Tomorrow" would adjust the balance of urban explosion and rural decay, moving both cities and small towns along a path that could only be beneficial. Dominated by an essentially architectural vision of the well-ordered society, this first USDA argument in 1967 anticipated the style of subsequent advocacy: a national urban growth policy could satisfy the Pareto criterion of increasing well-being without anyone suffering.

Whereas the USDA group saw a national policy as stimulating rural development, other participants in the policy community focused principally upon the creation of new communities within metropolitan spheres. Robert Weaver, who was to be the first secretary of the Department of Housing and Urban Development, believed that the expansion of these new communities would seriously address a variety of urban problems and that they were worthy objects of federal assistance. Like their rural counterparts, they would have a radiant regional impact.[9]

In 1968, the Advisory Commission on Intergovernmental Relations and then, in 1969, an *ad hoc* National Commission on Urban Policy, provided the links between the USDA initiative and the new community movement. The two groups developed the major features of a program to stimulate the articulation of new centers within metropolitan areas, to revitalize small towns in rural areas, and (in the ambitious version of the National Commission) to create 100 freestanding new towns and 10 substantial new cities.

Between 1968 and 1970, the policy community generated endorsements for a national urban growth policy as if moved by a giant invisible hand. By 1970, only 2 years after the first statements of a synthetic idea of a national urban growth policy, it was engraved in legislation. The Housing and Urban Development Act of 1970 was intended, in the words of its preamble, to "provide for the establishment of a national urban growth policy." Title VII of the act called upon the president to report regularly on recommendations for programs and policies needed to carry out such a policy.

There was virtually no substantive policy direction in the act. Its passage was a hollow victory for what was certainly a poorly developed and, as it was overcome by analysis and events, a short-lived idea. It was clear when the first mandated report was presented in 1972 that the

[8]U.S., Department of Agriculture, *Communities of Tomorrow* (Washington, D.C., 1967), quoted in Wingo, "Issues," p. 6.
[9]For a critical view of this position, see Edward P. Eichler and Marshall Kaplan, *The Community Builders* (Berkeley, 1967), pp. 160–182.

ambitious hopes of the National Commission would not be quickly realized. The report was met with howls of frustration from serious advocates of a comprehensive policy.[10] The 1974 and 1976 documents were even farther from the actual formulation of programs, and the latter was virtually ignored by the policy community.[11]

Critics of the series of reports in the Republican administrations frequently charged that the collapse of the dream of a national urban growth policy stemmed from a lack of presidential commitment.[12] The magnitude of effort inherent in any global attempt to optimize the distribution of population certainly did not fit within the framework of the so-called New Federalism as imagined by Richard Nixon.

The idea of a national urban growth policy was, however, beset by more than a lack of commitment. The moment the general strategic posture was employed to guide the design of specific programs, it collapsed. A committee of the Domestic Council was entrusted with the preparation of the first report under the 1970 act. "The whole thing was impossible to get hold of," staff member Jerry B. Waters later reported.

> First of all the technical information base simply wasn't there. Comprehensive data and economic and sociological models needed to evaluate alternative models were lacking. Secondly, there had simply not been enough political dialogue. There was little clear understanding of what was politically acceptable and what was not. The Council had been given a mandate, yet in trying to fulfill it, it found itself operating largely in a vacuum.[13]

The same problems beset the Commission on Population Growth and the American Future, chaired by John D. Rockefeller III. Although chiefly concerned with the size and demographic profile of the American population and the development of population policies, the Rockefeller commission, which reported in 1972, also examined the idea of distribution. Only the most modest recommendations emerged from this examination. The commissioners beat a graceful retreat from both the ambitious hopes and the Pareto assumptions of their predecessors. The marching orders for the retreat were drawn not by political leaders but by a group of regional scientists acting as consultants to the commission. The

[10]U.S., Congress, House of Representatives, Subcommittee on Housing, Committee on Banking and Currency, *National Growth Policy*, 92nd Cong., 2d sess.

[11]The process of preparing the reports and their reception are described by Kermit C. Parsons and Pierre Clavel, *National Growth Policy: An Institutional Perspective* (Ithaca, 1978), pp. 4–12.

[12]For an insider's view, see William Nicoson, "The United States: The Battle for Title VII," *New Perspectives on Community Development* ed. Mahlon Apgar (New York, 1976).

[13]James L. Sundquist, *Dispersing Population: What America Can Learn From Europe* (Washington, D.C., 1975), p. 8.

consultants killed—at least for a while—the bastard child of their own discourse.

The Uses of History

My purpose in recounting the recent history of the idea of a national urban growth policy is to provide a framework for a closer examination of the manner in which historical assertions were employed in the deliberations of the policy community. The Advisory Commission on Intergovernmental Relations, National Commission on Urban Policy, and Rockefeller commission report provide a convenient textual record of these deliberations.

In an earlier typological essay I distinguished three characteristic forms of policy-related historical argument.[14] The first form deals with the moral relationship between the past and the future; the second, with the direction and pace of change; and the third; with models of systems and their environments. These three forms are commonly interwoven in policy discourse. Advocates of a particular position are prone (understandably) to argue not only that we should do something but also that there are precedents for the proposed action and that it both fits the moment and is within our ken. Powerful arguments for moral legitimacy and precedent suffocate qualms about the difficulties of modeling, as if the assertion that one *should* have a policy ensured that one *could*. Assertions of modeling competency similarly work backwards, as if adequate knowledge established the legitimacy of an activity: If one *can* have a policy, one *should*.

At one level, both the ACIR and the National Commission addressed the problem of establishing the normative worth of a national urban growth policy without explicitly historical statements. The ACIR report, with characteristic judiciousness, included a series of arguments against the formulation of a national urban policy. On balance, these arguments were rejected, however, for reasons that suggest that they had not been seriously considered. Not to have a policy would, as it were, deny the efficacy of the federal system that the ACIR is directed by law to enhance.[15]

The National Commission as an *ad hoc* group recruited on the basis of already declared policy preferences was less disposed to balance arguments than was the ACIR. (The members and staff of the commission

---

[14]"The Past in Service to the Future," *Journal of Social History* 11 (Winter 1977): 193–204. See also Karl-George Faber, The Use of History in Political Debate," *History and Policy* Beiheft 17 (1978): 36–67.

[15]ACIR, *Urban and Rural America*, p. 129.

included several committed operating officials, but no skeptical academic planners and social scientists.) Its report, *The New City*, [16] is an enthusiastic, graphically appealing, and well-written work of advocacy, which leaps easily from the static photographic image of the well-designed town to the conception of a well-designed nation. If it is possible—see the picture before you—to create an appealing urban environment, must it not be possible and wise as well to create an equally attractive nation?

At a second level, both the ACIR and the National Commission launched into extensive historical arguments in which each of the three forms of statement appeared. The reports of both groups designed the past with the same care that we usually (naively) expect to be granted only to the future. In each, the burden of legitimation obscured the limited capability of modeling by adopting an essentially narcissistic historical vision.

The ACIR report opens with a description of long-term patterns of urbanization to demonstrate five "paradoxes" of American urban history. I am concerned here only with the first—"the emergence of an urban nation in a country that has a rural bias against cities"[17]—since it reveals the major intellectual simplification underlying the commission's idea of a national urban growth policy and dictated the manner in which historical arguments were employed. The paradox is a familiar one among urban historians. In a slight expansion it takes the following form: There is a peculiarly urban consciousness or program that would certainly have shaped American cities in a different pattern from the one that emerged. The absence of that pattern indicates an antiurban bias that could only be based in the animus or ignorance of rural residents or in the inappropriate rural heritage that urbanites were, unfortunately, unable to shed.

The expanded paradox defies empirical validation. It is a political argument asserting that there is a unique match between certain gross attributes of settlements and their social and physical form. For good reason, however, the argument is commonly stated as a series of mismatches or problems: If a city is to include a million people, it is antiurban to prefer that each household live on an acre lot; it is similarly antiurban to throw garbage out the window. A long list of mismatch assertions offered one at a time implies that opposite policies or designs form a uniquely powerful set in which environmental demands are met by appropriate urban forms and processes. If rural depopulation is bad,

---

[16]National Commission on Urban Growth Policy, *The New City*, ed. Donald Canty (New York, 1969).

[17]ACIR, *Urban and Rural America*, p. 1.

then new growth centers are good; if sprawl is wasteful, then new communities are efficient.[18]

The force of this argument depends upon acceptance of the general credibility of this loose form of logical obversion and of the particular set of problem or mismatch formulations. Rejecting the argument on either general or particular grounds, a designer or policymaker is forced to adopt a more complex conception of the process of choice. Problems are subject to alternative definitions, and preferences may be variously matched or mismatched. Governments usually fall into serious difficulties, for example, if they try to centralize employment while reducing residential densities and cutting travel time and costs. They are necessarily forced to trade among preferences, rather than to assume that each may be fully realized on the same urban surface. There are, however, a great many internally consistent patterns of settlement. For an individual with a stable and reasonably explicit and coherent welfare function, it is difficult to distinguish the acceptable patterns and to select one among them. For a social group, the task, if begun de novo, may be impossible.

The ACIR simplification generates a small positive set of programs and then bolsters them with a two-sided historical argument. The first side, like a lawyer's brief with its listing of precedents and works of historical scholarship, describes a long record of national attempts to influence urban and rural settlements, from nineteenth-century land policy to more recent federally sponsored new towns and regional development programs. (The National Commission added to this list a fuller treatment of European new town and population distribution policies.) Such a sustained history of activity constitutes a tradition that cannot be excluded from the legitimate domain of governmental activity.

The second side of the historical argument infers the existence of a policy from the regularities in the distribution of the population and the obvious spatial impact of a great many justifiable governmental activities. A nation that already builds great highways and allocates billions of dollars in contracts, stimulating employment here and shutting plants there, can hardly boggle at increasing the self-consciousness of its own practices.

The argument that there is an established implicit policy later emerged

---

[18]The design method described by Christopher Alexander, *Notes on the Synthesis of Form* (Cambridge, Mass., 1964), depends on the relative ease of specifying "misfit variables." Most United States environmental legislation has a similar character, prohibiting a long list of noxious conditions with little sense of the shape of the remaining surface for development. See John H. Noble, John S. Banta, and John S. Rosenberg, eds., *Groping through the Maze: Foreign Experience Applied to the U.S. Problem of Coordinating Development Controls* (Washington, D.C., 1977).

as important in the debate over regional shares. In both the ACIR and National Commission reports, this implicit policy is contemned rather than described. If the United States has a policy, it is repeatedly portrayed as "aimless" and "haphazard." The very process of rapid change suggests a failure to achieve "painless, planned, and productive land use." Planning, in contrast, implies stability and balance, a meshing of interests so that new community programs in one city conform to "areawide, regional and national plans and objectives."[19]

The National Commission extended the critique of established processes. It projected a United States population growth of 100 million by the year 2000 and argued that distribution in the current pattern would intensify metropolitan problems and rural decay. It proposed to treat those 100 million as a largely footloose resource, to be distributed (although by incentives, not by coercion) so as to maximize the well-being of the nation. In order to justify such a wrenching of individuals from the social fabric, they (or their institutions) were stripped of essential cognitive abilities. Despite the pervasive evidence of stability on the one side and purposive variation on the other, the current pattern of settlement was treated as if it were random. In the words of Douglas Canty, editor of *The New City:*

> So far we have been willing, by and large to see the shape of the nation be determined by a random accretion of individual decisions, with little regard for the end result. We have been building urban America as if there were no tomorrow.
>
> It doesn't have to be that way. There is nothing in our history or traditions which says the nation cannot take a hand in its future, cannot decide what it wants to be and how to get there.[20]

Large-scale models of intermetropolitan migration and differential growth or the form of individual cities may, indeed, use a random element to simulate variations at a microscale. Attributing randomness to the entire system avoided the problem of modeling its highly constrained dynamics. It also avoided—with the wave of a political fiction—the description of the shift in control implicit in the assertion that the "nation" should decide "what it wants to be and how to get there."

For all the mass of evidence on urban patterns in these reports, the two groups were left, in essential matters, with a self-reflective history of their own enterprise. They were in much the same situation as urban

[19]ACIR, *Urban and Rural America*, pp. 69, 99.
[20]*New City*, ed. Canty, p. 75.

reformers who could study only reform and not cities, because that was all the history provided for them.

In the 3 years after 1969, the policy community devoted a considerable amount of energy to correcting both the historical and the planning analytic flaws of the first efforts of the ACIR and the National Commission. The assumptions underlying the implicit economic models of the two reports were formalized and tested. The idea that there was an optimum size for cities and that the largest were uneconomic was poked at unrewarding data until researchers were heartily sick of it.[21]

Much of the work in these 3 years was supported by the Rockefeller-chaired Commission on Population Growth and the American Future. Unlike its predecessors, the Rockefeller commission fully engaged the scholarly community. The abiding invisible college of regional scientists and urban policy analysts and planners had temporarily lost control of an idea. In the Rockefeller commission they recaptured it, shaping the formal consensual recommendations while—in seven thick volumes of reports and hearings—strengthening their own intellectual claims.

The scholars' influence on the commission was dramatic. The apparatus for simplifications was dismantled in favor of a complex view of urban and regional dynamics. The stability and adaptive character of present distribution modes were exposed, and the assumption of unlimited plasticity was abandoned. Values that the ACIR and National Commission had treated as amenable to simultaneous optimization were quite sensibly shown to be, at least in part, contradictory. Accelerated growth in small towns might deflect population from the largest cities, but "at that point, one must ask if the cure is any better than the disease."[22]

The commission did not entirely abandon the idea of guiding the distribution of population. It suffused it, however, in a general endorsement of metropolitan regional planning, the reduction of racial segregation, rural revitalization, and the reduction of information barriers to migration. A national growth policy, the report concluded, will emerge in an unspecified future. For now, the commission recommended only the development of a set of "guidelines" and a continued effort to monitor the spatial impact of federal expenditures and other governmental decisions.

The consultants' reports elaborate the intellectual context of these recommendations in what may be taken as a form of C. P. Snow's cultural war. In effect (and perhaps in intention), the proponents of a national

---

[21]For a summary of the discussions of the scale issue, see Alan Gilbert, "The Arguments for Very Large Cities Reconsidered," and the critical comment by Harry Richardson, *Urban Studies* 13 (1976): 27–34, 307–310.

[22]*Population and the American Future* (New York, 1972), p. 40.

urban growth policy had expressed the hope that there was a way of avoiding the dense tangle of city–suburban, class, and racial issues for which "urban policy" had served as a rubric. This strategy of avoidance rested upon the marriage of an architectural vision to a commitment to specific images of the good society. Against this marriage the consultants mustered the classic weapons: a highly developed critique of geographic or spatial determinism and an elaborate defense of dynamic "want-regarding" markets and political systems. The weapons had been honed in several decades of warfare between planners and their social science friends on the one side and architects on the other. The attack might appear remote, critical rather than innovative, unduly delighting in its own complexity, and more useful in the trenches than stirring at the heights. By largely ignoring the problem of legitimacy so as to focus on the adequacy of the growth models, it did, however, define a new set of historical issues.

In a forcefully argued essay, subsequently published in *Public Interest*, William Alonso picked up one part of this attack. The control advocates, he lamented, were ignorant and perhaps worse:

> Many of the current proposals are naive either because they do not recognize the realities of the working of the sytem or because they propose geometrics of population.... Geographic radicalism seems misplaced when we are uncertain of the purposes, of the processes, and of the effectiveness of the instruments.[23]

Advocates of a national policy assume, he argued, that because systems have spatial implications, they can be controlled by regulating land use. (The photographs in *The New City* expressed this assumption.) A long history, which he only sketched, suggests that this assumption is false: "Direct policies to modify this geographic distribution have been generally ineffective and sometimes counterproductive because they have underestimated or misjudged the connections among elements of the system along dimensions other than geographic."[24]

Edgar Hoover proceeded in the same vein. Public policies, he argued, should enhance market processes rather than replace them. Whereas some efforts might be made to reduce the wildest swings of rapid growth and decline, the historical record of movement, for Hoover, was a sign not of systemic failure but of creative adaptation. Static distri-

---

[23]William Alonso, "Problems, Purposes and Implicit Policies for a National Strategy of Urbanization," in *Population, Distribution and Policy*, ed. Sara Mills Mazie, Research Reports prepared for the Commission on Population Growth and the American Future, vol. 5 (Washington, D.C., 1972), pp. 631–647 (quote on p. 635).

[24]*Ibid.*, p. 646.

butional formulas imposed upon dynamic processes involve "costly misallocations of resources and sometimes confuse equity among individuals and equity among regions."[25]

Finally, Brian J. L. Berry argued that we could not have explicit policies until we commanded explicit models that could deal with the spatial pattern and value implications of alternative federal spending programs. In the absence of such models, he argued, we are likely to distract attention from fundamental shifts in the urban pattern in order to "induce growth in small lagging peripheral zones where population decline is associated with either resource depletion or increasing agricultural efficiency, and from which the population remains so eager to emigrate."[26]

A counterattack to the Alonso–Hoover–Berry position would have abandoned the narcissistic history, the conflict-obscuring Pareto assumption, and the view of an "unplanned" population pattern. They would have been replaced with an explicit normative model and an associated distributional calculus. Who would benefit and who would lose from one change or another? The implicit "urban policy" would be seen not as haphazard or as embedded in the diversity of the market and in a pluralistic political system but as the result of discrete, discernable, and changeable acts and actors.

These specifications are difficult to meet. Insofar as the growth control position rests on evidence at all, it depends ultimately not on its legitimate predecessors or even a tally of modest successes and failures but on implicit answers to a series of sweeping counterfactual questions: "What if the urban hierarchy in the United States had been centrally planned over a hundred and fifty years?" "What if, over the same period, suburban growth had been concentrated and the social profits returned to inner-city development?" Posing these questions suggests interesting lines of inquiry, but it is difficult to be confident of the answers since the actual historical relations within a simulated system would be radically altered.[27]

The specifications are, of course, also difficult politically. Government

[25]Edgar M. Hoover, "Policy Objectives for Population Distribution," in *ibid.*, pp. 649–664 (quote on p. 651).

[26]Brian J. L. Berry, "Population Growth in the Daily Urban Systems of the United States, 1980–2000," in *ibid.*, pp. 229–270. The warning against responding only to the squeaky wheel appears on p. 245.

[27]On the historical method for using counterfactual arguments, see Jeffrey G. Williamson, *Late Nineteenth Century American Development: A General Equilibrium History* (London, 1974), pp. 10–19. For their role in planning, see William C. Baer and Skye M. Fleming, "Counterfactual Analysis: An Analytic Tool for Planners," *Journal of the American Institute of Planners* 42 (July 1976): 243–252.

planners and analysts are not likely to embrace them easily. The writers of the biannual reports on policy were caught up in the same search for models and indicators as were the Rockefeller consultants. No "mainstream" counterattacks were launched. Radical scholars, for their part, did not find "national urban growth policy" a comfortable mantle for their concerns.

After 1972, the discrete bands with the policy community moved apart again. The coalition of new community builders and rural revitalizers was shattered by the failure of analysis, by the rise of interest rates that inhibited construction, and by the rapid increase in nonmetropolitan population that promised to do "naturally"—and, many moaned, overdo—what Orville Freeman had urged in 1966.[28] A portion of the same group that had advocated a national urban growth policy moved over into the fight for a national land use policy, recapitulating in their early statements the forms of the ACIR and National Commission arguments and ending (at least for the moment) with an unsuccessful bill that, like the 1970 act, had no substantive content.[29] The policy community as a whole found new points of convergence, including, by 1975, the relations between the Sunbelt and Snowbelt. Because the relational issue, from the very beginning, involved an explicit conflict of interest and a distributional struggle, the use of history never had to play through the Pareto fantasy and the simplification methods of the national growth policy idea.

REGIONAL SHARES AND URBAN POLICY

The First Rounds

In 1975, Kirkpatrick Sale, in this well-publicized book, announced a *Power Shift: The Rise of the Southern Rim and Its Challenge to the Eastern Establishment*.[30] In the Winter 1976 issue of *Dissent*, David Muchnick, playing out a similar theme with a different evaluation, argued that the real national urban policy that had emerged from the Nixon and Ford administrations was a "death warrant" for the cities of the Northeast

---

[28]Gene F. Summers et al., *Industrial Invasion of Nonmetropolitan America: A Quarter Century of Experience* (New York, 1976); W. Patrick Beaton and James L. Cox with the assistance of Ron M. Morris, "Toward an Accidental National Urbanization Policy," *Journal of the American Institute of Planners* 43 (January 1977): 54–61.

[29]See Noreen Lyday, *The Law of the Land: Debating National Land Use Legislation 1970–75* (Washington, D.C., 1976); Michael Zisser, "The Design of a Public Policy: National Land Use Planning and Organizational Theory" (Ph.D. diss., University of Pennsylvania, 1979).

[30](New York, 1975).

and Midwest.[31] In May, *Business Week* characterized the debate over the relations between the regions as the "Second War between the States."[32] The *National Journal* in June provided extensive (although not unchallenged) documentation of the flow of federal funds from the North to the South.[33] The northeastern governors' meeting in Saratoga, New York, in November took up the same argument, and the Southern Growth Policies Board girded its loins for the northern counterattack.[34] Uncounted New Yorkers—some accepting, other refuting, the dominant history of municipal welfare expenditures gone wild—adopted the regional theme. Jack Newfield's and Paul Du Brul's devastating picture of the faults of New York City's "permanent government" was set within the context of "large" and "inexorable" forces that were draining jobs and capital to the Southwest and the Sunbelt. Quoting Robert Lekachman and Muchnick, they argue that the "major victim of the Nixon counter-revolution was American cities, especially the aging cities of the Northeast and Midwest."[35]

The issue of regional shares is not yet fully played out, and it is much too early to write its internal history. When this chapter was first written, I expected (as did many people) that the issue would be sharply drawn in a series of specific legislative arguments as the result of a major urban policy statement that President Carter promised for early 1978.

That expectation has not been fulfilled. Following the recommendations developed in his critique of the Model Cities planning effort, Marshall Kaplan guided the president's Urban and Regional Policy Group, through an unusually broad process of consultation. The URPG cast its net over problems of class, race, region, and neighborhood—and their partisans—that had been obscured by the issue of population redis-

[31]David M. Muchnick, "Death Warrant for the Cities: The National Urban Policy," *Dissent*, 23 (Winter 1976): 21–32.

[32]"The Second War between the States," *Business Week*, 17 May 1976, pp. 92, 95.

[33]"Federal Spending: The North's Loss Is the Sunbelt's Gain," *National Journal* 8 (26 June 1976): 878–891. For criticisms and replies, see "Challenging the Northeast's Plea of Poverty," *National Journal* 8 (27 November 1976): 1701, and C. L. Jusenius and L. C. Ledebur, *A Myth in the Making: The Southern Economic Challenge and Northern Economic Decline* (Washington, D.C., 1976).

[34]The central document prepared for the Saratoga Conference, 13–14 November 1976, of the Coalition of Northeastern Governors, was Jerry Hagstrom, "Regional Economic Stabilization Policies." For a report of the meeting, see Neal R. Pierce, "Northeast Governors Map Battle Plan for Fight over Federal Funds Flow," *National Journal* 8 (27 November 1976): 1695–1703. For a summary of the SGPB meeting, see the Winter 1976–1977 issue of its newsletter, *Southern Growth: Problems and Promise* (P.O. Box 12293 Research Triangle Park, North Carolina 27709). The *New York Times*, 18 December 1977, p. 21, reported the opening of an SGPB Washington office.

[35]*The Abuse of Power: The Permanent Government and the Fall of New York* (New York, 1977), p. 51.

tribution. The result, expressed in *A New Partnership to Conserve America's Communities: A National Urban Policy*, dated March 1978, is a predictable loss of clarity.[36] In speaking to every problem and attempting to meet every objection, the dramatically announced policy statement failed to mobilize any particular constituency. Major urban policies are still formulated and discussed in Washington, but *A New Partnership* has not framed or connected them in a new manner. Energy, trade, employment, inflation, housing, and community development all seem as separate now as they were in 1977.

The Uses of History

The current discussion of regional shares and urban policy has been intellectually sophisticated although not productive of new initiatives or strategic clarity. I distinguish five attributes of the current discussion, treating each in turn, so as to illustrate the complex demands that a historian must meet in dialogue with a policymaker.

DISCIPLINE

The first and perhaps most important attribute is the powerful manner in which the discussion is disciplined by preexistent scholarly traditions, data sources, and research institutions. The language of politics is always a little more careless than social scientists and academic planners would like, but scholars have little reason to complain about the manner in which regional and urban issues are currently debated.[37] The terms of political discussion are essentially the same as those employed in academic arguments over balanced and unbalanced growth, the dynamics of labor and capital migration, the renewal capabilities of real estate markets, and the normative claims of territorial units. Reports in *Business Week* and the *New York Times*, the deliberations of the Southern Growth Policies Board, and the Coalition of Northeast Governors—all have been controlled by the data provided by the Bureau of the Census and the Office of Management and Budget and disciplined by the

[36]The President's Urban and Regional Policy Group, *A New Partnership to Conserve America's Communities: A National Urban Policy, March, 1978* (Washington, D.C., 1978). Compare the process description on pp. P-7 to P-9 with the critique of the Model Cities planning process in Bernard J. Friedan and Marshall Kaplan, *The Politics of Neglect: Urban Aid from Model Cities to Revenue Sharing* (Cambridge, Mass., 1975), pp. 234–238.

[37]This chapter—and particularly this section—bears closely upon the relationship between professional social inquiry and social problem solving discussed by Charles E. Lindblom and David K. Cohen, *Usable Knowledge: Social Science and Social Problem Solving* (New Haven, 1979).

analyses of the Brookings Institution, the Congressional Budget Office, and the Economic Development Administration.

OPEN CATEGORIES

The political and analytic rigidity that might emerge from this consensual discipline is mitigated by the second attribute of the discussion: the openness of spatial categories. The political debate was initially phrased around "regional" policies. The data base that is used in the debate, however, comes in a disaggregated form: People and facilities are located at specific sites that can be combined and recombined in a great many ways. Through the construction of new spaces, it becomes possible to discover analytically that intraregional differences are more important than is the assumed interregional pattern.

A Congressional Budget Office study, *Troubled Local Economics and the Distribution of Federal Dollars*, illustrates the implications of a play of categories.[38] Instead of aggregated regional or even state accounts, the CBO analysts allocated federal expenditures to counties. They also distinguished a separate category of expenditures intended to "enhance development by investing in human and physical resources." The counties were categorized along dimensions of growth and income, as well as regional location. The pattern that is discerible in these new spaces is much more complex than the initial Sunbelt–Snowbelt dichotomy. If used to predict congressional voting, it would, I suspect, suggest the emergence of intersectional coalitions rather than of regional warfare.

The ultimate spatial unit is, of course, the ground occupied by a single individual. The regional debate touches a fundamental issue in the development of normative planning thought. Theorists in the 1930s had treated regions as moral entities. Homogeneous or tightly interdependent spatial units would generate consensual definitions of their social welfare function and enjoy legitimate claims to income, respect, and stability. This has been a powerful tradition that persists in assertions that once established, a neighborhood, city, or region is entitled to persist. The very idea of an "urban history" bolsters the classically conservative sense that "territory" matters.

The main line of liberal thought in regional science and planning in the United States has, however, moved in another direction.[39] Space, as in the CBO report, is viewed as a powerful but artificial construct. Enti-

[38](Washington, D.C., 1977).
[39]I am following the intellectual history of regional planning in John Friedmann and Clyde Weaver, *Territory and Function* (Berkeley, 1980).

tlements adhere principally to people, not to places. (Remember Edgar Hoover's complaint about the confusion of "equity among individuals and equity among regions.") The right of movement wholly dominates the rights of established sites. Indeed, constructive public policy should encourage the competition between places and the ready movement of labor, capital, and information.

For the president's Urban and Regional Policy Group—and similar bodies—the conflict between liberal and conservative views was a mine field of explosive possibilities. For the entire policy community, however, it is a rich intellectual resource. The ability to move back and forth analytically between places and persons opens apparently closed normative issues: Who, we may ask, will be harmed by the obviously desirable goal of "stabilizing" neighborhoods? Which town will die when we, with obviously good intentions, reduce the informational barriers to geographic mobility?

DEVELOPMENTAL PRINCIPLES

The third attribute of the current discussion—the search for developmental principles—appears in its simplest form in apparently straightforward accounts of the path of urban and regional development. The policy community, without being required to make any new intellectual investments, has inherited a strong tradition of historical study. The monumental account of population redistribution and economic growth by Simon Kuznets and his associates was published in 1957, and the complementary, although independent, volumes, *Regions, Resources and Economic Growth*, and *Metropolis and Region*, shortly thereafter.[40] A continuing flow of work tracked the "evolution" of metropolitan and regional relationships through a series of historical "stages."

The terms and perspectives of these histories have thoroughly shaped the current discourse. Seeing the past through a developmental model of stages in an evolutionary process simplifies the problem of policy design by focusing attention on the tasks presumed to be appropriate to the moment and on the inevitable constraints. Developmental models—to the frequent consternation of economists who employ them—are only weakly predictive. They do, however, have the advantages of a touch of historicism: What was, what must have been, and what will be are entangled in a web of restrictions.

The most extensive series of historical essays yet to emerge from the

[40]Simon Kuznets *et al.*, *Population Redistribution and Economic Growth, United States, 1870–1950*, 3 vols. (Philadelphia, 1957–1964); Harvey S. Perloff *et al.*, *Regions, Resources, and Economic Growth* (Baltimore, 1960); Otis D. Duncan *et al.*, *Metropolis and Region in Perspective* (Baltimore, 1960).

search for developmental principles is the collection edited by George Sternlieb and James Hughes after a 1975 conference at Rutgers University.[41] (At a second conference, in 1977, Sternlieb ruefully wondered why the speakers—including himself—seemed to be so much better historians than policy designers.[42]) The problem that runs through the essays is that of distinguishing secular from cyclic change. Cyclic fluctuations, as the editors describe them, either can attend to themselves or are relatively easily controlled; secular shifts in the urban hierarchy or the distributions of regional employment are not immutable, but they do demand more aggressive and far-reaching policy initiatives. Indeed, in many circumstances, they might as well be treated as unchangeable.

Brian Berry has the last word in the collection, arguing that when you discover a secular change, you are also likely to have discovered a system beyond your control:

> If some "we"—whoever that "we" is—would determine that continued deconcentration was undesirable then to turn around the very long-term and deep-seated process that has brought deconcentration would demand the kind of fundamental change in the nature of the value system that I would maintain is politically unacceptable because it's culturally unacceptable at this time, and we better well start realizing it.[43]

Berry's Burke is matched by David Gordon's Marx in a collection of essays on New York's fiscal dilemmas. The "current crisis," Gordon writes,

> is a general crisis of Old Cities in the corporate stage of capital accumulation. Capitalism has decreed that those cities are archaic as sites for capitalist aproduction. The process of capital accumulation is leaving them behind. Capitalists have found that they can better control their labor forces and make higher profits elsewhere. The logic of capitalism, in this ultimate sense, lies at the root of our current problems.[44]

Like the specification of mismatches in the urban growth reports, Berry and Gordon's historicism narrows the relevant policy options. The profound implications of this narrowing become apparent when a developmental history is transformed into a decision rule. The November

---

[41]*Post-Industrial America: Metropolitan Decline and Inter-Regional Job Shifts* (New Brunswick, N.J., 1975).

[42]The proceedings of this conference, also edited by Sternlieb and Hughes, were published as *Revitalizing the Northeast: Prelude to an Agenda* (New Brunswick, N.J., 1978).

[43]Sternlieb and Hughes, *Post-Industrial America*, pp. 266–267.

[44]David Gordon, "Capitalism and the Roots or Urban Crisis," in *The Fiscal Crisis of American Cities*, ed. Roger E. Alcaly and David Mermelstein (New York, 1972), p. 112.

1977 draft of the president's Urban and Regional Policy Group included a suggestion that we need

> a flexible set of policies which can be tailored to the specific needs of different types of cities. Where the processes of decentralization and decline are still nascent, Federal policies should be structured to help retard or stop them. *Conversely, where the processes of decentralization and decline have an extended history and are clearly impossible to change given reasonable options open to the public and private sector, Federal policies should be structured to allow cities to adapt to change, restructure their economies and provide a better life for their residents.*[45]

In the March 1978 version, the italicized sentences that depended upon operationalizing a developmental judgment were altered so as to suppress the difficult discrimination:

> We should help distressed cities and communities recover their financial stability and make certain that today's healthy cities do not become distressed in the future. We should also assist our older cities to restructure their economies and better adapt to change. A decent quality of life must be made available to their residents.[46]

CONFLICT

The debate over the plasticity of systems, necessary developmental principles, and immutable environments forms an essential part of the fourth attribute of the urban and regional policy discourse: a pervasive acceptance of the fact of conflict and, building around it, an elaborate structure of historical argument.

There is an inner dynamic to political controversy that keeps conflictual distributional debates open and honest, even if individual actors have reason to lie. Instead of some unique optimum as the obverse of every problem, there are benefits and costs that appear in many combinations. Moved by complaints and measures responsive to them, a quite ordinary flow of politics can proceed (its intelligence may even be enhanced) without everyone stopping to define national objectives.

The norms of the policy community discipline advocacy so that it is difficult to argue for unilateral or uncompensated advantages or devastating neglect. There is an important group of intermediaries who move back and forth between organizations, warning that there are complements where others see only competition and that no region can afford to go it alone.

Even the advocates of cooperation, however, must demonstrate the

---

[45]The November draft, which was widely circulated within the policy community, is entitled "Cities and People in Distress." See pp. II-3, 4.

[46]URPG, *A New Partnership*, p. P-4.

distributional impact of regional peace. In a context in which conflicting parties urge one or another national policy to shift resources, the conventional aggregate terms fairly beg for specific definition. A pamphlet issued by the Academy for Contemporary Problems (whose president, Ralph Widner, has been an important peacemaker) warns, for example, against turning the national response to the "post-industrial stage" of urban development into a "self-defeating, fractious conflict between the regions of the country." The academy suggests, instead, that the nation turn away from a conflict-provoking search for a national policy. Instead, states and localities should be encouraged to "work out their own solutions to their own peculiar problems in each region of the country," within "an equitable framework of federal policy."[47] The argument (attractive as it may be to those who want to avoid conflict) obviously hinges on an explicit and defensible conception of equity.

EQUITY

It is that problem of defining an equitable framework that dominates the historical arguments that whirl around the regional conflict. The debate over regional shares is largely free of the stigma of illegitimacy that burdened urban growth policy discussions. In a political system that allocates representation to spatial units, spatial coalitions are ubiquitous. It is impossible to deny the legitimacy of these coalitions without condemning the areal basis of representation and the entire pattern of American policies. In addition, by 1970, the idea of an implicit regional policy was well understood within the policy community, and the history of area development programs, widely known. The problem for the advocates of aid to the Northeast and Midwest was not legitimacy but right. Were those regions morally entitled to aid? The rich and varied answers to this question shape the final distinguishing attribute of the regional debate: the directness with which political actors address the issue of equity.

Claims to equitable entitlements have been asserted in three separate, although overlapping, forms, each evoking a somewhat different strand of historical argument. I call them, borrowing from Robert Nozick, entitlements in *patterns*, in *processes*, and through *deserts*.[48]

---

[47]Academy for Contemporary Problems, *Four Stages of National Growth: The Changing Roles of Our Cities and Regions* (Columbus, Ohio, n.d.).

[48]John Rawls, *A Theory of Justice* (Cambridge, Mass., 1971), is the principal contemporary theorist of patterned conceptions of justice; Robert Nozick, *Anarchy, State and Utopia* (New York, 1974), his principal process critic. There is considerable overlap between the terms I have chosen and the conceptions of need, right, and desert in David Miller, *Social Justice* (London, 1976).

The first of these is only weakly historical, because it consists of a prima facie assertion that the existence of an undesired distribution is sufficient grounds for equitable rectification. The lack of a minimum "human" level of income and any inequality or violations of the maximin principle are variously asserted as ground for complaint. The formula that defines the "need" for aid and allocates funds under the Community Development Block Grant program is a patterned entitlement. The only historical elements in such assertions consist of the demonstration of the existence of a maldistribution or the forecast that the dynamics of the present system will lead to one in the future.

The patterned claim to current entitlement—while sometimes vehemently urged—has already begun to crumble as a basis for regional policy. The South as a whole is still considerably poorer than is the northern manufacturing tier, although individual states within the regions have reversed long-standing ranks when income is adjusted for differences in the cost of living. I am not sure what judgment about the current distribution would flow from a Rawlsian conception of justice. I rather doubt, though, that on a large regional scale, it would favor the North against the South.[49]

The major patterned regional assertions of entitlement deal with the future, not the past or present, and are intertwined with process claims. Two rival assertions compete against one another. On the one side, partisans of the growth areas of the nation argue that since the transfer of people and activities from one site to another is legitimately and freely made, there are no grounds for denying the fairness of the resultant pattern or for entitlement to compensation. The history that is evoked describes the free flow of resources in a liberal nation and an open market.

Critics of the emergent regional pattern have argued, in reply, that the process of transfer has been neither as spontaneous nor as legitimate as its defenders contend. A cabal of southern congressmen and military officers and multinational corporations and a confluence of powerful but poorly understood national policies—together are portrayed as the source of the current problems of the North.

In both a scholarly and a street form—Daniel Patrick Moynihan in his senatorial role manages to combine both[50]—this history of federal activ-

---

[49]Carol L. Jusenius and Larry C. Ledebur, *Federal and Regional Responses to the Economic Decline of the Northern Industrial Tier* (Washington, D.C., 1977), p. 18, argue that the North's problems are severe enough to create an entitlement without any comparative referent: "Reference to other regions or demands for 'fair shares' or 'equity' are unneeded and may prove counterproductive."

[50]See Senator Moynihan's statement, "The Federal Government and the Economy of New York State," 15 July 1977, distributed by his office in the U.S. Senate.

ity meshes into a second argument. If the "secret" history of southern growth resulted in a satisfactory patterned distribution, many people would have difficulty complaining. Is it really wrong that a rich but "distressed" state or city sends more tax dollars to Washington than it receives in return, even if the result stems from a "trick" of power? The common negative answer to this question is constrained by an equally common belief that people and places are entitled to procedures that reduce the burden of change. They are entitled not merely to legal and political due process but to stable substantive expectations. Federal policy—whether toward central cities or the North—is attacked from this framework as having been either unsettling in itself or inadequately protective against external shocks.

Entitlements in patterns and processes stem from the current attributes of units or the way in which others have treated them. In the final form, equity is earned by the way in which units have behaved toward others. In his first newspaper column after the election of Jimmy Carter, Albert Shanker, president of the United Federation of Teachers, argued that the Northeast had aided the South in the 1930s and now rightfully claimed compensating assistance: "The Northeast looks to a son of the Deep South for the kind of regional help that area and others were given by the victor in 1932, a New York governor who went on to lead America for a dozen years, Franklin Delano Roosevelt."[51] The Coalition of Northeastern Governors in their Saratoga meeting presented the same argument in a form that combined claims to deserts and to stability:

> For many years, federal tax and spending policies have shifted the wealth of the older industrial states of the Northeast to the developing regions of the nation. This has amounted to a stabilization and development program for the South and West. . . . The movement caused little concern as long as the older, industrialized states continued to grow economically, and the traditional conditions of deep poverty in the South were being corrected. . . . But, around 1970, the shift accelerated with unprecedented speed. The economies of the South and Southwest had "come of age" and were no longer dependent on capital and factories of the Northeast and Midwest. . . . With the exception of a countercyclical aid program for states and localities suffering from severe unemployment, which Congress approved in 1976, the federal government has yet to develop regional stabilization policies which would alleviate the problems facing the Northeast.[52]

The history in the Saratoga statement is a peculiarly benign characterization of regional relationships. Whereas that portrait is not without

[51]New York Times, 11 November 1976, "News of the Week in Review," p. 9.
[52]Hagstrom, "Regional Economic Stabilization Policies," pp. 1–2.

its strong defenders and scholarly credentials, there is an alternative account that is widely known, at least to southern members of the policy community. Southern development, C. Vann Woodward wrote in 1951, was constrained by forms of colonial control that would have won the admiration of the pre-Revolutionary British Board of Trade.[53] Although the Woodward characterization of the "colonial economy" has taken its scholarly knocks in the last quarter of a century, recent discussions, even by southern liberals, reveal little sense of gratitude to the North. They are suffused with a persistent conception of the South as a poor region and a striking wariness about the imposition of external forms.[54]

Mancur Olson, in an address to the Southern Growth Policies Board in January 1977, provided his audience with a sophisticated version of the history of southern development in which there is no hint of northern entitlement.[55] Combining his own work in the logic of collective action with an empirical study of international growth patterns, Olson argued that the timing of southern development stemmed not from its own internal maturation but from the "institutional arthritis" of the North—a disease that the South has no reason to embrace. At a meeting of the National League of Cities in December 1977, James McCone, then mayor-elect of Houston, combined a claim to deserts with an attack on northern practice. "Why," he asked, "should we share our goodness when maybe we earned it" with cities that have had "trouble in the past with fiscal planning?"[56]

The attribution of desert or blame is an intrinsically historical argument. It depends, at its simplest level, on a moral evaluation of a past act. Even more deeply, it asserts (for the most part, implicitly) an historical model of a complex system and its environmental relations. When northerners argue that they are entitled to compensation for their past actions toward the South, they must mean that in the past, they (or predecessors from whom they derive their claim) might have acted in some other manner without diminishing their own advantage. Conversely, southern deserts depend upon the ability to distinguish regional contributions to growth independent to northern aid.

The American political system will not, of course, wait for the development of a consensual view of an equitable regional framework before it grinds out individual policy decisions. As events and the flux of

[53] *The Origins of the New South* (Baton Rouge, 1951), p. 317.

[54] Thomas H. Naylor and James Clotfelter, *Strategies for Change in the South* (Chapel Hill, 1975).

[55] "The Causes and Quality of Southern Growth."

[56] The comments were reported in the Philadelphia *Evening Bulletin* 5 December 1977, p. 2.

ideas in the policy community proceed, the embedding of assertions of entitlement in particular histories is likely (if the past is repeated) to soften the force of conflict. Tracking the impact of federal dollars over time, debating the degrees of historical desert, assessing blame—each in its way is a historical substitute for moral warfare. Nestled in problematic positive issues, normative assertions, as passionate men and women understand, lose their hard edge.

A CONCLUDING NOTE

The uses of history described in this chapter do not encompass all of the possible ways in which the past can be organized to serve the future. The two policy issues I have chosen to discuss are speculative and loosely bounded. A set of more circumscribed concerns, such as housing, education, or transportation, would have revealed (in ways not apparent here) historical arguments embedded in formal models, discrete program evaluations, and longitudinal measures of systemic performance. I have intended only to illustrate the density and ubiquitousness of historical argument and to point to the variety of hooks through which appropriate pasts are linked to policymaking.

Historians will, I hope, understand that my emphasis on the demanding requirements of dialogue is not intended to compromise the rhythm of serious research and independently guided careers. The history of the urban past is constantly enriched by new policy concerns. The dedication required for research and the long time span between a research design and final publication require that policy concerns, once embedded in the discipline, be pursued even though they are no longer prominent on the public political agenda. The policy community is composed of many free-marching bands, touching and then moving apart in fits and starts. Even the hard core of governmental decision makers search for programs, fasten on options, and then abandon them in a movement that is more like speculative research than their own hard-headed self-image allows. No large urban policy issue ever devolves into a single global decision for which the discriminating evidence is neatly packaged in advance. Instead, decisions are made and remade over and over again. Policy, in the words of David Cohen and Michael Garet, is a "grand story: a large and loose set of ideas about how society works, why it goes wrong and how it can be set right."[57]

[57]David K. Cohen and Michael S. Garet, "Reforming Educational Policy with Applied Research," *Harvard Educational Review* 45 (February 1975): 21.

As the loosely organized policy community moves irritably from one issue to the next, it spirals back upon itself, discovering a body of work that it has stimulated and then partially abandoned. The research that enters into policy deliberations is often, necessarily, a product of past interests—a trifle out-of-date and not quite appropriate. As the community circles back to the literature of urban history, it finds a record of past concerns, each cultivated over time beyond the point of initial policy interest and then repeatedly synthesized. The product of this layering of concerns, histories, and syntheses is a reservoir of information and insights. The reservoir suffers from the weakness of large, old cities: It is not well designed to serve any particular purpose and it protects obsolete technologies. It also shares the strength of such cities: Its variety and disorder support multiple demands and provide opportunities for idiosyncratic although disciplined personal reorganization. Unlike severe single-purpose accounts, the community can use the discipline "as it wills."

ACKNOWLEDGMENTS

I am grateful to the participants in the Russell Sage Conference on History and Social Policy for their assistance. I have also benefited from the extended comments of Rayma Feldman, Kenneth Fox, William Hengst, Dorothy Mandelbaum, Ralph Widner, and Michael Zuckerman.

10

HISTORY AND THE FORMATION
OF SOCIAL POLICY TOWARD CHILDREN:
A CASE STUDY

JOHN DEMOS

In the summer of 1972 one of the nation's leading private foundations, the Carnegie Corporation of New York, laid plans for a substantial new project in social policy investigation. The focus was to be America's children and especially its *young* children (defined as all those under 10 years old). The end in view was a general reassessment of current situation and future prospects. The means to this end was the establishment of a study group or "council"—the Carnegie Council on Children—with a core membership of about a dozen persons.

The procedural format would follow a pattern applied in many previous instances. The council would convene at intervals of several weeks, for perhaps 2 or 3 days at a time, over a span of 3 years. (Eventually, the council would extend its lifetime to nearly 5 years.) Meanwhile, a regular staff, embracing a similar number of people, would conduct full-time investigation at the behest of the council. The chairman of the council was also the director of the staff; otherwise, there was no overlap in the membership of these two bodies.

The charge of the Carnegie Corporation to the council was extraordinarily broad. The corporation had long been involved in promoting research on children's learning—their "cognitive development"—but now something more was involved. As the president of the corporation would later put it, "Increasingly we found ourselves asking whether the ability of children to learn was not linked to many other facets of child

SOCIAL HISTORY AND SOCIAL POLICY

301

development, and whether child development itself was not heavily influenced by its social context."[1] There was a feeling, too, that the country was on the verge of major policy decisions affecting the lives of the young. The recently concluded political struggle over the comprehensive child-care bill of 1971 had produced a negative result—a presidential veto—but new efforts along similar lines seemed likely in the future. Further ahead lay possibilities such as national health insurance, welfare reform, revision of the tax laws, in all of which the interests of children were profoundly concerned. Policymakers at various levels, and in both the public and the private sectors, might thus make good use of a reasoned overview of children's needs and circumstances. Or so it then appeared.

Reflecting the breadth of its assignment, the council and its staff comprised an unusual mix of professional and personal backgrounds. The members included only one certified specialist in child development; for the rest, there were lawyers, teachers, social workers, economists, anthropologists, a pediatrician—all broadly committed to the welfare of children and some with direct experience in one or another field of child advocacy.[2] There were also two historians—one on the council, and the other a member of the regular staff.

This chapter constitutes, in effect, an offering of retrospective testimony by the council's resident historian. It strives toward three somewhat divergent aims. An opening section summarizes the history *of* the project, to the point in the autumn of 1977 when the council's "core report" was officially published. A middle section explores the place of history *in* the project—that is, the use, non-use, and misuse of historical ideas by the council and its staff. The final section is more openly subjective, posing as it does some pointed questions about the role of a historian *on* the project. A short conclusion attempts to draw a few morals and lessons for the future.

Considered as a whole, the chapter is a literal "case study." It presents, therefore, no general viewpoint, and it needs testing against other, roughly similar cases. That such cases will multiply in the coming years seems likely, given current signs and trends. The architects of projects in one or another area of social policy seem increasingly inclined

---

[1]Alan Pifer, "Preface," in Kenneth Keniston and the Carnegie Council on Children, *All Our Children: The American Family under Pressure* (New York, 1977), p. ix.

[2]The members of the Carnegie Council were the following: Kenneth Keniston, Chairman, psychologist; Catherine Foster Alter, social worker; Nancy Buckler, teacher of disturbed children; John Demos, historian; Marian Wright Edelman, lawyer; Robert J. Haggerty, pediatrician; William Kessen, psychologist; Laura Nadar, anthropologist; Faustina Solis, social worker; Patricia McGowan Wald, lawyer; and Harold W. Watts, economist.

to incorporate historical "perspectives." Usually this takes the form of including one or more professional historians in staff positions and building historical study into project agendas. Since the pattern— perhaps we should call it simply a tendency—is so new, there is as yet little clarity about substantive goals and strategies. Indeed, in some projects the inclusion of history, and historians, may prove to be no more than a form of institutional tokenism.

However, it is worth noticing at the outset that discussions of public policy often refer to history without specific plan or intent to do so. One example may be worth at least brief consideration, by way of preface to the main business of this chapter. Shortly before the Carnegie Council came into being, many of the issues it would confront were spotlighted in the public debate over the child-care legislation of 1971. Even a quick review of this debate shows that both sides—supporters and opponents—sporadically cited the impact of historical trends on children's lives. The supporters repeatedly emphasized a sequence of social changes, which made their proposals seem desirable—even necessary. The growing participation of mothers of young children in the labor force and the increased numbers of single parents, for example, virtually required a commitment to the establishment of day-care centers. Meanwhile, opponents of the legislation detected a gradual erosion through time of traditional institutions and values. In their view, day-care centers in particular, and the "child development" viewpoint in general, threatened further damage and decay. Above all, the family stood in jeopardy—and they viewed the family as a prime source of whatever strengths and virtues Americans yet retained. There was in their pronouncements a note of alarm, almost of outrage, lest government action with respect to children should breach a sacred boundary.[3]

It seems promising, from the viewpoint of a historian, to find that history did indeed figure in this debate. But a second look at the material elicits doubts and questions. For one thing, both sides advanced historical ideas in a careless and self-serving way. The "conservatives" (those against the bill) invoked a highly idealized image of the family in the past, with which to contrast its modern "decay." The liberals cherished some sentimental notions of their own. One advocate of day care, writing in the *New York Times,* pinned her case to an alleged change in family structure from "extended" (formerly) to "nuclear" (nowadays):

[3]On the congressional legislation, see H.R. 19362, as noted in U.S., Congress, House of Representatives, *Congressional Record,* 91st Cong., 2d sess., 1971, 116, pt. 24:32820–3281. For testimony about the bill, consult *Hearings before the Select Subcommittee on Education of the Committee on Education and Labor* (Washington, D.C., 1970), *passim.* For congressional debate on the subject, see *Congressional Record,* 91st Cong., 2d sess., 1971, 117, *passim.*

> Once upon a time [the family] consisted of grandparents, uncles and aunts, cousins, and even friendly neighbors. . . . If we are to preserve the family's strengths for our children, then we must provide mothers with some of the help they used to receive from the extended family. A good day-care program acts as an extended family.[4]

It is not just that such views are inaccurate when measured against what scholars have learned about the history of the family; there is also a sense in which they converge. Both sides in the child-care debate agreed that American life had changed—in some respects for the worse—so far as families are concerned. Their disagreements involved the matter of *response* to change. Liberals proposed new policies to meet the inescapable reality of new circumstances, new pressures, new needs. Conservatives urged redoubled efforts to consolidate what was left of traditional family life. But the *historical baseline* in each case was similar, if not identical. Perhaps, too, it was in some sense irrelevant.

One more thought suggests itself from the welter of claims and assertions in this debate. Public discussion of childhood and the family seems, whenever it turns toward the past, to take on the roseate hues of nostalgia. Somehow this subject, these concerns, are invested with a collective charge of sentiment. The outcome hardly differs from what is often true of individuals, as they recall, with exaggerated fondness, some aspect of their personal pasts.

THE WORK OF THE CARNEGIE COUNCIL: AN OVERVIEW

The central business of early council meetings was, necessarily, to define the task. Strategic alternatives were faced, and judgments were made, that would shape the project irrevocably. Several of these bear careful consideration from the standpoint of the present chapter.

The first important judgment came, in effect, ready-made from the officers of the Carnegie Corporation. The council's charge was to "think broadly," to construct insofar as possible a "framework" within which policy programs might be organized, and to explore the "ecology of childhood." But, of course, this left much open territory. Actually, its chief import was to suggest what need *not* be done. The council would not assemble another "shopping list" of specific needs and problems. It would not produce detailed recommendations to deal with one or

----

[4]Elinor Guggenheimer, "Look Here, Mr. Nixon," *New York Times*, 21 December 1971, p. 37.

another situation affecting children. It would not undertake fresh research in child development, family sociology, community organization, or any comparable field. Instead, the project would make use of information already available and evaluate programs already in existence, in the course of fashioning larger perspectives.

But what was the appropriate starting point for this investigation: How even to *begin* reaching toward such large and lofty horizons? In fact, three different approaches were considred at length in early council meetings. The first entailed sustained effort to identify major and continuing trends in American life insofar as they affected children. The second was frankly visionary: One could try to define an "ideal world" for children and then devise plans and principles for making the real approximate the ideal. The third involved a focused examination of a single "problem area," not for the sake of developing programatic "solutions," but rather as a way of unraveling the complicated web of institutions, values, and scientific information bearing on *every* aspect of children's lives.

At one time or another, the council would make use of each of these strategies. The "problem-area" approach was tried very early, around the specific focus of children's nutrition. It was possible in this way to consider corporate industry (the food companies), advertising, scientific research (on various aspects of nutrition), social contexts (the "family meal"), and even some highly philosophical issues (such as food in relation to mind–body dualism).[5] Significantly, however, the council chose to abandon its nutrition studies within about 6 months. Many words were committed to paper, but none to print. (Indeed the paper has remained undisturbed in assorted office files ever since.) In retrospect, this appears to have been something of a warm-up for the council—an opening exercise that served to test various ways of working together and to flag certain issues and questions that would reemerge in other guises during the years ahead.

The notion of an "ideal world" did not figure largely in the council's substantive discussions. Perhaps it might have done so in a different setting and with different people, but the project as originally constituted was loaded with "real world" experience. Still, from time to time the council did seek to be "visionary," to glimpse something radically better than the existing order of things. Evidently, this expressed a felt need in all council members to reaffirm the seriousness of the task and to recapture an immediate sense of moral commitment.

[5]The main elements of this discussion are summarized in Carnegie Council on Children, Minutes of the Third Meeting, 1–2 December 1972. Carnegie Corporation, New York, N.Y.

The strategy of exploring cultural trends and tendencies proved, in the end, quite central to the council's work. Repeatedly, discussion moved out from the present and immediate experiences of childhood to the temporal flow in which all such experiences are carried along. This point will bear further consideration later in this chapter.

A second strategic judgment was of another sort. The council was asked to consider children, but where, so to speak, would it find them? Again, various possibilities suggested themselves. There was, for example, the possibility of a direct approach, an effort to hold children alone in view, trusting that help and support might somehow reach them directly. An obvious alternative was to target the child in the family, on the assumption that families are (and will continue to be) the most important setting for early experience. Still another possibility was to set a broad stage and direct attention to whole communities, if it seemed that the welfare of children was actually inseparable from that of other groups (the elderly, the poor, the racially oppressed—not to mention the affluent, the powerful, and those in the "prime of life"). Here, too, no absolute choice seemed prudent, or even possible; however, the strongest emphasis would fall on the *second* alternative. The Carnegie Council on Children became, secondarily, the Carnegie Council on Families. Parents, the council decided, are usually the best "experts" about their particular children; therefore, helping children inevitably means helping families.

A third question presented another difficult choice. Should the council concern itself with *all* American children, or should it concentrate on those who are most immediately and heavily at risk? Was it foolish, perhaps immoral, to link the children of backcountry hollows or inner-city ghettoes with the "comfortable" children of middle-class suburbs? In the end, the council compromised. Some problems affect all American children and families today; to this extent, it seemed important to "think national." But other problems chiefly involve specific groups: The victims of race prejudice and poverty, for example, disproportionately include children. The council's surveys, reports, and recommendations would therefore take aim in both directions.

These decisions on basic issues of strategy evolved rather gradually through the first 6–10 months of council work. During the same period, council members and staff initiated a variety of substantive investigations. As noted already, considerable effort was directed to a study of children's nutrition, and all staff persons were drawn into this to some degree. The staff included no single specialist in this field, so papers and discussions were built from reviews of the published literature and interviews with recognized experts. This would, in fact, become standard procedure for other aspects of the project as well. The staff, as originally constituted, was composed largely of able and resourceful "generalists." Most staff members had broad competence in one or another field (e.g., political science, history, health care, law), but not more specific forms of expertise. Consistent with the original conception of the project, they were expected to gather, sift, and blend together recent research, wherever it might bear on council aims.

In essentially the same spirit, early council meetings were planned as much to gather information from outside sources as to pool ideas from within. The meeting sites were notably varied: LaJolla, California; Davenport, Iowa; Jackson, Mississippi; Little Rock, Arkansas; Denver, Colorado; Madison, Wisconsin—among others. (One meeting was held outside the country, in Cuernavaca, Mexico, in order to foster international comparisons.) On each occasion, there was considerable effort to consult opinion in the immediate locale. In part, this was "expert" opinion (academic and/or professional), but in part, too, it involved lay persons from all parts of the community. The council sought, most especially, to hear from people who were active in advocacy groups at the local level.

After the completion of its first year, the project underwent a partial, and gradual, change of orientation. The early sorting phase was over, and the balance between internal discussion and external opinion gathering altered somewhat. The latter would never be entirely given up, but more and more the council concentrated on developing its own viewpoint, its own priorities, and its own style. Meeting arrangements reflected this change, in terms both of sites (New York, Boston, and Chicago were increasingly preferred) and of schedules (less time for "field visits" to day-care centers, health units, and the like). There was a complementary trend with respect to staffing. Certain of the generalists who had at the outset occupied central positions now left the project, and their replacements tended to be people of sharper professional definition.

Meanwhile, a sense of overall direction was gradually emerging in the discussions of the council itself. Time after time, consideration of some particular problem area led off to issues and themes of the largest sort. Periodically, council members sought to pull themselves back to the more immediate concerns of children (and families). Yet, the very persistence of this tendency seemed to express a truth of its own—or, if not a truth, at least a conviction in which most members shared. The deficits and the difficulties that most deeply affected children could not be addressed in piecemeal fashion, and the search for their sources led to the very center of the social and economic "system." What was called for, in the long run, involved nothing less than "structural change." (The political persuasion of most council members at the outset could reasonably be described as center-to-liberal, but the project seemed to move them, albeit rather quietly, toward much more radical positions).

Reflecting this structural orientation, the council staked out some broad areas of study. Questions of economics, most especially the distribution of jobs and income, assumed an absolutely central importance. The impact of technology, of mass society, and of racial and class distinction followed close behind. A provisional agenda of books and reports emerged accordingly. The council would issue a "core report" to summarize its major findings and recommendations. Two additional publications (written by particular staff members "for the council" and expressing council views) would treat at length the issues of inequality in American society and of socialization to American ways and values. Finally, three "background studies" would deal with more specialized problems and themes: handicapped children, minority children in the schools, and the implications for policy of recent research in child development. The actual completion of this agenda was a long and complicated process, and the details have little significance in the present context. However, it is necessary to say something of the outcome, if only to trace the perimeters through which historical ideas did, or did not, finally gain entry.

From the very start, the council had fastened on a set of discrepancies, or "tensions," in the situation of American children. Myths versus realities, ideals versus behavior, profession versus practice: such were the defining categories of its investigation.

The most obvious and fundamental of these discrepancies appeared to begin from the abiding belief of many Americans that ours is a "child-centered" nation. Typically—we like to think—our children are cherished, protected, nurtured, and offered a field of opportunity unmatched elsewhere in the world. We value children almost to a fault—often, indeed, we "spoil" them—but they are, after all, the hope and the promise of America's future. This rhetoric, these beliefs, are studded through our public professions no less than our private sense of ourselves. And yet, on closer inspection, they yield a painful sense of contradiction. Our public *policies* affecting the young, and the welfare of American children as measured by various social and medical indices, suggest an actual commitment to children substantially lower than that of other industrialized countries. Our patchwork of welfare programs does not amount to support for families with children. Our legal protections for children are meager and inconsistent. Our infant mortality rates are shockingly high. At each of these points of comparison, other countries stand well ahead of us.[6]

In spotlighting this gap between profession and performance, the council hoped to grasp a wedge for change. Recommendations could then be advanced in the name of living up to our national ideals. There was more here, however, than simply a tactical opening. The lack of consistent performance was, and is, a dilemma that must somehow be fathomed. What, in fact, are the *real* attitudes of our country toward children?

A psychiatrist who visited one of the council's early meetings suggested that it consider "whether Americans actually hate children."[7] The proposition seemed stark, and finally implausible, but it could not be ruled entirely out of court. At best, the council came to think, American attitudes toward children are deeply ambivalent. To some extent, of course, ambivalence is built into all intergenerational bonds. Growth and nurturing lead inevitably to separation; the old die, whereas the young live on; the sins of the fathers are visited on their sons, and vice versa. To some extent, the structure of all modern (i.e., industrial) society exacerbates these tensions. In premodern society, children repaid the costs of their care by contributing labor to family enterprise, but now they are massive financial liabilities. Yet with all this accounted for, there is a distinctly American residuum. Somehow, the young in this country seem especially likely to elicit a divided response from their elders.

In the long run, these ambivalent attitudes must be faced, and understood, if American children are to have maximally effective support. But they run so deep, and are so broadly diffuse, as to prevent the drawing of clear connections with substantive policy issues. Other conflicts seem much closer to the visible surface of contemporary American family life, and three of these would eventually become central to the council's "framework" of analysis. In each case, there seems to be great need for policy initiatives in response to real problems and pressures, but the need is obscured, and the problems themselves denied, by the presence of long-standing cultural "myths."

1. *The need for support versus the myth of self-sufficiency.* The prevalent anxiety today about the quality of American family life is not without foundation. Our own families differ from those of our forebears in significant ways, and some of the difference powerfully implicates children.

---

[6]On the deficiencies in current policy for children, see Keniston *et al.*, *All Our Children*, pp. 78–80.
[7]See Carnegie Council, Minutes of the Second Meeting, 3–4 November 1972, pp. 4–6.

The rapidly increasing participation of women in the labor force is a particularly striking case in point. Among women with school-age children, a clear majority now hold jobs outside the home; the figures leaped from 26% to 54% within the period 1948–1974.[8] Single parenthood is a comparably important phenomenon, given the rising curve of both divorces and out-of-wedlock births.

But the family has been changed in other ways as well. The widely noted loss of its traditional functions is real enough. Work and home no longer have much intrinsic relationship. Education is less and less a domestic affair, and the same can be said of health care. The larger point is that families today must depend on a variety of specialists for vital needs and services. Meanwhile, *expectations* have risen markedly. We want more education, and better medicine, than ever before. And the home itself has been "emptied": parents at work, children at school or elsewhere. The managerial aspects of family life have thus become enormously complicated. The "core report" of the Carnegie Council summarizes this trend as follows:

> In a sense parents have had to take on something like an executive rather than a direct function in regard to their children, choosing communities, schools, doctors, and special programs that will leave their children in the best possible hands. The lives parents are leading, and the lives for which they are preparing their children, are so demanding and complex that the parents cannot have—and often do not want—traditional kinds of direct supervision of their children.[9]

And yet these needs, these realities run directly against a powerful mythology of family life. The stay-at-home mother, the breadwinner father, and, above all, the family that confidently takes care of itself are enduring images that we all know well. For a family to require help is, by the light of American traditions, to *fail*. When things go awry, the individual family members must somehow be at fault. The price of such beliefs is paid in guilt, in lessened self-esteem, and in disorganized, wholly inadequate programs of social services. In fact, American families have never been the self-sufficient building blocks of society that the myth affirms. And they are becoming less so as time moves along.

[8] Keniston *et al.*, *All Our Children*, p. 4.
[9] *Ibid.*, pp. 12–13.

2. *The reality of the "stacked deck" versus the myth of equal opportunity.*
The council chose the metaphor of a "stacked deck" to designate some
of the deepest and most painful dilemmas in American life: the paradox
of poverty in the midst of affluence, the crippling burdens of prejudice,
the maldistribution of life's chances and rewards. Of all age-groups,
children are the most likely to be poor. Moreover, poor children experience, from the beginning of their lives, convergent streams of insult and
injury to body and mind. Their health is significantly worse than the
average for their age-mates; their rate of mortality is higher; their educational opportunities are far inferior. The odds that they can better themselves are low: According to one study, a child born into the topmost
level (highest 10%) of the national wealth hierarchy has a 1-in-3 chance
of remaining there, whereas a child born near the bottom (lowest 10%)
has a 1-in-250 chance of ever getting there. The blight of poverty is, of
course, frequently compounded by the bitter shafts of race prejudice.
Black children are four times more likely to be poor than are white
children, and native Americans suffer even more terrible odds.[10]

And yet statistics tell only half the story. The emotional scarring,
the wounds to soul and spirit, the denial of hope, the warp of expectations—such things cannot be measured quantitatively. Young
people willingly learn skills that they know they will be able to use;
conversely, they do not learn what seems irrelevant or disfunctional in
terms of their probable life pattern. These judgments, in turn, are based
on what they see around them and particularly on the experience of the
adults they know best.[11]

The "problems" of poverty and racism are familiar enough by now.
Yet their full measure is concealed, and change is hindered, by still
another pervasive cultural myth. Our society, we have long believed, is
an "open" one; our highest values, our noblest professions, consistently
affirm equality, or at least equal opportunity. Where poverty persists,
the fault must lie with the individuals involved. Our "solutions" to
poverty are fashioned accordingly. Reduced to their common de-
nominator, they amount to this: Change, uplift, "reform" the
individual—help him to get started in helping himself.

3. *The perils of the "technological cradle" versus the twin myths of
technological progress and the laissez faire economy.* There is no avoiding the
impact of technological change on all our lives. Indeed, the scope of this

---

[10]*Ibid.*, pp. 32–33.
[11]This point is explored at length in one of the council's background books, John U.
Ogbu, *Minority Education and Caste: The American System in Cross-Cultural Perspective* (New
York, 1978), especially chaps. 1, 5, 6.

change is so vast as to defy any simple characterization. One can dip into the experience of individuals, or families, at almost any point and find a maze of effects, all stemming in one way or another from technology. The council elected, in its final report, to single out three such points: television, the "new diet," and nuclear energy.

In each instance, thanks to technology, Americans have been offered large apparent gains. Television "expands our horizons," especially those of children. (According to many studies, children now spend more time with this ubiquitous electronic companion than with either their parents or their schools.) The new diet makes food "cleaner" and its preparation more convenient than ever before. Nuclear power holds out the prospect of a dramatic solution to our chronic energy problems. And yet, in each instance, there is vast uncertainty about long-range implications and cause for immediate concern about some of the short-run effects. What is the hidden message to children from television, with its "quick takes" and instant (often violent) solutions for all manner of personal and social problems? What will be the eventual result for their health of the new diet? And what about the risks of nuclear energy— risks that in many respects we cannot even conceptualize?

The country has scarcely begun to take these issues seriously, and once again the lag has much to do with myth. We have, as a nation, a deep and abiding faith in technology as the engine of progress. Our very identity has been shaped by this faith. To be an American has meant participation in a culture of triumphant self-assertion, of mastery within both the natural and the social environment, and the means to this end has been, in large part, a distinctive national gift for technological ingenuity. Many Americans, therefore, now receive the warnings of risk inherent in technology with a special sense of surprise, of indignation, and of panic.

A second myth, also pertinent here, affirms the benign workings of the laissez faire economy. Free enterprise, and most especially the free choice of consumers, are its central tenets. If television programs are not what they should be, then viewers will switch channels, advertisers will shift their contracts, and producers will come up with something better. If processed foods, laden with cosmetic additives, are dangerous to health, then shoppers will express their preference for something else. If nuclear energy threatens the genetic integrity of future generations, then planners in both the public and the private sectors will react accordingly. These beliefs—they are, in fact, less cognitive than purely instinctive—presume free and informed choice. Yet most of us cannot possibly inform ourselves about such complex matters, and we are far less free than we sometimes imagine. Increasingly our "laissez faire" economy is controlled both from within and by government; to depend on "market forces" is therefore patently ill-advised.

The foregoing "tensions" obtained a central place in the discussions of the council, and eventually in its "core report." They directly undergird the opening part of that report—the analysis entitled "Children and Families: Myth and Reality." A second part—"What Is To Be Done?"—offers a variety of policy recommendations. The latter are too numerous and complex for easy summary here, but they embrace the issues of full employment, income supports, flexible work schedules, services to families, health care, and the legal status of children. A concluding chapter discusses ways and means of "Converting Commitment into Politics".

The report was published in September 1977 under the title *All Our Children: The American Family under Pressure*. One additional "council book," *Small Futures: Children, Inequality, and the Limits of Liberal Reform* was published in 1979. One of the "background studies," *Child Care in the Family: A Review of Research and Some Propositions for Policy*, appeared in December 1977; the other two, *Minority Education and Caste: The American System in Cross-Cultural Perspective* and *The Unexpected Minority: Handicapped Children in America*, were published in 1978 and 1980 respectively. This completes the council's publishing agenda.[12]

With the appearance of its final report, the council ceased to exist as a formal entity. However, the members and the staff continue to be active as individuals on behalf of council ideas and recommendations. A last meeting of all those connected with the project was held in Washington, D.C., and interviews were obtained with leading figures in government and private organizations of child advocacy. A small public affairs unit, based in New York, has been helping to funnel speaking invitations to appropriate council members. The director of the project has appeared several times on national television and has testified before a congressional subcommittee on children and youth.

These ongoing activities express a shared conception of the council's work as essentially a form of "consciousness raising." There was never much ground to expect that the publication of books and reports would

---

[12]The full citations for those works not already cited are as follows: Richard Delone, *Small Futures: Children, Inequality, and the Failure of Liberal Reform* (New York, 1978); Alison Clarke-Stewart, *Child Care in the Family: A Review of Research and Some Propositions for Policy* (New York, 1977); John Gliedman and William Roth, *The Unexpected Minority: Handicapped Children in America* (New York, 1979).

lead directly to policy change. Rather, the hope is to enhance discussion by concerned citizens everywhere of the forces that actually do, and the principles that ideally should, govern the lives of American children.

HISTORY IN THE WORK OF THE COUNCIL

The appointment of historians to the council and its staff signaled a clear intent on the part of the officers of the Carnegie Corporation. Historical experience—that is, the experience of children in the past—was deemed relevant to the situation of children in the present and the future. The questions of *where* history fitted in and *how* to make it meaningful for the project as a whole were not so easily resolved. Most council members seemed to feel that historical knowledge might offer a useful "background" from which to approach the crucial present-day, policy-oriented issues. And there was a general sense that such knowledge should be deployed at the beginning of the council's work.

So it was that various parts of early council meetings were set aside for consideration of history. How were children viewed in the past? How were they valued? How were they treated? What was the nature of their family experience? How easily, and in what contexts, did they move between their particular domestic settings and the community at large? Questions like these were raised for the entire group by those whose prior experience qualified them for the task. The discussion was distinctly open-ended, and there was little attempt at connection with the substantive problems of contemporary American children.

There were other manifestations of the same impulse. The director of the council began, at an early stage, an extensive study of attitudes toward children in the past. (The result was a manuscript of several hundred pages.) A staff member with particular training and interest in history was asked to review the outcome of the various White House conferences on children from 1900 to the present. (The same person would subsequently undertake to research the history of day care.) Other staff members began to investigate poverty from a historical perspective and the changing workroles of women during the past 2 centuries. The early emphasis on nutrition sparked a modest foray into food history. In fact, all of these studies fell by the wayside as the council's work reached a more advanced stage. A few may well find their way into print at some future date, but their immediate priority in terms of council goals did not prove in the end to be high. Were they, therefore, entirely without significance? On the contrary, they appear to have entered, in numerous small ways, the larger flow of ideas that the council was gradually generating. But this result is clearer in retrospect than it was at the time.

One particular meeting, midway through the project, elicited a substantial exchange of views on the "uses of history." The director had circulated several "pre-draft" chapters from his ongoing study of children in the past, and the council was asked to react. One member—the only real skeptic in this connection—doubted "the relevance of history to the problems of children and families in American society now.... People do not decide to do things by taking account of historical findings; instead they look at economics, politics, and the immediate social context... in order to determine how and what to do." (This, and succeeding quotations, are taken from the meeting minutes.[13]) But others, from both the council and the staff, took an opposite view. History was "important... as a means of dispelling fears of change." History would be helpful "in identifying the needs of children, and the sources of those needs." History might serve to "unveil certain nostalgic myths" that had traditionally frustrated or distorted policy efforts. History would teach by example, spotlighting "those programs [which had been] tried time and time again with almost no success." In effect, the council reaffirmed a generalized interest in history, even while setting aside specific inquiries about the past.

There was one additional sign of affirmation, indirect and unintended, but hardly unimportant. Repeatedly, the council historian noticed his policy-minded colleagues opening some new line of discussion with a brief reference to the past. An argument for expanded daycare facilities would be introduced with the thought that day care was not, after all, so very new; the "day nurseries" of the nineteenth century and the federally sponsored preschool centers of the World War II era could be seen as approximate precedents. A comment about the need for additional "family services" might start from a notion that the mobility of Americans, in the geographical sense, is now greater than ever before. A discussion of the impact of divorce on small children would explicitly presume that family separations were rare long ago. This tendency amounted, indeed, to an almost automatic instinct or impulse— let us call it the Impulse to the Historical Preface. For many council members, it was as if the record of the past conferred a certain legitimacy on ideas about the present.

These prefaces were not always accurate—at least by the light of academic research—and some of them had no necessary bearing on the policy positions with which they were linked. If American children of

[13]Carnegie Council, Minutes of the Sixteenth Meeting, 13–14 December 1974, pp. 3–4.

the 1970s can benefit from day care, does it matter much whether similar arrangements have existed in the past? If contemporary families truly need expanded "services," must policymakers decide whether or not an increased rate of geographic mobility is the cause of this need? If millions of children are adversely affected by the rising divorce rate, what difference does it make (for policy) that such occurrences may have been less common in the past? But, within the context of council discussion, it seemed immaterial whether such connections could actually be demonstrated. Somehow, the preface was its own justification.

Meanwhile, the larger flow of the council's work was reaching toward history in ways far more substantial, if less immediate and obvious. The priorities, the assumptions, the "strategic decisions" described earlier in the chapter carried important historical implications. The council would adopt an "ecological" approach, as opposed to that of the "problems list." The former was by definition multidimensional, and one of the dimensions, quite clearly, was time. The council would interpret its charge to comprehend all children, not simply the most disadvantaged, and would key its investigation to continuing trends and tendencies, not a utopian vision of an ideal world. Such notions had little meaning apart from comparisons of the past with the present.

Most of all, the family focus reached out to history—indeed depended on history. It is not impossible, in the decade of the 1970s, to imagine that the family system itself is disintegrating. Divorce, illegitimacy, the burgeoning technology of contraception, a new brace of "countercultural" standards and values—these undoubted landmarks of contemporary life suggest to some that families are virtually outmoded. If that were truly so, policy discussion about children would have to begin from new and "radical" premises. The council, however, elected to think otherwise, and history was strongly implicated in its decision. The record of the past, at least by this reading, powerfully displays the durability of the family system. Concern for the family has reached high levels before; yet its inner structure, and its fundamental integrity, has remained largely intact for centuries. Change it has indeed experienced, and further changes can be expected. There are few grounds, however, for predicting its imminent demise or the *kinds* of change that would lead to something genuinely new.

The council returned often to the problem of cultural ambivalence toward children, and here, too, history was asked to supply understanding. The roots of this ambivalence invited extended exploration—more extended than the council could reasonably undertake and more, certainly, than is feasible within the compass of a single chapter. But a brief sketch may serve to exemplify the mode and manner of such discussion.

Consider as a way of approaching the problem the special situation of one type of American family—the immigrant family. It is a commonplace of social science research that immigrant families are liable to inner stress and tension.[14] For one thing, the children—those who are raised here—may prove to have certain advantages over their Old World parents. They are, in general, more adaptable: They learn the language more quickly, as well as the mores, the values, the prevalent *nuances* of social style. At some points, the parents may actually have to depend on their children for advice and assistance of a sort that has traditionally flowed the other way. Is it not plausible that these reversals may seem, at least in part, unwelcome to the parents?

Here, then, is one potential source of resentment in the older generation, and there are other things that may trouble them as well. *Guilt* is a factor that seems intrinsic to immigrant experience, and directly pertinent to family life. The parents feel that the decision to migrate has placed all members of the family at risk; in particular, it has robbed the children of their proper birthright in a stable and rooted community. Of course, many immigrants have justified their coming in terms of the gains expected for the children, but at some level they recognized that there was also a loss. This tacit recognition has prompted, in turn, a further response, a compensatory pledge that they as parents would subordinate their own interests to the future prospects of the young. Here, incidentally, one encounters the *positive* side of the cultural ambivalence toward children. Enormous sacrifices have, in reality, been made by many parents for many children in this country; to this extent, the myth of our "child-centered" society finds confirmation. And yet there is still another twist. The immigrant parent who has sacrificed all understandably expects a return. "My own life has been foreshortened," he seems to say to his children, "but you will live for me; the luster of your success will redeem my bitter struggles." This, most assuredly, is an open door to intrafamilial tension of various kinds, and to potentially deep disappointment.

The foregoing sequence has been presented as specific to immigrant families, but, in truth, many of the same themes can be associated with American family life more generally. Immigration has been a central and dynamic element in our history from the very start; the Puritan settlers were, after all, the first immigrants. Moreover, millions of Americans who are certifiably "native stock" have shared with their foreign-born neighbors the experience of sudden geographical movement. In short,

---

[14]The fullest and most insightful exposition of the argument summarized in these paragraphs is found in Oscar Handlin, *The Uprooted*, 2d ed. (Boston, 1973).

they are migrants, if not immigrants. The motion in *their* lives has raised some of the same expectations, and fueled some of the same tensions, that have often characterized immigrant families.

To these pressures from social experience was added the impact of ideological forces, dating back well over a century. Beginning in the period 1800–1850, for example, Americans developed a special and highly optimistic view of social evolution—their own version of the "idea of progress." The country had made a successful revolution and come through a difficult period of adjustment in the generation or so after independence. The westward movement was in full swing; the economy was expanding dramatically; the political system appeared to have a "vanguard" status in relation to other parts of the world. Americans of all sorts were congratulating themselves on their "go-ahead spirit" (a familiar period cliché), and they truly did believe that they had launched a wonderful experiment in human improvement.

According to this view, the present was inherently better than the past, and the future was certain to be better than the present. And who were the representatives of the future? Who else, of course, but the nation's children. In a sense, the younger generation could claim a moral edge on the older one, as the flow of history moved along. And to the extent that the young asserted this claim, family relations, or even social relations generally, were unsettled. In premodern society, the superiority of age had been everywhere recognized, but now much of that was turned around.

Another ideological innovation of the same historical period lay in the meaning and emphasis given to human achievement. This was part, to be sure, of a larger climate of "individualism," in which the worth and talent of each person became a touchstone of social value. But the key development was the so-called cult of success. According to the premises of this cult, life was a race, open to talent and with tangible prizes for the winners. The central figure here was the "self-made man," the man whose success was attributable solely to his personal strivings.

The implications of these values for the relation of parents and children were profound. It was accepted from this time forward that the way for a young person to move ahead was to leave the world of his parents and strike out on his own. (For "young person," we should probably substitute "young man," since these formulas were applied chiefly to males.) Ties to family, attachment to the community of his birth—all this could only hold him back. Would his parents' experience at least serve as a guide, a model, as he made his way in the wider world? At best, the answer was ambiguous. The ethical teachings of parents might prove a valuable "rudder" for him as he veered hither and yon—and nautical metaphors were common in this connection—but other aspects of the parental experience would be irrelevant. He would choose his own occupation, his own friends and colleagues, his own place of residence, wherever the main chance seemed to beckon. In short, getting *ahead* meant getting *away* from one's parents.

And there was more. How would the young person's achievement be measured? His achievement was measured, his "success" evaluated, by comparing his ultimate social position with the point from which he had started out. In short, success meant surpassing one's father. So it was that a deep strain of competitiveness entered the relation of parents and children in nineteenth-century America. It has remained with us, indeed in us, ever since.

This is a fair specimen of council inquiry specifically embracing historical circumstance. It begins from a question or problem founded in present-day experience. (Whence comes the characteristic American ambivalence toward children?) It proceeds at a high level of generality and requires no direct acquaintance with "primary" data. It draws, at least implicitly on the research of whole legions of scholars. And it suggests no solutions, carries no direct implications for policy, since it purports to express the accumulated experience of an entire culture.

Much the same could be said of the place of history in the council's final report. Historical ideas figure quite prominently in the opening sections of that report, in the "analysis" that precedes the offering of particular recommendations and findings. Recall the quartet of cultural "myths" presented in counterpoint to problematic social "realities." The myth of self-sufficiency, for one, is clearly a legacy from the past. Much depends on the growth, especially in the nineteenth century, of an inside–outside view of the family in relation to the larger community. The modernization of American society raised deep, and often unadmitted, anxieties among many of those most centrally involved. The new world of commerce and industry seemed chaotic, impersonal, and amoral; the home, by contrast, was idealized as a bastion of traditional virtue. The boundaries were maintained with ever-increasing vigilance, and "self-sufficiency" became the means to this vital end. (The echoes of this view, with its shrill emphasis on boundary maintenance, can be heard in the opposition to the child-care legislation of 1971 discussed earlier in the chapter.) The hallowed division of sex roles (breadwinner and housewife) was similarly founded. The "cult of true womanhood," as one historian has called it, was founded on a belief that maternal care alone guaranteed the safety and virtue of children.

The myth of equal opportunity, which prevents our full confrontation with structural poverty and racism, also dates from the early nineteenth century. And, at the outset, it contained at least a kernel of truth. From well before the War of Independence, American society was more homogeneous in its social and economic structure than was its mother country overseas. And the Revolutionary ideology helped to convert these "facts" into values. After 1800, as the national economy entered a "take-off" stage, there were indeed unusual opportunities for enterprising (and lucky) folk to get ahead. Perhaps the single strongest boost for the myth of egalitarianism came from the creation of a free, and later compulsory, public school system: Schools would be the starting line from which all competitors might equally begin. That this mythology has survived so long, and in the face of so much evidence to the contrary, seems nothing short of incredible. But it carries the dreams, and softens the disappointments, of whole generations of Americans.

The historical derivation of the final pair of myths—those that shroud our "technological cradle"—is so transparent as hardly to need comment. The myth of technological progress encapsulates more than a century of extraordinary economic growth, of manifold "invention," and of ever-expanding comforts and "conveniences." For most Americans, technology was, and remains, the tangible expression of the confidence, the resourcefulness, the practical bent that together have created our modern "life-style." The myth of laissez faire has a not dissimilar set of roots. The energy of individual producers needed only to break free of traditional restraints in order to yield its most bountiful possible result. The public interest was the sum of many personal interests, no more and no less. English writers of the seventeenth and eighteenth centuries, like John Locke and Adam Smith, had forged the philosophical underpinnings of laissez faire, but American *do*ers of the nineteenth century effected its social application.

The later sections of the council's final report offer fewer, and markedly smaller, openings to history. Specific recommendations for policy look naturally to the present and the future. Nonetheless, these chapters are dotted at intervals with brief references to the past, which do bear some consideration.

Most such references can be divided among three different categories. One group invokes history on behalf of policy. (Hence, e.g., the following: "It is consistent with almost any interpretation of American traditions and values to insist that parents' efforts to secure an adequate income for their family not be thwarted by the brute fact that there are no jobs for them."[15]) A second group serves to highlight particular features of the present. In some cases this is achieved by way of contrast.

[15]Keniston *et al.*, *All Our Children*, p. 85.

(E.g., " 'Services' is the catchall term for many of the kinds of help that parents use now that life is not the simple family affair it was on eighteenth-century farms."[16]) In others, the emphasis is on continuity—that is, the power of a linear tendency over time. ("Barring a dramatic reversal in the trend that decreased the proportion of self-employed workers in the labor force from 20 percent in 1940 to about 8 percent in 1970, changes in the working conditions of the 92 percent who work for others will have the greatest impact."[17]) A third group of these references presents the past in a darker light. Here the emphasis falls on the burden of inherited practices and principles, whose very longevity belies their worth. (Thus, "For far too long we have applied to the job problem the same old solution—uplift and reform the individual—that has proven so difficult to achieve in other realms."[18]) In short, the "problem" and its purported "solution" are both of considerable duration; hence the latter must be deemed ineffective.

In all the above-mentioned instances, the purposes served are essentially tactical. The substance, for the most part, is left rather vague; the tone is usually rhetorical. There is little intrinsic relation between the cited historical circumstance and particular policy recommendations. Indeed, we are back to the matter of "Prefaces," and it is no coincidence that many of these references appear at the beginnings of paragraphs or of the larger textual subdivisions.

THE ROLE OF A HISTORIAN:
PERSONAL REFLECTIONS

What, now, can be said of the role of the historian *on* the council? And how can the council's experience be used to illuminate the uses of history, and of historians, for similar policy investigations in the future? In turning to these questions, it seems appropriate to speak in the first person. There is no way finally to escape the subjective aspect of my participation in the work of the Carnegie Council. And I cannot at this point be sure how much my role, and my conclusions about that role, may parallel the experience of other historian participants in projects of a similar nature.

I must admit, in the first place, to some unease about my contribution to the council virtually throughout. It seemed from the start that most of

---

[16]*Ibid.*, p. 135.
[17]*Ibid.*, p. 124.
[18]*Ibid.*, p. 91.

my colleagues were more immediately and tangibly connected with the task than I was. In effect, they represented particular constituencies—disturbed children, poor children—by virtue of much professional experience, or else they represented some distinct expertise—pediatrics, law, economics—with direct bearing on the lives and prospects of children. My constituency, if such it can be called, was the children of the past, and they were clearly beyond reach. My expertise seemed inherently less practical, more diffuse, and more esoteric than the others. None of my fellow council members wished to make me feel uncomfortable about this—quite the contrary—but nonetheless my role continued to seem problematic.

Several possibilities emerged, and to varying degrees I tested them all. The project began, as noted earlier, with efforts to use history as "background." My own part in these efforts was necessarily prominent: the preparation of a general paper on the history of family life and extended comment on the history of childhood in particular. The immediate results were disappointing, to say the least. My rendering of history seemed to lead nowhere in particular, and the reaction around the table was understandably diffident. Such background presentation seemed vaguely comparable to the tunes piped into supermarkets and airline terminals. To this point, it could be said, mine was the role of *the historian as music maker*.

The background had only a limited claim on the council's attention, and quite soon I was searching for new forms of participation. The aforementioned Impulse to the Historical Preface apparently offered a way. I could, and did, become an occasional spokesman on behalf of historical accuracy. From time to time, as the comments of my colleagues created opportunity, I would correct the record—*the historian as gadfly*. "But wait," I would interrupt, "it really wasn't quite that way; recent studies have shown . . ." At the same time, I would suppress my sense that such historical corrections were often irrelevant to the policy questions immediately at hand.

But this, too, was a function of minimal reward, both from my individual standpoint and for the project as a whole. And increasingly I drifted toward the position of a "generalist"—*the historian as intelligent layman*. I sought to understand at least something of the specialities that my colleagues variously represented and to assist in melding them into a larger viewpoint. Historians are practiced in the arrangement of facts and the construction of arguments; so I might serve as a sounding board against which others might bounce their ideas. Historians are also practiced in writing, and when the final report had been drafted (mostly by other hands) I spent several days poring over it with a red pencil, as a self-appointed editor.

By this time, however, I had actually done some service from out of my own specialty—*the historian as historian.* And, curiously, this happened almost without my noticing it. As the council fashioned its analysis of children's experience in the present, questions about the past regularly popped into view. It seemed important, above all, to locate the origins of the various "myths" to which the final report would assign such significance. Here I could contribute directly, albeit in a rather piecemeal and unsystematic way.

The belated and roundabout entry of historical ideas into the mainstream of council work implies a general point of some interest. Perhaps we erred in approaching history in the way it is usually approached by scholars—that is, moving from the remote past, to the more recent past, to the present. Indeed, I suspect that history's relevance to policy is most easily appreciated along a route that *reverses* chronology—that is, from present to past. And if this is true, then historical investigation belongs to a later, rather than an earlier, stage in the work of a group such as ours. One needs questions to put to history, and questions arise only as policy itself receives shape and substantive definition. To proceed otherwise, as the council initially did, is to invite discussions that become "academic" in the literal sense.

The largest of the questions that the council put to history reflected its overall "ecological" orientation. Effective advocacy for children, so we concluded, requires far-reaching social change. Hence we asked, What elements of our culture facilitate change, block change, distort and inhibit change? Which of our traditions can be marshaled on the side of new policy initiatives, and which serve merely to maintain the status quo? The council sought to make these inquiries by counterpointing inherited "myth" with immediate, and problematic, "reality." As such, our analysis reached out to one branch of history in particular: the history of values, of custom, of ideology.

It is worth noticing, in conclusion, what the council did *not* attempt by way of historical investigation. The evolution of cultural "myth" is an important matter for any project concerned with policy change, but it hardly covers all relevant possibilities. The council might, for example, have used history to reflect more fully on its own place and function. What have similar projects achieved in the past? What does the historical record suggest about professional advocacy for specifically targeted groups, such as children, within the larger population? Are there often unintended results that may rival in importance the ostensible "findings" and recommendations? Can one discover—again, from historical inquiry—meaningful implications in the fact of foundation sponsorship, or in the social position of the project members, or in the inevitable dealings with government, the media, and other institutional structures?[19] Answers to any or all of these questions might possibly have altered the council's view of itself and its subsequent mode of operations.

There is, moreover, a second route toward the past that the council also avoided. It may well seem odd to some readers of *All Our Children* that the book presents so little history *of* policy for and about children. Health programs, nutrition programs, the whole vast record of public education—are there no lessons to be learned here that might guide policy for the future? What of the history of the Children's Bureau, of local agencies for child and family services, and of private philanthropies in this same connection? And if indeed the record of policy specifically for children seems at many points rather thin, what might be learned from studying past programs for other groups (e.g., the elderly)?

Perhaps with a different membership, a different staff, and, in particular, a different historian, the council would have tried such approaches. But not *this* council, as originally constituted. An extended effort to reflect on the context of our own work—a process of institutional introspection—would, I suspect, have made most of us quite impatient. An agenda of research around the details of past policy would have seemed inordinately tacky and esoteric. In fact, few studies of the latter sort have been made by anyone, so the council would have had to start almost from scratch. Furthermore, historians themselves are skeptical about using the past to read lessons for the future. The context shifts, the characters come and go, the equation of cause and effect is never the same—such, at least, is our usual profession.

Still, it is far too early for closure on any of these questions. Historical inquiry and policy formation make a new, awkward, and necessarily uncertain tandem. But practice may yet bring greater synchrony and increasingly substantial results.

---

[19]A provocative book by Christopher Lasch sketches one set of parameters for such discussion. See his *Haven in a Heartless World* (New York, 1977).

SUBJECT INDEX

A

Abbott, Grace, 186–187, 198

Abortion, Comstock Law against, 226

Academy for Contemporary
    Problems, 295

ACIR, *see* Advisory Commission on Inter-
    governmental Relations

Advisory Commission on Intergov-
    ernmental Relations
  on antiurban bias, 282
  community movement and, 379
  historical arguments by, 282
  report of, 282–284
  use of arguments by, 281

Affirmative action, resistance to, 92

Africa, blacks from, 262–263

Afro-American family, 239–273, 261–262,
    see also Afro-Americans
  destruction of, 240–241
  in Harlem, 244–245
  marriage after emancipation, 243–244
  maternal, 240, 269–270
  misconceptions about, 241–242
  in New York City, 245–246

Afro-Americans, *see also* Africa; Afro-
    American family; Emancipation;
    Exslaves; Slavery; Slaves

Christianity of, 253–254
clergy of, 258
disfranchisement of, 255–256, 259
forced expatriation of, 259
Frazier, E. Franklin, on, 239–240
isolation of, 268, 269, 270, 271
kin networks among, 243, 244, 272, 273
marriages of, 251–252, 254, 258, 264–270
migration of, 239, 244–245, 270, 272–273
misrepresentations about, 255
morality of, 255–256
Odum, Howard, on, 261–262
and "opportunity model," 266, 268, 270
policy toward, in 1960s, 239, 252, 272
sexuality among, 257–258
social processes and, 266, 267, 268, 271
as unchanging Africans, 260–261
urbanization and, 239, 245, 273

Alameda County, Calif.
  plea bargaining in, 218–220, 221
  probation in, 207–208

Alonso, William, 286

American Association of Child Hygiene,
  199

American Child Health Association, 199 n.

American Federation of Labor, Los Angeles
  firemen and, 156